A PARISIAN'S GUIDE TO PARIS

A PARISIAN'S GUIDE TO

PARIS

Henri Gault and Christian Millau

Translated by PATRICIA ALLEN DREYFUS

Drawings by NATHAN GLUCK

RANDOM HOUSE [*New York*

Contents

INTRODUCTION

Every year, a very strange scientific phenomenon can be observed in Paris on the first fine days of spring. Another city arises in the very midst of town. It is both a part of and completely apart from its surroundings—a foreign city with its own monuments, stores and restaurants, laws and customs. For almost six months the inhabitants of these two cities, who are as close and as isolated from each other as red and white blood corpuscles, will pass each other, brush against each other, sometimes even meet and talk to each other, but almost never will they feel that they belong to the same city.

An "invisible wall" is said to come between the foreigners and the Paris of the Parisians. This wall exists for every tourist in every city, but rarely is it so obvious and its presence so oppressive as in Paris. Here the tourists really are a world apart, under the thumb of a little group of intermediaries: travel agents, tour organizers, souvenir vendors, hotel concierges, taxi drivers, who fasten onto them like leeches and imprison them in a Paris which is almost fictitious or, at any rate, absolutely artificial and terribly disappointing.

No book, not even a masterpiece, could claim to transform mere passing travelers into full-fledged Parisians on the strength of its advice. To grasp a city takes time and a good deal of skill. Still, it's important not to start off on the wrong foot, and we are scandalized by the way tourist organizations usually show Paris to their clients. They treat them like morons or very young children. We don't know whether the percentage of stupid, shy, indifferent and lazy American tourists is the same as among their counterparts from France, Germany, Switzerland or anywhere else, but this is still not a sufficient reason to pretend that *all* tourists are like that. Unfortunately, this is exactly how the tourist industry operates. As if by magic, the tours always manage to select and recommend the worst restaurants, the worst night clubs and the worst stores. The reason for this is extremely simple: The bad places are snubbed by local customers, and since they need business, they are ready to make any kind of deal, to cheat on the quality of their products and to forget all the basic rules of their profession.

So don't be surprised to discover wide gaps in this book. For instance, you won't find a word about the restaurants on Montmartre's place du Tertre, although this is the first place where tourists are sent—which is exactly why we prefer to forget it. Still, in all fairness one must admit that not all tourist haunts are necessarily bad. The important thing is to know which are the good ones . . . and that is the aim of this book.

Our main ambition, however, is to avoid treating our readers like tourists, at any cost. Whether they stay in Paris two days or two months, they will, we hope, no longer be mere foreigners. A glass of wine at the bar of an old bistro, a brief tour of the antique shops off the beaten paths, a good dinner in a restaurant known only to Parisians, and the charm is already beginning to work. You leave without once clambering up the Eiffel Tower or seeing Napoleon's tomb. You're a little bit ashamed? Come on, now! Do you really think any true Parisian ever goes up the Eiffel Tower or visits Napoleon's tomb?

So you will find only a limited number of suggestions in this guide. The listings are by general area, in turn divided by neighborhood, and the *arrondissement* numbers are always listed after the name of the *quartier*. We could have given you a lot more, for we have been systematically exploring Paris for over four years, and it's a spot we are getting to know rather well. Still, we thought it wiser to restrict ourselves to a relatively modest but extremely careful selection of good addresses. It would give us the greatest pleasure if accepting us as your invisible guides could make you feel a little more at home in Paris.

Henri Gault and Christian Millau

Part I

RESTAURANTS

EXPLANATION OF SYMBOLS

Quality
- -

****
***
**
*

We give one, two, three or four* stars to a certain number of restaurants for the quality of their food, regardless of their luxuriousness or décor. If a restaurant hasn't been awarded a star, this in no way means it is not recommended, merely that it is not on a sufficiently high gastronomic level to justify this honor. Nevertheless, for the restaurants with no star, in order to differentiate one place from another, we have graded their cooking on a scale from 0 to 20.

Wine cellar, reception and service, atmosphere and décor
- -

These are likewise ranked from 0 to 20. "Atmosphere" has to do with a place's charm, gaiety or picturesqueness.

---

* Four stars stand for culinary perfection. We haven't found any restaurant in Paris consistently worthy of this distinction, which, on the other hand, we

Prices

V.E. (very expensive): at least $13 per person
E. (expensive): $8 to $12 per person
I. (from rather expensive to inexpensive): $4 to $7 per person
V.C. (very cheap): under $4 per person

Can you still get a good meal in Paris?

People often ask us where the best restaurants in Paris are. And our invariable answer is: In the provinces.

This isn't just a wisecrack. Paris has a fantastic world-wide reputation for gastronomy. Nevertheless, painful as this admission is, our experience with close to a thousand restaurants has convinced us that it is the provinces—Burgundy, Périgord, Lyonnais, the Landes, Alsace—which have best preserved the great traditions of good eating and the art of living.

For centuries France was like the Seal Woman displayed in circus side shows: a huge head on an almost nonexistent body. The huge head was Paris—Paris, where everything happened and all decisions were made: in politics and economics, literature and entertainment, social life and gastronomy. People in the provinces ate well and abundantly, but the ultimate refinement was cultivated in Paris. The great chefs worked for the Court, for the nobility and old families who staked their honor on the excellence of their table. This was the origin of the French fine art of cooking: skillful, incredibly complicated, insanely taxing and at least as concerned with how things looked as with how they actually tasted. This rather crazy way of life (no one would have dared serve fewer than ten dishes in the course of a supper) was the monopoly of a certain class of society. Under the Ancien Régime, restaurant meals were much less refined and Parisians ate at home or at friends'. But with the Revolution, and especially after 1792, these great chefs

----

unhesitatingly award to Troisgros in Roanne, Paul Bocuse in Lyons, and a few others.

found themselves out of a job, since their masters had either emigrated or lost all taste for food on the gallows. The chefs took their savings (they were experts at padding bills) and opened restaurants. After the Revolution, under the Directoire, these restaurants were such a hit that new ones kept opening right and left: at the beginning of the nineteenth century Paris had more than two thousand restaurants. Some of them were of unimaginable luxury and refinement. Amid the sumptuous décor at Méot's, formerly chef to the Duc d'Orléans, ecstatic customers selected their food from a list of a hundred dishes and could even take baths in champagne. Beauvilliers, who had been the chef of the king's brother, the Comte de Provence, strolled among tables loaded with silver dishes and crystal, his sword at his side and his jabot unfurled on his chest. Later, under Napoleon I, Véry was to offer, in a setting of staggering richness, thirty-one poultry dishes, twenty-eight of veal and lamb, fifteen kinds of roast meat and forty-four varieties of *entremets* (side dishes). Under such conditions it is easy to see how Grimod de la Reynière (one of the greatest French gourmets) never spent less than four hours at the table.

Parisian restaurants kept up a rather heady pace throughout the entire nineteenth century. Balzac has given a magnificent account of the feasts at the Rocher de Cancale, where he himself would down twelve dozen oysters just to whet his appetite. Veritable fortunes—in the form of truffles à la serviette, lobster, woodcock, pheasants à la Sainte Alliance—were consumed every day at the Café de Paris and at the Café Anglais, presided over by the great chef Dugléré. Bills of the time make one's head spin: in 1875 the Duke of Brunswick paid 2,250 francs ($450) for a dinner for four at the Petit Moulin Rouge. Restaurateurs didn't care a fig for costs. Why should they, when their customers were willing to pay 400 francs ($80) to sample one of the first melons of the year?

An end to madness

These eating orgies continued to some extent until World War II, but four years of German occupation, plus a 52 percent income tax (practically unknown in 1900) and, finally, a radical change in living habits (the discovery of dietetics and new ways of spending money, such as on automobiles, vacations, travel and weekend homes) all dealt a terrible blow to the luxury restaurants. Larue, Voisin and Le Café de Paris were forced to close down in the face of almost total indifference. A few of the great establishments—La Tour d'Argent, Lasserre, Lucas-Carton, Le Grand Véfour, Ledoyen, Maxim's, Lapérouse—are still holding out, but neither the menus nor the service are anything like they were in the old days. They still look quite impressive, all the more so since the public—which is continually less refined and demanding—is easily dazzled. But there as elsewhere, things are simplified, reduced, replaced. If, for example, truffles and foie gras were to be served as generously as they were forty or fifty years ago, no luxury restaurant would be able to survive.

In the end, the cuisine in the great restaurants is becoming less and less distinguishable from the food served in less luxurious establishments. This trend is encouraged by the customers themselves, who today are quite capable of ordering cabbage soup at Maxim's.

The finest restaurants used to be temples where a great religion was celebrated with wildly complicated rites. To the extent that they must strive for wide appeal in order to survive, they tend to lose their spectacular originality.

The provinces seem to be doing better.

Paul Bocuse in Lyons, the Troisgros brothers in Roanne, the brothers Haeberlin at Illhauesern in Alsace are among the chefs who embody the profound spirit of great French cooking. The first thing you notice is that each one is his own boss, which is almost never the case in Paris. Then, they enjoy greater assets: the provincial idea of luxury is more modest than in Paris. The cooking is noble but the style of life is down to earth. This means that less money has to go for interior decoration and salaries; these sums can be spent exclusively on the food. Family life is more important and the desire to make money is doubtless less pressing. You will also notice that the menus in these great provincial establishments are even more limited than in Paris. The chefs stick to their specialties, a few dishes whose number they increase on Sundays and on days when they expect a crowd. They therefore incur few risks or losses.

In addition, provincials make less fickle customers than Parisians. Once they get used to going to a particular restaurant, they keep on going back. The fads which fill one restaurant in Paris and empty another do not wreak their havoc. It is obviously easier to prepare food well under these conditions than when you have no idea in the morning whether your restaurant will be half-empty at dinner or whether you will have to turn customers away. Finally, people in the provinces, who are calmer and less rushed than Parisians, have remained more or less faithful to gastronomy's true rhythm. They don't mind waiting forty-five minutes for a dish and find it quite natural to pop around to the restaurant the day before to enlist the owner's help in planning the dinner they'll be ordering on the following day. It's all handled in a friendly, neighborly way. A visit to the Troisgros, for example, will give you an even better idea of what we mean. The owners are in constant touch with their customers, who are their friends by now, and they keep the greatest gourmets among them posted on what comes in. They telephone one to let him know that some Gypsies have brought in a magnificent Adour salmon or that they have a wonderful brace of woodcock all ready to be eaten. They operate a little like some antique dealers and rare-book sellers. Only the provinces foster such delicious customs.

But let's get back to our great Parisian restaurants. Far be it from us to disparage them. They do their best to live up to their image; it's not their fault if this is becoming more and more difficult. Such as they are, they are as indispensable to Paris as the Vendôme Column or the quais along the Seine. The memory of woodcock at Lucas-Carton, duck at La Tour d'Argent or a bottle of Cristal Roederer 1959 at Maxim's is one of the most precious souvenirs that a man of taste can take with him from Paris.

Little restaurants sometimes surpass the big ones

As we said earlier, the owner and the chef are never the same man in large Parisian restaurants. This is impossible because of the very size of the establishment and its attendant responsibilities. Personally we regret this, for cooking is a matter of temperament: it is much too personal an art not to suffer from having to comply with the injunctions of even the most enlightened administrator. It's another example of the perpetual conflict between the artist and the businessman. A miraculous union does sometimes come about between the two, with admirable results, but usually they pull in opposite directions.

This is why we think that, as gastronomy now stands in Paris, the places run by an owner-chef are, with certain exceptions, in the best position to preserve fine culinary traditions. It is easier for them to foster the cult of sincere cooking: decorating and service costs are reduced to a minimum, the menu revolves around a few specialties (often good home-style dishes like braised beef, pot au feu, etc. that are not harmed by being prepared in advance; indeed, they often benefit by it). Finally, there is a limited number of tables and the clientele is usually more knowledgeable and more demanding than in luxury establishments. Prices generally run just as high, sometimes even higher, as, for example, at Denis, which is the only little restaurant in Paris where they still practice the "noble" cooking of fifty or a hundred years ago. At least you have the satisfaction of knowing that your bill covers only what's on your plate and not what's on the walls.

These little places, with their strong provincial flavor, are unaffected, as it were, by the fads and fashions which blow now hot, now cold. Their one weak point is that they rarely survive the loss of their owner, except when he has had the wisdom to start molding his successor far in advance, as was the case with Allard.

The price myth

We're not telling you anything new when we say that Paris is an expensive city. But is it fair to claim that its restaurants are more expensive than those in New York or Chicago? Knowing both sides, this assertion strikes us as most unjust. Then how does this notion come to be so widespread among American visitors?

We see three explanations. The first is that inhabitants of a rich country always have a hard time accepting the fact that prices in a poorer country can be just as high as at home. This feeling goes so deep that when French people go to Spain, where life is very inexpensive for them, they spend their time arguing about prices. All it takes to make them scream out loud is for a hotel to cost 10 percent more from one year to the next, while back home the same sum would be just enough to rent a bed in a flophouse.

The second reason, which is a corollary of the first, is that a considerable number of Americans live on a higher level than usual when they come to Paris. They head straight for the most famous restaurants, these being the only ones they have ever heard of. Well, we'd like to know how many of them make it a habit to eat lunch or dinner every day at La Caravelle, Lutèce or the Pump Room. Do they really think that Parisians have their every meal at Lasserre or Garin? Of course not. In Paris, as in New York or Chicago, dinner in a great restaurant is for most people a rather rare occasion, an unaccustomed feast.

The last reason is that people still drink relatively little wine in American restaurants. In France, on the contrary, an American doesn't dare refuse wine, either out of curiosity or because he is somewhat dazzled by his surroundings. The picture of the "typical" American tourist drinking Coca-Cola with his tournedos Rossini, is funny but not true to life. All the wine stewards in the great restaurants agree: most of their prestigious (and therefore extremely costly) bottles are ordered by foreigners, and by Americans in particular.

Even if wine is cheaper in France than in the United States, you mustn't forget that a single bottle can easily double your bill. So if you want to compare the price of a meal in Paris and New York, you should do it honestly and not throw in a bottle of Haut-Brion and a glass of Martini vermouth. You'll then see that a great meal costs just as much on either side of the Atlantic.

What is absolutely true, on the other hand, is that you get better food for less money in an American snack bar than in its Parisian equivalent.

To wind up the topic of prices, here's a little trick to enable you to calculate the price of your meal quickly, as you read the menu. If you triple the price of the entrée, you'll get a figure close to your total bill, including the wine (if it's a reasonable vintage).

Lunch or dinner?

Contrary to United States practice, French prices are not generally higher at dinner.

If this is your first visit to Paris, it is obviously preferable to go to the great restaurants in the evening. Uninformed foreigners go to Maxim's for lunch, which is a little like meeting Brigitte Bardot for the first time with her make-up off and her hair in curlers. (This is a slight exaggeration: Maxim's has a certain charm at lunch, but it's nothing compared to the evening.) However, there is one exception to this rule: Lucas-Carton, which is much livelier at noon than at dinner. As for Lasserre, it is equally busy early and late. It is nonetheless true that the charm of a pretty spot is always more effective at night, and that supper at La Tour d'Argent, with Notre-Dame illuminated in front of you, is a picture that will long remain in your memory album.

In the other restaurants and bistros, lunch attracts an overwhelming proportion of men. Women stay at home or nibble a sandwich as they shop, while their husbands gorge themselves, building a better world on a foundation of Beaujolais.

What time should you arrive?

For lunch, from twelve-thirty to two o'clock. Dinner, around eight-thirty; later (between nine and nine-thirty) in luxury restaurants. In any case, and perhaps due to Spanish influence, Parisians are acquiring the habit of having dinner later and later. Opening and closing times of restaurants, bars and night clubs are subject to changes, and we suggest that you verify these by a telephone call.

Are reservations necessary?

As a general rule, yes. Even when a restaurant isn't full, a reservation assures you of a better table. If you are alone and want to dine in a large restaurant, our advice is to fib a little and reserve a table for two. Single diners are a thorn in the side of restaurateurs, who often seat them any odd place.

What should you wear?

You will undoubtedly be surprised to learn that people show up every day at La Tour d'Argent, Lapérouse or even Maxim's, who have to be loaned a tie and a jacket. This is rather unusual all the same, though the truth is that Parisians dress more casually than they used to. Only Maxim's (and only on Friday night) requires black tie. Everywhere, people show less and less concern with formalities. At Lucas-Carton we saw two young men in turtleneck sweaters at the table next to Onassis and La Callas, and at Lapérouse a shirt-sleeved guest slipped his shoes off under the table in order to be more comfortable. One shouldn't generalize, but the reputation of Paris for elegance has become somewhat debatable.

What should you order?

A good rule to follow is: Trust the owner or maître d'hotel and let them make suggestions. At the Lyonnais, for example, it would be out of the question to do otherwise; if you wish to stop anywhere short of open rebellion, you eat what the *patron* decides. And it works out much better that way, since he is always right. We must admit, however, that very few owners take the trouble to compose a meal; it's an art that demands both time and love.

If the menu includes a *plat du jour* (daily special) you generally can't go wrong by ordering it. As a rule it is guaranteed not to have languished in the kitchen or refrigerator. This is especially true at lunch. If the dinner "special" is, for example, a leg of lamb that is already three-fourths gone, refuse it: it's had more than enough time to dry out since lunchtime.

It is wise to take the time of year, and even the time of day, into account. If you are offered game out of season, it will be imported, frozen and of abysmal quality. You should know, for example, that it is extremely difficult to get freshly killed native hare in Paris after the month of October, and that when Christmas is past, young partridge becomes old partridge, and can only be eaten stewed with cabbage. Once the season is over, why bother ordering cèpes, which are marvelous when they're fresh and mediocre when they come from a can or, dried, from a bag?

Since you can't possibly know the right season for everything, the simplest solution is to ask the waiter or owner whether or not something is a *produit de saison* (in season). There is a world of difference between a stringbean picked that morning or the day before and a bean that comes out of a can. And if you can't tell the difference, rush this book back to the store this very minute . . .

The day of the week is important, too. Fish is freshest on Fridays (when the demand is greatest), whereas meat and shellfish are sometimes not as fresh on Mondays, when restaurants use up their odds and ends and the markets of Les Halles are closed.

Take your time reading the menu and ordering. If the waiter tries to rush you, complain, call the owner, if necessary walk out. Waiters are there to serve you, not vice versa. And don't let yourself be cowed by surly bistro waiters. Tell them, with a smile, to stop bugging you. Once they know who's boss, they'll bend over backward for you.

Don't be afraid to order a single dish for two if you're not particularly hungry. After the hors d'oeuvres, for example, share one fish and one meat course. You won't be overeating, and your meal will have a pleasant note of variety. Some restaurants, like the Ami Louis, serve such enormous portions that sharing is indispensable, even if it isn't suggested to you.

Gourmet restaurants always have two or three *spécialités de la maison,* usually underlined in red on the menu. These are often worth looking into. Not always. We therefore take the liberty of advising you to make careful note of the dishes we recommend at each of the restaurants mentioned in this book. As you will see for La Tour d'Argent, these are not necessarily their most famous dishes.

If there are complete, *prix fixe,* lunches or dinners, make sure that the superiority of the gourmet menu, *menu gastronomique,* over the "tourist menu" does not consist solely of an extra course. Thus, the two meals might be as follows: For 12.50 francs ($2.50) you get hors d'oeuvres, chicken, cheese or dessert, and for 22.50 francs ($4.50), hors d'oeuvres, truite au bleu, the same chicken, cheese and dessert. In that case you will have been had, since they are charging almost as much for trout and cheese (the additional items on the second menu) as for the entire first meal.

Both French and American customers (especially women) have a habit of diversifying their orders. One has one kind of fish, another takes a second kind, a third orders meat, etc. Gastronomically speaking, this is a deplorable custom. A good cook need only read over the orders to know whether or not he's dealing with connoisseurs. If you really want to eat well, you mustn't be afraid of uniformity. The chef will be grateful to you, and you even more grateful to him, since a nice joint of beef or a fish for three or four people is not only easier to prepare but, most important, will be a lot better.

For a great, an unforgettable meal, don't think twice about ordering it that morning or better yet the day before. The restaurant will prepare special dishes, the wines will be at just the right temperature, everyone will make a fuss over you, and the bill won't have any hidden surprises. (There should be no less than four in your party.)

One last bit of advice: good cooking takes time. You can't eat both fast and well.

What to drink before the meal

If you dare drink martinis or whiskey before a fine meal, we'll kill you! How do you expect to appreciate good cooking when your palate has been numbed by alcohol? It might even be all right if people were satisfied with one drink, but they have to have two, three, four. They get to the table with a heavy head and coated tongue, incapable of discerning the flavor of a dish or a wine. If you absolutely must drink something, order a goblet of champagne, a glass of port, a kir (red or white wine with a dash of black-currant liqueur) or simply open the nice cool Beaujolais, Muscadet or fine Sauterne which you will be drinking with your meal.

How to select your wine

We are not about to review all the wines of France. The subject has been covered many times and deserves a volume all to itself. Our more modest aim is to call your attention to a few points which authors generally forget to mention.

If you are in a restaurant that has a wine steward (*sommel-*

ier), do not insult him straight off by asking for the wine list. One can't help thinking Monsieur Henocq of the Grand Véfour is right: whenever this happens, he puts the wine list on the table and leaves it to the waiter to take your order. The *sommelier*'s role is to advise, to help you profit from his knowledge, not to bring you a piece of cardboard. You should therefore tell him what you are having (and in what order) and ask what he suggests. At this point it's his task to indicate the wine's vintage and price on the wine list. If it later turns out that you don't care for that wine, you'll only feel easier about changing it.

Some *sommeliers*, spoiled by the incompetence of their customers, have a tendency to be remiss. If, for example, the wine steward can't make a more intelligent suggestion than champagne or rosé, on the pretext that you are having both fish and meat, you have a perfect right to ask him to be a little more imaginative. A dinner accompanied by champagne, although undoubtedly pleasant in hot weather, is debatable gastronomically. Champagne is very good with light meals, but is not at all suited to rich dishes like flamed woodcock or hare à la royale. As for those rosés which "go with everything," they actually go with nothing, since these Provençal wines are absolutely undistinguished and often horribly adulterated.

The sacrosanct fear of mixing wines is absurd: no one has ever died from starting off with a Corton-Charlemagne or a Meursault and following it with a Chambertin or a good Pomerol. The essential, as in everything, is not to overdo it.

A number of good restaurants have a "house wine," generally served in a carafe. It comes directly from the barrel, is reasonably priced, and without being a very great wine, is more often than not a good, honest one. For several years Beaujolais has been "the" wine. Beaujolais (Beaujolais-Villages, Morgon, Chiroubles, Juliénas, Fleurie, Brouilly Côtes de Brouilly, Moulin-à-Vent Chenas, Saint-Amour) is full bodied and delicious. It is best when young and cool. The trouble is that two or three times as much "Beaujolais" is sold as is actually produced. Some restaurants—especially the good bistros—serve authentic Beaujolais (we'll point them out as we go along), but in general you should be wary of the Beaujolais sold by wine

merchants. On the other hand, if the name on the label is followed by the words *viticulteur* (winegrower) or *propriétaire-
récoltant* (owner-producer), the wine stands a good chance of
being honest and pure. Origin is important for other wines
besides Beaujolais. In Burgundy the vineyards (with the exception of the Romanée-Conti estate) belong to a multitude of
owners. There is not any one particular kind of Gevrey-Chambertin or Pommard (whereas in the Bordeaux region there is
only one Château Lafite-Rothschild, one Château Pétrus, etc.)
so that the same name may apply to two very different wines.
This is why the dealer and estate are so important. At present,
the list of dealers one can trust almost blindfolded (which
doesn't preclude an occasional unpleasant surprise) is headed
by Louis Latour, Louis Jadot Drouhin-Laroze and Drouhin,
who handle almost all the Burgundies, followed by estates of
varying importance but uniformly high quality, such as Comte
de Moucheron, Marquis d'Angerville, Comte de Vogué, Bou-
chard père et fils, Ropiteau, Leroy, Paul Rouleau, Grivellet père
et fils, Moingeon, Lupé-Cholé.

If you are determined to treat yourself to a prestigious bottle,
try to act like a true connoisseur. Ideally, you should telephone
a few hours in advance so that your bottle can be uncorked and
the wine become thoroughly aerated while it waits. This may be
difficult to do; in that case, select your wine as soon as you get
to the restaurant and don't hesitate to postpone sitting down at
the table. In an hour the wine will have rounded out and recaptured its full fragrance. Nothing is more distressing than to
see a venerable Château Latour 1928 served the moment it is
uncorked. Great wine is a religion; if you don't respect the
ritual, you had better convert to Mohammedanism. Finally,
you should realize that you needn't think twice about sending
a wine back, regardless of its price, if it tastes corked, sour, past
its prime or very inferior to what the vintage or year led you to
expect.

Some jokers get a kick out of having precious bottles opened
and immediately sent back under false pretexts. This gives rise
to little ballets in which the wine steward, the cellarman and
finally the owner take turns tasting the wine and assume an

astonished expression. But they are helpless in the face of such bad faith and are forced to capitulate. The only thing is that you can never play this joke twice in the same place. (This is why some establishments open certain especially old and dear bottles only at the customer's risk.)

Since we are on the subject of old wines, it's a good time to warn you about the excessive idolatry from which they often benefit. Aging a wine for thirty, fifty or sixty years doesn't necessarily make it wonderful; on the contrary, it risks getting the wine past its prime. It can be sublime, but it's often disappointing. So don't have any misgivings about drinking a great Burgundy which is under twelve years old (even less for the whites, since, with some exceptions, these keep very badly). Bordeaux, however, improves with age, since it loses its harshness, but it is perfectly drinkable five or seven years after bottling.

To close the subject, do not allow anyone to serve you a red wine that is too warm. This may mean that the bottle was *chambréed* by being put near a hot stove or, who knows, even in a basin of hot water, which is guaranteed to "break" it. An old wine should be drunk at room temperature, which implies that it should be a few degrees below that when it is brought out, since contact with your hand will warm it up very quickly in the glass. On the other hand, a young red wine should be drunk at the temperature of the wine cellar. The Troisgros serve their marvelous Gevrey-Chambertin (which can be found in Paris at Raffatin et Honorine) quite cool, in pewter pitchers. This isn't to every gourmet's liking. You can judge for yourself.

How much to tip

The service is always shown on the menu, and can be 12, 15 or 18 percent, depending on the class of the establishment. If you are very pleased with your meal and the way it was served, it is an elegant touch to leave a few franc pieces on the table, but nothing obliges you to do so. Leave two or five francs for the *sommelier* if you have had a fine bottle of wine, but you can be sure that his behavior will in no way indicate that he expects something from you.

THE RIGHT BANK

Champs-Elysées (8ᵉ)
- -

Lasserre ***
WINE: 18
DÉCOR: 15
RECEPTION AND SERVICE: 19
ATMOSPHERE: 15
PRICES: V.E.

Maxim's, La Tour d'Argent and Grand Véfour have to refuse customers in the evening but are half-empty at lunch. Other restaurants are very busy at lunch but have painful evenings. Of all the "greats," only Lasserre always has the "Full" sign out (with the possible exception of Saturday forenoon).

The man behind this undeniable success of almost twenty years' standing is a former dishwasher, René Lasserre, who started at the age of thirteen and gradually worked his way up through the ranks of the profession. Equally capable of directing his restaurant's finances as of telling the chef precisely what a dish needs, Lasserre has given his restaurant the stamp of absolute consistency.

Lasserre is located in a small town house near the leafy Champs-Elysées and is generally admired for its décor. Private dining rooms occupy the first floor while the main dining room is on the second. Satin, chandeliers and Dresden porcelain abound. It is gorgeous and impressive, especially if you can't really tell an authentic Louis XV commode from an imitation.

But we have no complaint about the big movable roof, which lets in cool air during the summer, nor about the table appointments, for the linen, glassware, silver and antique aiguières really partake of a most refined luxury.

The clientele includes many foreigners, but also prosperous-looking French manufacturers and businessmen, whose bills, neatly folded at the end of the meal, will soon be added to their expense accounts. André Malraux lunches here almost every day. The French Minister of Culture and author of *Man's Fate* eats very little but tolerates nothing less than perfection in cooking as in art.

Lasserre's menu, rather ugly to look at, is strictly classical. The belon oysters are among the finest in Paris and we count chicken Grand Palais, sea bass with sorrel and duck à l'orange (the most popular dish) among their triumphs. Most restaurants underestimate the importance of dessert, but Lasserre offers an impressive choice; to our taste, the most remarkable is the crêpe Grand Marnier.

The wine cellar is an utter joy (140,000 bottles) and the head *sommelier* knows how to decant your Chambolle-Musigny or Château Latour in high style, pouring it cautiously into a magnificent crystal and silver aiguière before your eyes.

You won't get away for much under 75 to 100 francs ($15 to $20)—or even a little more if you are moved to carry off the little copper casserole which serves as an ashtray. René Lasserre has had to resign himself to charging for them since his customers used to "borrow" so many.

Lasserre, 17 avenue Franklin Roosevelt (8e), 359.53.43. Closed Sundays and in August. Dinner served until 11 P.M.

Ledoyen **

WINE: 15

DÉCOR: 16

RECEPTION AND SERVICE: 18

ATMOSPHERE: 14

PRICES: V.E.

The worst judges, the coarsest palates have opinions about everything and peremptorily declare their disappointment in the potted quail au foie gras when they couldn't tell a quail from a hormone-fattened chicken or distinguish foie gras from rillettes. And we let ourselves be swayed in spite of everything; we begin to have our doubts and almost go so far as to repeat the slander. This is why, despite and apart from an ever-growing reputation, Ledoyen is denied the patronage of part of its natural following, and even we ourselves rarely think of going there to sample the baby chicks en chemise, the duck with peaches or the feuilleté of truffles.

This is a great mistake. There is, to be sure, a certain amount of truth in everything they say about Ledoyen. It's the other side of its gold medal. One cannot be both wildly luxurious, serve candlelight dinners worth $20 a person in vermeil dishes, be surrounded by the foliage of one of the noblest gardens in the world, welcome guests from every seminar, congress, symposium, colloquium, council, conference, briefing, synod, trainee program and any other excuse for banqueting in Directoire salons, and at the same time have the cozy charm of a Lyonnaise bistro where one eats tripe among friends.

In short, you have to take Ledoyen for what it is and enjoy the showy but refined pleasures it is able to offer. The great wines, respectfully decanted and served in silver aiguières, are exquisite, and a good number of the specialties deserve distinguished compliments. From the cassoulet and simple roast fresh ham (tastier than many a braised excuse for York ham) on through the pheasant à l'orange and the famous sole soufflée, we were in the presence of cooking that is unquestionably the equal of restaurants with a more brilliant gourmet reputation and less brilliant décor.

And, strange as it seems, one can have meals there which are almost simple. An American girl whom we lunched with the other day even managed to eat onion soup with a silver spoon.

Ledoyen, Carré des Champs-Elysées (8ᵉ), ANJ 47.82. Closed Sundays. Dinner until 10:30 P.M. Parking.

Taillevent **

WINE: 18

DÉCOR: 15

RECEPTION AND SERVICE: 16

ATMOSPHERE: 14

PRICES: V.E.

Taillevent is one of the three or four Parisian restaurants whose name rings a bell in the United States. (Guillaume Tirel, known as Taillevent, was a cook at the court of the kings of France in the fourteenth century, and the author of the oldest French treatise on cooking.)

The setting—a town house in the *grand bourgeois* manner, decorated with Louis XV furniture—does not lack style. The dining room, where young Monsieur Vrinat welcomes you, is extremely comfortable. The well-spaced tables allow businessmen to exchange secrets, and waiters and maître d's to slip by unnoticed. Our only possible criticism of this symphony of good taste is that the amosphere is rather cold, as befits a distinguished establishment.

The very classical cuisine is generally most satisfactory. We miss the days when Taillevent used to feature regularly the specialities of the French provinces, a different one every time. Of the wide variety of dishes available we especially recommend the suprême of turbot Guillaume Tirel, trout cooked in Arbois wine, veal cutlet en papillotte and iced raspberry soufflé. The wine cellar is a real curiosity: 130,000 bottles and 512 different wines, including such collector's items as Romanée-Conti 1899 ($80), Château d'Yquem 1869 ($250) or Lafite-Rothschild 1806 ($140), of which Taillevent has twenty-seven bottles (which it will probably still have for quite some time). Fortunately, there are many other less risky and less impressive wines: Château Haut Brion white (1964) and red (1948), both of which are admirable, or simply some very good little wines served in carafes for $2.

Between $12 and $15, with a reasonably priced wine.

Taillevent, 15 rue Lamennais (8e). Closed Sundays and in August. Dinner served until 10 P.M.

Laurent *

WINE: 16
DÉCOR: 15
RECEPTION AND SERVICE: 15
ATMOSPHERE: 13
PRICES: V.E.

The food you'll taste here, amid a luxurious setting of circular salons or out on the marvelous flower-covered terrace in the tranquil groves of the Champs-Elysées, in the company of the best Parisian and international society, is usually prepared with care, occasionally great and always traditional: duck livers in Muscadet, stuffed baby chicken, remarkable broiled scampi (there is a strong Italian influence at Laurent), sole with tarragon and wine from one of the finest cellars in Paris. But don't expect to get all this elegance and gastronomic splendor for nothing: you should plan on spending easily 70 francs ($14).

Laurent, 41 avenue Gabriel (8e), ELY 14.49. Closed Sundays. Dinner until 11:00. Reservations necessary. Free parking.

Relais Plaza *

WINE: 14
DÉCOR: 13
RECEPTION AND SERVICE: 16
ATMOSPHERE: 16
PRICES: E

The Relais Plaza is probably the one very elegant spot in Paris where you can have a quick late supper after an evening at the Théâtre (or Studio or Comédie) des Champs-Elysées. This means you'll be in with theater people with lots of style, or at least lots of money. (The bill can be a whopper if you choose your food indiscriminately; you should generally count on spending about 40 to 50 francs ($8 to $10). You'll also meet some late-starting South Americans from the Hotel Plaza and some lovely nocturnal creatures. Late at night the food may not always be as awe-inspiring as some people claim. There are some brilliant dishes, however, like the the lobster soufflé; others of a rustic nature, such as braised beef in aspic, make an excellent late meal with a carafe of pleasant wine. In the summer we recommend that you have lunch or dinner in the hotel's little cool and flower-filled courtyard.

Relais Plaza, 25 avenue Montaigne (8ᵉ), BAL 14.90. Open until 1:15 A.M.

Le Berkeley *

WINE: 14

DÉCOR: 14

RECEPTION AND SERVICE: 15

ATMOSPHERE: 14

PRICES: V.E.

Nothing ever changes at the Berkeley—except the price of oysters, which continues in majestic ascent and always makes us feel that those oysters, plump and good as they are, should certainly contain a pearl.

There is always the same very elegant clientele: rich businessmen, pretty, slender girls (actresses, famous models, etc.) who make up for other excesses with a grilled sole, a simple fried whiting or a comforting steak-frites (steak with French fries)—all of the finest quality.

But you can also order more complicated dishes and drink good wines (excellent champagne) amid surroundings reminiscent of a luxury train with red-covered walls, or on the peaceful terrace so close to the seething heart of Paris (50 to 120 francs—$10 to $24).

Le Berkeley, 7 avenue Matignon (8ᵉ), BAL 47.79. Open daily until 11:00 P.M. Reservations necessary.

Trocadéro, Avenue Victor Hugo, Avenue Foch (16ᵉ)

Jamin ***

WINE: 12

DÉCOR: 10

RECEPTION AND SERVICE: 15

ATMOSPHERE: 13
PRICES: E

Raymond Jamin's greatest virtue is his modesty. He came up through the ranks to become manager of the Grand Véfour, and Raymond Oliver's partner. He learned to respect his customers, to heed advice and to act on good suggestions, and when, eight years ago, he bought the restaurant at 32 rue de Longchamp, he had the good sense not to rely on an inexpensive menu and run-of-the-mill clientele. After one year he and his excellent young chef, Saboureau, had created the restaurant we know today. Its quality and success have quietly but steadily increased to the point where it is now absolutely first-rate.

Chef Saboureau has an almost perfect record of successful dishes. Among our own personal favorites are scrambled eggs with lobster, stuffed sole, soufflé of salmon, veal kidney Marceron, his incomparable hare with brown game sauce, squab chicken with tarragon, and crêpes Masprone, as well as Bordeaux lamprey, foie gras of duck, lobster salad or his simple salad of asparagus tips and artichoke hearts. The cooking carefully holds to the Bordeaux traditions dictated by Jamin, who is a native of that region.

The wine list is rather weak in Burgundies but includes some fine Bordeaux: Latour 1937, Ausone 1955, Haut-Brion 1955, Cheval-Blanc 1955, Yquem 1959, as well as such pleasant wines as Château-Peyrabon, Smith Haut-Lafite, Pouilly-Fumé, a sort of pink champagne, and a very nice "crémant," an exceedingly light wine.

The only thing wrong with Jamin's is the dining room, but this is not his fault. He was expropriated from his former location at Number 32, and for another year or two will have to make do with a long little room shaped like an English bar, where his customers are squeezed in practically on top of each other. They accept their misfortune with good grace, however: Jamin has to turn people away every evening. About 50 to 70 francs ($10 to $14).

Jamin, 36 rue de Longchamp (16e), PAS 12.27. Closed Sundays and in August.

Le Petit Bedon ***

WINE: 13

DÉCOR: 9

RECEPTION AND SERVICE: 14

ATMOSPHERE: 12

PRICES: V.E.

For a long time this was one of the most popular restaurants in Paris. Nothing could top having chatted with Chef Bernard over your duck with peaches.

Bernard went into cooking after receiving his *baccalauréat* and was trained by his uncle, then chef at Voisin. He served first as apprentice and later as cook all over France, trained in deluxe gourmet cooking, and was more successful than he had dreamed possible when he opened Le Petit Bedon ten years ago. But Bernard's head swelled up higher than his chef's hat. He was soon off demonstrating *haute cuisine* throughout the world. He opened another restaurant at Vienne and somewhat neglected his Petit Bedon.

But for some time now this big prodigal son with the mustache and slate-blue eyes has had the good sense to spend as much time as possible in front of his customers and his oven. And his restaurant is again becoming one of the most popular places in Paris.

The spotless little room is undeniably comfortable (there is no smoke or cooking odor, even though the kitchen is practically in the same room; the dining room is air-conditioned), but the décor is ghastly. The "rustic" chandeliers are horrible, the lighting makes any woman look ugly, the tablecloths are yellow and ordinary, the flowers few and the yellow leatherette chairs would be rejected by any self-respecting snack bar. Monsieur Bernard and his wife are now reconsidering the problem.

The clientele, which completely fills the restaurant at dinner, is elegant, cosmopolitan and rich (and boasts many famous names from the blue book: the Aga Khan, the Shah of Persia, Albert de Liège and Princess Paola, well-known actors, politicians (Didn't Prime Minister Edouard Herriot write Bernard, "Your restaurant would be a credit to Lyons"?) and, of course,

Curnonsky, who was very fond of Bernard and died in the act of writing him (the last word he wrote was "cuisine").

Some of Le Petit Bedon's preparations are absolutely extraordinary, like the belon oysters au champagne: oysters lightly poached in old champagne, served in their shell and swathed in *beurre blanc* made with the reduced champagne and oyster liquid. The duckling with green peppers, noisette of lamb with tarragon, woodcock, famous écrevisses omelet and the broiled lobster are all very great dishes and prove that Bernard is really a first-class sauce cook.

The wine list, on the other hand, is not very thrilling.

If the restaurant isn't too crowded and you don't look too poor, Bernard can be a very agreeable person—jovial, very attentive, perhaps a bit gabby. His chef's hat gives him a stagey look that can get on one's nerves. In any case, he possesses the essential virtue: respect for his clients. The waiters are well schooled and quite efficient.

This is a very expensive restaurant, despite Bernard's efforts to hide the fact by giving his customers' guests menus with no prices (he sometimes makes a mistake and gives the blank menu to the host, thus causing him considerable embarrassment). Still, you can figure that the high quality, and therefore high cost, of the products and sauces he uses justify the 65-odd francs ($13) which is the least you can expect to pay for a meal at Le Petit Bedon.

> Le Petit Bedon, 38 rue Pergolèse (16ᵉ), PAS 23.66. Open every day. Reservations necessary.

Prunier-Traktir ** (See *Concorde, Madeleine*, p. 48.)

Le Vivarois **

WINE: 12

DÉCOR: 15

RECEPTION AND SERVICE: 10

ATMOSPHERE: 9

PRICES: E

Whereas restaurant owners (whose taste is not always their strongest point) usually opt for imitation Louis XV when they have lots to spend, imitation Louis XIII (with exposed beams *e tutti quanti*) when they have average means, and country-style (homey curtains, checkered tablecloths) when their budget is limited, Claude Peyrot, prompted by a natural and rather surprising impulse, has been daring enough to ask Florence Knoll to decorate his restaurant.

Some of you will surely be surprised, and perhaps not very pleasantly, by the chairs (Saarinen's white tulip chairs), Florence Knoll's long banquettes, the airy multicolored curtains and an abstract sculpture which we took for a duck on a spit and which actually represents the trumpets of glory.

Personally we like it a lot, though we think that colored tablecloths would lend more warmth to the room's solid whiteness. And we would encourage restaurant owners to be brave enough to choose contemporary furnishings, as they do in the United States.

There is one thing, however, which requires no encouragement but only applause: Claude Peyrot's cooking. It bears the unmistakable stamp of Fernand Point, Vienne's famous cook; Peyrot has inherited his finesse, distinction and refined simplicity.

Vegetables à la grecque are generally a pretty dull dish; here they are marvelous and surprising. But it's the sweetbread pasty with cream sauce that comes a moment later which carries one across the boundary between good and great cooking, and the dodine of duck with truffles and pistachios, à la Fernand Point, that carries one to the very heights of great cooking after another five minutes. We remained at these heights in the company of a few snails Dumaine style, and then of a superb veal kidney with Cornas wine, backed up by a splendid braised beef with shallots which would tempt a vegetarian to eat meat. And finally, scalloped potatoes. Very few chefs know how to make an authentic gratin à la dauphinoise. They slice their potatoes too thick, or overdo the grated cheese or the cream. Peyrot's gratin is "definitive": it is both firm and succulent and, above all, allows the potato (the *bintje*) to retain all its natural flavor.

We still had the courage to order the fruit brioche, but we

couldn't face the chestnut baba. Forgive us. Around 50 francs ($10).

> Le Vivarois, 192 avenue Victor Hugo (16e), TRO 94.31. Closed Mondays and in August.

Pavillon Russe

CUISINE: 10

DÉCOR: 13

RECEPTION AND SERVICE: 16

ATMOSPHERE: 17

PRICES: E

The most charming, intimate and comfortable of the "little Russian places" in Paris. The cooking is classically Slavic, read: dullish. But the caviar is good and the zakouskis aren't a mediocre hodgepodge of ill-defined, sorry-looking items but really authentic little hors d'oeuvres (including caviar and smoked salmon), after each of which it is proper to drink a glass of vodka, neat, to clear the palate.

This restaurant has many habitués, whom Ludmilla Lopato embraces as the salt of the earth and who sometimes join voices and relive the unforgettable evenings of the Russian princes, far into the night.

A mustachioed gypsy violinist screws up his eyes and warbles away, but without upsetting the customers by waving his bow under their noses, as is sometimes the case elsewhere. The young Yugoslav guitarist has talent and uses his nice voice to teach us odd, unfamiliar songs. But above all it's Ludmilla herself, with her glowing, velvety eyes, proud chin, extravagant and sincere hospitality, unflagging high spirits and triumphant voice, who makes the Pavillon Russe an inimitable spot, where the gaiety is charged with violence and nostalgia. At least 50 francs ($10).

> Pavillon Russe, 4 rue Lauriston (16e), KLE 83.79. Open every evening until 2 A.M.

Ternes, Péreire (17ᵉ)

Chez Denis ***

WINE: 19

DÉCOR: 13

RECEPTION AND SERVICE: 10

ATMOSPHERE: 11

PRICES: V.E.

He's crazy.

If he were in the theater he would send calvary charges flying across the stage of the Opéra; if he were a multimillionaire
he'd try to buy Versailles. If he were an emperor he'd set fire to
Rome—and wouldn't spare the matches. He's crazy because
we have become too sane. Denis picked the wrong era: he
should have appeared in the middle of the nineteenth century.
At the Rocher de Cancale he would have served Balzac twelve
dozen oysters to whet the great author's appetite and brought
salads of fresh truffles to Alexandre Dumas. He would have
been a real lord, the toast of all Paris.

Denis is a unique case, a phenomenon. Do you know any
European restaurants with the gall to put a 40-franc ($8) filet
of beef on the menu, or a $9 veal kidney or a $12 dodine of
duck? Yes: Denis. It's a deliberate outrage to Parisians who
think only in terms of grillades and that unbeatable little rosé.
All right, but that filet is topped with a marvelous duck liver;
that fantastic dodine of wild duck (a whole duck for each person) is bursting with foie gras, and when you order the lamb
with Sarlat potatoes, Denis quite simply puts in a layer of potatoes, a layer of truffles, a layer of potatoes, a layer of truffles. . . . This is the way our grandparents lived, if they were
lucky enough to have money. Customers of the Café Anglais or
Foyot found it perfectly normal to pay 200 or 250 francs ($40 to
$50) a person. Today the "high liver" is at large and the V.I.P.
eats lightly. A few great lords of the table still exist, however,
and it is altogether possible that Chez Denis will one day become a sort of club, every bit as exclusive as the Jockey, where
freemasons of a vanished art of living will find a haven in

which to abandon themselves to their gourmet rites. And even now, if both you and your wallet are subject to fits of insanity, you really must go to Chez Denis. There will always be philistines who are thrown into a sudden rage by the sight of their bill and who squawk that Denis is nothing to get excited about. Forget about them. Once you have tasted a slice of pheasant salamis with hazelnuts or a bit of fricasséed rabbit in aspic, once you have sampled the superb terrine of truffled sweetbreads, gotten your fingers gooey with lobster à la bordelaise, dispatched a nice plump ortolan in one swallow and succumbed to the delicate fragrance of the dodine of duck, it is impossible—yes, impossible—not to award Denis the culinary Légion d'Honneur.

Denis' wine cellar—coming from a good Bordeaux family, he was raised a wine lover—is just as insane. It requires no less than half an hour to read through the prodigious, extravagant wine list, with its one hundred-sixty vintages of Bordeaux, its great Burgundies and its extremely rare cognacs. Denis is an absolute tyrant in his dizzying kingdom—like all great chefs with any self-respect. It is out of the question to ask him for a couple of radishes, a steak-frites and a beer. He is quite capable of grabbing you by the collar and throwing you into the street. And don't get any ideas about ordering your partridge well done (the meat should be pink) or a young Bordeaux: you'll get them with a quiet sneer.

No, you must put yourself in Denis' hands with your eyes closed, your wallet open, your pride forgotten (Denis can't stand being wrong, and indeed he almost never is), and the feeling deep in your heart that you are going back to a century you thought was dead and gone.

> Chez Denis, 20 rue Rennequin (17ᵉ), WAG 40.70. Closed Mondays and in August. Dinner until 10:30 P.M.

La Mère Michel **

> WINE: 13
> DÉCOR: 10
> RECEPTION AND SERVICE: 12
> ATMOSPHERE: 13
> PRICES: I

Like many famous discoveries, beurre blanc (white butter) was the result of a mistake.

Before World War I a great epicure, the Marquis de Goulaine, lived in the vicinity of Nantes. One of his servants was a superb cook named Clémence, who spent her days simmering tasty little dishes, much to the Marquis' delight. Well, there came a day when the good Clémence forgot the eggs in a béarnaise sauce she was preparing. Upon realizing her mistake she burst into tears and went to beg her master's pardon. The Marquis examined the sauce, dipped a spoon into it once, twice, and finally said: "Why, that's good . . . why, that's very good indeed! Clémence, you have just invented something remarkable. We'll call it beurre blanc nantais." Clémence dried her tears and later opened a restaurant, and Mère Clémence's "white butter" became a classic of French cooking.

In the thirties Mme Michel, a native of Rouen married to a man from Nantes, in turn opened a little bistro on the rue Rennequin in Paris. She had met Mère Clémence, and the latter had told her the secret of her famous beurre blanc. It's a very simple secret, which Mère Michel, now a delightful grandmother with her hair in a bun, summarizes in a few words: "Beurre blanc, well, it's very easy. The recipe is all in the wrist."

White butter is Mère Michel's whole life and world. When she talks about it you forget that it's a sauce and come to think of it as a living thing. "You can't imagine how sensitive it is. You leave it alone for a second and oops! it's gone. And then it has its rebellious days, when you have to coax it with a spatula. So you don't want to thicken, you little rascal! We'll see about that. There, and there! No indeed, it never fools me. Oh well, maybe once or twice. Life's like that. . . . But then it's all over with, it's no good. You know, sir, you can patch up anything, but not a beurre blanc!"

Don't think of asking her if she uses anything but butter, shallots and vinegar. Our question thoroughly disconcerted her: "On my word of honor, I swear there's nothing else in it. Oh, no! I'm not like some people, who put in starch, flour, who knows? maybe even eggs. No, sir! I'll tell you right now, I'd rather hang up my apron for good."

As you can see, the secret of Mère Michel's beurre blanc is love. And it's the secret of all her cooking, one of the last and most authentic examples of "home cooking" to be found in Paris.

For instance, when the season is over for Brittany langouste, Mère Michel would rather drown herself in her beurre blanc than buy any "wretched Canadian lobsters" from her fishmonger (she has utter contempt for Les Halles where, she says, retailers and the big restaurants always get first pick). But then she triumphs with her pike, the simplest and most delicious brochet au beurre blanc imaginable. Or then again, with turbot, sea bass, John Dory or mullet, which constitute her daily bill of fare, depending on what comes in. Don't let this make you pass up her scallops, though. They are prepared without theatrics or unnecessary ingredients (and to the best of our knowledge are among the finest in Paris). And don't miss her exquisite chicken which—what do you know?—tastes like chicken. Her olive oil salad dressing, as women alone (and rarely restaurants) know how to make it, is even more of a must. May one add that Mère Michel is also as honest as can be? Her prices have not gone up one penny over the last three years. About 30 francs ($6). Let's hope there is a special heaven for cooks.

> La Mère Michel, 5 rue Rennequin (17e), WAG 59.80. Closed Sundays and in August. Dinner served until 10:00. Make your reservation a day in advance.

La Marée **

> WINE: 15
>
> DÉCOR: 13
>
> RECEPTION AND SERVICE: 14
>
> ATMOSPHERE: 10
>
> PRICES: E

For awhile La Marée was an unsuccessful sort of place, where you selected your fish at the counter before eating it broiled, fried or prepared in a more complicated manner. But this kind of outlandish idea had no future in Paris.

Marcel Trompier, a former movie actor and a great fan of

the sausage-and-Beaujolais combo, took over La Marée and succumbed to Pomerol and Vieux-Certan. The sea here has flooded the hillsides of Burgundy.

In Paris La Marée is one of those that is second only to Prunier as a seafood restaurant. This is important to know since we live at a time when the ocean's fruit spills over perhaps a little too freely onto our table. It is also the only place in Paris where one can eat splendid Belon oysters during the summer months.

The simplicity of the marvelous sole Colbert, which manages to reconcile breading and frying with preserving the full flavor of the fish, does not preclude more complex, and less maritime, dishes like filet of lamb en croûte, with a crust that would do a pastry cook proud. The pastries—made right in the sophisticated kitchen—are remarkable, as is the cheese.

Prices are high: around 50 francs ($10) a person, including a good wine and service. One is obviously paying for the comfortable red velvet surroundings and the extravagant sums which have been sunk into the stained glass of the façade.

> La Marée, 1 rue Daru (17e), WAG 52.42. Closed Sundays and in August. Reservations necessary.

Dessirier *

> WINE: 12
>
> DÉCOR: 10
>
> RECEPTION AND SERVICE: 10
>
> ATMOSPHERE: 12
>
> PRICES: I and E

Dessirier no longer has to worry about establishing its reputation as the best oyster house in Paris; only Prunier can compare with it. Rather, it has to convince people (especially in the months without an "r") that they can get something else to eat there besides those marvelous belon and "special" oysters, so wonderfully fresh and carefully opened, or those little sea urchins with their subtle flavors. It's worth noting that the interior, which is expensive-looking but done in outdated, flashy "modern" (in spite of some touches of better taste of late), prompts many passers-by and even some habitués to look down on the cooking as limited to sauerkraut and cold cuts. Even without the shellfish, however, Dessirier counts as one of the fine restaurants in Paris, with its blood pudding and tripe sausage (andouillette), tripoux (lamb's intestines), crayfish, crab salad, its broiled red mullet and the tender, delicate pot au feu served on Thursdays. (About 25 francs—$5—without oysters; much more with them.)

> Dessirier, 9 place Péreire (17ᵉ), GAL 74.14. Open daily until 1:30 A.M. Closed in August. Free parking at lunch. Reservations necessary.

Chez Fred *

> WINE: 14
>
> DÉCOR: 11
>
> RECEPTION AND SERVICE: 10
>
> ATMOSPHERE: 12
>
> PRICES: E

You don't stand a chance of getting a table Chez Fred unless you have reserved it at least three or four hours in advance. (As far as we can tell, Chez Allard holds the Paris record for advance registration: you have to make your reservation about thirty-six hours ahead of time.)

This is easy to understand. The food that Mme Fred cooks up, in a kitchen that would make the devil perspire, is among the most reliable and consistent in Paris. No casseroles, no sauces—just meat, broiled or roasted, with French fries like they used to make. There is an extraordinary joint of Charollais (or is it Limousin?) beef, seared by hell's flames but tender, juicy and flavorful on the inside, served in portions that could do for four; an admirable lamb steak, or if you are lucky enough to be there on the right day, a little roast leg of lamb cooked to order and to perfection and served with white beans that melt in your mouth; or else an enormous plat de côte (boiled upper ribs of beef) or, then again, a little broiled chicken.

They are all perfect, as are the hors d'oeuvres (dodine of duck, hard salami and Lyons "rosette" sausage) and the entrées like scallops meunière, the best we know of, provided you like the garlic and lemon juice which Mme Fred adds so provocatively.

After a good glass of the marvelous Saint-Amour, Juliénas or Chiroubles, every one a pedigreed Beaujolais, you will have enough courage to confront and congratulate Mme Fred. She will welcome you to her lair with her hands on her hips, a sly but tender smile on a face spotted with sizzling oil or butter. Or then again, she may not welcome you at all, for she has other things to do, and she has her moods.

Fred is there to iron things out for his brilliant clientele (Tout-Paris) and to bring you a bill of about 40 francs ($8).

> Chez Fred, 190 *bis* boulevard Péreire (17e), ETO 20.48. Closed Saturday evenings, all day Sundays, holidays, and from July 14 through August 31. Reservations are a must.

Tsarevitch

CUISINE: 10

DÉCOR: 15

RECEPTION AND SERVICE: 16

ATMOSPHERE: 15

PRICES: V.E.

This is the Russia of the boyars and grand dukes. Gold-framed portraits of Peter the Cruel and Catherine the Great adorn walls covered with damask velvet. The luxurious, pampered atmosphere of Great Russia, schooled in the ways of France, reigns beneath the red silk canopy. Chef Vartan has just returned from a trip to the USSR. His caviar and salmon, served with delicious blinis, are worthy of a prince. His dishes are typical of a rather spectacular style of *grande cuisine*. There is a good cellar of wines and champagnes. The obliging maître d', Nicolas Smirnoff, stands at attention, just as he did when he was a lieutenant in the Army of the Czar.

To make one forget her non-Russian origin, Mme Paoli, the owner of Tsarevitch, has surrounded herself with the best and most authentic Slavic ensembles in Paris. This means that the orchestra and entertainers are no longer in short pants. It also tells you how talented they are. The violinist Pali Gesztros will melt the lady next to you with three strokes of his bow, and she becomes Natasha in St. Petersburg under the spell of Oleg Arepoff's deep voice. Then there are the Dimitrievitchs, who once numbered thirty and are now only four. You must see the fabulous Valia, the fat mama of these genuine Russian gypsies, with her black tresses, coal-black eyes, aquiline nose, calico gowns and hoarse voice, alternately veiled and violent, which is still enough all by itself, to make you head for Russia. (About 100 francs—$20—and from 120 to 150 francs—$24 to $30—with champagne and caviar.)

> Tsarevitch, 1 rue des Colonels Renard (17e), GAL 72.99. Closed Mondays and in August. Open all night.

Concorde, Madeleine (Ier, 8e)

Lucas-Carton ***

> WINE: 19
> DÉCOR: 18
> RECEPTION AND SERVICE: 14
> ATMOSPHERE: 12
> PRICES: V.E.

It is ten in the evening. You are at the back of the dining room, to the left, sheltered from prying eyes. A waiter has placed a little footstool beneath the feet of the lovely lady with you, and you are sinking blissfully into the plush-covered banquette which casts a red glow over the maple and sycamore paneling in one of the last authentic holdovers from the Paris of the 1900's. The La Tâche 1937, which Fernand has meticulously poured into your glasses, has left you definitely convinced that God is not dead. Now two young waiters have brought a little side table upon which Mario, handsome and solemn as a Roman emperor, starts preparing your woodcock with a surgeon's skill and a lover's gentle hand. And at that moment you are convinced that you are reliving a precious moment from an era which grows more distant every day, and of which Lucas-Carton is one of the last, greatest and most moving witnesses. Every season Lucas-Carton's woodcock flambé appears at the first November chill and rules the roost until February or March, leaving gluttons like us with ineffable memories.

For over forty years the "Queen of the Marshes" has been the pride of this restaurant on the place de la Madeleine. Monsieur Allegrier, whom the staff calls Monsieur Alex, has served it to the most illustrious gourmets. His woodcock's reputation even spans the ocean: one evening he was host to two Americans from Los Angeles who had just gotten off the plane and explained: "This is our first time in Europe. A friend of ours told us there were three things that make the trip worthwhile: Malaga, the port of Amsterdam, and the woodcock at Lucas-Carton. We've seen Malaga, yesterday we were in Amsterdam, and now we're here." And each of them sat down to a woodcock.

Some co-called connoisseurs say and write that woodcock should be eaten very well hung. A few declare that you can tell if the bird is ready to eat when the beak comes off in your hand. For Monsieur Allegrier (and we completely agree) this is a stupid heresy, not to mention the risk of food poisoning incurred by eating game that is nearly rotten. Gamey, no; aged, yes. Monsieur Allegrier buys his woodcocks right after they've been killed. (Did you know, by the way, that the most reliable "hunters" are Brittany lighthouse keepers? The unfortunate birds are blinded by the beam of light and crash in the lighthouse yard.) He hangs them, unplucked, in a very cold and well-ventilated room and four days later—five if it's a very severe winter—they are "done."

This is where Mario comes in. Flamed woodcock happens to belong to what is known as "chafing-dish cooking" or, with a hint of (highly unjustified) contempt, as "maître d'hotel cooking." The operation is enacted before your eyes. Here is the recipe, a simple one as you will see. Let half a bottle of good Burgundy, to which a lemon peel has been added, cook down to a glaze in a sauté pan. Cook the well-larded woodcocks for fifteen or sixteen minutes and bring them out to the table with their juices running. Save the drippings. Prepare toast rounds by lightly frying bread in the butter used for the birds; keep them warm. Remove the bird's intestines, chop them finely and blend them with three ounces of purée de foie gras, a cup of the finest butter available, salt and pepper. Remove the thighs and breasts, place them in the pan with the reduced red wine, heat gently, pour in a cup of Fine-Champagne and flame. Arrange each woodcock half on a toast round, surrounded by the larding strips and the heads, which have been split in two and generously peppered. (The head is a delight fit for a king.) Return the mixture of intestines, foie gras, butter and drippings to the pan, heat until it reaches the desired consistency and pass it through a fine strainer over the woodcocks.

But Lucas-Carton's reputation does not rest on woodcock alone. The rather short menu includes such bravura morsels as lobster à la nage, flamed veal kidney, crayfish casserole Allegrier, hare à la royale, Brie cheese and peaches Lucas. These dishes cannot be too highly recommended, although some deplorable lapses occasionally occur in the *plats du jour* and service. The wine cellar (about 150,000 bottles) is one of the most splendid in Paris. Ask Fernand (a marvelous *sommelier* who performs his function without putting on any airs) to serve you a cool bottle of real Beaujolais or a more prestigious wine like Corton-Charlemagne, Richebourg or Romanée-Conti, and as a finishing touch, an old Calvados or an incomparable 1913 marc brandy.

The elegant and distinguished clientele is sparse at night, whereas you absolutely must have a reservation at lunch. The second floor has private rooms with individual entrances (the bell is hidden in the third step). Average price, all inclusive, is 75 francs ($15).

> Lucas-Carton, 9 place de la Madeleine, ANJ 22.90. Open daily until 11:00 P.M.

Maxim's ***[1]

WINE: 18
DÉCOR: 20

---

[1] These three stars are awarded to Chef Humbert when he is having a good day. Otherwise the food at Maxim's is very uneven; it sometimes deserves two stars, sometimes one and sometimes none at all.

RECEPTION AND SERVICE: 18

ATMOSPHERE: 19

PRICES: V.E.

Tuesday. Your wife refuses to admit she was wrong. You're annoyed. You long to make up with her, but she's as stubborn as a mule. And this makes you furious. It's a stalemate.

No, there's still one possibility. Pick up the telephone, dial 265.27.94 and ask for Roger. He's not a procurer, but Albert's successor.

Just ten years ago Albert, who is no more, would have answered. You would have had to list your titles. And it was rough going if you didn't have any. Albert's order of preference happened to be: nobility, then wealth and finally beauty. Good manners were taken for granted, as was elegance. Fame was trivial, even if your record had sold a million copies.

Today Maxim's is somewhat less exclusive, if only because nobles are getting scarce or trying to pass for useful members of the bourgeoisie. How can one put on airs about being a duke and at the same time hire out one's name and sad spaniel face to an advertising agency? Moreover, Roger doesn't have the same hidebound insolence or hippopotamuslike contempt that Albert flaunted before John Doe (or his brother Monsieur Dupont) and even fashionable actors. Roger served under Albert and was satisfied to learn how to judge whether a customer deserved a table for dinner on Tuesday from his voice, tone and ease of manner, as well as by the time of day and what was ordered.

Let's state right off that your little domestic crisis could occur equally well on a Wednesday or Thursday. But not on Friday. It's true that black tie is required that night, but the means have been mistaken for the end. Maxim's did not foresee social progress when it hoped to make the last day of the week more lavish by requiring formal dress. Friday is now like the English Saturday. John Q. Public can look forward to sleeping late the next day and has the money to buy himself a tux off the rack. The plan misfired.

So, there is Roger on the other end of the wire. You mention your name in a distinguished, offhand way: a common enough name but at least it's not Dupont—unless it happens to be Dupont de Nemours. You casually request a table for two on the banquette to your left as you enter the main dining room. You haven't the slightest chance, or right, to such a table, since all of the tables across from the orchestra are reserved, in order of priority, for disabled royalty, women expecting a (multimillionaire's) baby and heiresses accompanied by their darling "boys." Roger replies that he'll do what he can.

Now go tell your tear-stained wife that you're taking her out to dinner. . . . Not a chance. . . . To dinner at Maxim's. Her sobs stop. The miracle is already working; as far as we know, no woman has ever refused a dinner at Maxim's.

In a last fit of pride she declares she has nothing to wear. As a matter of fact this is always false, for Maxim's is precisely the one spot in France where your wife can wear those dresses which made you see red when she bought them—those insane sleeveless, backless, skirtless and topless dresses which you swore she would wear only over your dead body.

You too can be a bit daring. The carnation which all men dream of wearing in their buttonhole will not look ridiculous. Wear tails if you like, and even a ruffled shirt. Distinguished extravagance is permitted.

Thus attired, you drive up to Number 3 rue Royale about nine o'clock (not at seven, like some uninformed foreigners, who dine seated between a Luxemburger and a Swiss and go away convinced that they have been in the thick of Parisian high life). Georges and Paul won't make any unkind remarks if you don't happen to own a Rolls-Royce, and will smilingly park your Bentley on the place de la Concorde.

It is hard not to be solemn as you enter Maxim's. There is something papal about the purple and gold entrance hall. You won't be fooling anyone, but try to act a little casual all the same. A lady, perched high behind a sort of counter, stretches out her arms to you. It's Paulette. She's been there for over thirty years, has seen every mink in the world and rules over footmen and porters. She doesn't give anyone a coat check and has never once made a mistake.

You are now in costume and have to act your part. Go up the stairway on your left to the Impériale, the second floor, where a bar and cocktail lounge have replaced the private rooms. Gone are the days when a fine supper would bring together Boni de Castellane, the Duc de Morny, the journalist Henri de Rochefort, Robert de Montesquiou and the tastiest "daily dishes," as the ladies of the main dining room were referred to, with a fine caddishness. Our era, with its paper eroticism, knows little about those frank debauches and fears the very memory of them. The respectability game has made a mockery of all our most natural, and therefore most scandalous, impulses.

You sit at the bar, which is a very odd affair of marquetry and bronze, or in a comfortable Louis XVI armchair covered with Nattier blue velvet, and drink an old sherry or, better yet, an iced Sauterne, surrounded by the muffled din. Your wife is still annoyed but surrender is near. The perfect lighting, which brings out the shadows of her throat and takes the edge off her glance, is beginning to win her over. She luxuriates in the soft light like Poppaea in her bath of asses' milk. And when she has to make her entrance at the foot of the stairs, she is going to cling close to you.

Roger stands at the intersection between the main dining room and the Omnibus. Formerly Albert was there, casting the cold eye of an obese bishop on the petitioners, indicating his opinion of them with an imperceptible moue or motionless gesture. ("Everybody wanted to speak to Albert, but Albert spoke only to the Aga Khan.") Roger, a younger man, gives you a somewhat warmer welcome, although he will be quick to show an excessively vulgar customer to the door.

Of course, your table is not in the Omnibus, which at night is reserved for hoi polloi of total unknowns whom Maxim's deigns to shelter, doubtless out of charity. The Omnibus is the elegant spot, with the grill room, appropriate for lunch. Never let them put you there at dinner.

A strange fate has befallen the narrow room to your right off the hall, which connects the main dining room and the old bar, now a grill. During the *Belle Epoque* all the celebrities on Maxim's roster, that is, all of society, from grand dukes to great men about town, sat face-to-face and shoulder-to-shoulder on the banquettes of the Omnibus. The great courtesans (Liane de Pougy, Caroline Otéro, Emilienne d'Alençon, Cassive, Marthe de Kerrieu), who sometimes had a perfect right to their aristocratic names, sat enthroned in their trappings of jewels, lace and silk. "Sacred scarabs with asparagus tongs for claws," said Cocteau, who added: "The idea of undressing one of these ladies was an expensive business, and called for preparations worthy of a moving day." All these creatures have left their soft, perfumed stamp on the Omnibus, one which will never be effaced by their present-day replacements—the pretty little darlings of film and fashion, insignificant courtesans whose multiple minuscule lovers give the title of "fiancée."

You have been seated on the banquette to the right in the main dining room (let us note in passing that the banquettes at Maxim's are rather hard). This is better than out on the floor, where you would have been dispossessed a little before midnight to make room for the dancers hopping around to the strains of the jerk (which André Ekian's clarinet interprets as a sort of lame one-step. But then, it would be ill-bred for the orchestra to play too well. On the other hand, you can request any tune you like; it will be performed for you in such a way as to make it indistinguishable from the one before and the one after).

Not a single table is empty beneath the ceiling's incomparable stained-glass window and between the 1900's volutes of copper and mahogany. The Maharanee of Baroda, Callas and Onassis, Grace and Rainier of Monaco are gossiping sweetly at their tables. Their only apparent privilege is that they are seated over on the left, but the maître d's perform a no less elaborate ballet in front of you as in front of them. Winged, soundless, impalpable and perfect service.

Now for the menu, the great menu where almost no one any longer seems able to notice pheasant Souvarov, saddle of veal Orlov, caviar or ortolans. Naïveté, inexperience or narrow-mindedness usually make diners at Maxim's blind to anything but smoked salmon, oysters ($6 for only six, and no pearl), saddle of lamb, the dull and pretentious sole Albert and the sherbets.

Order whatever you like; it won't make much difference as long as Chef Humbert (who would undoubtedly be the greatest cook in France if he were given the means and had a better disposition) is not personally at work in the kitchen, which for a long time was one of the most obsolete and grubby in all of France. As a rule—and the exceptions are divine—he is satisfied to direct operations like an orchestra conductor and gives a solo performance only when a dish has prudently been ordered ahead of time (his coquilles Saint Jacques are a dream). Then too (and this is especially true after the theaters let out, when Humbert has already left for the day), Maxim's gastronomic level does not rise to such heights that deciding what to order need be a heartbreaking experience. Everything will be perfect, but not too perfect, for good eating must not be allowed to take precedence over the other areas of good living.

When you deal with Pommier, whose devilish eyes undergo spontaneous combustion in the thicket of his eyebrows whenever one describes the charms of a particular wine, you'll be tangling with a crack *sommelier* who will not stupidly let you have a run-of-the-mill "little Bordeaux." Since this is a reconciliation, perhaps you should obey the champagne rule, which has proved its merit.

And the feast, your feast, begins. Quiet, understated. Our era no longer produces eccentric characters who made their bad taste look good by their nerviness and style. There was the one who rode a horse into the dining room in the early 1900's; the one who ordered a jeroboam of champagne brought to him in a coffin to bury his bachelor days; Grand Duke Ivan, who drank eight liters of Mumm champagne one right after another, before falling over, as stiff as a poker, under the fierce eye of the cartoonist Sem who was sketching away on the corner of a tablecloth; those Hungarian princes who snatched the musicians' violins in order to play a *czardas* on top of a girl's table, or that French manufacturer who had a naked woman brought in on a platter for dessert. . . .

No, tonight you are almost in 1970. The fun is milder, less brilliant. But even if the women are no longer luscious, they are still pretty, and the champagne, the little pink lamps, the music, the mingled perfumes, the murmurs and the laughter, the décor like that of some fabulous subway, all take hold of you like sleep overtakes an honest man. And as you absentmindedly sign a check for $40 or $50, your eyes meet those of your wife: she is asking you to forgive her.

Maxim's, 3 rue Royale (8e), 265.27.94. Closed in August and on Sundays. Supper served after midnight. Black tie required on Friday evenings and recommended on Tuesday evenings.

Prunier **

WINE: 15

DÉCOR: 16

RECEPTION AND SERVICE: 17

ATMOSPHERE: 11

PRICES: E

This is the temple—or rather, temples, since there are two Pruniers, one on rue Duphot and the other on avenue Victor Hugo—of seafood. Everything here is of exceptional quality and may indeed be the finest in the world. The oysters, sea urchins, clams, even the little cultured mussels (served raw) and the caviar (excellent Gironde caviar in May), are all infinitely recommendable.

You have to love your work as much as Monsieur Barnagaud, the owner, to maintain 1900's standards in 1968. Dragnet fishing has destroyed "fine" fish; the sole caught at sea in a dragnet has nothing in common with the sole you hook from a little boat just off shore. So M. Barnagaud only buys his fish from old retired sailors who live in nice little coastal ports like Grandcamp or Port-en-Bessin and work for him all year round. The fine fish available at his restaurants are at the most two days old, whereas commercial fishing boats stay out for four to ten days before sending their catch to Paris. Also, you mustn't fail to sample his Dieppoise chowder, filet Boston (filet of beef with oysters), filet of turbot Verilhac (with champagne and lobster), stuffed sea bass à l'angevine, crayfish, and baby lobsters à la nage. This doesn't mean that the entrées (the veal kidneys, especially those prepared in a casserole—*en cocotte*—or simply broiled; hen pheasant with sour cream) or roasts are devoid of interest.

The charming downstairs rooms, with the bar and 1925 mosaics in Prunier-Traktir and the famous *lavabos* and carved panels in the oyster bar at Prunier-Duphot are really museums of the finest prewar and postwar (World War I) styles. However, the main and private dining rooms lack both warmth and imagination in their paintings (often uninspired), lighting (indirect) and walls (pale).

Monsieur Jean Barnagaud is personally in charge at Prunier-Duphot and helps his son Claude run Prunier-Traktir. He is a very great *patron,* extraordinarily conscientious and well informed. Absolutely nothing escapes him. In addition, his restaurants are full of very paternalistic control systems which allow him to make an instantaneous check on how things are going: suggestion boxes, pneumatic tubes, "intercoms" like they have on ships. His son Claude runs Prunier-Traktir with a gentler, shyer, more rigid hand. But he is completely on top of his job and the sea holds no secrets from him.

The clientele is very elegant, in a prewar way. Distinguished foreigners. Businessmen at Duphot. Tout-Paris at Traktir in the evening, in the large 1925 bar.

The wine cellar is not very large but has some great vintages (especially among the white Burgundies), at prices which may be the lowest in Paris.

Shellfish restaurants are always expensive. You know what scandalous prices oyster breeders charge. At Prunier they cost no more than anywhere else although they're much finer and more attractively served. (You can even get extremely fresh shellfish at Traktir during the summer.) The cooked dishes are also reasonable for a restaurant of this class. For example, an excellent meal consisting of six "fine" belons, crab pilaff, quail with grapes, a soufflé, coffee, half a bottle of Muscadet and a Gaffelière '43 came to 70 francs ($14), including cover. You can go way beyond this, however: a customer came in with a friend for several weeks' running. Each and every time they both ordered: two portions of caviar, lobster, turbot, lamb saddle, cheese, sliced oranges, half a bottle of vodka, a bottle of champagne and after-dinner cordials.

> Prunier-Duphot, 9 rue Duphot (Ier), OPE 11.40. Closed Mondays and from July 15 through September 1. Prunier-Traktir, 16 avenue Victor Hugo (16e), PAS 01.45. Closed Mondays.

Karpoucha

DÉCOR: 12

RECEPTION AND SERVICE: 12

ATMOSPHERE: 16

PRICES: E

A long, narrow little room, quite elegant, with everyone sitting more or less on top of his neighbor. Ter Abramov, a balalaikist emeritus, places his stool in the middle of the guests and throws himself into his music with an ease and virtuosity that leave one gasping. This extraordinary old man, who rarely smiles, has achieved such mastery in the course of his eighty some-odd years that the Soviet government invited him, a White Russian, to make a tour of the USSR in order to inspire interest in balalaika playing, which is a dying art. When he's in good form and the audience is with him, the atmosphere at Karpoucha can reach a kind of frenzy. (Very classical Russian cuisine, fortunately better than it was a few years ago.) At least 50 francs ($10).

> Karpoucha, 12 rue Pasquier (8ᵉ), ANJ 53.10. Open until 2 A.M. Closed on Sundays.

Lescure

CUISINE: 11

DÉCOR: 10

RECEPTION AND SERVICE: 11

ATMOSPHERE: 14

PRICES: I

Independent and nonconformist, Lescure has no telephone. And it's not easy to get a table. In that case the owner, a rough-edged Limousin whose bark is worse than his bite, will have you wait at the bar over a glass of *blanc cassis* (white wine with a dash of black-currant liqueur) or port, and you won't mind a bit since the dining room always presents a colorful spectacle.

Lescure is still an absolutely unspoiled bistro, in spite of its décor and the very touristy customers. Both the cooking and the atmosphere are completely authentic. The waiters, who

aren't exactly close-mouthed, serve you hard salami, good Limousin duck with cabbage, rabbit with olives, Sarthe blood sausage, boeuf bourguignon, dandelion salad and excellent tarts.
The prices, unfortunately, have assumed Parisian airs: 30 to 35
francs ($6 to $7).

> Lescure, 7 rue de Mondovi (Ier), no telephone. Closed Sundays
> and in August.

Palais-Royal (Ier)

Le Grand Véfour ***

> WINE: 15
> DÉCOR: 19
> RECEPTION AND SERVICE: 18
> ATMOSPHERE: 17
> PRICES: V.E.

At the beginning of the French Revolution some ladies of
easy virtue, "house" owners and their clientele, were fired with
patriotic and democratic ardor and selected the arcade and gardens of the Palais-Royal as the setting for their own particular
enterprises. Hundreds of these most generous creatures set
themselves up as laundresses or down near a window from
whence they exhorted the nation's manhood to fulfill its highest function. A guidebook was even circulated, giving the
names, addresses, fees and specialties of the girls of the Palais-
Royal.

It may be because love-making whets the appetite, but at any
rate the Palais-Royal section became a gourmet center at the
same time. The Café de Chartres, located under the arcade,
had opened its doors a score of years earlier. Jean Véfour, formerly chef to Philippe d'Orléans, nicknamed Philippe-Egalité
(that fine fellow voted for the death of his relative Louis
XVI), turned it into a restaurant. Its customers were freethink-
ing aristocrats and middle-class intellectuals, who planned the
revolution between mouthfuls.

The Café de Chartres was to have an exceptional fate. Re-
baptized Le Grand Véfour, it and the Procope are the only

restaurants which have come down to us with their original décor. And an exquisite décor it is, a transition between Louis XVI and Directoire, where the paneling and the painted and etched glass which enhance the walls and ceiling make it the prettiest restaurant in all Paris. Completely abandoned at the end of World War II, Le Grand Véfour was reopened by a strapping, bearded fellow just in from his native Bordeaux country, Raymond Oliver. Oliver was briefly connected with Maxim's but quickly regained his freedom and was glory-bound. Jean Cocteau and the great novelist Colette were instrumental in making him famous. They used to drop in regularly (both lived close by) and were soon followed by every celebrity in Paris. The food was extraordinary and the owner's personality fascinating enough to make one want to go back.

Boisterous, a walking encyclopedia of cooking (he has the largest gastronomical library in France), lordly, witty and a tireless businessman (his marked fondness for publicity makes him an easy target for critics), known throughout France for his televised cooking lessons, Raymond Oliver has only one serious failing: he spends more time in Tokyo, New York or Montreal (he ran the French restaurant at Expo '67) than in his own kitchen, and in any case he has announced his imminent retirement.

The cooking sometimes suffers from the boss's absence. But when it's good, it is remarkable indeed. Subtle, original, even astonishing, it can reach the heights of culinary artistry. Thus, choosing to forget a few unpleasant experiences, we cherish fond memories of fried eggs Louis Oliver (two eggs on a bed of foie gras, sprinkled with truffles), lamprey bordelaise (a kind of eel cooked in red wine), coulibiac of salmon or that masterpiece of sophisticated simplicity: the timbale of macaroni, lobster, truffles and foie gras. And if you take the trouble to order them, the chicken with lobster, hare à la royale, rib of beef with green pepper, young guinea hen Jean Cocteau, and crêpes Balzac are marvels you will not soon forget.

When Oliver is criticized for the lapses in his cooking he very adroitly retorts: "Cooking is a fickle and faltering art. Didn't Rembrandt ever ruin a picture? Then why shouldn't I have the right to ruin a dish?"

Some of his customers make him roar with indignation at their ignorance. One day a lady ordered a steak, *very* well done. It was brought to her. She called for the owner (he was there, for once): "This isn't fit to eat!" "Madame," replied Oliver, "if any *very* well done steak were fit to eat, what would I be doing here?"

The other star of the house is Monsieur Henocq, the wine steward. At eighty-five he still darts about like a quick fish. He is against expensive wines and partial to the Bordeaux *en carafe,* which is always excellent and skillfully chosen. For all his expert knowledge, however, his rather limited cellar cannot compete with La Tour d'Argent or Lucas-Carton.

Lunch at Le Grand Véfour is a very pleasant experience. The place is quiet—too quiet for Oliver, who has to turn people away in the evening.

Prices are slightly lower than in other restaurants of the same class: around $13 all told. But then there was the night some ten years ago when the Marquis de Cuevas, the dance patron, invited everyone in the room to be his guest: they managed all the same to present him with a bill for $2,000!

Should nature's call make you visit the *petit endroit,* don't bother complaining about the lack of room. Le Grand Véfour has been classed as a historical monument and enlargements are strictly forbidden.

> Le Grand Véfour, 17 rue de Beaujolais (Ier), 742.58.97. Closed Sundays and in August. Dinner served until 10:00 P.M.

Opéra, Place Vendôme (Ier, 2e)

Drouant ***

WINE: 15

DÉCOR: 16

RECEPTION AND SERVICE: 17

ATMOSPHERE: 12

PRICES: E

Ever since 1903 this has been a restaurant that makes news once a year—because this is where ten novelists meet at the end

of November to award the famous Prix Goncourt. Then
Drouant sinks back into the shadows, if not into absolute ano-
nymity. All of which is rather senseless. If the Goncourt jury
(which has always included both guzzlers and gourmets, from
Léon Daudet to Francis Carco) has selected and retained
Drouant not only for their awards dinner but also on the first
Tuesday of every month, you can rest assured that it's not so
they can nibble some potato chips and an endive salad. It's
obviously because Drouant has been a good place to eat for the
past sixty years.

Drouant is a restaurant dynasty whose empire extends to
Fouquet's and, in the Bois, to the Pré-Catelan, the Pavillon
Royal and the Buffet at the Auteuil track. But the old establishment on place Gaillon is still their emblem, fortress and
research department.

When we said that Drouant remains in the shadows except
for the Goncourt dinners, we didn't mean it's not a "going
concern." One hundred and fifty to three hundred lunches are
served every day, a figure many famous places merely dream
of. We simply mean that it's a quiet place run by quiet people
who are mainly interested in preserving firmly established traditions.

The extraordinary Café de Paris—probably the greatest restaurant in the world and of all time—remained firmly in the
hands of Grandfather Drouant until the very last. It is not surprising, then, that his descendants, trained in that school,
should have nothing but contempt for all the little tricks which
some fledgling restaurateurs use in an attempt to cover up
their incompetence. Here, if one may say so, the menu calls a
cat a cat, and the admirable jugged hare in the French manner
turns out to be just that: the real, the classical civet de lièvre à
la française. This menu hasn't much appeal for the imagination. The names are not very thrilling. But Pascal, the head
maître d' (he commands six maître d's as well as a regiment of
master and apprentice chefs), can explain the exact meaning of
filet de sole Drouant or mignonette de pré-salé à la Chartres.

If none of the ten charming private rooms tempts you (they
are either small or medium-sized, some having been designed

for two or three guests, and all of them have a décor straight out of 1925), try to get a table in the room on your right as you come in. It is known as the Flower Room because of the delightful way it is decorated with dried flowers arranged under glass, the curious, delicate work of Maurice Delacroix. When you make your reservation, however, be sure to speak to the manager, Monsieur Saint-Simon, who will help you plan the details of your meal.

Drouant happens to be a restaurant where one really ought to order one's meal in advance. The chef, Jules Petit, has to serve dozens and dozens of meals a day and for this very reason you should give him a chance to serve you the best food under the best conditions at the appointed time. This is what the Goncourt jury does, and we should all follow their example. Don't make the mistake of thinking that Drouant disdains elaborate dishes (especially game) just because it is primarily a seafood restaurant; its *plats du jour* (blanquette of veal à l'ancienne, paupiettes of Bresse chicken, lamb stew) are always excellent. And those are the dishes which it is always preferable to order in advance.

The same holds true for the wine. Drouant's cellar is rich in old vintages (it also has an immense stock of Bordeaux, too young for our taste) which shouldn't be opened at the last minute. We would be doing gastronomy a service if we could help revive the intelligence and courage shown by ordering a meal in advance. How can one expect to serve a large fish, a joint of meat or a piece of game properly if they have been ordered in a hesitant, random way? But how can this be brought home to a people who were once the greatest gourmets in the world and who now distractedly snatch bites of food which can only have been intended for Hottentots or infants?

Drouant, place Gaillon (2ᵉ), OPE 53.72. Open daily until 10:30 P.M., except on Saturdays. Closed in August.

L'Espadon du Ritz **
WINE: 18

DÉCOR: 17
RECEPTION AND SERVICE: 18
ATMOSPHERE: 14
PRICES: E

Parisians are convinced that hotel restaurants are always very dull. This is a rather silly notion, at least when it applies to the Espadon, which is one of the prettiest restaurants in Paris. The lack of Parisians is compensated by exiled kings, British duchesses, American millionaires and Audrey Hepburn—in a word, the usual Ritz customers, among the most elegant clientele in the world.

The décor is delightfully baroque. The ceiling has false beams painted in the Italian manner and on one wall there is a trompe l'oeil seascape by Carzou. The small-scale dining room (which opens onto the garden, weather permitting) is bathed in a golden, unreal glow from the clever lighting designed to flatter every woman alive.

At the beginning of the century the great Escoffier was the Ritz chef. His recipes have not been forgotten, and one can still enjoy his divine foie gras in port that César Ritz used to send as a Christmas gift to all the courts of Europe. His heir Charles Ritz, a great trout fisherman, has given a decided maritime flavor to the Espadon menu, which admittedly is somewhat brief. The young turbot with mustard sauce, filet of sole Ritz, John Dory (fish) Héloise and turbot Monique are perfect, as are the oysters, but other dishes are less successful. The chef will prepare a sublime coulibiac of salmon to order. Have the stuffed crêpes for dessert; they are divine.

The wine steward at the Espadon is an authentic and great sommelier whose choices are always intelligent. The great wines are surprising for their (relatively) low prices; we especially recommend the 1950 second growths from Médoc (Pichon Longueville, Ducru-Beaucaillou, Montrose, Léoville-Lascases) for about 30 francs ($6) a bottle, the first growths (Margaux and Lafite) at 45 francs ($9) and the superb white Burgundies (Corton-Charlemagne, Chassagne-Montrachet, Meursault des Hospices de Beaune) from the best years (1955, '61, '62, '64) for between 25 and 35 francs ($5 to $7), prices which are almost unbeatable anywhere in France. Figure about 60 francs ($12) for a well-lubricated meal.

L'Espadon, Hotel Ritz, 38 rue Cambon (Ier), OPE 53.11. Open daily until 10:30.

La Tour de Jade *

DÉCOR: 12

RECEPTION AND SERVICE: 16

ATMOSPHERE: 12

PRICES: I

Owner Monsieur Nhung, a perfect man of the world and a charming and attentive host, was Indochina's minister of health under Emperor Bao-Dai. He wasn't exactly sure how to run a restaurant when he opened La Tour de Jade, but it is now one of the two or three best Vietnamese restaurants in Paris.

Vietnamese restaurants usually have some very quaint ideas about lighting and décor; the more the lighting resembles a merciless glare and the room a bazaar full of horrors, the prouder they are. Fortunately this is not the case with La Tour de Jade, which, without being sumptuous, is extremely comfortable and metes out the lighting in intelligent doses. (If there are six or eight of you, reserve the pleasantly isolated rear table.)

Two cooks, one Vietnamese and the other Chinese, prepare Sino-Vietnamese specialties which are among the best to be found in Paris. We especially recommend the egg rolls, the five-flavored chicken and the tabanh-lu, which is a sort of fondue bourguignonne (you dunk little vegetables and pieces of meat into a boiling pot), but if you want dishes that are even more unusual, place an order in advance for crab stuffed with bird's nest, broiled mullet with anchovies, duck stuffed with lotus seeds, red mullet with tamarind or pork balls in soy sauce. This is Vietnamese cuisine in the grand manner. Between 25 and 30 francs ($5 to $6).

La Tour de Jade, 20 rue de la Michodière (2e), RIC 07.56. Open every day until 10:30.

Lindt Munchner Keller

CUISINE: 10

DÉCOR: 11

RECEPTION AND SERVICE: 12

ATMOSPHERE: 14

PRICES: I

Lots of good hearty laughter to set the heady Pschorrbrau gushing. And good sauerkraut and cold plates after eleven at night. A certain kind of subtle pleasure, like you find in Munich, whose atmosphere and cheerful décor have been recreated here.

Lindt Munchner Keller, 5 rue Danielle Casanova (Ier), OPE 66.25. Closed Sundays. The brasserie is open until 1 A.M.

Les Halles (Ier, 2e, 3e)

Les Lyonnais ***

WINE: 17

DÉCOR: 10

RECEPTION AND SERVICE: 13

ATMOSPHERE: 13

PRICES: I

We know quite a few restaurants in Paris and discover new ones every week. But there also comes a time when we eat just for our own pleasure . . . and so, like everyone else, we have our favorites, our pet spots which we keep coming back to. Les Lyonnais is one of them, and for a very obvious reason. Not only is the food good; it is consistently good. This is an amazing, perhaps even a unique accomplishment in the restaurant business. Customers at Les Lyonnais are in the habit of saying that this incredible consistency comes from the waitresses' fondness for the food they serve, Mme Viollet's smile, and the constant, questioning presence and rare qualities of the redoubtable and gentle owner, Monsieur Viollet. This is certainly correct, but incomplete. You have to get to the heart of the matter.

One day we chanced to go there when dinner was proceeding full-steam ahead, which is an apt description because one wife knocked over some chicken bouillon, delicious on the palate but scalding on the arm. The finest home remedies, including the efficacious one of dabbing the burn with wine vinegar, were immediately suggested. For reasons of decency the operation took place in the kitchen—at the very, very back of the kitchen. And that is where we discovered the secret of Les Lyonnais success: Old ladies, adorable grandmothers appeared from everywhere like little black mice and gathered around the patient. They were, quite simply, mothers, those wise, heroic, unobtrusive Lyonnais *mères,* alchemists who can transform a cabbage leaf into gold leaf and tripe into velvet.

Lyonnais cooking, and conspicuously that at Les Lyonnais, which is the most authentic in Paris, is a miracle of moderation and craftsmanlike good taste. It has no use for brilliant Parisian affectations, clever southern tricks with spices or the southwest's stick-to-your-ribs consistencies, nor for Touraine's elegant fussiness, Lorraine rusticity or heavy Norman graces.

Here it's all refined simplicity, with long-overdue homage to good vegetables and respect for real Beaujolais, free from incongruous sugar or suspicious aromas. And with this go the moderate prices, which are not the least of Lyonnais virtues.

You probably won't see a menu at Les Lyonnais. We ourselves gave up consulting it long ago. Monsieur Viollet makes this unnecessary by firmly suggesting a limited and always unexpected choice with which it is best to concur. According to his mood, the season and the consignments, your meal will consist (among hundreds of examples) of sheep's trotters, chicken with coarse salt and pot cheese; or scallops à la nage with mustard cream sauce, roast young wild boar and almond tart; broiled fresh anchovies, blood pudding with spinach and strawberries in Beaujolais; braised tripe in white wine, loin of lamb with marvelous white beans and a full-flavored cheese; hot salami, partridge on a bed of fresh cabbage and blackcurrant sherbet; and so on. The number of successful combinations is infinite. And each time all this superb food is better than one dreamed.

There are no great wines. "They'd be too expensive," says the owner. But there is some fine Beaujolais from little winegrowers, priced very low considering their unwavering quality: 6 to 8.50 francs—$1.25 to $1.75.

We knew Les Lyonnais when a thick brown layer of soot, cooking fumes and human odors dating back to the old "greasy spoon" at 32 rue Saint-Marc covered the walls and the 1900's gingerbread. It gave the décor the fatherly charm of old seasoned pipes. Monsieur Viollet thought (alas!) that it would be more elegant to destroy that precious patina and paint the room in a grayish shade which only emphasizes a hideous stripe committed in "crushed raspberry" ("The color of Beaujolais," he says as an excuse). But it still has its funny little ceramic tiles, the large bar made of dark wood and an indelible bistro atmosphere. (Around 30 to 35 francs—$6 to $7; service is left to the customer's discretion.)

> Les Lyonnais, 32 rue Saint-Marc (2ᵉ), RIC 65.59. Dinner served until 9:30 P.M. Closed Sundays and in August. Reservations necessary.

L'Ami Louis **

WINE: 14

DÉCOR: 6

RECEPTION AND SERVICE: 12

ATMOSPHERE: 14

PRICES: V.E.

Monsieur Magnin was born in Paris and perfected his cooking (which is basically that of the Landes, despite its Burgundian accent) in Switzerland. This lends breadth to his ideas. Since he only uses products of the highest quality (so much so, in fact, that this sometimes has a very painful effect on prices) and has such an extensive knowledge of gastronomy, he manages to prepare dishes which are at once very simple and very refined.

Foie gras is his great specialty. It is served in great slabs (accompanied, if you wish, by a remarkable Bayonne ham), but the rib of beef, roast leg or saddle of spring lamb, and marvelous potatoes boulangère are all delectable. (His French fries are too thick and a little mushy for our taste.) Monsieur Magnin is a great fan of early vegetables, and you'll find he has the first real morels, strawberries, asparagus, etc., depending on the season.

You can't haul a bistro over the coals for looking like a bistro. L'Ami Louis is undoubtedly the only restaurant in Paris which has not yielded to the temptation of ridiculous or horrible "renovations." Here, in this dark, out-of-the-way little street, the peeling brown paint, baleful light, stovepipe and even the black air-raid curtains are "of the period." The "toilets" are more uncomfortable and wretched than in the worst café of any whistlestop. We won't go so far as to congratulate the owner on this, since his conservative bias borders on the most elaborate faddism. (Rumor has it, however, that he recently gave them a once-over with a paintbrush.) Anyhow, this doesn't offend the clientele from the big hotels and avenue Foch; quite the contrary. (It seems, however, that people from the Ritz give a sudden start backward the minute they open the door.)

Mme Magnin is very gracious to customers she considers worthy of a smile. These are not necessarily the richest ones, but rather the finest gourmets and steadiest customers. She has her moods. Other people are likely to be treated with contempt, and many of them are hurt by it. At the end of the meal the owner steps out onto the ramp and casts his pale eye over everything. His fine seafarer's head is an impressive sight. His conversation is affable if somewhat distant. The waiters are efficient and they like their work.

Wines are expensive (the cheapest is the Fleurie Beaujolais) but good. The choice is limited: simple Bordeaux, and some Burgundies and Bordeaux of excellent vintage. We consider it indispensable to have a mellow, chilled Sauterne with the foie gras.

L'Ami Louis has a reputation as the most expensive restaurant in Paris. This isn't completely justified, for with a little effort you can spend more at Denis or Maxim's. One the other hand, we feel that the prices are not at all justified, even if the ingredients are often very rare and the portions lavish (too lavish for many women): at least 70 francs ($14).

> L'Ami Louis, 32 rue du Vert-Bois (3ᵉ), TUR 77.48. Closed Tuesdays and from July 14 through September 15. Reservations necessary. Open until 11:00 P.M.

L'Escargot **

> WINE: 13
>
> DÉCOR: 17
>
> RECEPTION AND SERVICE: 14
>
> ATMOSPHERE: 12
>
> PRICES: E

If the Escargot Montorgueil were put on stage, with its black and gilt façade, exquisite beams and ceiling moldings, red banquettes reflected in immense mirrors, painted staircase and potted plants, the audience would applaud the inspired designer who had dreamed up such a little marvel.

L'Escargot, like the Véfour, is one of the few restaurants in Paris which has kept its nineteenth-century décor almost intact. It is a very pure example of 1830's style. When you enter, don't forget to look up at the ceiling. You will see an allegory of cooking, full of chubby little cooks: it used to adorn Sarah Bernhardt's dining room.

It is easy to see why Americans, enamored of a certain France and its art of living, come in such numbers to see this Escargot, nestled in its nineteenth-century shell. They have nothing in common with the hordes who gloomily invade the oh-so-quaint places on both banks. They are distinguished, often gourmets, and always rich. They constitute a brilliant but not flashy clientele who lend the subtle and utterly chic flavor of "café society" to dinner at L'Escargot, where the Tout-Paris, from Louise de Vilmorin to Marie-Laure de Noailles, can always be found.

At lunch this festive atmosphere is much less apparent. The tables are occupied by businessmen and manufacturers whose appetite is as serious as their conversation.

L'Escargot does not have an omnipresent *patron* (like those at Allard or Les Lyonnais) who puts his own personal stamp on the place. But the manager, Monsieur Pacaud, is no mere employee, even if he does do his best to pass unnoticed; he has been supervising the kitchen for over twenty years. So when he recommends a dish, he knows what he's talking about.

It would be a mistake to think that L'Escargot is a bistro. Don't expect to find the veal casserole or lamb stew which are the pride of Le Grand Comptoir or La Grille. The customers are, to a large extent, the same as those at La Tour d'Argent, Lasserre, Véfour and Maxim's. Home cooking is something absolutely unknown to them. Even the snails, which rightfully should be king of this domain, occupy a very inconspicuous place on the pretty menu. Although there are a good ten ways to prepare snails (à la chablaisienne, à la poulette, à la comtesse Riguidi, skewered, with hazelnuts, larded, sautéed, breaded, fried, etc.), they are served here in their most commonplace form: with garlic butter.

The customers down snails in great quantities, but their taste runs more to lobster à l'américaine, curried sole or châteaubriand béarnaise. Fish makes a good showing: we found the stuffed filet of turbot somewhat disappointing, but there is no question that the sole maison is a great dish. For once the sauce does not dull the flavor of the fish. The calf's liver aux fines herbes is excellent. The scalloped sweetbreads are magnificently succulent, if somewhat drowned in their sauce. The desserts sin by the omission of imagination (crêpes suzette, fruit in wine, etc.). All in all, the cooking, despite a few weaknesses, is more than honorable thanks as much to the top-quality ingredients as to the way the dishes are prepared. There is a very fine cellar of great wines (Bordeaux is more popular than Burgundy), as well as some very good Beaujolais bottled at the restaurant.

This is also one of the most expensive of the "great bistros": a meal averages 55 francs ($11), everything included. But the prices are justified, to some extent, by the setting and service.

> L'Escargot, 38 rue Montorgueil (Ier), CEN 83.51. Closed Mondays and in August.

Le Grand Comptoir **

WINE: 13
DÉCOR: 13

RECEPTION AND SERVICE: 10

ATMOSPHERE: 14

PRICES: I

At the end of August we had dinner once again at Le Grand Comptoir. The famine which was ravaging the Parisian desert had driven the wild beasts from the elegant sections—businessmen making use of their secretaries for one last evening, hatted actresses, lawyers from recessed courts—to gather in this simple "tavern" in Les Halles. No fad had prompted them to come in such droves to this unpretentious *bar-tabac,* nor was it the room done in a charming Louis XVI-1900 style, nor the hearty, lively, jovial waiters who occasionally bumped into the distinguished and overcrowded tables. They were neither titillated nor annoyed by the presence of more modest diners, people from Les Halles eating in their neighborhood restaurant. They were simply happy in that sea of noise, Chiroubles and smoke.

And for that matter, Le Grand Comptoir didn't pay any more attention to these elegant creatures than to the market porters who come there at dawn for a rum coffee. Nothing changes Le Grand Comptoir, which is only concerned with serving good food to hungry people. And this lack of affection makes the hot Limousin salami, sautéed rabbit, Clamecy tripe sausage, Corrèze sausage, scalloped potatoes, cherry clafoutis, Beaujolais and Sancerre taste even more unusual and authentic (30 to 35 francs—$6 to $7).

Le Grand Comptoir, 4 rue Pierre Lescot (Ier), GUT 56.30. Closed Sundays and in July. Dinner until 10:00.

La Grille **

WINE: 14

DÉCOR: 15

RECEPTION AND SERVICE: 15

ATMOSPHERE: 13

PRICES: I

Together with Le Grand Comptoir, Pharamond and L'Escargot Montorgueil, La Grille is the most intact and genuine bistro in the "belly of Old Paris." Its hard to imagine just what it will be like when Les Halles moves out of the city. The building, which was erected in 1544, is certainly one of the most authentically old houses in the section. It had been a wineshop since 1830 until, some thirty years ago, a former butcher, Monsieur Lenoble, turned it into a restaurant which he named La Grille in honor of the wonderful iron grille protecting the window near the front door.

With a lover's devotion he preserved the charming old-fashioned décor exactly as it was, with its ancient bar worn down by all the hands that have gripped it, its mirrors, leatherette banquettes and floor of half-effaced tiles.

When lovers of Paris the world over dream of a real bistro, the image that comes to mind looks very much like La Grille.

Monsieur Lenoble has a sentimental attachment to Les Halles, but their imminent disappearance hardly disturbs him, at least not as far as business is concerned. As a matter of fact, you'll find a lot more reporters, painters, writers, brokers and textile merchants from the rue du Sentier here than agents or porters from Les Halles.

Ever since 1932 the newspapers in the neighborhood have adopted La Grille as their deluxe soup kitchen. Vaillant-Couturier, Gabriel Péri and the staff of *L'Humanité,* the official Communist organ, sat side by side with Léon Daudet and the editors of the ultramonarchist *Action Française,* eating andouillette.

At lunch the ground floor and upper room are besieged by a rather noisy crowd of men, and one rarely catches sight of a feminine silhouette.

In the evening the attack is mounted by foreigners, under good Monsieur Lenoble's slightly amused glance. But La Grille has such a strong personality that neither their minks nor their occasional desire to drink milk with snails have had the slightest effect on it.

Although he hails from Burgundy, Monsieur Lenoble confesses to being not much of a cook. This is a nice little fib, for we have heard that he's no dud when he occasionally has to confront a stove. Nor is his wife, for that matter. It's true, however, that for the last five years a young chef, Marcel Clay, who learned his trade at Lasserre, has been responsible for the cooking.

Clay handles his job with infinite talent. We've never been the least bit disappointed with La Grille. As our readers know, we have a weakness for home-style food and good old household recipes. Well, this is heaven. True, Monsieur Lenoble's menu doesn't offer as diverting a choice as Monsieur Viollet's at Les Lyonnais, but his Sarthe andouillette, his lamb stew or petit salé (corned pork) leave us admirably satisfied every time.

The same *plats du jour* reappear imperturbably all through the year: lamb stew and coq au vin on Monday; loin of salt-meadow lamb and boeuf bourguignon on Tuesday; club steak with scalloped potatoes on Wednesday; braised Beaujolais ham on Thursday; corned pork with lentils on Friday, and top ribs with coarse salt on Saturday. In addition, chicken with morels, veal sautéed with tarragon or stewed chicken appear from time to time.

Monsieur Lenoble has some old and delectable bottles (1928, 1937, 1945) stuck away in his stately vaulted cellar. But his warhorse is Chiroubles, a Chiroubles pure as gold which he himself goes to buy at the estate. (About 30 francs—$6, everything included.)

> La Grille, 50 rue Montorgueil (2ᵉ), CEN 24.64. Closed Sundays and in August.

Le Cochon d'Or *

WINE: 10
DÉCOR: 7
RECEPTION AND SERVICE: 10
ATMOSPHERE: 13
PRICES: 1

The sidewalk on the rue du Jour is the color of steer's blood, which broad-shouldered, white-clad men in skullcaps swill off without much concern for the feet of passers-by.

Next door in the rue Montmartre, men cart pork quarters, sheep's trotters, blocks of foie gras, pyramids of chicken. It's a section where you have a right to demand good food.

Still, it isn't easy to get a good meal here, especially at night. Luckily, there is Le Cochon d'Or, which is now open for dinner—a sign that this minuscule restaurant is partially deviating from its traditional policy of serving only the market set, and is attending to the Jet Set as well.

We recommend the magnificent club and rib steaks, but particularly advise you to order a dish that is rare despite its extreme and delicious simplicity: grilled pork (the neck muscles, done with a bit of garlic).

Since the game pâtés are very decent, the munster flavorful and the Beaujolais-Villages beyond reproach, you can enjoy yourself here for some 20 francs ($4), in very diverse company and in surroundings that are not likely to take your mind off your food.

Le Cochon d'Or, 31 rue du Jour (Ier), CEN 38.31. Reservations necessary at lunch. Closed Sundays and in August.

A la Forge d'Eloy *

WINE: 12

DÉCOR: 13

RECEPTION AND SERVICE: 10

ATMOSPHERE: 10

PRICES: I

Bernard Eloy has nothing to fear from the imminent relocation of Les Halles. A number of restaurateurs feel some anxiety as they picture the day when they'll have to attract customers who no longer have much call to be in that half-deserted section (although we'll finally be able to get a look at that admirable district then).

Eloy and his wife have created something more than just an honest bistro, using their own hands, dogged courage and discerning taste. The décor of this ancient house has been nicely handled: a long room with walls of large rough stones bordered by an antique grille, a tall marble cashier's desk (the kind they have in dairies), and a thick table d'hôte covered with cold cuts and hors d'oeuvres whose excellence is apparent to both eyes and nose. Then the room narrows around a "forge," a grill where oak logs are burning and good Chef Eloy is at work, his chef's hat on his head.

He is a pale young man with startled eyes, an expert in his

field, a connoisseur of fine ingredients; quick (his leg movements are remarkable), attentive and affable. He wasn't interested in turning this (or the little vaulted dining rooms in the
basement—clean, arranged with elegant simplicity, illuminated
by extravagant glass rosettes) into an antique dealer's masterpiece or a modish, self-conscious eatery.

You'll soon be convinced by the taste of the first dishes: the
extraordinary rillettes of duck, for example, or the blood pudding (hot or cold) and andouillette which he gets from an old
charcutier from Vouvray, or the stuffed pig's trotters; and then
the *plats du jour* like blanquette of veal with calvados, lovingly
cooked on a corner of the grill, or again, the pear tart, sherbets,
flamed pineapple crêpes and profiterolles. And finally, Eloy has
a very acceptable Beaujolais and an excellent "Gentilhommes"
Burgundy along with some brilliant vintages. A well-rounded
meal need not take you over 30 francs ($6), which proves that
nice things still happen to nice people in Paris.

A la Forge d'Eloy, 62 rue Greneta (Ier), LOU 95.63. Closed on
Sundays. Dinner served until 11:00 P.M.

Louis XIV *

WINE: 12

DÉCOR: 13

RECEPTION AND SERVICE: 10

ATMOSPHERE: 12

PRICES: I

This is a real old bistro, in one of the prettiest houses on the
place des Victoires, which they have finally decided to clean
and restore so as to give the place Vendôme a little run for its
money some day.

The clientele, which is always numerous, consists mainly of
reporters, brokers and people from Les Halles. Evening finds
pretty Parisiennes mingled with provincial and foreign types.
(It is always a good idea to have a reservation at lunch. Dinner
isn't so busy.)

The service is friendly, familiar, efficient and honest (if not
too tactful: the other day a waiter explained to a dissatisfied
customer that there couldn't be anything wrong with his coffee

"because it was made less than two hours ago and has been kept warm the whole time . . ."). Tony, the owner, looks exactly like a bistro owner in the movies. That shouldn't keep him from smiling.

Food: the scallops are admirable, prepared simply with fines herbes, and the foie gras is of good quality. But in our opinion the basic dishes—home cooking with the accents of Burgundy and Lyons (except for the oysters, which are always excellent) —are still your best bet: dandelions (real ones) with bacon, boeuf bourguignon, hot salami, the firm and very flavorful mitre-joint of beef (onglet) which butchers usually put away for themselves, accompanied by a good Sancerre and a pitcher of Beaujolais, which may not be particularly outstanding wines but won't bring your bill over 30 francs ($6).

Louis XIV, 1 *bis* place des Victoires (Ier), LOU 07.35. Closed Saturday evenings and Sundays and in August. Dinner until 9:30.

Pharamond *

WINE: 10

DÉCOR: 14

RECEPTION AND SERVICE: 11

ATMOSPHERE: 11

PRICES: 1

Pharamond? Oh, yes—the tripe place. That bizarre name, which should call to mind a legendary Frankish chief and maybe Egypt too, instead makes one think primarily of Les Halles and the mode de Caen. And nothing else.

This is really a shame since, just between us, tripe will never rank as great cooking, even when it is perfectly prepared and kept hot (even too hot) in a saucepan over a charcoal burner. It's a shame, too, because the fact—or misconception—that one doesn't care for tripe (women frequently turn up their noses at these innards, imagining them to be intestines; actually, they are the stomachs of a steer) keeps one from going to Pharamond, which in fact holds many other pleasures in store.

First of all there is the décor, whose charming moldings, naïve ceramics and little staircase winding its way up to the second-floor dining room have been admirably preserved since the turn of the century; and then the efficient waiters in their big blue aprons, the ironic but smiling owner and the relatively sensible prices (under 30 francs—$6, all inclusive).

And then, the food. It doesn't stop with tripe, which, by the way, is the finest classical tripe in Paris. It also includes many examples of that family-style gastronomy which now is so often imitated and so rarely genuine: sweetbreads with cèpes, boeuf bourguignon, duck with turnips, saddle of lamb with salsify, strawberry tartlet and some good, pure wines like the Chablis and an honest Pomerol. And a very unusual specialty which must be ordered in advance: the surprising trout with leeks.

Pharamond, 22 rue de la Grande Truanderie (Ier), GUT 06.72. Closed on Sundays during the summer.

Au Bougnat Blanc

CUISINE: 10

WINE: 11

DÉCOR: 4

RECEPTION AND SERVICE: 10

ATMOSPHERE: 13

PRICES: V.C.

René Rousseau would be at a loss to give you even an approximate date for the transformation of this long off-beige room dominated by its high counter of purplish-blue mahogany. The heavily silvered bas-reliefs are adorned with flowers, and a peculiar notice proclaims that a Chinese proverb, translated into pidgin French, says that all honest tradesmen owe it to themselves to consider credit dead.

Jean, whose freshly shaven chin matches his blue apron, brings you onion soup, corned pork, an excellent blood pudding with pommes en l'air, or tripe. Although he might appear to be preoccupied, he is merely scrutinizing the pattern on the oilcloth, through eyes dimmed by Beaujolais.

Bottles of Beaujolais are quickly emptied while Jean calculates your appetite. Tripe sellers (both sunny and shady) read and comment on the evening papers. The atmosphere of Au Bougnat Blanc, where you can get a decent meal for a song, is very special and rather down and out. But mainly it's an engaging place whose robust and touching simplicity is already threatened by Tout-Paris gone slumming.

Au Bougnat Blanc, 5 rue Sauval (Ier), CEN 38.15. Closed Sundays. Open from 9:30 P.M. to 3 A.M.

Au Cassoulet

CUISINE: 10

WINE: 9

RECEPTION AND SERVICE: 11

ATMOSPHERE: 13

PRICES: I

How would you like to have a sunny outdoor lunch in a huge flower and vegetable garden right in the middle of Paris?

The garden is Les Halles, of course, but this is one of its more secret nooks, at the corner of rue de la Grande-Truanderie and rue Pierre Lescot, where tourists rarely dare to stray.

Every noon the owner of Au Cassoulet clears the sidewalk somewhat of the clutter of hampers and sets up ten tables. These are immediately claimed by well-dressed and well-fed gentlemen, mostly stock exchange types. Still, we did sit next to a more original table, occupied by three retired generals who come to the peaceful Cassoulet once a month to recall campaign memories. When weather permits, the customers remove their jackets and the owner serves them an apéritif of a little white Saumur wine, Château-Parnay, of which our late lamented friend Edward VII said (it's written on the label): "If the alchemists had known this wine, they wouldn't have looked any further for gold." After which they come to serious terms with the dozen terrines and sausages placed on their table.

There are three hundred and twenty-five restaurants in Les Halles. The owners all know where to get the finest products, but hardly more than fifteen of them make any use of their knowledge. Monsieur Orsal is one of the latter. He doesn't claim that his cooking is as refined as that of the neighboring Pharamond or Le Grand Comptoir, and his humble bistro is not the place to go for elaborate dishes. Fine ingredients in all their honest simplicity are his special province, whether they go into fricandeau, rillettes, duck pâté or neck of pork, marvelous pickled herring with a slightly smoky taste, bavette, calf's liver, fish or pear tart. About 20 francs ($4).

> Au Cassoulet, 2 rue Pierre Lescot (Ier), CEN 15.75. Lunch only; closed Sundays and Mondays.

Le Pied de Cochon

CUISINE: 8

WINE: 10

DÉCOR: 5

RECEPTION AND SERVICE: 9

ATMOSPHERE: 14

PRICES: I

When you read these lines, Les Halles may already have completed their sad migration to Rungis. What will then have become of this little Parisian temple, where the flotsam of the night, mink and provincial chic weren't always shown much respect, where the onion soup, oysters and breaded pig's trotters wouldn't make your heart skip a beat, but where all the revelers in Paris drifted in one night or another, to soak up a little light and warmth?

> Le Pied de Cochon, 6 rue Coquillière (Ier), CEN 11.75. Open every day and all night.

Quai du Louvre (Ier, 2e)

Le Bistroquet*

WINE: 10

DÉCOR: 14

RECEPTION AND SERVICE: 15

ATMOSPHERE: 15

PRICES: E

The fad for this charming Left Bank restaurant on the Right Bank seems to have waned a little. But you still frequently run into Rothschilds, politicians, pretty little actresses and reporters who make an honest meal of écrevisses à la nage and splendid pastry. The décor is always attractive and in good taste (it changes with the season) and extends onto the sidewalk for lovers of the Louvre, the Palais Mazarin and the Vert Galant. Albert, the owner, a former bartender and a native of England, is talkative and extremely attentive. (Around 50 francs—$10.)

> Le Bistroquet, 26 quai du Louvre (Ier), CEN 49.52. Open daily until 12:30 A.M.

Place des Vosges (4ᵉ)

Coconnas

CUISINE: 10

WINE: 12

DÉCOR: 15

RECEPTION AND SERVICE: 11

ATMOSPHERE: 14

PRICES: E

On summer evenings the place des Vosges used to make you think you were in some Spanish or Italian town. The concierges set out their chairs under the arcades, the shopkeepers gossiped on their doorsteps, an occasional tourist strolled by. Now the Festival of the Marais and the illuminated mansions bring scores of starving music-lovers and esthetes to the admirable pink and white square every night.

The luckiest ones will sample the stewed chicken or whiting at Coconnas, as they sit on the sidewalk terrace or inside, in the elegant Louis XIII dining room. They pay 40 or 45 francs ($8 to $9) for a meal, about which little can be said, one way or another.

> Coconnas, 2 *bis* place des Vosges (4ᵉ), ARC 58.16. Closed on Tuesdays. Dinner served until 10:30 P.M.

La Chope des Vosges

CUISINE: 9

WINE: 9

RECEPTION AND SERVICE: 12

ATMOSPHERE: 12

PRICES: V.C.

At noon this modest café-restaurant serves as soup kitchen for the architects working to rehabilitate this maimed district. In the evening society has its turn. The music festival draws crowds of fervent, authentically young people and bejeweled society women with somewhat overly refined old "youths" in tow. There they all are, squabbling over a café table and a paper tablecloth. No gourmet orgies here, but good plain food served with a smile.

La Chope des Vosges, 22 place des Vosges (4ᵉ), ARC 64.04. Open until 10:30 P.M.

Grands Boulevards, Gare de l'Est, Gare du Nord (9ᵉ, 10ᵉ, 11ᵉ)

Cartet *

WINE: 10

DÉCOR: 7

RECEPTION AND SERVICE: 10

ATMOSPHERE: 12

PRICES: I

Mme Cartet and her nostalgic glance rule over a restaurant no bigger than a postage stamp. The place won't hold more than five tables. And this good lady's nightmare is that she will have to turn away customers, who knows, maybe even old regulars who haven't been far-sighted enough to reserve a table. This has already happened to her on several occasions, and her respect for her customers is so great that it causes her acute suffering every time. This is a change from those fashionable eateries where they slam the door in your face without the slightest excuse or friendly word.

So be sensible for once and don't descend on Mme Cartet out

of the blue. Telephone her and give her enough time to make you a good lunch (the restaurant is closed at night).

Mme Cartet is no cooking "giant." She is content to preserve the precious tradition of what used to be called "home cooking" with great constancy and honesty—which is already something. Her menu is as unpredictable as the arrivals and prices in Les Halles.

She will return from the market one day with a nice shoulder of mutton, which is then artfully stuffed and made to give off delicate aromas. Another day it will be some lovely rock mullets, a pike or possibly a hare, but every time the ingredients will be of the finest quality and prepared with all the love of which an old-school cook is capable.

In her closet of a kitchen Mme Cartet also makes big tarts. They may not look very spectacular, but your first bite will remind you of the tarts grandmother used to make, which we all have tasted at least once during our childhood.

> Cartet, 62 rue de Malte (11ᵉ), VOL 17.65. Lunch only. Closed Sundays and in August.

Le Chateaubriant *

> WINE: 14
> DÉCOR: 13
> RECEPTION AND SERVICE: 13
> ATMOSPHERE: 11
> PRICES: E

When we first discovered the Chateaubriant a few years ago we were immediately worried by its location, for the rue de Chabrol isn't especially famous for its ravenous hordes.

Our worry turned out to be justified. Despite the quality of its Franco-Italian cuisine, despite the graciousness and savoir-faire of the owners, Monsieur and Madame Forno, despite the unusual décor of lithographs signed and dedicated by Picasso, Lorjou, Villon, Cocteau, Braque, etc., the Chateaubriant comes to a standstill at dinner while the most wretched pizzerias in the Latin Quarter or along the Champs-Elysées are mobbed. Alas, one can't overestimate the role which a restaurant's location plays in its success.

Well, the Chateaubriant is still around. And so you'll be doing both it and yourself a favor by having dinner there. Contrary to most of his compatriots, Monsieur Forno contrives to prepare unfamiliar Italian dishes and is not afraid to apply great French techniques.

Try the maltagliatti, for example—big fresh noodles served with Parma ham; the seafood brochettes with beurre blanc; the polpettone (pasta stuffed with spinach, eggs and pot cheese, then rolled up, poached and served with melted butter or cream); the remarkably light fritto misto; the ribs of beef au fer or the herbed squab chicken Val d'Aoste.

In all honesty, however, we must mention one little point which is a stumbling block for many prospective customers: the Chateaubriant, like almost all the good restaurants in Paris, is not cheap. It would be difficult to eat here for less than 35 francs ($7), especially since Monsieur Forno not only has new Beaujolais but also some very great French vintages and the best Italian wines, which are never given away.

> Le Chateaubriant, 23 rue Chabrol (10ᵉ), TAI 58.94. Closed Sundays and in August.

Roggero *

WINE: 6
DÉCOR: 7
RECEPTION AND SERVICE: 10
ATMOSPHERE: 14
PRICES: V.C.

You may not be aware that the Mediterranean has wandered as far as Belleville's door. To prove it you have only to open that of a little green-fronted café, which is the hiding place of an amazing restaurant.

For that matter, "restaurant" is too ambitious a word for the five oilcloth-covered tables where local workmen come to have a bite. But there is also Marius, Marius Roggero, who is everybody's idea of a Toulonnais and who, together with his wife, lovingly preserves the good recipes of his native region.

A menu is something unknown to them. You simply take potluck. One day this will mean a magnificent, authentic bouillabaisse or a delicious-smelling daurade; another day it will be aioli, which is like a ray of sunshine in your stomach. In each and every case, however, it will mean delicious home cooking, the likes of which have not been seen for many a moon in the artsy-craftsy restaurants on the Côte d'Azur.

Marius' fine traditions have not faded in the pale sun of Belleville. He is determined not to kill himself with overwork and is only open for lunch. And on the stroke of three, if you are a fan and if Marius has taken a liking to you, he will escort you to his "office." This is the bowling green on place Colonel-Fabien where Marius is a nimble contender in expert matches of *pétanque,* a bowling game. (Approximately 15 francs—$3.)

> Roggero, 37 avenue Claude Vellefaux (10ᵉ), BOL 30.01. Lunch only. Closed Sundays. Bouillabaisse must be ordered a day in advance.

Brasserie Flo

CUISINE: 10

WINE: 11

DÉCOR: 14

RECEPTION AND SERVICE: 11

ATMOSPHERE: 13

PRICES: 1

In the eighteenth century the tangle of passageways between the rue des Petites Ecuries and the rue du Faubourg St. Denis was the site of the Little Royal Stables (*Petites Ecuries Royales*), and the great courtesan Ninon de Lenclos is thought to have had a country house nearby. Absolutely nothing remains of that glorious past, yet this courtyard does have a certain mysterious charm, with its old buildings, workshops and cobblestone pavement. At any rate it's a surprising place to find a great old-time brasserie which rivals Lipp as the most picturesque beer-house in Paris. The façade was recently repainted—much to the sorrow of the old habitués—but, except for replacing the old light globes with Dutch-style chandeliers (a questionable improvement), the owners have scrupulously respected the interior and left all its 1900's paneling and bronzes intact. Still, at a time when brasserie owners can't wait to sacrifice their décor to neon and formica, Flo (soon to celebrate its fiftieth year) happily preserves the magic of the past.

It certainly has some of the best brasserie food in Paris: foie gras with Riesling; the special, real sauerkraut, carefully prepared and garnished with good pork products: sausage, shoulder, ham and bacon, *plats du jour* like beef with coarse salt or duck nantais (accompanied by turnips that unfortunately are nothing to write home about) and the plum tarts (mirabelle or quetsche). Have a small carafe of Gewurtz-Traminer as an apéritif and follow it up with a carafe of good wine (Alsace or Beaujolais) or some excellent draft beer. A terrible crush at lunch but much quieter at dinner. Around 25 francs ($5).

> Brasserie Flo, 7 cour des Petites Ecuries (10e), PRO 13.59. Closed on Sundays and in August. Dinner served until 10 P.M.

Au Petit Riche *

> WINE: 14
> DÉCOR: 14
> RECEPTION AND SERVICE: 12
> ATMOSPHERE: 12
> PRICES: I

The Little Rich Man: what a marvelous name from another age of business and restaurants!

You can't really call this a bistro, despite the 1900's bistro décor (authentic, of course) with its moldings, colored ceilings, etched windowpanes and dark-brown pillars, despite the good-natured waitresses who mother all their customers, and the authentic provincial cooking.

This long, ornate string of little dining rooms, where lunch[1] finds tradespeople, businessmen (the Rothschilds are often seen here, since their bank is right around the corner) as well as auctioneers and bidders from the nearby Hotel Drouot, shoveling in the food and sloshing down the wine, is closer to a category of restaurants now on the verge of extinction but which occupied a place somewhere between an eatery and a deluxe restaurant over a hundred years ago.

---

1 At night the restaurant is very quiet—too quiet in fact.

Au Petit Riche specializes in Touraine food and has only one drawback, as you might guess from the name. Although it's an economical place where your bill never amounts to very much (say 25 to 30 francs—$5 to $6 including wine and service), the portions are somewhat scant, at least for hearty eaters.

The good rillon du Vouvray (veal and pork cracklings, done up like eggs in aspic) is not too small, but a slice of their excellent terrine is slim pickings indeed.

The grilled Vouvray andouillette is scarcely bigger than your thumb; the way the roast lamb melts in your mouth makes you even sorrier that you get only a shaving instead of a slice; the beautifully cooked rib of beef would do nicely for just one person; the pork shoulder (with a nice salad of whole fresh vegetables) could easily be slipped into a wallet like a dollar bill; and the delicious geline (chicken fricassee in the Touraine manner) is all too quickly gone.

The only thing one can get one's fill of here is wine—charming Loire wines, which are so little appreciated: spirited, first-growth Vouvray (available either plain or sparkling; the 1947 is admirable), untamed Bourgeuil Grand-Clos, a perverse Anjou and tangy Champigny, as well as a Lafite 1945, priceless as hundred-carat rubies.

Au Petit Riche, 28 rue Le Peletier (9ᵉ), PRO 86.50. Closed Sundays and in August. Open until 9:30 P.M.

Paprika

CUISINE: 10

DÉCOR: 14

RECEPTION AND SERVICE: 15

ATMOSPHERE: 14

PRICES: E

The fine Gypsy orchestra doubtless has something to do with it, but the varied and original Hungarian cooking also does its share to make the Paprika a cozy, likable restaurant. Have the fantanyeros, a sort of Magyar mixed grill, served on a wooden plate; but also sample the rather rich stuffed goose neck, and the excellent "peasant's plate" of eggs, cervelat and kidneys. The Tokay and the sweet barrack (apricot liqueur) are expensive. (Around 45 francs—$9.)

> Paprika, 14 rue Chauchat (9e), PRO 19.01. Dinner served until 2 A.M. Closed on Sundays and in July.

Pigalle (9ᵉ, 18ᵉ)

Proust **

> WINE: 13
> DÉCOR: 7
> RECEPTION AND SERVICE: 16
> ATMOSPHERE: 12
> PRICES: 1

It smacks somewhat of magic to be able to find the best cassoulet, the best preserved goose, the best foie gras and the best truffles in Paris all in one little hotel in Pigalle.

Right: Monsieur Lamazère used to be a magician. Some ten years ago this energetic and intelligent-looking Toulousain was still running around France pulling doves out of his pocket and guessing where the ace of spades was hidden in a deck of fifty-two well-shuffled cards. But he had just gotten married and his young wife dreamed of peace and quiet. Paradoxically, their provincial innocence led them right to the middle of the most dubious section in Paris: Pigalle. In spite of everything there was at least one hotel where respectability and good manners flourished, and which bore the name Hotel Proust (rather intriguing for readers of *Remembrance of Things Past*). It was for sale. The magician was transformed into a hotel owner.

Like any good Toulousain, he looked all over Paris for a restaurant where one could get a cassoulet as good as the one his mother used to make. He couldn't find any. This disappointment is at the root of his success—one might even say his glory. This man, who had never before given a thought to cooking, decided that this undiscoverable cassoulet would be found at Proust.

During the Gay Nineties the writer Anatole France used to

sing the praises of the cassoulet which Clémence, a little bistro in the rue Vavin, had been cooking up for the past twenty years. If he were alive today he would certainly immortalize Proust's cassoulet (which, just between us, is a lot more substantial than the famous madeleine of the same name . . .). Today the cassoulet, as it is still described by some backward writers, is little more than a myth. Gone are the days when different schools argued the comparative merits of cassoulets from Castelnaudary (dominated by breast of lamb, salami, pig's knuckle and pork shoulder), Carcassonne (which also included braised partridge or roast lamb) and Toulouse (the same base as the Castelnaudary, plus preserved goose or duck, lamb, Toulouse sausage and bacon). With very few exceptions, restaurateurs from Carcassonne to Montauban now serve only one type of cassoulet, the kind based on preserved goose.

Monsieur Lamazère, too, has yielded to the demands of simplification. But his secret, his uniqueness reside in having nothing to do with the canned *confit* which now prevails even in the best-known inns of the southwest. The only one of his kind in Paris, he makes his own conserves down in the hotel cellar and puts it into large earthenware jars brimming with goose fat, which allows the meat to keep for several months or even years. (The longer it stands, the better it is.) Earthenware has none of the disadvantages of metal: it allows the meat to "breathe." When treated in this way the meat is both firm and succulent, and imparts its inimitable flavor and aroma to the entire dish (baby white beans, homemade salami and sausage).

The foie gras, too, is exceptional: there's none better in Paris. Monsieur Lamazère has whole livers shipped directly from the Landes rather than Périgord, where the peasants tend more and more to force-feed the birds for too long, which makes the livers rather mushy. In the Landes, on the other hand, where the geese are not force-fed for more than four weeks, the livers are firm, with very little fat.

The foie gras at Proust is admirable because it is perfectly natural. Monsieur Lamazère needs six days to obtain this result: the livers are cured for forty-eight hours, then poached in goose fat for five or ten minutes (depending on their size). Thanks to this method, the cells do not break down and the liver, which for once has not been overcooked, retains all its mellowness. But after that it must be eaten within the next week and a half, which is possible only when the demand is intense—as it is in this little restaurant, where M. Lamazère sells a good ton of foie gras per year.

Finally, to transport his guests heavenward permanently, he has recently perfected a very simple technique (which we will keep secret) which keeps truffles "fresh" all year round. Truffles, which are delicious in season (December and January), subsequently lose much of their aroma and velvety texture. The canned ones, although still terribly expensive, most of the time are very disappointing since they are too dry and have no fragrance. Lamazère's truffles, on the other hand, which are served whole and plain, are quite simply sublime throughout the entire year. Eat them with a bit of foie gras and a glass of Sauterne; it will be one of your stomach's fondest memories of Paris. Your happiness will be so complete that it will make you forget the rather depressing décor of this hotel dining room. And when the meal is over, you can ask M. Lamazère, who has not forgotten his former profession, to show you a few tricks. But you won't need this to be convinced that he is truly a magician (35 francs—$7).

Proust, 23 rue de Ponthieu (8ᵉ), ELY 66.66.

Chez Haynes

CUISINE: 10
DÉCOR: 9
RECEPTION AND SERVICE: 14
ATMOSPHERE: 12
PRICES: 1

Leroy Haynes, a 250-pound Negro from America, has a degree in sociology, a captain's stripes from the United States Army and professional acting experience; he is also a good cook.

Whenever Louis Armstrong, Ella Fitzgerald or Duke Ellington come to Paris they dine at Haynes'. The Negro writer Chester Himes is a steady customer as, unfortunately, are very few French people as yet. They are mistaken: Haynes' salads, spareribs, Mexican chili and southern fried chicken are well prepared, and you'll be happy to find them when you're feeling homesick.

The cooking is American, or rather Southern. It is Negro cooking, known as "soul food" because it is warm, rich in contrasts, flavorful . . . and sometimes staggeringly spicy.

> Chez Haynes, 3 rue Clauzel (9ᵉ), TRU 40.63. Open until 2 A.M. Closed Sundays.

Kortchma

> CUISINE: 10
> DÉCOR: 7
> RECEPTION AND SERVICE: 14
> ATMOSPHERE: 13
> PRICES: V.C.

This is an inn—as its name indicates—straight out of a Gogol novel, a little *izba* decorated with chromos and naïve folk paintings. The cooking is homey: borscht, piroshki, home-style shashlik. You must taste the exquisite vatrouchka cheese cake and of course the vodka: white, red or yellow.

Everyone feels at home and among friends here, laughing, dancing, swallowing his vodka neat. Everyone joins in singing the whole pseudo-Russian repertory like "Kalinka," "Dame, Dame," gypsy songs and the ballads which Sandra sings with such verve. She's wonderful, full of fun, no longer so very young, with a haughty little nose and a terrifying accent when she calls you "Doucherki." She fills your heart with joy. Serioja on the guitar and Loya on bass are her talented accompanists. Joseph Kessel, Serge Lifar, Prince Youssoupoff (Rasputin's assassin) and other Franco-Russian celebrities sometimes visit this little lost inn in the heart of Pigalle. (Around 25 francs—$5.)

> Kortchma, 4 villa Guelma, on the corner of place Pigalle, (18ᵉ). ORN 18.52. Open from 9:00 P.M. to 2:00 A.M.

Old Vienna

> CUISINE: 9
> DÉCOR: 13

RECEPTION AND SERVICE: 15

ATMOSPHERE: 13

PRICES: E

Old Vienna recaptures the authentic, snug atmosphere of Vienna. The drapes, lighting and refined service are all Viennese. But wait, Hungary is here too: the tender, violent music and heavy goulash come from Budapest and create a profound, indefinable charm. (Around 40 francs—$8.)

> Old Vienna, 48 rue Saint-Georges (9ᵉ), TRU 46.09. Dinner served until 11:30.

Montmartre (*18ᵉ*)

Relais de la Butte *

WINE: 15

DÉCOR: 9

RECEPTION AND SERVICE: 12

ATMOSPHERE: 12

PRICES: E

You are in for a merciless dose of "little old Montmartre": rustic, turned furniture, checkered curtains and tablecloths, paintings of the place du Tertre variety (although a few talented young painters do occasionally exhibit one or two attractive canvases), culinary maxims written on the walls in Olde Frenche (on the pretext that the inn supposedly dates from 1672). And yet both the little ground-floor room and second-floor dining room, which you reach by a tiny spiral staircase, have a cheerful atmosphere that is much pleasanter than in many restaurants where the décor is more high-falutin'. And anyhow, the Montmartre folklore ends right there. The cooking at the Relais de la Butte doesn't make any concessions to the local style.

Monsieur Tresicq is from Languedoc, which gives his cooking a certain style: he is fond of garlic and of casseroles. He always mans the stove himself, with the help of a single assistant, and he doesn't get things going until he has your order in his hand. The dishes we recommend are: garlic soup au gratin (this is absolutely unique in Paris: light, safe for one's neighbors and very healthy). Truffled foie gras, fresh all year round and lovingly prepared by the chef in the Périgord manner, but with a highly individual and sophisticated touch. It is exquisite-tasting, and although extremely rich, can be eaten in considerable quantities (and the portions are rather generous) without upsetting even the most delicate stomach. The port jelly that goes with it is remarkable. The casseroles: sweetbreads with spring vegetables, golden-fleshed quail, guinea hen and the marvelous woodcock which is cooked to perfection and flamed. The buttery brandade of cod. The écrevisses à la nage (although these are white clams, they are among the best in Paris, firm and flavorful, cooked to order in a strong, superb court-bouillon). And the rich little lobster Newburg. Very fine cheese, especially the fresh Roquefort which comes straight from the official cellars and is selected according to Southern taste, which prefers a much milder flavor than Parisian taste. There is a good vacherin and interesting caramelized oranges. A very fine wine cellar: quality Muscadet, great Sauterne, honest Beaujolais and, here and there, some magnificent, mature Burgundies from Lupé-Chollé (Corton, Chambolle-Musigny, etc.) kept at room temperature on the shelves. (Around 40 francs—$8.)

Le Relais de la Butte, 12 rue Ravignan (18e), MON 16.18. Closed on Thursdays and in August. Dinner until 11:00 P.M.

L'Assommoir

CUISINE: 10

WINE: 5

DÉCOR: 14

RECEPTION AND SERVICE: 10

ATMOSPHERE: 15

PRICES: 1

Philippe Larue used to be Maria Callas' photographer. He jilted the diva and transported his angelic and somewhat ambiguous smile behind the counter of Montmartre's last authentic snack bar-grocery-restaurant.

The reading done in the course of a Christian education had left a few solid traces, and he named his establishment L'Assommoir in honor of Zola's novel. And all of thinking, singing or dancing Paris immediately adopted this bistro from another age.

Does your eye wander carelessly over the African masks arranged on the shelves, thinking they're right from the factory? Well, you're wrong. Philippe Larue has put together a remarkable collection in this thoroughly unusual spot, and naturally he keeps the finest pieces out of his customers' reach.

The dishes which a friend of Philippe Larue's prepares out in the kitchen will undoubtedly have a harder time getting into a great gourmet collection. It is casual cookery, pleasant if somewhat amateurish, and as so rarely happens on the Butte Montmartre, it is perfectly straightforward, despite a few annoying traces of culinary "chic" on the menu, like calf's liver flamed with vodka.

For 15 or 20 francs ($3 to $4) it would be a mistake to skip L'Assommoir, one of the nicest bistros in Paris—provided you steer clear of its tasteless Beaujolais.

> L'Assommoir, 12 rue Girardon (18e), ORN 55.01. Closed Mondays. Dinner served until 1:30 A.M.

Chez Jean

> CUISINE: 11
>
> DÉCOR: 10
>
> RECEPTION AND SERVICE: 14
>
> ATMOSPHERE: 13
>
> PRICES: 1

Melanie and Louisette, who look as if they stepped straight out of a Lautrec drawing, have been in Paris for over thirty years, but you'd think they just got off the train from Languiole. Aunt and niece have brought and preserved the savory perfume of their native Aveyron in their tiny little restaurant, Chez Jean, at the bottom of the Butte Montmartre.

Governments and Montmartre dwellers come and go: these two women remain solidly attached to their accent, their gratins, their terrines, which are piously prepared "back home," and their indestructible kindness.

They are wonderfully natural in their lack of interest in Paris fads and the short-lived enthusiasm for fashion's darlings. And when they fall all over an old customer, they're not just doing it for show; that's how people act where they come from, and it makes them happy to see people who appreciate the trouble they take.

Paris has lots of other places where you can get an equally good roast lamb, cassoulet, rabbit and almond tart, and drink just as good a Saint-Amour, but few where they are served with as much friendliness and genuine simplicity.

It goes without saying that at Melanie and Louisette's the bill, too, comes straight from a region where people don't sit down to a meal with the idea of ruining themselves.

> Chez Jean, 24 rue Durantin (18ᵉ), MON 64.79. Closed Mondays and in August. Dinner served until 10:00 P.M.

Nation (20ᵉ)

- -

Chez Léon *

WINE: 9

DÉCOR: 6

RECEPTION AND SERVICE: 12

ATMOSPHERE: 15

PRICES: V.C.

This bistro is more real than real life; it's even more real than the movies. But believe us, Léon, the king of beef with coarse salt, didn't set up shop in a gloomy little side street near the Porte de Montreuil in order to compete with movie directors. Léon is the real thing, the genuine article, and anyone who doubts it will soon find his chin in contact with Léon's large hands and brawny arms.

A few years ago Léon "retired," as he puts it, from the rue du Volga in order to enjoy a little rest now that he was over sixty. The eventful life of a bookmaker and bistro keeper is not always easy (his Rascasse on the rue Lemercier was the most notorious bar in Paris, and the clientele of his Boule Argentée at Epinettes was rather touchy on questions of Corsican honor). The shadow of the peeling walls in this joyless street seemed likely to provide the calm he craved for this huge Parisian scrapper.

But you can't escape your fate. The "Organization" left him alone, and for a while Léon thought he was going to find peace with his boeuf gros sel. He was betrayed by horses. His whole life had been devoted to horses. His father used to sell them on the boulevard de l'Hôpital. Léon ran them, played them and took bets on them. And the world of horses—owners, racing fans and toughs—soon smelled him out. Famous actors found their way to the secret little bar. His old pal, actor Jean Gabin (who hardly eats anything), spread the word about the admirable top ribs, so huge and so tender, the big flavorful vegetables, the seven kinds of terrine and the plum tart, about the little Beaujolais, about Léon's stories and his white hair.

Reporters—we were the first, by the way—glorified this royal chow at cafeteria prices (10 francs—$2—for an enormous and always equally delicious meal; but Léon says he's beginning to feel the bite of price supports . . .). And you'd see Sam Spiegel, counts and cuties, and women loaded with jewels devouring beef in this run-down section where they never even thought human beings could live. They drank champagne after the Brie (Dom Perignon, and it wasn't free).

But Léon hasn't changed. He stands there with his huge hands on his wide hips, surrounded by yellowish walls which no one ever considered decorating. His shrewd little eyes look at all those beautiful people begging for a scathing comment, an anecdote or possibly some marvelous pickled herring. He gives it all to them, takes his success as it comes, and laughs to think of his miserable colleagues in Saint-Germain-des-Prés with their exposed beams, herb-broiled menu and bleak calculations at the end of the month.

> Chez Léon, 70 rue du Volga (20e), DID 96.58. Closed on Sundays. Lunch only.

La Villette (*19e*)

Au Cochon d'Or **

WINE: 14

DÉCOR: 12

RECEPTION AND SERVICE: 13

ATMOSPHERE: 13

PRICES: I

It's wonderful how even the worst areas always have one eccentric who loves his profession and manages to remain uncontaminated by the surrounding mediocrity. They exist in Montmartre, on the Champs-Elysées, in Pigalle, even in La Villette.

Whereas no one in this section can resist treating tourists—and particularly Americans—like dirt, the owner and staff of the Cochon d'Or are charming and courteous. And it's a spontaneous, not a commercial, kindness which doesn't seem to vary with the size of their customers' wallets.

As in all the eating places in La Villette, it takes a good quarter of an hour to read through the overly abundant menu. But you are quickly repaid for your effort.

Choosing your appetizer and entrée is always a problem in a meat restaurant like this, where you know that quantity is no laughing matter. Unless you're starved when you get there, you'd prefer to start with something light. Well, the menu at the Cochon d'Or is fairly limited in this respect. Quailing before the pâtés (which looked extremely appetizing), the snails or the eel stew with Châteauneuf-du-Pape, we foolishly ordered hors d'oeuvres à la grecque, which turned out to be rather uninteresting, and an egg in aspic. Now, an egg in aspic isn't terribly exciting, but when it's prepared as intelligently as it is here and when the aspic is real aspic, it can be very good indeed.

Then came the broiled rib of beef with marrow sauce. It was suitably enormous, but so tender that it disappeared in a twinkling, together with a dish of wonderful souffléed potatoes, followed by magnificently light strawberry and raspberry puffs.

Au Cochon d'Or has a feature that is rather unusual today: a real *sommelier*, not one who starts off by suggesting a "blanc de blanc," a "light little Bordeaux" or a "nice cool rosé." Désiré —that's the name of this likable little bald man—did not hesitate to recommend the Burgundy, not the most expensive one on his list but the one he considered the best: a Volnay Santenots 1959 from the Hospices de Beaune which did indeed make us believe in perfection for a moment (37 francs—$7.50).

As one might suspect, the bill is somewhat more substantial than the pastry puffs: 30 to 35 francs ($6 to $7) without the wine. But it is money you can cheerfully spend, happy to be reconciled with avenue Jean-Jaurès.

> Au Cochon d'Or, 192 avenue Jean-Jaurès (19e), NOR 23.13. Open every day.

The Islands (Ile Saint-Louis and Ile de la Cité) (Ier, 4e)

Le Vert Galant **

> WINE: 15
> DÉCOR: 14
> RECEPTION AND SERVICE: 14
> ATMOSPHERE: 11
> PRICES: E

Monsieur Bos, the owner of the Vert Galant (and Laurent) has finally finished work on the second floor, where three pretty Louis XIII salons now overlook the marvelous spectacle of the Seine. The dining room has been entirely redecorated in the same sober, elegant style and the magnificent terrace still attracts the cream of the legal profession. They need only descend the steps of the Palais to treat themselves to a taste of tripe with madeira, soufflé of brill, oysters, milk-fed lamb à la sarladaise and great Bordeaux, as well as the stewed chicken which always makes one wonder if good King Henri would have approved of its being so expensive. A meal at the Vert

Galant, always excellent and prepared with great care by the new chef, is very hard to get for under 50 francs ($10).

Le Vert Galant, 42 quai des Orfèvres (Ier), Ile de la Cité, DAN 83.68. Open daily until 10:00 P.M.

Au Gourmet de l'Isle *

WINE: 11

DÉCOR: 12

RECEPTION AND SERVICE: 12

ATMOSPHERE: 10

PRICES: V.C.

Not every restaurant on the Ile Saint-Louis is a camouflage expert, hiding some pitiful meat under a blanket of "herbes de Provence." This one has no pretentions to medieval quaintness or profitable rusticity, although the natural setting of its magnificent vaulted cellars might well have inspired them.

The meals have fixed prices that never exceed 20 francs ($4), including all the wine you like.

Come on and admit that a fresh artichoke heart with a soft-boiled egg and a light sauce, or calf's head followed by daube de boeuf, or duck with new peas, salad, cheese, strawberry tart and lots of Auvergne wine are a welcome change from all the singed thyme in the vicinity.

Au Gourmet de l'Isle, 42 rue Saint-Louis-en-l'Ile (4e), DAN 79.27. Closed on Thursdays.

L'Orangerie *

WINE: 9

DÉCOR: 16

RECEPTION AND SERVICE: 9

ATMOSPHERE: 14

PRICES: E

This restaurant caters to the specific needs of Parisians enamored of elegant late suppers, a pleasure which is generally denied to those who are not taken in by gimcrack refinements —particularly in the Ile Saint-Louis, which is beginning to be a regular pirates' den.

It is not so much a *prix fixe* restaurant as one with a unique formula. Hot toast and a big bowl of herbed cream cheese are to be found on every table. Then charming (almost too charming) waiters bring you a long wooden platter covered with slices of excellent smoked ham and, finally, a huge dish of raw vegetables straight from the Marché Forvil at Cannes, since you couldn't possibly find fresh baby artichokes, fennel, celery, peppers, radishes, etc., in Paris on a regular basis. These are to be munched salted with hard-boiled eggs, or dipped in vinaigrette sauce.

Afterward you have to choose among three main courses. Two are always the same: ribs of beef and leg of lamb cooked over a wood fire as fashion now demands. The third is a *plat du jour:* broiled chicken, rabbit with mustard sauce, etc. Then comes cheese, tarts or chocolate mousse, coffee and liqueurs. This would be as banal as it is elegant if it were not the perfect expression of its genre. Everything is abundant, attractively presented and perfectly prepared from excellent ingredients. Thus the surge of irritation which people, infuriated by the food of starlets and delicate young men, feel when they first hear the menu is transformed into unblemished satisfaction.

And there is the added pleasure, almost unique in Paris, of not spending a penny more than what you're led to expect. This means a rather stiff but unalterable bill of 45 francs ($9), which covers everything, absolutely everything, no matter how much you put away, even of the wines (a nice Bordeaux and straightforward Beaujolais).

But even if the food at L'Orangerie were poor, we'd still be tempted to recommend dining there. The décor, you see, is absolutely delicious. The decorators have deliberately avoided the 1880's, a style which is beginning to bore us, and have shown very discerning taste by using only eighteenth-century appointments, often genuine and never overstated or cloying, in the long dining room.

The glassware, china and silver are no less refined, and the background music is not just another rehashing of Albinoni's *adagio,* but elegant harpsichord pieces instead.

L'Orangerie, 28 rue Saint-Louis-en-l'Ile (4ᵉ), MED 93.98. Open every day for dinner, from 8:00 P.M. to 3 A.M.

La Rose de France

CUISINE: 10

DÉCOR: 11

RECEPTION AND SERVICE: 10

ATMOSPHERE: 14

PRICES: I

This charming and tasteful little restaurant offers lunch out-side on the terrace or dinner by candlelight, with a view of the place Dauphine. The dishes are few but appetizing (lamb cut-lets à l'ardechoise, daurade with herbs, tournedos Henri IV). Every night the young and generally elegant clientele storms the ten tables which the owner refuses to reserve. Expect to pay 25 to 30 francs ($5 to $6).

> La Rose de France, 24 place Dauphine (Ier), Ile de la Cité, ODE 10.12. Closed Thursdays. Dinner served until 10:00 P.M.

La Tassée du Chapitre

CUISINE: 11

WINE: 8

DÉCOR: 15

RECEPTION AND SERVICE: 11

ATMOSPHERE: 13

PRICES: E

The Ile Saint-Louis harbors so many high-falutin' eateries that one is tempted to lump all its restaurants together in the same category. There are some which should be spared, how-ever.

La Tassée du Chapitre opened three years ago and was the first antique shop-cum-restaurant in Paris.

The pretty shop, full of curious objects, and the very beauti-ful cellar, where excellent grills and marvelous ices could be enjoyed to a background of Vivaldi, got it off to a good start. Everyone knows the usual life span of this kind of restaurant, which is soon destroyed by the same chic fads which create it.

Today the antiques have only a decorative function, while the menu has been filled out by a series of dishes—some of them highly original—whose quality will satisfy the severest critics.

We know that cucumbers in sour cream, herbed cheese and marinated daurade are not great cooking, but when they are good they can be very nice indeed, which is the case here.

We doubt that "old-style" chicken stew (stuffed and cooked in a pot au feu with oxtail and salami) or Indian rice (lamb curry with peanuts, coconut, bananas marinated in pimento sauce, candied citron, chutney and raisins) belong on a classical menu. But we were delighted as much by their quality as by their originality.

The ices come from Chez Berthillon across the street, which is the finest gourmet reference. The plain champagne has lots of character. The candlelight succeeds for once. The delightful, friendly way in which the owner welcomes you is very winning. We have only one complaint: the silverware. Rustic china is fun but aluminum tableware is a disaster. It's really too bad. Around 40 francs ($8).

La Tassée du Chapitre, 36 rue Saint-Louis-en-l'Ile (4ᵉ), MED 56.09. Dinner only. Closed on Mondays.

LEFT BANK

Saint-Germain-des-Prés, Rue de l'Université (6e, 7e)

Le Galant Verre **

WINE: 11

DÉCOR: 12

RECEPTION AND SERVICE: 14

ATMOSPHERE: 11

PRICES: 1

Before Guy Girard started his own place on the rue de Verneuil, he was the chef at the Petit Navire, one of the good little restaurants in Paris. Don't let his extreme modesty and shyness fool you: Girard is worth any number of the great cooks strutting around in restaurants which are much more famous than his. He is driven by an explorer's zeal which constantly leads him to perfect new dishes, either rediscoveries of ancient, long-forgotten recipes like ribs of beef toulousaine (with butter blended with ground hazelnuts, walnuts and almonds) or innovations like his ingenious crab and grapefruit salad. Even old customers are not bored by reading the menu, for it always has surprises in store.

Girard is from Toulouse, but his culinary tastes wander far afield of its *Capitole* (the hôtel de ville). He gives his origin its due with his fresh foie gras of duck and his cassoulet, but he also remembers that he worked in Marseille, where he acquired the secret of a perfect, light bourride, with lots of saffron and very little garlic. His menu makes a detour through Burgundy for coq au vin and sole in white Beaujolais, and ends with a bang in Périgord with filet of beef Prince Albert, cooked with foie gras and old port. And these dishes all have one thing in common: their finesse. Girard's cooking does not try to overwhelm you; its unobtrusiveness and delicacy are the perfect expression of Girard's own personality.

Our own favorites are: hearts of artichoke with duck liver, Baltic herring in sour cream, grapefruit stuffed with crabmeat, tapenade, bourride, filet of beef Prince Albert, preserved duck with sorrel, ribs of beef toulousaine, pear flan with walnuts and chocolate mousse.

At lunch the clientele consists mainly of editors and antique dealers from the neighborhood, while dinner attracts people from the "nice sections."

The prices are very reasonable considering the quality of the food; 25 to 30 francs ($5 to $6) will cover a good bottle of Beaujolais-Villages with appetizer, meat, dessert, coffee and service.

> Le Galant Verre, 12 rue de Verneuil (7ᵉ), BAB 37.81. Closed Mondays. Dinner until 10:00 P.M.

La Broche d'Or *

WINE: 14

DÉCOR: 13

RECEPTION AND SERVICE: 13

ATMOSPHERE: 15

PRICES: E

This is a vaulted room in a sixteenth-century house. The waitresses, dressed in Louis XIII style, are foreign students. Candles are burning on the polished wooden tables and the fireplace holds spits rotating under the weight of succulent meats. It's a little theatrical, to be sure, but it doesn't go overboard, and in any case it's one of the few places in Saint-Germain-des-Prés where you can take an elegant creature for an excellent grillade. The meal is still rather expensive, since you end up paying about 50 francs ($10) for antipasto plate, ribs of beef, dessert and a decent Bordeaux.

> La Broche d'Or, 5 rue Bernard Palissy (6e), LIT 55.16. Closed Sundays. Dinner served until 11:15. Reservations necessary at dinner.

Bistrot de Paris *

CUISINE: 10

WINE: 14

DÉCOR: 17

RECEPTION AND SERVICE: 16

ATMOSPHERE: 17

PRICES: I

One thing is certain: Michel Oliver (son of the owner of the Grand Véfour) has scored a bull's-eye with his décor. Taking advantage of the incredible vogue for bistros, he wanted to create one with a chic, sophisticated atmosphere. He was brilliantly successful. Slavik's 1880's décor, with its mirrors, *Belle Epoque* mosaics, marble tables and little conservatory, is perhaps the most attractive interior done in Paris since the war. Tout-Paris was absolutely right in swarming to such a pretty, custom-tailored bistro. But even more surprising is the fact that its popularity has not declined, as usually happens with fashionable restaurants. Quite the contrary; Michel Oliver turns away a crowd of people every evening (except for very pretty girls, whom he can always manage to squeeze in. . .). A very "in" crowd, naturally, provides a brilliant, heady evening for admirers of pretty girls and beautiful clothes.

The cooking is as rustic as the clients are chic (another form of snobbism). Michel Oliver's menu is carefully calculated to be fun, clever and appetizing: lentil salad with bacon, veal tongue, tripe with plums, pot au feu, trout with pine nuts,

lamb stew, excellent Brie or delicious caramel ice cream. The
way it is cooked is less reliable: on some evenings the food is
very satisfactory indeed; at other times unfortunate errors crop
up (but these are getting rarer and rarer). In any case, there is
no risk of disappointment as far as the wines go (especially the
Burgundies), which are always perfect. (Around 35 to 40
francs—$7 to $8.)

> Bistrot de Paris, 33 rue de Lille (7ᵉ), LIT 32.44. Closed Sundays
> and in August. Dinner until 11:00 P.M.

Chez Castel—Club Princesse *

WINE: 13
DÉCOR: 16
RECEPTION AND SERVICE: 17
ATMOSPHERE: 18
PRICES: E
(See "Discothèques")

We will talk about the famous Castel's, the most celebrated
private club in Paris, later and in more detail. In principle, you
don't stand a chance of getting in here unless your name is
Rockefeller or Sammy Davis, Jr. But we discovered—and it
was no mean trick—that a few concierges at the big Parisian
hotels have the magic power to procure a table for some of
their Anglo-Saxon guests. As a matter of fact, if you are staying
at the Ritz, Plaza or San Régis, Castel deems you worthy to
enter his place—surreptitiously. If, on the other hand, you
happen to be at the Hilton or George V, it becomes a very
touchy business indeed.

For a long time the food was pretty bad in Castel's charming
1900's dining room decorated with little bronzes, zany photographs and the prettiest girls in Paris. What's more, Castel—
gourmet that he is—never set foot in it. He has since hired a
new chef and need feel no apprehension about eating his own
food every night. And he's not wrong, for, without being
fabulous, the cooking is extremely agreeable and made with
top-quality ingredients, as, for example, the country ham, an-
chovy spread, cold jellied chicken, steak au poivre, and the

pastries. It's a pleasant surprise to find such down-to-earth food and friendly service in a place as snobbish as this. About 40 francs ($8) with a good Beaujolais or a nice little Bordeaux.

Chez Castel–Club Princesse, 15 rue Princesse (6e), DAN 90.23. Closed Sundays. Dinner served from 9:00 P.M. to 1:00 A.M.

La Chaumière *

WINE: 12

DÉCOR: 12

RECEPTION AND SERVICE: 14

ATMOSPHERE: 11

PRICES: I

La Chaumière, a country inn with lots of flowers and pictures, is one of the best and most dependable restaurants in the area, at the price. The owner, Monsieur Richard, is remarkably careful about where he buys his ingredients. There are four different specialties every day, all standbys of fine home cooking as, for example, tongue in piquant sauce, lamb stew, pot au feu, corned pork with lentils, rabbit with prunes, veal chop en brioche or Irish stew. All in all, a good hundred *plats du jour* are offered in the course of a year. Monsieur Richard is also an expert at preparing game. Hare, young boar, roe deer and venison are all magnificently handled in season at La Chaumière.

This is the headquarters for the antique dealers in the neighborhood, but from time to time a famous face, like Cary Grant, also shows up. Lunch is very crowded; dinner less so. Monsieur Richard, an active, smiling host, knows all the preferences of his customers, who have in time become his friends.

La Chaumière also deserves to be cited for the exemplary moderation of its prices. For a meal consisting of a lamb's lettuce salad, venison stew, cheese tray, tart maison and half a bottle of Bordeaux, your bill barely comes to 25 francs ($5). A single criticism: the tables are too small and too close together.

La Chaumière, 35 rue de Beaune (7e), LIT 46.64. Closed Sundays. Dinner served until 10:00 P.M.

Le Petit Zinc *

WINE: 11

DÉCOR: 13

RECEPTION AND SERVICE: 16

ATMOSPHERE: 13

PRICES: 1

Everywhere else in the *quartier* you are suffocated, strangled and have your nostrils clogged with thyme and basil, but Le Petit Zinc stays calm. There still are lots of people—on the ground floor, first floor and right out onto the sidewalk in the summer—but the waiters keep cool and serve you in a matter of seconds. Their aprons are always neat and their palms dry, even if their customers are ruffled and perspiring.

Don't expect any white damask tablecloths or crystal goblets (even though the cool Beaujolais is served in huge bubble glasses which let the wine breathe), and don't expect really plain food, either, although this is what the owners—three brothers from the Aveyron—are obviously aiming at. There are very few dishes: green salad prepared with walnut oil and electrified by a sliver of lemon, very nice roast lamb which is still juicy at eleven o'clock at night, and chicken that remains respectable even though it leaves a lot of its kick in the bottom of the pot.

On a whim we asked the waiter for more of the garlic with which the lamb was studded, and it was immediately brought to us without any obsequiousness or that artificial, conniving smile which waiters put on when they are angling for a fat tip.

We only hope that this unpretentiousness and good nature, however fundamental, will last a little longer than a Left Bank fad. (Around 25 francs—$5.)

> Le Petit Zinc, 25 rue de Buci (6e), ODE 79.34. Open until 3:00 A.M. Closed Sundays.

L'Auberge Basque

CUISINE: 10

WINE: 8

DÉCOR: 10

RECEPTION AND SERVICE: 12

ATMOSPHERE: 13

PRICES: V.C.

Pierrot is certainly the only restaurant owner in Paris who can boast a great Surrealist painter as his restaurant's godfather.

Fourteen years ago, in fact, Max Ernst personally inaugurated the little Auberge Basque on the rue de Verneuil and marked his unusual passage with two drawings which, together with works by Foujita and Mané-Katz, are the pride and joy of this modest establishment.

Pierrot (we don't know his last name) is not the fourteen-carat art collector one might expect. It's simply that five years of cooking on the Côte d'Azur brought him in contact with painting's "upper crust" and he quite naturally transported his passion to Paris.

The other original feature of this likable place is that the same formula has been strictly applied from the day it opened: it has one fixed price (12.60 francs—$2.50—today), including cover and service, and starts serving lunch at twelve thirty and dinner at seven.

The formula is certainly an inspired one, for the inn has never had a slow day as long as we've known it (for those who are interested in such things, lots of deputies go there for lunch). Pierrot's cooking owes an obvious debt to his native town, Saint-Jean-de-Luz, and can pretty well be summed up by the following dishes: tuna basquaise, tripe à la basquaise, piperade, crêpes with ham, broiled chicken Spanish style and Basque cake.

Shall we even mention the wine list? That "list," alas, consists entirely of one Bordeaux "supérieur," one Muscadet and one rosé. But here again one must go along with the "formula," and in any case these wines are far from unworthy.

L'Auberge Basque, 51 rue de Verneuil (7e), LIT 51.98. Closed from December 20 to January 6 and from July 20 to September 20.

La Bricole

CUISINE: 9

WINE: 6

DÉCOR: 10

RECEPTION AND SERVICE: 5

ATMOSPHERE: 14

PRICES: I

Saint-Germain-des-Prés has a little restaurant-cum-gallery where night brings together a collection of comedians of every stamp, actors, a few starlets and reporters who will laugh at anything after eleven o'clock at night.

The two pretty Mulard sisters—brunette Martine and blonde Brigitte (who appeared on Broadway in Robert Dhéry's *La Plume de Ma Tante*)—have chosen an old grocery store as the setting for La Bricole.

The décor holds no surprises. It looks, appropriately enough, like the stage set for an inn. Its simplicity is echoed in the dishes: lamb chops, veal chops, steak au poivre or tartare. The meat is charcoal broiled with herbs, but you can stay the heavy hand of the Chief Herb Sprinkler if you like the taste of meat, which happens to be thick and excellent.

This charming little restaurant is officially open from eleven in the morning until almost midnight, but customers would be well advised to take the service into their own hands if they want to get home before dawn. It is one of the liveliest and most unusual gathering places on the current Saint-Germain scene, where the incomparable atmosphere generated right after World War II is as vital as ever, no matter what people say.

La Bricole, 5 rue Perronet (7e), BAB 87.53. Open until 11:30 P.M.

Chez Coquin

CUISINE: 9

DÉCOR: I

RECEPTION AND SERVICE: 5 or 15

ATMOSPHERE: 15

PRICES: V.C.

What in the world could ever have brought Bretons to this little alley in Saint-Germain-des-Prés, which used to be a hot-bed of ribaldry in the days of the monks, and now slumbers beneath an honorable layer of dirt? It's a real mystery.

But be that as it may, in a space of less than a hundred yards there are, one right after another: a notions shop called Pays Breton where all the expressions of Breton thought are piously collected, from bed lamps shaped like a lighthouse to the *Breton Sailor's Almanach,* which a little notice stuck onto the windowpane tells us has finally arrived; a *crêperie* with the simple name Toullig Arc' Hramponez; and last, Mme Coquin's restaurant. And it's really something, this Mme Coquin's. We'd even say it's something else.

The place is cleaned once a year. This does not include the walls, however, whose successive incrustations bear the imprints of genius or dirty fingers casually left by generations of cartoonists and painters.

But even if you can get over the decorative hurdle, you still have to get by Mme Coquin. If this sixty-year-old Bretonne happens not to take to you, or to have taken to her bottle a little too much, you'll find yourself out on the sidewalk.

On the other hand, if you look like a good sort and not too proud, Mme Coquin will shower you with a wealth of kindness while her guardian angel Jo, a little snip of a woman dressed like a kingfisher(man), with a cigarette and a curse always in her beak, will affectionately install you at an oilcloth-covered table, and seconded by a slack-clad German girl who is studying for some degree or other, will bring you Mme Coquin's treasures.

As a matter of fact, Mme Coquin is frequently a good cook. And that isn't the least surprising thing about this place.

Experts on the subject are well aware that Bretons always come in families. Since Mme Coquin's family fishes for all it's worth, oysters, mussels, lobsters and crayfish are delivered here directly at unbelievable prices.

We won't tell you how much we paid for a dozen delicious fines de claire oysters; you'd accuse us of lying. Who would believe, for example, that for 5 francs ($1) Mme Coquin served us two enormous and succulent soles? That for 3.50 francs she'll bring you a plateful of curried mussels or that for 4.50 francs, beautiful, juicy slices of roast lamb will fall copiously onto your plate?

We swear that Mme Coquin's bill is the most genuine Breton article to be found in Paris.

Chez Coquin, 15 rue Grégoire-de-Tours (6e), DAN 49.64. Closed Sundays. Dinner served until 1:00 A.M.

Lipp

CUISINE: 10

WINE: 10

DÉCOR: 15

RECEPTION: 0–16

SERVICE: 15

ATMOSPHERE: 18

PRICES: I

A revolution is always proportionate to its setting. It was revolutionary for Roger Cazes, the owner of Lipp, to shave off his moustache. All Paris was involved, from Bernard Buffet to Yves Saint-Laurent, not to mention Darryl Zanuck. A mustache or a new clock is a major event in this historical monument.

One thing that is not about to change, at any rate, is the vigilant guard mounted every evening by Roger, the son of Marcellin ("Old Man Cazes"), at the entrance to his "digs," together with Michel, his smiling nephew and future successor.

"You always have the feeling that he's going to ask you for proof of identification," noted one of our colleagues. And this is more or less just what is required of provincials and foreign tourists who naïvely turn up at Lipp's. But if you are one of the few thousand elite whose features are etched in Roger Cazes' amazing memory, you have the right to a smile (which varies in size according to the customer's personality) and, optimally, to a handshake.

When he unbends, Roger Cazes can be the most charming of men, and, surprisingly, he even turns out to be chatty. His restaurant is his world. He is absolutely indifferent to what goes on in Saint-Germain-des Prés: it's been ten years since he set foot in the rue Saint-Benoît just across the way. He dreams of having his morning coffee regularly on the terrace of the Deux Magots, but is afraid that this would set tongues wagging in the long run and that the quarter would be full of talk that Monsieur Cazes wasn't happy "at home."

Léon-Paul Fargue, who was one of the first habitués, wrote that "Lipp is definitely one of the places, and perhaps the only one, where you can get a faithful and complete summary of a French political or intellectual day for the price of a beer."

Times have changed on the political scene. It's the fault of the Fifth Republic. Ministers used to unwind over a choucroute at Lipp's; today Parliament is in a coma. Only a few nostalgic politicians, like François Mitterand, are left. And of course De Gaulle never comes here any more (he used to have his lunch at Lipp's under the R.P.F.).

Sartre, too, has disappeared. He never leaves Montparnasse. But, on the other hand, the list of famous "Lippians," from the Comtesse de Paris to Georges Pompidou, keeps right on growing.

When you ask Roger Cazes to tell you who has never been to his place, he sinks deep in thought before answering: "I've had Benoît-Frachon [Secretary-General of the Communist organization], but except for him, the Communist leaders don't dare. It must be some kind of snobbism . . ."

For years no illustrious "Lippian" would have agreed to "sink so high" as the first floor, which was reserved for tourists. But ever since the princesses of France dined there with their fiancés, you can go up the stairs without any loss of self-respect . . . which doesn't prevent actors, starlets and fashionable designers from turning on their charm full blast to get a table near the entrance or in the back room after ten o'clock at night. Anyhow, everything depends on what time it is. The merely curious and the foreigners arrive with beating heart around seven thirty or eight, when nobody famous is ever there. . . . They eat by themselves and leave convinced that they have experienced a great moment in *la vie Parisienne*.

If you tell Cazes that he has one of the most limited menus in Paris, he replies that Lipp is strictly a brasserie. When Marcellin Cazes bought the Brasserie des Bords du Rhin from the Alsatian Lippmann in 1920, he put cervelat with remoulade sauce, sauerkraut (rather undernourished), two daily specials and munster cheese down on the menu. In 1926 he added Baltic herring, somewhat later, beef with coarse salt, and finally, rib steak. Almost nothing has changed. Not even the tart (which, by the way, is excellent), which has been supplied by the same bakery since 1913.

Enormous quantities of beer are consumed at Lipp. It, too, is invariable: nothing but dark and light Kronenbourg on draft. Order a *distingué* (a quart) if you want to look like an habitué. Darryl Zanuck adores it too, but is satisfied with a *sérieux* (a pint).

> Lipp, 151 boulevard Saint-Germain (6e), LIT 53.91. Closed on Mondays and in July. Dinner served until 1:00 A.M.

L'Oenothèque

CUISINE: 11

WINE: 16

DÉCOR: 11

RECEPTION AND SERVICE: 12

ATMOSPHERE: 10

PRICES: I or V.E.

The owner, a likable gourmet, has devoted his life to the propagation, not of the faith, but of French wines. He makes his loving and discriminating selection right at the wineries. The choice is immense for such a little place, and few restaurants can boast such a wide variety of half-bottles. It's true that wine keeps less well in half-bottles, but this formula does allow you to vary your pleasure without spending a fortune. To go with the wine there is a limited number of dishes, such as boeuf bourguignon or rib steak bordelaise, and some fine cheese. You'll spend 20 to 25 francs ($4 to $5) with a lesser wine, but who goes to L'Oenothèque to drink lesser wines?

> L'Oenothèque, 37 rue de Lille (7e), BAB 41.37. Open daily until 11:00 P.M. Closed around Christmas.

Le Procope

CUISINE: 9

WINE: 8

RECEPTION AND SERVICE: 10

ATMOSPHERE: 13

PRICES: 1

Paintings of Voltaire, Rousseau and the short-story writer Piron occupy three oval medallions in the ground-floor dining room of the place they made famous. Indeed, this café (now a restaurant), which is the oldest in Paris, can thank them for being the most prestigious as well. We are talking about the Procope, of course.

The "Florentine" Francesco Procopio dei Coltelli was actually born in Palermo. In 1686 he set up shop here selling coffee, drinks and sherbets. Then bright young men started coming, attracted by the "actresses" from the Comédie Française, which had converted a tennis court across the way into a theater three years later.

Old La Fontaine is believed to have been the first habitué of this shrine of pleasure, which later became a hotbed of liberalism. Anyone who was anyone in Paris frequented the Café Procope during the Enlightenment. An adolescent watchmaker used to see Rousseau, Voltaire and all the Encyclopedists here, before becoming known as Beaumarchais. Danton, Marat and Robespierre sat at tables which had once been occupied by those revolutionary agitators (and which can be seen on the first floor) and tried to strengthen their own as they paid homage to a fellow named Franklin, momentarily holding court here.

A hot-blooded lieutenant—Bonaparte—laid his hat down on a wager, among the oranges, cookies and jars of "sweet spirits."

Hugo, Balzac and their friends learned to sip black coffee at the Procope, where Verlaine used to spend many hours making the "green fairy" dance inside long, thick glasses.

The Procope became a restaurant in the early 1950's. Jean-Paul Sartre and Simone de Beauvoir went there regularly for quite some time without managing to attract their imitators. Today the Procope is enjoying a measure of its former success.

Foreigners go there at midday or in the evening to sample quail with grapes, duck with cherries—the recipes for which figure in all eighteenth-century cooking manuals—or simply for a grillade.

You can get a very acceptable meal here for very little (even as low as 7.50 francs—$1.50). Eleven waitresses contrive to make the dishes arrive in the right order and with the proper dignity.

But above all the Procope deserves a visit for its unique, exquisite setting: the mirrors which have reflected the most illustrious faces, the carved doorposts, red walls and pearly blond light from the crystal chandeliers.

Le Procope, 13 rue de l'Ancienne Comédie (6e), DAN 99.20. Closed Mondays and in July. Continuous service from noon until 11:30 P.M.

Santa Lucia

CUISINE: 10

DÉCOR: 10

RECEPTION AND SERVICE: 13

ATMOSPHERE: 12

PRICES: 1

Although Signor Vincenzo has been dishing out pizza and scampi in Paris for over ten years, his new place in Saint-Germain-des-Prés preserves the smiling simplicity and homey, cheerful atmosphere of his native Naples.

There is no double-dealing in his two narrow little rooms. The six or eight kinds of pizza are as big as your plate, the scampi are real shellfish and not some codfish in disguise, and the "daily specials"—canelloni, veal scallopini Milanese, saltimbocca, osso bucco, calamari and scallopini Fiorentine—are as abundant as they are tasty. The fresh pasta is homemade and Monsieur Vincenzo is rightly proud of having no refrigerators, since it proves that he makes a daily trip to Les Halles.

But your greatest pleasure (expecially in this neighborhood), even greater than that afforded by the humming waiters, the compliments they unfailingly pay the ladies or the glass of grappa on the house which you often get, comes when you get the bill. A real feast, even one washed down with Valpolicella or Orvieto, never costs more than 15 francs ($3).

Santa Lucia, 13 rue des Canettes (6ᵉ). Open until 3:00 A.M.

Vagenende

CUISINE: 9

WINE: 7

DÉCOR: 16

RECEPTION AND SERVICE: 10

ATMOSPHERE: 13

PRICES: I

This undoubtedly has the purest *fin-de-siècle* décor of any public place in Paris. But even if the owner, Mme Vagenende, has lovingly memorized the history of her restaurant (which opened in 1885), her customers—mostly young lawyers, old lovers, students, vagabonds from Germany and America—don't fully realize that they are snatching a quick lunch in a museum which is nothing less than a poor-man's Maxim's.

This décor, rich in Art Nouveau paneling, ceramics, Tiffany glass, gramophones and marble-topped tables, is the reason you should go to Vagenende. Waiters in black jackets and long aprons serve fairly good *cuisine bourgeoise* at fairly reasonable prices. About 20 to 25 francs ($4 to $5).

Vagenende, 142 boulevard Saint-Germain (6ᵉ), DAN 68.18. Open daily.

Le Wagon-Salon

CUISINE: 10

WINE: 3

DÉCOR: 10

RECEPTION AND SERVICE: 11

ATMOSPHERE: 12

PRICES: I

The owner confines his talent to light food. He does it so nicely, however, that one hates to complain about the minuscule menu, which contains nothing more nor less than salami, antipasto, chicken roasted on a spit (excellent), lamb cutlets (rather disappointing) and above all a very noteworthy rib of beef.

One could, on the other hand, ask him to try a little harder with the wine. Having a cellar with only two vintages, one of which is a rather mediocre Beaujolais, is really a little too casual, even in times like these.

You often see pretty women and incurable night owls at Le Wagon-Salon, where they are served—always with a smile—at the most ungodly hours.

> Le Wagon-Salon, 8 rue des Ciseaux (6e), MED 69.49. Open every evening until 2:00 A.M.

Odéon, Place Saint-Michel, Quai des Grands-Augustins, Quai de la Tournelle, Halles au Vin (5e, 6e)

Allard ***

> WINE: 16
>
> DÉCOR: 13
>
> RECEPTION AND SERVICE: 15
>
> ATMOSPHERE: 16
>
> PRICES: E

Whereas Parisian bistros have an unfortunate tendency to let decorators and antique dealers turn them into parodies of themselves, Allard remains humbly faithful to his marble-topped tables, dark-brown walls and finely crafted zinc counter, not to mention the sawdust scattered over the tile floor where the Aga Khan, Brigitte Bardot, Prime Minister Georges Pompidou, actor Jean Gabin and many other celebrities from Paris and New York have left their (fleetingly) famous footsteps. And when Allard enlarged his quarters last year to include a little, warmly elegant dining room, he did it without any ostentation.

Marcel Allard, the restaurant's founder, died several years ago, but his son André had already been running the place for some time. His crew-cut hair and beaming face make him one of the most affable *patrons* in Paris. The reputation of his often famous and always cosmopolitan clientele has not gone to his head. He is always on hand, and his tact is equaled only by his efficiency.

Women traditionally do the cooking at Allard's. André Allard's mother, a cordon bleu from the Morvan region, used to be in charge of the stove. Since her retirement, her daughter-in-law Fernande has taken over. Fernande was born near Saulieu in Burgundy, which everyone will agree is almost a God-given boon.

If women are rarely at home in the kitchen of the so-called "great restaurants," where one feels compelled to prepare complex, sophisticated dishes, they are ideal for a great bistro like this, where people come for good, plain home cooking.

Year in, year out, Allard always puts one *plat du jour* on the menu: on Monday it is cassoulet; on Tuesday, veal à la berrichonne in red wine sauce (we had lost our taste for veal, but this superb dish won us back); on Wednesday, coq au vin and roast leg of lamb; corned pork with red kidney beans on Thursday (we haven't had any as good as this except at Lucas-Carton); on Friday there is braised beef and lamb stew (that marvel which most restaurateurs have forgotten even exists); and finally on Saturday, as on Wednesday, coq au vin and roast lamb.

All of these dishes can be taken on trust. But the guinea hen with lentils, duck with olives, or even better, with turnips—an absolutely sublime creation—and, in season, partridge with cabbage or simple roast woodcock, are all equally unforgettable. Rush over to Allard's in June when raspberries are in season: his raspberry cake is a marvel.

When you ask André Allard for a bottle of Bordeaux, he usually replies that he's all out of it. This is the pious fib of a real Burgundian—a Burgundian who lovingly and expertly selects his wines on the spot and bottles them himself in the priceless seventeenth-century cellar which you reach by a very steep stairway a stone's throw from the counter. Allard specializes in Côte de Nuits. (If you order a "great" bottle, he will undoubtedly suggest his own personal favorite, Bonnes Mares '61, which he nicknames "the beurre blanc of Burgundies.")

You can't expect to have a really fine meal here for less than 40 francs ($8) per person. That's somewhat stiff, but remember that you don't have to pay anything for the service. You can leave a few coins in the saucer, of course, but even if you don't, the waiters will always be just as attentive and just as delightfully courteous.

> Allard, 41 rue Saint-André-des-Arts (6e), DAN 48.23. Closed on Sundays and from July 20 to September 1. Dinner served until 10:00 P.M. Make your reservations thirty-six hours in advance.

Garin (Le Colbert) ***

WINE: 14

DÉCOR: 13

RECEPTION AND SERVICE: 13

ATMOSPHERE: 12

PRICES: V.E.

You wouldn't expect to find such a haven of costly refinement just a few steps from the Skid Row of Paris. As a matter of fact, only a few years ago Le Colbert was still just a hangout for bums who came there to trade cigarette butts. Then Monsieur Garin took over in 1961 and with dizzying speed achieved a success the likes of which no restaurant had ever known (two Michelin stars after two years in business).

Monsieur Garin looks like a big rosy baby with gray hair. After serving as manager and chef of an excellent restaurant in Burgundy, he went into business for himself for the first time here in rue Lagrange. He got through an uncertain first year and then sent his restaurant's fortunes soaring by means of the only trick which seems to have any lasting success in Paris, if you know how to prepare *la grande cuisine,* i.e., high prices.

His success continues today amid recently enlarged and agreeably redecorated surroundings despite Garin's own prediction: "Our kind of quality restaurant, small and expensive, has been doomed by those taboo 'temples,' the snack bars and pseudo-bistros."

Garin's has the smallest menu of any restaurant in its class. There are half a dozen fish or shellfish dishes, half a dozen meat or poultry dishes, and rare, delicate puréed vegetables.

Garin is an inspired and often original cook. You don't come here for fried sole and a grillade, but for lobster fricassee with port, pan-fried scallops bordelaise, steamed chicken with Meursault, pepper steak wrapped in an airy pancake or thick, buttery, wonderful calf's liver with grapes.

Garin is a skilled technician in "genteel" cooking. He has definitely chosen between the two gastronomical poles of *haute cuisine* and great, plain, home-style cooking. One may of course prefer simplicity to complexity and a trout au bleu to a trout soufflé, which is delicious but no longer tastes like trout. It's a question of schools, a simple matter of taste.

The wine list is rather short and unbalanced, but worth reading for a few great names: Haut Brion '53, Latour '53, La Tâche '59.

The clientele is the finest in Paris, people who have the means to dine high on the hog and who prefer subtlety to false simplicity. Lots of businessmen at lunch; evenings find pretty women dining with manufacturers, lawyers, doctors and politicians.

Monsieur and Madame Garin are very friendly, competent hosts. They wisely refrain from disagreeing with their customers' tastes or wishes. Everything proceeds calmly and quietly. The service, on the other hand, is somewhat cold and anonymous. The waiters lack "human warmth."

Your first glance at the menu instantly reassures you, if that is the right word: you know you're not going to get off lightly. The average bill at Garin comes to 65 francs ($13), for everything but service. It seems one can manage to go below 50 francs ($10), but rarely over 100 francs ($20).

Garin (Le Colbert), 9 rue Lagrange (5e), ODE 13.99. Closed Sundays and in August.

La Tour d'Argent ***

WINE: 19

DÉCOR: 18

RECEPTION AND SERVICE: 19

ATMOSPHERE: 17

PRICES: V.E.

From the roof of a building on the banks of the Seine, 385 years of gastronomy contemplate more than eight centuries of faith: the Cathedral of Notre-Dame de Paris, aglow with a thousand lights, is the unique spectacle which Claude Terrail, a dandy with a carnation flowering in his buttonhole, offers to his guests at the top of La Tour d'Argent. The story of what this apparently frivolous man has done with an inn that was built at the end of the sixteenth century and was immediately taken up by clergy and court before becoming a fashionable eighteenth-century rendezvous, deserves more space than we can give it. It is true that this playboy, who is Barbara Warner's ex-husband and who knows America like the palm of his hand, was preceded here by a very talented father, and before that by Frédéric, whose duck in blood sauce made him famous at the beginning of the century.

Dinner at La Tour d'Argent is a journey into the past. The ground floor houses Claude Terrail's unique collection of documents and objects pertaining to cooking through the ages. Here, for example, is the menu—complete with Grand Duke Vladimir of Russia's scribbled comments—for the "Three Emperors" dinner which brought William I of Prussia, Emperor Nicholas of Russia, the Tsarevitch Alexander and Bismarck together at the Café Anglais on June 7, 1867. They merrily put away two soups, three relevés, four entrées, two roasts and four entremets, washed down with prestigious wines. Several showcases hold glasses, soup spoons, forks (tradition has it that this was the first place in Paris to use forks), and silver dishes—all rare and precious—for you to admire. But now it is time to climb into the sort of sedan chair, which is actually an elevator decorated in *Grand Siècle* fashion, that quickly carries you to the very top of La Tour d'Argent.

The door opens. A very tall, very elegant and very friendly man is there to welcome you: Roland, the dining room director. You have of course taken the precaution of reserving your table; you even had the foresight to do it a day early so as to get a table near the picture window, giving you a better view of the Seine, the Ile de la Cité and Notre-Dame.

You are shown to your table. The china, glassware and table linen are of good quality but much less sumptuous than what you have just been admiring downstairs. The menu, on the other hand, is a work of art. You'd love to take it home as a souvenir. Well, go right ahead: Claude Terrail is resigned to having scores of them stolen every week (deep down he is delighted: it is excellent advertising).

Right now your head is in the clouds. But the main order of business is still at hand—the dinner itself. There's no use hiding it: much as the décor and service are unanimously praised, the cooking is sometimes criticized. Of the fifteen or so meals we have had at La Tour de'Argent, two have been frankly disappointing, two or three absolutely perfect, and the rest good. That seems a very respectable average.

Chef Pierre Descreux' cooking is subtle and original. It has style, as one might say of a beautiful interior or an elegant woman. Our own personal taste inclines toward simpler food, which proves to be more complex when you come right down to it. (Today, real luxury consists of eating freshly picked vegetables.) But some of La Tour d'Argent's dishes do deserve our wholehearted enthusiasm. Start with brill in Dugléré sauce (to order), for example, or quenelles of pike, which can be so tasteless and here are truly perfect. Their great specialty, as you already know, is duck in all its forms. The duck in blood sauce has won many medals for France, so we risk being hacked to pieces for confessing that this famous fowl, numbered and served in two parts (slices of meat in sauce, followed by the roast drumsticks), leaves us rather indifferent. We much prefer the duck au poivre vert, which is more tender and not the least bitter. Last of all, the game in winter—partridge, roebuck—is always of the finest quality.

The wine cellar is inexhaustibly rich: 150,000 bottles selected by expert old Félix, who lives in his cellar like Diogenes in his barrel. Follow wine steward Marcel's advice if you want to win his esteem. It is always judicious, whether pertaining to a minor vintage (the least expensive is a Fleurie for $2.50) or a great one, whose price he will discreetly indicate to you. By the way, you usually won't get to see that great wine in its bottle since it is brought to the table in a decanter. Drink it religiously and not like that smooth-talking Texan sitting next to us one night who poured his Musigny 1906 like beer and polished it off in a single gulp. The Texan might have been French, for that matter, since the number of French people who no longer have any respect for wine is growing at an impressive rate.

In the summer we recommend a refreshing drink which can only be had here: hanap, a mixture of Sancerre, Chablis or Champagne with curaçao, cognac and fruit.

Once dinner is over (to the tune of about $15 including the wine but not the service; $12 or so at lunch), the only thing left to do is to turn a little charm on the maître d' or Roland so that they'll have you taken to the wine cellar. The elevator will let you off next to a well where an eighteenth-century noble drowned himself after being sentenced to the galleys. But water is beside the point here; wine is what inspired Claude Terrail's little "light and sound" show, which you admire over a glass of old liqueur. The epic story of wine is told by the bottles themselves—some of which are over a hundred years old—as the light falls on them one by one. Take a good look; you'll never taste them. Which may be just as well. . . . These priceless flagons (Pierpont Morgan had one pinched when Claude Terrail's father refused to sell it to him) may now contain nothing but vinegar. No, they hold the most precious of all commodities: dreams.

> La Tour d'Argent, 15 quai de la Tournelle (5ᵉ), ODE 23.31. Open throughout the year except on Mondays. Dinner served until 10:00 P.M.

Lapérouse **

WINE: 14

DÉCOR: 18

RECEPTION AND SERVICE: 18

ATMOSPHERE: 16

PRICES: V.E.

Americans adore this old restaurant reminiscent of an era which people will never stop dreaming about. A profound antiquated charm emanates from the little downstairs room with its dark woodwork, the narrow stairway, the maître d' and waiters of the "old school," who seem to be posing for a Gay Nineties photographer, the low-ceilinged dining rooms, the pier glasses and sconces which are half Louis XV, half 1900, and finally, the private rooms whose mirrors bear the names of turn-of-the-century belles, scratched there with the diamonds that gentlemen with monocles and large incomes gave them between goblets of champagne. It is a charm which no one can escape, despite all the criticism leveled at Lapérouse.

Indeed, every time we come here we experience some more or less serious disappointment with either the food or the wine. The menu does include some subtle, time-tested specialties like timbale des Augustins, delights of sole pepère, duckling Colette or kidneys "never better." The sad thing is that when we enter Lapérouse we always wonder if we are going to have a superb meal (which has happened at least once, with braised Loire salmon) or, on the contrary, be cruelly disappointed. So that you won't have to run the same risk, we recommend that you order foie gras des Landes (available from November to May), the salmon, of course, the kidneys and any of the vegetables, which are always perfectly prepared. (Complete dinner at 40 francs; à la carte, about 70 francs—$14.)

> Lapérouse, 51 quai des Grands Augustins (6e), DAN 68.04. Closed on Sundays and the first three weeks in August. Dinner served until 10:00 P.M.

Le Pactole **

WINE: 9

DÉCOR: 10

RECEPTION AND SERVICE: 12

ATMOSPHERE: 11

PRICES: I (lunch); E (dinner)

Monsieur Manière is a hefty fellow with pepper-and-salt hair; a chatty, passionate, incurable perfectionist. Didn't he just invent an omelet with truffled foie gras after perfecting crêpes filled with smoked salmon and chicken stuffed with lobster? He's not low on daring, either, since his greatest trick is a 20-francs ($4) luncheon menu which is short and simple, but extremely refined. And this a stone's throw from La Tour d'Argent!

This idea, which runs contrary to general developments. (inferior quality and high prices), is going to make good, almost low-priced lunches possible for a whole category of people (a few at a time, though, since Manière can only accommodate forty) forced to choose between a little steak with frites or a big bill. For example, they can try the raw chopped mushrooms in paprika sauce or Manière's excellent homemade terrines, followed by the daily special (stuffed chicken, miroton, lamb stew with spring vegetables, ham in pastry crust, etc.) or, for weight-conscious lady executives, noisette of lamb or club steak, and then dessert. And it is all exquisite.

In the evening Manière once again becomes Midas in his solid gold Pactole with the great dishes named above and many others, such as a superb foie gras, duck, steak with green pepper, lobster omelet, accompanied by a great Bordeaux or a good plain Château des Graves. Dinner will cost about 45 francs ($9), including service to which Monsieur Manière himself often lends a hand. Indeed, he has a hand in everything, from mornings at Les Halles until ten o'clock at night in his tiny kitchen and modest dining room.

> Le Pactole, 44 boulevard Saint-Germain (5e), DAN 92.28. Closed Sundays. Dinner served until 10:00 P.M.

Le Petit Chatelet **

> WINE: 14
>
> DÉCOR: 10
>
> RECEPTION AND SERVICE: 10
>
> ATMOSPHERE: 10
>
> PRICES: E

One might well feel a twinge of apprehension at the sight of Le Petit Chatelet, given its location right across from Notre-Dame and near the Latin Quarter, the most beatnik- and camera-ridden section in Paris. Nor will the sign "Maillard, Innkeeper" do much to reassure people who have already been stung once too often by places of that sort. And what's more, Monsieur Maillard was accused of the crime of refusing Americans, especially during the crazy fifties, and was condemned to lose almost all of his French customers because of it. Almost all the Americans, too . . .

So Maillard's is not too crowded, and it's high time we made up for our negligence. A friend of ours practically had to drag us there for lunch the other day, after a drooling description of five of Maillard's great specialties: foie gras, beef with carrots, blood pudding, duck à l'orange and apple tart flamed with calvados.

The tiny little room makes a good impression right away because of the décor, which is neither slick nor pretentiously picturesque. Instead, it is simple and intimate, full of appealingly understated elegance. Monsieur Maillard modestly inquired what we would like, in his low, somewhat formal voice (he doesn't waste words). We chose the dishes mentioned above, neglecting others (which also looked excellent), like scallops, rib steak marchand de vin and veal kidneys with mustard.

It was a superb meal, served zealously and not too slowly, washed down with perfect Bordeaux. (Monsieur Maillard has some Cheval Blanc '53 and Lafite '55.)

The foie gras, streaked with pink and green, was delicate and extremely flavorful. The blood sausage de la Mayenne had that slightly sweet taste and feathery lightness which we had forgotten about since wartime rationing had made it impossible to get anything but ghastly *boudin* stretched with bran. The pot roast (tender slices of meat served with a generous helping of succulent little carrots) wasn't just some vulgar slop floating in the dregs of a sauce.

As for the duck à l'orange (braised whole to order for one person), it was a marvel which has eradicated our frequently low opinion of that great, mistreated dish. The apple tart was fun (but the calvados is really excessive); the bill rather less so since Monsieur Maillard uses top-quality products for which he himself has to pay a lot (count on spending about 40 francs —$8).

Le Petit Chatelet (Maillard Aubergiste), 39 rue de la Bucherie (5ᵉ), ODE 17.95. Closed Sundays.

Le Relais de Porquerolles **

WINE: 11

DÉCOR: 10

RECEPTION AND SERVICE: 13

ATMOSPHERE: 13

PRICES: V.E.

This restaurant was the scene of a very ususual drama. For some mysterious reason, two years ago the *Guide Michelin* withdrew the two stars it had awarded to Le Relais de Porquerolles, run by the two Zick brothers. One of them committed suicide a few weeks later, and the press immediately saw a cause-and-effect relationship between the loss of the stars and that desperate act.

Be that as it may, Le Relais de Porquerolles, now run by the surviving brother, has not gone downhill. Amid a Provençal and somewhat hokey-folky setting, it still has one of the best bouillabaisses in Paris, real Mediterranean sea perch with fennel, delicious shellfish and exquisite fish soups (round off your meal with a coffee ice). Lunch is much too quiet, while dinner is so mobbed that you absolutely must have a reservation. When you get there, be sure to walk to the end of the rue de l'Epéron for a glance at the Cour de Rohan. This courtyard, unknown to most Parisians, is only a hundred yards away from the rumble of boulevard Saint-Germain but sixteenth- and seventeenth-century houses covered with Virginia creeper, beautiful grilles and a few old trees make it a haven of peace and charm.

To get back to our bouillabaisse: the only thing wrong with the Relais de Porquerolles is the size of the bill. You can easily spend 60 or 70 francs ($12 to $14), and sometimes even more, for a good "shore" dinner.

Le Relais de Porquerolles, 12 rue de l'Epéron (6ᵉ), ODE 44.30. Closed Sundays and in August. Dinner served until 10:30 P.M.

Le Clos des Bernadins *

WINE: 11

DÉCOR: 14

RECEPTION AND SERVICE: 14

ATMOSPHERE: 13

PRICES: I

Le Clos des Bernadins is located right in the middle of what used to be the garden of the famous Cistercian monastery, some remains of which can still be admired at the firehouse at 21 rue de Poissy. Since Monsieur and Madame Darremont took over, it has become a most engaging gourmet outpost. The main room, cleared of its disfiguring accessories, has recaptured the former nobility of its superb beams and brick partitions. Bouquets of flowers and the owners' pleasant smiles add a note of friendly gaiety to what might otherwise be a somewhat austere décor.

But it is not just a treat for the eye. You can also get a very pleasant meal here, and even if the choice of dishes is relatively limited, everything from the buttery piperade to the individual soufflés, passing through cheese fondue, filet of beef in pastry crust, leg of lamb and purée of spinach, is prepared and served with the utmost care. Every day a different *plat du jour* (cassoulet, stew, joint of beef, etc.) is wheeled out on a steam table. The food at the Bernadins certainly has style, even though, as one can see, it's hard to pin down exactly what style that is.

There are some fine classical vintages in the wine cellar, but if you don't want to go overboard, stick to a pitcher of this year's Beaujolais or Macon Viré. (About 35 francs—$7.)

Le Clos des Bernadins, 14 rue de Pontoise (5e), ODE 70.07. Open until 11:00 P.M.

Relais Louis XIII *

CUISINE: 11

WINE: 15

DÉCOR: 16

RECEPTION AND SERVICE: 12

ATMOSPHERE: 12

PRICES: V.E.

When a man meets an adorable creature and asks her out to dinner, he looks through his address book for the ideal restaurant, one that is at once fashionable, elegant, good and not too expensive. The Relais Louis XIII fulfills all these conditions, except for one small (and important) detail.

This is undeniably the most refined and prettiest of all the picturesque restaurants that have opened in the last few years. And it has the most sensitive and winning décor.

It was in this noble house, formerly part of the Augustinian monastery, that Marie de Medicis was named regent after the death of Henri IV. Her portrait, which manager Odette Delanoy discovered at an auction, hangs on the wall next to those of Louis XIII, Henrietta of England and Anne of Austria, beneath the ceiling's beautiful heart of oak beams. Everything is genuine here, from the superb sixteenth-century staircase leading to the private rooms, to the Louis XIV (or Regency) candlesticks on every table.

The reception, too, true to the traditions of those great centuries, is quiet and gracious. Thus everything invites one to spend an exquisite hour at table. And indeed, André Marfeuille's cooking doesn't lack panache. We would criticize him for putting too much vermouth in the scallops, and for his somewhat offhand treatment of the vegetables which accompany the herbed lamb. All in all, it seems that greater simplicity could be nothing but an improvement in this spectacular, and let's not forget to add, abundant and sometimes inspired food.

The wines, some of which come from the cellar of the late lamented "Chapon Fin" in Bordeaux, are magnificent, and the wine steward, one of the best in Paris, gives very intelligent advice.

The bill, unfortunately, is distressingly "regal." You can blithely spend 70 francs ($14) per person. At those prices, they should at least leave the coffeepot on the table instead of making you pay 10 francs for four cups of coffee.

Relais Louis XIII, 8 rue des Grands-Augustins (6e), DAN 75.96. Closed on Sundays.

Moissonnier *

WINE: 14

DÉCOR: 10

RECEPTION AND SERVICE: 13

ATMOSPHERE: 10

PRICES: 1

Some of the great bistros like Les Lyonnais, Allard and a few others are just naturally full at almost every meal. Moissonnier is another. There is a sort of grapevine in Paris which needs no help from advertising to keep a refined (but not necessarily sophisticated) clientele informed of those addresses where they can expect to be taken seriously.

Moissonnier isn't cheap, but it's not terribly expensive either: 30 francs or so for extraordinarily plentiful and substantial food with the accents of Burgundy and Lyons. This includes sheep's trotters ravigotte, Lyons "rosette" sausage, snails, Jésus de Morteau (liver sausage), quenelles of pike, marrow toast, sweetbreads à la franc-comptoise, pot cheese and strawberries Melba.

Everything is prepared with that loving care which Lyonnais "mothers" know so well how to apply, and supervised by the owner's unchanging, youthful smile. His Beaujolais is still one of the best around.

Moissonnier, 28 rue des Fossés-Saint-Bernard (5ᵉ), ODE 69.27. Closed Mondays and from August 10 to September 10.

Raffatin et Honorine

CUISINE: 10

WINE: 12

DÉCOR: 11

RECEPTION AND SERVICE: 14

ATMOSPHERE: 12

PRICES: E

If François and Robert didn't exist, we would have had to invent them so that people from Holland, Texas and Carpentras could flock to Paris for evidence that our capital is indeed that of the little country bistro complete with terrace, where the laughter is loud and the food just like in the good old days. As a matter of fact, they were invented by Monsieur Raffatin himself, who knew his tourists inside out and could tell just what kind of wool pulled over their eyes would tickle them the most. When François and Robert succeeded him, they wisely got rid of the more obvious stage of machinery and developed a more modest notion of what constitutes quaint rusticity—even if the hams are still hanging from the rafters and the farandole of appetizers, charcuterie and desserts is still in full swing; even if they still give you a drink of Kir in a little earthenware mug and still like to waft the smoke of flamed plums in the customers' faces in order to tempt them, and even if their prices are just as substantial as ever (about 40 francs—$8). In fact, they have been so successful that even Parisians feel at home here. The food, which is typical of Auvergne and Berry, is honestly prepared. We sampled with pleasure an amazing little rack of baby rabbit served in a light sauce of fresh herbs, and a tasty chicken with noodles. Don't miss the owner's remarkable red Burgundy.

Raffatin et Honorine (Pouilly-Sancerre), 16 boulevard Saint-Germain (5e), ODE 22.21. Closed Sundays. Reservations necessary at dinner. Open until 10:30 P.M.

Aux Deux Marches

CUISINE: 10
WINE: 8
DÉCOR: 6
RECEPTION AND SERVICE: 8
ATMOSPHERE: 13
PRICES: 1

Even the most "with it" decorator wouldn't dare come up with a place like this. If it weren't absolutely authentic, "Victor the Corsican's" grocery-restaurant could easily pass for the height of faddish chic.

You go up two steps and find yourself in a grocery store the likes of which can only be found in the most out-of-the-way provinces. A group of solidly rooted habitués stand leaning on the little bar in the middle of the room. To the left is the kitchen where "Spanish Dolores" bustles about. At the back is a little room devoted to the memory of Napoleon. This is where you sample the famous Dolores' beef Corsican style, paella or osso bucco. And neither she nor Victor ever loses his bearings, since the bill easily sails past the 30-franc mark ($6) all the same.

Aux Deux Marches, 15 rue Gît-le-Coeur (6e), DAN 29.44. Closed on Sundays. Dinner until 9:30 P.M. Reservations necessary.

Le Port Saint-Bernard

CUISINE: 11

WINE: 12

RECEPTION AND SERVICE: 12

ATMOSPHERE: 11

PRICES: I

Monsieur and Madame Peyssens are one of the most charming couples that the Aveyron ever deposited on the banks of the Seine. They were taking a risk when, some time ago, they opened their Port Saint-Bernard on quai de la Tournelle. (It was given this name in memory of the port which functioned nearby during the Middle Ages.)

When you settle in a neighborhood besieged by so many temptations, it takes a certain courage to decide that you will be sensible, won't set your sights too high, won't try to victimize your fellow-men, won't compromise quality and won't be carried away by fads.

It's true that Le Port Saint-Bernard hasn't escaped the Left Bank's obligatory beams, but it has been able to impose reasonable limits on the décor's rusticity. The hostess loves flowers and puts armfuls of them everywhere, a pleasure which too many hotel and restaurant owners deny their customers.

Monsieur Peyssens has very definite views on food. He has no fondness for the fireworks involved in flamed sea perch, nor does he fall into the "cooking with herbs" trap, the flagrant abuses of which will forever ruin one's taste for those herbs, which are so exquisitely fragrant when used in moderation.

When, not guessing who we were, he declared, "Rosé de Provence will be served here only over my dead body," we came very near kissing him—except for that tremendous mustache of his.

With that he brought us a rosé du Tarn, a little wine from the Labastide-Levis cooperative, which won't change your life but is certainly pure and honest.

Monsieur Peyssens' cooking is, of course, a love song to his native Aveyron. This cult, a discreet one, takes the form of cracklings, stuffed goose neck and nice big terrines which are generously left on the table. It's a shame that so few restaurants think of serving bavette, which is one of the tastiest cuts of beef. Le Port Saint-Bernard is one exception, together with the Louis XIV and the Cochon d'Or. The beef comes with Bordelaise sauce and Auvergnat potatoes fried in goose fat, which are absolutely superb.

Follow that with a delicious salad with walnut oil dressing, a tart and coffee, and your bill for this pleasant meal will not amount to more than 25 francs ($5); there is also a very plentiful complete dinner for 18 francs ($3.60), including a nice little wine.

> Le Port Saint-Bernard, 29 quai de la Tournelle (5e), DAN 37.28. Closed Saturdays until dinner. Dinner served until 10:00 P.M.

Restaurant de la Mosquée de Paris

CUISINE: 10

DÉCOR: 13

RECEPTION AND SERVICE: 12

ATMOSPHERE: 12

PRICES: 1

It used to be that whenever a tourist landed in Paris, he went to dine in the Mosque. It was an obligatory stop on the tourist circuit.

Then, with the war, and particularly the Algerian crisis later on, this great monument, where the muzzein calls five times a day in one of the most moving old parts of Paris, was transformed into a disturbing sanctuary which one no longer dared come near (quite mistakenly, for that matter, since no incidents ever occurred here).

A few Parisians are now timidly going back to sit around large copper trays to which waiters, dressed (alas) in European fashion, silently bring pots of minted tea. But it is far, very far from crowded.

In this row of little rooms where, everything considered, picturesque local color is rather neglected, you quickly forget Paris and are filled with the peace, mystery and silence that hang over this place.

The couscous is admittedly less sumptuous than at Aïssa; the sauces are a bit insipid and could certainly use a few raisins but the semolina is remarkably light, and if you take care to precede the couscous with brik (an egg in a delicious pancake) and kefta (shish kebab made with a variety of meats), for some 15 francs ($3) you will have had a nice meal in the cool, quiet shade of a Moorish café.

And in the afternoon you can enjoy the beauty of the patio done in blue mosaics and white marble, and the opulent prayer room with a ceiling as pricelessly ornamented as a retable, magnificent carpets and a fabric partition screening off the women's section.

Thus you'll spend several pleasant hours amid the battlements and green tile, especially if a ray of sunshine happens to make the walls as white, the pools as transparent, as those we remember seeing in Cordova.

Restaurant de la Mosquée de Paris, 39 rue Geoffroy-Saint-Hilaire (5e), GOB 18.14. Open every day and all year.

La Venta

CUISINE: 11
DÉCOR: 12
RECEPTION AND SERVICE: 12
ATMOSPHERE: 14
PRICES: E

We can't recommend a better Spanish meal than a peppery, sunny dinner at La Venta on rue Guénégaud.

You watch thrilling flamenco dancers from a balcony aggressively decorated with Basque artifacts. In addition, you'll find a choice of Spanish dishes cooked in good virgin oil, such as tapas, which unfortunately doesn't include percebes, a kind of seafood at which French people foolishly turn up their noses because it is as ugly as a lizard's leg.

Try the chilled soup, eel in pepper sauce and deep-fried shrimp. Try also the criadillas, which are what bulls have and steers don't; dipped in flour and fried, they taste like kidneys and have the texture of sweetbreads.

You won't mind the substantial sum which you will be smilingly asked to pay (45 to 50 francs—$9 to $10).

La Venta, 33 rue Guénégaud (6e), DAN 69.83. Closed on Sundays. Dinner served until 1:00 A.M.

Panthéon, Rue Mouffetard (5ᵉ)

Luu Dinh *

DÉCOR: 7

RECEPTION AND SERVICE: 12

ATMOSPHERE: 10

PRICES: I

Luu Dinh is a Vietnamese bistro a stone's throw from place de la Contrescarpe, which is a paradise for bums, students and poets but not—as yet—for tourists. The décor is reduced to its simplest form, and except for the chopsticks on the tables and the (oil) portrait of a mandarin executed by the owner's skillful brush, there's not a trace of Vietnamese exoticism—or whatever is left of it. . . .

Monsieur Luu Dinh is a charming, smiling young man who has spent most of his life in France. Fortunately, this has not made him forget the savory recipes of his native Tonkin. He does everything single-handed in his little dining room, hopping from one table to another, serving with one hand and clearing with the other. On crowded nights you'd think you were watching a Mack Sennett movie.

But the real show takes place in the miniature kitchen on the other side of the partition where his mother, aided by a few young relations, turns out the good things that Monsieur Luu Dinh serves in hurricane fashion.

These women, whom one never sees, put loving care into the preparation of light egg rolls, spicy soup, Peking duck, chicken with ginger and especially the more rare and remarkable specialties: chicken in buttered paper (which will definitely make you a friend of chicken), stuffed pigeon or suckling pig Peking style, which we think is even more savory than Peking duck (You should always check on the specialties ahead of time.)

The food is unpretentious but authentic and unfailingly honest. (It would be hard to go over 25 francs—$5.)

Luu Dinh, 6 rue Thouin (5ᵉ), DAN 91.01. Closed on Mondays. Dinner until 10:00 P.M.

Le Berthoud

CUISINE: II

WINE: IO

DÉCOR: I4

RECEPTION AND SERVICE: 9

ATMOSPHERE: I4

PRICES: I

After all the pseudo-bistros, pseudo-taverns and pseudo-country inns, the latest fad in restaurants seems to be taking a very original turn, following the example set by the Caves du Square.

The décor is sophisticated in its simplicity: adjustable 1920's lamps with beaded fringes are suspended over the tables and charming, old-fashioned, faded frescos run around the walls.

A window which looks a little like a mirror opens onto a second room. Kitchen china, a few friendly, casual waiters. Young patrons falling somewhat haphazardly into each other's arms.

What makes Berthoud's cooking unique is that it resolutely refuses to have anything to do with such fashionable fakery as grillades with herbs.

Here, on the contrary, you get crazy little Russo-Swiss (?) style dishes bedizened with deliberately precious and mystifying names: lots of soups, egg dishes and unusual desserts. There are little chicken liver pâtés, raw vegetables that you dip into strange sauces, a plump chicken in a basket, a sort of raclette (broiled potato rolled in melted cheese), Irish coffee, nice little wines. And contrary to all expectations, the bill is modest: about 25 francs ($5), which is modest indeed when you add that the prettiest women in Tout-Paris, from Ursula Andress to Jeanne Moreau, have made Le Berthoud a fashionable place to eat.

Le Berthoud, 1 rue Valette (5ᵉ), ODE 38.81. Closed Sundays and in August.

Le Coupe-Chou

CUISINE: IO

DÉCOR: I4

RECEPTION AND SERVICE: 15

ATMOSPHERE: 14

PRICES: I

Oak heartwood beams, Louis XIII mantelpieces, fashionable customers (Brigitte Bardot comes here now and then)—it all can be loathsome. But at Le Coupe-Chou the dishes have a sophisticated simplicity (eggplant casserole, mushroom salad with lemon juice, a slab of beef with herbs or boeuf bourguignon) and are served by very urbane young men, most of whom are actors. This is not gourmet cooking, but at least it has the merit of being sincere.

Le Coupe-Chou—named after a sixteenth-century barber who slit his clients' throats before selling them in pâté form to a nearby *charcutier*—couldn't be less cutthroat. (About 25 to 30 francs—$5 to $6.)

> Le Coupe-Chou, 9 rue de Lanneau (5e), MED 68.69. Open every evening until 2:00 A.M.

La Folie d'Or

CUISINE: 9

DÉCOR: 2

RECEPTION AND SERVICE: 12

ATMOSPHERE: 13

PRICES: V.C.

This could be a "fancy lady's" bedroom, the throne room of an operetta principality, a boudoir for wordly adulterers, a provincial night club from the thirties or the dining room in an Italian palace.

Gold flocked velvet ennobles the walls and the imitation Louis XV chairs, while the ceiling and windows are hung with moiré, also gold. The bronze chandelier, the armoires and even the telephone all wallow in their gilt. It's an Oriental Versailles crammed in twenty-five square yards.

You'd probably expect the worst, since the owner is Tunisian, the chef Greek and the specialties Tyrolian, Russian and Tunisian. Not at all: the beef stroganoff isn't bad, the shashlik leaves you with a pleasant memory, the lamb chops are large and fresh and the 10-franc specialties dinner, including stuffed grape leaves, chackchouka-merguez and baklava, is very decent.

> La Folie d'Or, 35 rue des Ecoles (5ᵉ), DAN 38.69. Open daily until 1:00 A.M.

Mouf 5

CUISINE: 7

DÉCOR: 2

ATMOSPHERE: 14

PRICES: I

Day or night, this is the new refuge for bums, students, artists and even tourists astray on the Contrescarpe of an evening.

Mouf 5 is a minuscule grocery-restaurant installed in two little back rooms. For the sum of 8 francs ($1.60), including wine, you have a choice of three appetizers and three main dishes, topped by cheese tray and dessert.

Thus you can have an after-dinner supper in the Contrescarpe area for a very modest sum. The supper, too, is modest but still no insult to the digestive system.

You can also listen to long-haired singers from the neighborhood who drop in to air their latest innovations to their own guitar accompaniment. The manager, Bobosse, specializes in starting new restaurants (he has opened five in London). He doesn't want Mouf 5 to become a cabaret, but rather a cheap, original restaurant where you'll run into just as many housewives picking up their quart of red wine as diners in pursuit of the picturesque.

> Mouf 5, 5 rue Mouffetard (5ᵉ), ODE 97.33. Open until 2:00 A.M.

Montparnasse (6ᵉ, 14ᵉ, 15ᵉ)

Chataigner **

WINE: 13

DÉCOR: 10

RECEPTION AND SERVICE: 10

ATMOSPHERE: 10

PRICES: E

Everything's in order at Chataigner's. . . .

Five years ago the illustrious Doctor of Beurre Blanc from the rue du Cherche-Midi abandoned, without a word of warning, her ovens, her pikes and her famous club chairs where all the gourmets of Tout-Paris, from the Comte de Paris to the Duke of Windsor, had sat at least once.

Everyone who ever ran aground of Mme Chataigner's iron-clad personality will be pleased to learn that three years of retirement have given her a renewed appreciation of smiling faces.

We couldn't help admiring her angelic patience as she tried to explain the meaning of the word *pintadeau* (guinea hen) to a couple of Americans.

As for the food, we would be lying if we claimed that Chataigner's beurre blanc surpassed La Mère Michel's. Both are excellent.

The reason that good beurre blanc has become such a rare commodity is that most of the time chefs throw in starch, egg yolks and cream. Chataigner sticks to tradition, and this holds true for the entire menu.

You don't have to be a genius to serve melons that are as fragrant and ripe as can be, nor to make a good chocolate cake or excellent coffee. Still, the best restaurants don't always have the longest menus or the most intricate dishes. At Chataigner's, talent resides in simplicity.

It's a shame, though, that this simplicity comes so high. You can judge from our bill: three covers (without the slightest trace of luxury), a melon, a dish of prawns (marvelous, it's true), a terrine, three pikes, two cakes, three coffees, a Muscadet and an Evian: 130 francs ($26) for a meal without any extravagance.

> Chataigner, 75 rue du Cherche-Midi (6e), LIT 82.74. Closed Sundays and in August.

Aïssa **

WINE: 7
DÉCOR: 8
RECEPTION AND SERVICE: 8

ATMOSPHERE: 13
PRICES: I

As long as he was still the unrecognized king of Moroccan couscous there was never any controversy about Aïssa. (He was not so unrecognized, however, that most political, fashionable and even religious circles—the Apostolic Nuncio was a steady customer before becoming Pope John XXIII—didn't intersect at his restaurant.) But when a name is on everyone's lips, a few crabs can always be found to complain "It's not what it used to be."

Well, we can assure you that everything is exactly like "it used to be." The same appalling Moorish décor and stucco walls, the same long wait in the somewhat stifling little dining room.

Then finally (to order) the superb pastilla, that sweet, flaky pigeon pie into which it is customary to plunge one's entire hand to seize pieces of pigeon.

Then comes the couscous: light, made with homemade semolina and smelling deliciously of the butter and milk vapor in which Aïssa has cooked it. It is accompanied by raisins and chick peas and is moistened with a light vegetable broth and a peppery sauce. It is served, according to your preference, with tagine, stewed lamb with lemon (incomparable), shish kebab (without peer) or tender slices of roast lamb and, of course, savory meatballs and merguez.

This is usually the moment that Aïssa, the chef in sultan's clothing, chooses to make the most theatrical entrance possible.

This amazing character—multifaceted, boisterous, full of epic memories (captain in the French Army, godson of Marshal Lyautey)—catches you up in a whirlwind of laughter, compliments and wisecracks. And your meal ends in a Moroccan fantasia.

Aïssa, 83 avenue Denfert-Rochereau (14e), ODE 99.86. Open daily until 10:30 P.M.

Dominique **

WINE: 13
DÉCOR: 13

RECEPTION AND SERVICE: 14

ATMOSPHERE: 13

PRICES: E

People who go to Russian restaurants to share in the famous flights of the Slavic soul will be surprised to learn that the chicken Kiev or Pojarsky, even the Russian salad to which they are treating themselves, are all French inventions! As a matter of fact, almost all the great Russian dishes—at least those served in top-flight restaurants—were created during the last century by French chefs at the czar's court or in the great houses of Moscow or Saint Petersburg. And the French influence becomes more marked as the restaurants become more luxurious. On the other hand, the tiny little restaurants in the 15th *arrondissement,* where tourists never go, serve rugged food which is certainly more typical but much less good.

Although we know almost all the Russian places in Paris, we still never tire of going to Dominique.

This is where you get the best Russian food in Paris, served in a red and gold setting amid the silken tapestries and precious souvenirs of Saint Petersburg's Gay Nineties. This is where you come to eat ollivier salad (chicken, ham, pickles, vegetables and mayonnaise) which French restaurants have degraded into "Russian salad," coulibiac of salmon, sturgeon, some of the finest smoked salmon in Paris and, of course, caviar, served by waiters who seem to have stepped out of a picture book on Old Russia (the maître d' kisses the hands of his faithful lady customers), as you sit either in the back room or near the entrance, perched on a stool at the counter.

Dominique has given up Russian caviar, which is too uneven in quality, in favor of all varieties of Iranian caviar, packed with jealous care.

It's obviously better to have a comfortable bank account if you want an orgy of these little black grains, which can easily retail for 500 to 600 francs per kilo ($50 to $60 per pound). But the infinitely less expensive pressed caviar (a paste which looks a little like shoe polish) is much more appropriate with blinis.

You are served three of these steaming little pancakes, together with melted butter and sour cream. Spread a layer of caviar, then butter, then sour cream, on each, stack them one on top of another, "rinse out your mouth" with vodka (Ukrainian gorilka is the best) and off you go into paradise.

Dominique, 19 rue Bréa (6e), DAN 63.92. Open every day. Dinner served until 10:30 P.M.

Chez Joséphine *

WINE: 13

DÉCOR: 12

RECEPTION AND SERVICE: 14

ATMOSPHERE: 14

PRICES: I

Every Parisian with any taste for fine food knows this bistro on the rue du Cherche-Midi, a bistro more real than life itself where evening finds mink coats hanging on coat hooks around the room.

After his Joséphine's death, old Papa Duranton, a loud-mouthed, open-hearted, foxy old man, turned the business over to a very nice young cook, Jean Dumonet, who used to ply his talents at the Galant Verre. But Papa Duranton, broken-hearted, still comes back once a week, on Wednesdays, to do the roast lamb.

Southwestern France and Burgundy share the honors for the specialties: fresh foie gras of duck, Landes ham, pike with beurre blanc and sorrel, Castelnaudary cassoulet, preserved goose, scalloped duck liver with grapes, preserved goose with Landes apples, rabbit with mustard. The cheese is always excellent and the wines come from good sources (we particularly recommend the Savigny-Vergelesses 1964, which you should follow with a glass of rarest old Armagnac after the sherbet or chocolate soufflé. Monsieur Dumonet also has a few old bottles with some rather extraordinary dates: 1928, 1887.) About 30 to 35 francs ($6 to $7).

Chez Joséphine, 117 rue du Cherche-Midi (6e), LIT 52.40. Closed Sundays and in August.

Le Logis Saint-Vincent *

WINE: 11

DÉCOR: 12

RECEPTION AND SERVICE: 12

ATMOSPHERE: 10

PRICES: 1

Le Logis Saint-Vincent used to have the sad look of places whose existence has been forgotten. Owner Georges Vigué gave it a spruce, discreetly rustic look, dramatized by superb beams that look as if they've always been there—which can't help coming as a surprise in a very bourgeois building which must have gone up around 1910. Don't rap those beams too hard: they're hollow. They are such superb reproductions that you don't notice the fraud even when you're right on top of them, but they are made from staff by young Montparnasse artists.

The cooking hasn't completely repudiated its Burgundy and Lyons origins, but it's a discreet heritage: besides the excellent hot salami (the potatoes are peeled just before serving), there are ballotine of turkey, truffled sausage patties, delicious dry rillettes (grillons), stewed beef and duck with green grapes. The list of fish and shellfish is a fine and tempting one: judging by the skate with black butter (few restaurants in Paris still are daring enough to sell this fish, which is delicious when fresh and abominable when it's a day too old), the owner knows the right addresses. A good strawberry or lemon sherbet rounds off the meal and an unusual, light and inexpensive wine ("Green Seal," simply a Beaujolais which can't officially use the name) goes with it.

So here's one place in Montparnasse (which isn't exactly overrun with them) that serves good food without too many pretensions, since we spent 50 francs ($10) for the two of us, everything included.

Le Logis Saint-Vincent, 145 boulevard du Montparnasse (6e), DAN 63.39. Small terrace. Closed on Sundays.

Le Caméléon

CUISINE: 10

WINE: 7

DÉCOR: 10

RECEPTION AND SERVICE: 10

ATMOSPHERE: 13

PRICES: I

Maurice, who is of Russian origin, and Ginou, from Picardy, already had a very honorable reputation among the painters and sculptors of Montparnasse, who had been enjoying their cooking for several years. They've left their Chaumière on rue Léopold-Robert and resettled nearby, in the short rue de Chevreuse where Paul Cézanne lived for a time.

Behind the large macramé curtains shielding the narrow window is a huge room whose floor is tiled with little pink flagstones and whose walls, accentuated with antique copper sconces, are covered with a delightful wallpaper, patterned in blue and white on a black background. Everything from the pale-marble tables to the simple chairs is perfectly calculated to contribute to the relaxing atmosphere of an old Parisian bistro —revised and corrected, to be sure, so as to harmonize with the current taste of the artists who were led here by the sculptor César and the very refined painter Clavé, and who have been seized with a sudden passion for the accessories of turn-of-the-century brasseries. The assiduity of those two hearty and particular eaters seemed a good sign, so we followed their example and can now confirm the accuracy of their judgment.

The range of home-style dishes, from mackerel in white wine maison to rabbit bonne femme, that Maurice and Ginou serve from noon until very late at night, make for very pleasant eating, considering the price. (About 20 francs—$4.)

Le Caméléon, 6 rue de Chevreuse (6e), MED 63.43. Closed on Sundays. Open until midnight.

Closerie des Lilas

CUISINE: 10

WINE: 13

DÉCOR: 14

RECEPTION AND SERVICE: 14

ATMOSPHERE: 14

PRICES: E

"J'aime pas les *z*'haricots." The strains of this song accompanied the birth of the Closerie des Lilas, which was the favorite shrine of French thinkers for over a century.

The boldest artists and intellectuals in Paris, from Murger to Jean-Paul Sartre, from Verlaine to Samuel Beckett, from Béranger to Georges Brassens, from Séverine to Simone de Beauvoir, came here to exchange ideas and to empty glass after plate.

It all started with a dance. Here, across from the old Charterhouse, people used to abandon themselves to the joys of the quadrille. Seamstresses flowered amid the lilacs which Bullier had planted in the spring of 1847. This wealthy merchant took no pleasure in seeing the sign "Closerie des Lilas" go up a little later over a nearby pub frequented by bearded poets.

Came the year 1903. There also came Francis Carco, Charles Cros, André Gide, Paul Valéry, then Georges Braque, and finally Lenin and Trotsky, silently preparing the coming of the Russian soviets, sat over a chessboard which can still be seen.

The young Surrealists, for their part, were a lot noisier when they made long, scandalous speeches here in the days after World War I. Hemingway, wedged in near the bar, paid no attention to their projected reforms and only had (blue) eyes for strong drink.

After going through a drowsy period, the Closerie des Lilas is now a restaurant-bar where Parisians are always certain to spot a familiar face. The rather showy cooking is not beyond reproach, especially as regards the prices: at least 50 francs ($10) for a meal. But on a beautiful day the charm of the sidewalk terrace hidden beneath the foliage will make you forget those defects.

> Closerie des Lilas, 171 boulevard du Montparnesse (6e), DAN 70.50. Open daily until 2:00 A.M.

La Coupole (*See Cafés and Bars,* p. 187)

Rosebud

CUISINE: 7
WINE: 10

DÉCOR: 12

RECEPTION AND SERVICE: 12

ATMOSPHERE: 14

PRICES: V.C.

Drawn from the neighborhood between Port-Royal and the place de Rennes, from the hub of Saint-Germain-des-Prés and the rue d'Alésia, everyone who writes, paints, sculpts, makes prints or has made a name in the movies or avant-garde theaters on the outskirts of town, seeks refuge in the Rosebud at nightfall.

Thinking Montparnasse does its thinking from midnight to the wee hours in this spot with the name from Orson Welles' *Citizen Kane*. It's a place to see and be seen, even though it's stingy with the light.

The owner—a pretty woman—looks very genteel. She almost seems out of place in the midst of those elite drinkers: Sartre, Marguerite Duras, Ionesco.

Not much bourbon is consumed here. Scotch, beer, wine (very good red Loire wine) seem to be preferred as an accompaniment for the chili con carne flanked by a generous helping of thickly buttered bread, or the grillades which Gilles, present-day Montparnasse's most glorious bartender, serves far into the night. Gilles may be the ringmaster in the pleasure circus of Tout-Montparnasse, but he remains seriously concerned with the fate of the young artists who come to confide their nocturnal doubts and fears. And to the famous cocktails which he composes from his palette of flavors, he dutifully adds a few drops of hope, to brighten the new day.

Rosebud, 11 *bis* rue Delambre (14e), DAN 95.28. Open from 7 P.M. to 6 A.M.

Convention, Vaugirard (14e, 15e)

Bistrot 121 **

WINE: 14

DÉCOR: 10

RECEPTION AND SERVICE: 13

ATMOSPHERE: 12
PRICES: E

Today's readers—and we don't just mean the ladies—are under a constant barrage of "minute" or "miracle" recipes: for madame, for monsieur, for the cat. We don't intend to follow suit. Still, if a very complicated recipe can make your mouth water without wreaking havoc in your own kitchen, and if you can test its superiority seated in a restaurant instead of standing over a hot stove, we think it's our duty to tell you about it. We're talking about the hare à la royale to be had at Bistrot 121 during the winter.

The owner, Monsieur Moussié, hasn't absolutely respected the classical recipe (which is very controversial anyway), whereby one removes the ribs from the hare, leaving all the other bones, stuffs it with foie gras and truffles and cooks it very, very slowly down to a sort of royal mush, to be eaten with a spoon. Moussié completely bones two hares, marinates them overnight and makes a concentrate from the bones and marinade. He prepares a stuffing with the liver, heart, bread centers soaked in the concentrate, foie gras, truffles and a little bacon. The two hares are stuffed after being placed head to foot (to keep the meat evenly distributed), rolled up, tied, and wrapped in pork caul. Bistrot 121's lièvre à la royale is then slowly browned on a mirepoix of spices, moistened with the concentrate (which has been thickened with the blood) and served with braised chestnuts, poached pear halves glazed with gooseberry jelly and, possibly, parslied cèpes. And that's all there is to it.

We advise Bistrot 121's occasional detractors, whose letters hint that we are overly indulgent with this restaurant, to give careful consideration to the rare, perfectly balanced, exquisite flavor of this fabulous dish, fittingly accompanied by a Musigny 1949. Maybe we're just lucky, but the simpler dishes that we've sampled there have provided us with outstanding meals every time: fricasseed kidneys and sweetbreads, ham cooked in ashes with leaf spinach, the marvelous and extremely satisfying stewed chicken Figeac style, salmis of duck with madeira and truffles, frittot (scallops, Bouzigues mussels and crayfish fried in puff paste and served with a choice of three sauces: paprika mayonnaise, tartar sauce or garlic mayonnaise), Tatin tart or the superb tangerine sherbet.

Not everything is on the credit side at Bistrot 121, however. The lighting is rather raw, the décor is more "little brasserie" than "great bistro" and it's too crowded for our taste. This, plus the bill of some 40-odd francs ($8), which is the least you can expect to pay (hare à la royale alone costs $5), may be enough to deprive nitpickers of all the pleasure which the Lot cuisine has to offer.

> Bistrot 121, 121 rue de la Convention (15e), VAU 13.85. Closed Mondays and in August. Dinner served until 10:30 P.M.

Aux Bonnes Choses *

WINE: 9

DÉCOR: 8

RECEPTION AND SERVICE: 12

ATMOSPHERE: 11

PRICES: I

Mme Pannetrat is a delightful old lady. You have only to see her nice, homey face, hear her zesty Lot accent, and above all eat her cèpes or preserved duck to want to pack your bags at once and dash off to that blessed province where they worship friendship, beauty, hospitality . . . and truffles.

She goes back home every year, partly to rest but mainly to lay in her supplies with the local farmers. For decades she has been buying ducks, turkeys and geese, which she herself puts up into delicious preserves, together with the foie gras, cassoulet and cèpes that you eat in the humble and rather dim little dining room at Aux Bonnes Choses.

These preserves are made with love (and ingredients of the finest quality) and for this reason they are better than lots of supposedly fresh dishes.

Three of us shared two truffle omelets, six fine pieces of preserved duck accompanied by exquisite little beans, nut cake (good but a little filling) and a bottle of old Cahors 1961, for which we paid 87 francs ($17.50), not counting the service. (As you see, these prices are more at home in Paris than Quercy.)

If we had to criticize one thing about that perfect meal, it would have to be ourselves. We really were wrong to have Cahors. This wine is becoming very fashionable, but unless it's very old, it lacks bouquet, body and character. We should be hearing more about Bourgueil or Champigny instead, which are a lot more satisfying for the same price.

Aux Bonnes Choses, 8 *bis* rue Falguière (15ᵉ), SEG 81.77. Closed Saturday evenings and all day Sundays, and from July 15 to September 15.

Restaurant du Marché *

WINE: 12
DÉCOR: 9
RECEPTION AND SERVICE: 12
ATMOSPHERE: 14
PRICES: 1

After 8:00 P.M. the rue Dantzig gives a pretty good imitation of a desert and makes one wonder whatever got into Monsieur Massia to make him open up a restaurant there. Maybe it was his love of a joke, or maybe it was simply chance. He would certainly be coining money in a more accessible district. The Restaurant du Marché is, in fact, one of the most genuine bistros to open in recent years.

There used to be an old bistro with off-beige walls here, one of those old bistros which came to have a sort of rare nostalgic charm in the face of the neon invasion. Instead of ransacking the Flea Market and sending out distress signals to interior decorators, Monsieur Massia left everything just as it was and was satisfied to give it a good once-over with a broom. On the other hand, he arranged to have a group of small farmers from the Landes mail him a daily supply of eggs, vegetables, chickens, cèpes and doves according to season, as well as foie gras and potted meats—in short, all those unadulterated, natural products which some day will belong to history.

And after that he sent for an amazing old cook, Mme Descats, a woman of passion and the Landes, schooled in the fine Mimizan tradition of goosefat cookery (the lightest in the world).

A few days ago Mme Descats opened a drawer and pulled out a Landes recipe that is very unfamiliar to Parisians: "lou magret." As you most certainly have already guessed, this is a duck steak. Not wanting to shock the convention-bound mentalities of his customers, the proprietor only wrote "broiled red meat" on the menu. And one might indeed take this grilled meat, nice and red on the inside and surprisingly tender, to be an unknown variety of beefsteak. We shared this thought with the august cook, adding that we thought too much of duck to allow that anyone could make it lose its flavor.

Five minutes later she came trotting back with another little duck steak. It was sheer delight from the first bite: juicy, flavorful meat, this time with a real taste of duck. Instead of using a grill she had prepared it her own way, i.e., cooked very rapidly —three or four minutes—in a cocotte. Simply superb. So don't forget the "lou magret," but "en cocotte."

A word, too, about the tourtière that M. Massia has been getting lately. Ah, good old pie! A rustic, naïve air that brings back childhood, evenings by the fireside and dear old granny, if you haven't been completely spoiled by city living. An old country woman from Saint Justin in the upper Landes still makes this amazing pastry (she's the last of her kind in the region), which reminds one a little of a *pastilla* and requires hours of work as well as strong arms.

Every product, from the preserved goose to the good country eggs, and including the Sauternes and the exquisite Monbousquet Bordeaux which sells for 7.50F, is selected with loving care. All the dishes are tempting, but we especially recommend the preserved goose omelet, Landes ham, goose or duck liver, Landes stew, potted pork, and braised chicken with Armagnac. And when we add that the bill doesn't come to more than 25 or 30 francs, you'll agree that the Restaurant du Marché is well worth a detour to rue Dantzig.

> Restaurant du Marché, 59 rue Dantzig (15ᵉ), VAU 3.155. Open every day.

Le Clos du Moulin

CUISINE: 10

WINE: 10

DÉCOR: 13
RECEPTION AND SERVICE: 11
ATMOSPHERE: 12
PRICES: I

In the eighteenth century this whole section bristled with windmills, and the Green Mill stood on this very spot. All were destroyed, except for one, parts of which can still be seen in the Montparnasse cemetery. Among the casualties was that same Moulin Vert. A pub called Auberge de la Mère Saguet was erected on the site during the last century and soon became a gathering place for the Tout-Paris of Romanticism: Musset, George Sand, Victor Hugo, Beranger, Nerval, etc. The inn subsequently went downhill; its leprous façade could still be seen only a few years ago.

Monsieur Louis Delrieu, a Méridional and ardent sea perch fisherman, brought this memory-laden place back to life. We think he would have been better advised to attempt a sincere recreation of a Romantic inn, as long as everything pointed in that direction.

He preferred to rebuild a sort of farmhouse, very *House and Garden,* with exposed stones, giant spit, barbeque and turn-of-the-century curios. It's extremely sophisticated and, we must admit, not at all pretentious. Quite the contrary: it's fresh and appealing even if this style doesn't especially thrill you. The more or less Provençal cooking is steadily improving. You quickly round the 45-franc ($9) mark, but Le Clos du Moulin has a very acceptable 15-franc ($3) menu, plus wine and service, which entitles you, for example, to a little fried fish, chicken in Beaujolais, cheese, tart or sherbet.

Le Clos du Moulin, 34 *bis* rue des Plantes (14ᵉ), SEG 31.31. Open every day.

Pouteau

CUISINE: 11
WINE: 12
DÉCOR: I
RECEPTION AND SERVICE: 0–17
ATMOSPHERE: 14
PRICES: I

Is the dining room ten yards square, as some claim, or twelve yards square, as we would be generously inclined to believe? This historical and geometrical point won't soon be settled, for Monsieur Pouteau isn't a man to let himself be measured. He rules over the smallest restaurant in Paris with the virile assurance of a sovereign who brooks neither argument nor excessive zeal. When we told him the other day that we wanted to have photographs taken of him and his establishment, he haughtily replied: "Well, all right, I'll do you the favor. I'm glad to help you fellows get ahead."

It's not easy to have a conversation with Monsieur Pouteau. You never know whether this fast-drinking Norman is joking or serious. He seems to be pulling your leg when he mysteriously whispers in your ear that he used to work at the Elysée Palace during Auriol's presidency, that he was on close terms with such important people that he'd rather not reveal their names, that he never stops jetting around the world. Then a minute later he's nothing but a regular fellow again, squeezing a pheasant to show you how fresh it is, with no greater ambition than to have you share his love of good food.

The restaurant which this odd character rules over in rue de la Croix-Nivert is just like him: zany. Picture four tables jammed in around a bar behind which the autographed smile of Tino Rossi and photos of some less important stars are slowly yellowing. At the back, almost within arm's reach, is an old stove, undoubtedly army surplus from the first Russo-Japanese war. Until a few months ago it was still the domain of Mme Pouteau, a lady with yellow hair and lots of lip. She has commended her soul and her apron to God. Under Père Pouteau's watchful eye, a buxom creature with a German accent is now simmering the little dishes which an enthusiastic group of habitués eagerly devours. What's written on the menu doesn't always correspond to what's actually available that day. It all depends on what the lord and master unearthed at Les Halles. If it was pheasant or hare, it will be out on a table. He waves it under your nose: "Have this!" There's no use arguing. It will be prepared for you in an hour, in the proper sense of the word, and you won't regret it. The owner's whims always stem from a judicious choice, and be it frog's legs, flamed guinea hen or joint of beef, you never stop wondering how such wholesome products managed to turn up between those yellow walls.

The only criticism to be made about Pouteau's cooking is that he overdoes the alcohol somewhat. The liquid element admittedly plays a very decided role here. . . . But you can't complain when you discover Lafite-Rothschild 1953 on the laboriously handwritten wine list at the pleasantly absurd price of $7.50 a bottle. (Pouteau hides his best bottles in his first-floor bedroom.) Anyhow, Monsieur Pouteau doesn't give the impression that he wants to make a fortune in this vale of tears: the bill rarely exceeds 25 francs ($5).

> Pouteau, 236 rue de la Croix-Nivert (15ᵉ), VAU 31.77. Closed on Sundays.

Le Serin

> CUISINE: 10
>
> WINE: 7
>
> DÉCOR: 9
>
> RECEPTION AND SERVICE: 12
>
> ATMOSPHERE: 13
>
> PRICES: V.C.

If, some fine evening, you don't want anything more than a nice cheerful, relaxed meal, go take a seat behind the cane fence on the terrace of Le Serin, on little place Falguière. For 10 francs ($2) you will be given a dinner that is more than satisfactory both in terms of variety and in the freshness and preparation of the products. You can choose among fish soup, red mullet, Toulouse sausage, spaghetti or couscous. And you won't be disappointed.

> Le Serin, place Falguière (15ᵉ), SEG 12.24. Closed Mondays and in August. Dinner served until 10:00 P.M.

Parc Montsouris, Cité Universitaire (14ᵉ)

Le Pavillon du Lac

> CUISINE: 10
>
> WINE: 9

DÉCOR: 12

RECEPTION AND SERVICE: 12

ATMOSPHERE: 12

PRICES: I

An old tradition, which has proved correct hundreds of times, has it that one always gets terrible food in what today's officialese terms "green spaces." One park restaurant is free of this curse, however, for it is fortunate enough to function—and even to function well—all year round. It's the one in Parc Montsouris.

In the thirties Le Pavillon du Lac was a very popular restaurant. Montparnasse had nothing but impecunious painters, and people like Braque had taken over the quiet streets like rue de Douanier, rue Gazan and rue du Parc Montsouris, which border on this slightly crazy park.

Le Pavillon du Lac profited from this little fad. At night you would find artists and writers there like Fernand Léger, Aragon, Man Ray, Blaise Cendrars, André Breton, and Giacommeti, who had no idea that their names would some day wind up in the encyclopedia. Then Montparnasse declined in prestige and pulled the food at Le Pavillon du Lac down with it. It had become a sorry-looking, uncomfortable and empty place by the time Monsieur Massouline took charge some ten years ago.

That energetic fellow set to work reducing the pavilion's ugliness, struggling with the municipal government to have a terrace built across from the charming artificial lake, and, most important, raising the quality of the food to a very honorable level.

Today Le Pavillon du Lac is full day and night, summer and winter. Customers are given a nice welcome, friendly service and very good treatment.

Monsieur Massouline, who also owns a little fish restaurant on rue Mademoiselle in the 15th *arrondissement,* has a special weakness for seafood. He has therefore put a very acceptable bouillabaisse on the menu, as well as broiled fish like the absolutely delicious turbot with hollandaise sauce, for example. The cooking isn't breath-taking, but it is honest, clean and consistent, and 25 francs ($5) will put you on the best of terms with "park cuisine."

> Le Pavillon du Lac, 29 rue Gazan (14ᵉ), GOB 38.52. Reservations necessary. Open daily until 10:00 P.M.

Invalides, Latour-Maubourg, Suffren (7ᵉ, 15ᵉ)

Chez Les Anges **

WINE: 16

DÉCOR: 12

RECEPTION AND SERVICE: 14

ATMOSPHERE: 11

PRICES: E

The rich sauces and wine-simmered meats of bourguignon cooking may make this hearty food seem rather a challenge to delicate stomachs. When it is prepared with neither scruples nor talent it can send a fellow reeling as surely as a cannonball. On the other hand, in loving, skillful hands it becomes, if not exactly light, at least completely inoffensive to the stomach, and a joy to the palate in any case.

You couldn't do better than going to eat this fine Burgundian food at Chez les Anges, a pretty, elegant restaurant much appreciated by businessmen. After whetting your appetite with a glass of champagne to which a dash of fresh raspberry juice has been added, try the eggs en meurette (in red wine), for example, or the parslied ham, excellent vegetables in vinaigrette sauce or crabmeat salad. You will then have a choice of several bravura morsels: oxtail, marvelous calf's liver served in thick, slightly pinkish slices with scalloped potatoes, rib steak bourguignonne, coq au vin or superb chartreuse of pheasant.

Accompany this with a Rully white or a great red wine from Côtes de Beaune or Côtes de Nuit, follow it with goat cheese (they have the widest selection in Paris), flaky tarts and a glorious Burgundy marc-brandy, and you will have had a meal fit for an angel. (About 35 to 40 francs—$7 to $8.)

> Chez les Anges, 54 boulevard de Latour-Maubourg (7ᵉ), SOL 89.86. Closed Mondays. Dinner served until 10:00 P.M.

Le Petit Niçois

CUISINE: 10

WINE: 8

DÉCOR: 10

RECEPTION AND SERVICE: 11

ATMOSPHERE: 12

PRICES: 1

Ever since the television people discovered Le Petit Niçois near their studio on rue Cognacq-Jay, it has lost some of its simplicity, and the price of a meal is nearer 20 francs ($4) than 10 francs, as used to be the case. And it has become almost indispensable to reserve your table in one of the three little rooms decorated in Provençal fashion.

It's still a cheerful, appealing place, frequented by a motley crowd of people who are bizarre, cosmopolitan, happy and often broke. And the cooking—plentiful, gay, loaded with garlic—hasn't changed. The bouillabaisse is always excellent, the little hors d'oeuvres nice and fresh, the steak à la marseillaise tender and spicy, the daily specials are tasty and original, and the Provence wine is full of life.

Le Petit Niçois, 10 rue Amélie (7e), INV 83.65. Closed Sundays and in August. Dinner served until 9:30 P.M.

DRUGSTORES AND SNACK BARS

Bar Belge, 75 avenue de Saint-Ouen (17e). See CAFES AND BARS, p. 178.

Bar des Théâtres

CUISINE: 6

SERVICE: 5

ATMOSPHERE: 15
PRICES: E

Theatergoers from the three Champs-Elysées theaters gather here during the between-the-acts confusion. Almost all the tables are taken either by stripling couturiers accompanied by haughty girls or by other striplings trailing ladies whose age betokens their experience and whose brilliant jewels bespeak their means.

It's a real free-for-all in this noisy bar-restaurant (steak, osso bucco, welsh rarebit and other French gourmet specialties), so noisy in fact that the old waiters dressed in blue blazers (and with a gait that rolls as much as their *r*'s) have formed the habit of not hearing your order until the sixth time around.

When the curtain falls, actors, playwrights, conductors and virtuosos come here to rejoin their attentive public, whose exaggerated enthusiasm then reaches the boiling point. The harassed stagehands cool things off again. They fill the places left by musicologists, critics and autograph hounds, and exchange views on what's wrong with the country. The conversational level progressively declines until daybreak, when road workers come in to have "fortified" coffee with their morning snack. These highway workers seem little inclined to discuss the clarity of von Karajan's attack in the last movement of Mahler's Third, and fill each other in on the latest exploits of the farmer's daughter until dawn floods the metamorphosed terrace. Then a waiter sets to work washing last night's traces from the floor before the Dior mannequins arrive for breakfast.

> Bar des Théâtres, 6 avenue Montaigne (8e), ELY 34.88. Open daily until 2:30 A.M.

La Boutique à Sandwiches

SANDWICHES: 13
DÉCOR: 2
SERVICE: 10
ATMOSPHERE: 9

All snack bars are gray at night, but even though this one is no more charming or attractive than any of the rest, it does at least have a little color and warmth, so sorely lacking in this section's neon-lit *boîtes*. You are treated like a human being, there even are a few little *plats du jour* and the sandwiches (twenty-five varieties, priced from 1.50 to 3 francs) have both flavor and personality.

La Boutique à Sandwiches, 12 rue du Colisée (8e), ELY 56.69. Closed on Sundays. Open until 12:30 A.M.

Drugstore des Champs-Elysées and Drugstore de Saint-Germain-des-Prés

CUISINE: 7

DÉCOR: 15

RECEPTION AND SERVICE: 12

ATMOSPHERE: 15

PRICES: 1

It may seem paradoxical, but relatively few Americans ever go into these two drugstores, which the French see as the reflection of the American way of life. This is because the drugstores, created by the large advertising agency Publicis, are offshoots of a very French invention, which consists in combining pleasure with triviality. You'd be hard-pressed to find drugstores like these two in New York, San Francisco or Chicago. And far from disdaining them, American tourists ought to find them extremely interesting, for they have become little bits of the soul of Paris like Lipp or Maxim's, little artificial, exaggerated, bastardized bits which nevertheless count for a lot in the evolution of Parisian customs. The French-style drugstore is closed-circuit Paris. You could practically live in one without ever going outside. You can have breakfast there, buy newspapers from all over the world, telephone Cannes or Miami, get your shoes shined, have a whiskey, pick up the latest books, select a perfectly humidified cigar, buy perfume, send flowers to your girl friend, buy your children the latest toys, pick out a Japanese television set, eat lunch, see the latest film by Antonioni or Godard, have dinner, have supper, and with a little luck, top it all by leaving with a pretty girl on your arm, not without having previously bought a bottle of vodka and a tin of caviar.

The drugstores thus put on a running show which is one of

the most entertaining in Paris. You catch sight of Marlene Dietrich, her arms full of packages (and she's back the next day to exchange everything; the salesgirls in the Champs-Elysées drugstore dread her like the plague). Then there's Belmondo buying a teddy bear for Ursula Andress, Sammy Davis autographing his autobiography for some frenzied girls, starlets nourishing their hopes with ice cream, kids gotten up like Carnaby Street clowns, very serious businessmen consulting the stock market reports, pickpockets, voyeurs who stay there for hours without eating or buying a thing; in short, an absolutely motley population which is a mixture of every age and class.

As in any show, the décor obviously plays a very important role. Both places were conceived by Slavik, who managed to create a rather successful sort of "popular luxury." Of the two, Parisians concur in their preference for the décor at the Champs-Elysées, although Americans will certainly find it less novel. Slavik's inspiration for the bar-restaurant's furnishings and décor is in fact based on the theme "Winning the West": Winchesters, old posters and gleaming copper. It's blond, attractive, comfortable and very ingenious. At Saint-Germain-des-Prés he was handicapped by lack of space, and the maze-like corridors and mezzanines all get a little confusing. The general theme here is a very free interpretation of the 1830's, to which some modern touches—like the bronze molds of famous movie stars' lips (Brigitte Bardot, Sophia Loren, etc.)—have been added.

And the food?

You might guess that no restaurant whose best-selling beverage is Coca-Cola is going to inspire us to dithyrambic comments. But these drugstores can't simply be ignored, what with fifteen hundred people eating there every day.

Instead of a real drugstore menu, these places serve food that is neither fish nor fowl, since the point of having typically American dishes (hamburgers, chicken salad plate, tunafish salad, banana splits, etc.) is lost by adding French or other foreign touches. And even the fact that the Champs-Elysées and Saint-Germain drugstores owe their undeniable success to the exoticism of their American-Swedish-Russian-Italian-French-Swiss menus doesn't make us any happier with the food. On the other hand, it doesn't prevent us from finding the

oysters excellent and some of the daily specials pleasant, nor
from having our childish hearts' delight in the gigantic desserts
covered with whipped cream. (The ice cream, however, is far
inferior to Howard Johnson's.) As far as prices go, we must
have been unlucky, since people assure us that a meal never
averages more than 10 francs ($2); each time we've gotten a
bill of at least 25 francs ($5), plus the feeling that we hadn't
had much to eat.

Drugstores, 133 Champs-Elysées (8e), BAL 94.40; 149 boulevard
Saint-Germain (6e), LIT 42.63. Open daily until 2:00 A.M.

Au Sauvignon, 80 rue des Saints-Pères (6e). See CAFES
AND BARS, p. 184.

Le Village, 7 rue Gozlin (6e). See CAFES AND BARS,
p. 185.

SUBURBS IN THE IMMEDIATE VICINITY OF PARIS

We don't want to give you too many addresses on the outskirts of Paris. And anyhow, there aren't too many that deserve
to be mentioned. We have chosen to limit ourselves to places
whose food or charm, or sometimes both, make them really
exceptional.

Barbizon

Hostellerie du Bas-Bréau **
WINE: 15

DÉCOR: 16
RECEPTION AND SERVICE: 16
ATMOSPHERE: 13
PRICES: E

This is the prettiest, most refined, most hospitable hostelry in the region south of Paris.

Back in 1867 a lumber dealer named Siron had an inn here called Auberge de l'Exposition. That fine fellow had the idea of installing a permanent exhibit of paintings. The following year he received a visit from Napoleon III and the Empress, and soon canvases by Millet, Diaz and Rousseau were hanging beside paintings by Corot, Chaigneau, Bodmer and other masters of the Barbizon School. A crowd of artists and writers, including Robert Louis Stevenson, formed the habit of staying at hospitable Monsieur Siron's.

Monsieur and Madame Fava have turned that historical, timeworn dwelling into a haven of peace and charm. They have put up little "colonial" summerhouses in the huge blossoming garden, and Mme Fava herself has furnished and decorated them with rare taste and a remarkable sense of harmony.

This charming couple welcomes its rich customers with the exemplary courtesy of true hosts and has created an atmosphere that combines genteel elegance with rustic simplicity.

Unfortunately, you need a very fat wallet to sample all the pleasures of Bas-Bréau. You have to be prepared to spend from 75 to 180 francs ($15 to $36), plus 15 percent service, to sleep in one of those lovely rooms or elegant apartments. And if you want to sit in the shade of the tall trees and eat the jellied quail stuffed with foie gras, curried chicken or rack of hare (all accompanied by the finest wines), which have helped make this the best restaurant in Barbizon, you have to be able to face a bill of at least 50 francs.

Hostellerie du Bas-Bréau, Barbizon (Seine-et-Marne). Telephone: 937.40.05. Closed from November 15 to December 15. (About forty minutes from Paris on the Autoroute du Sud.)

Chevreuse

Le Prieuré Saint-Saturnin

CUISINE: 10

WINE: 10

DÉCOR: 15

RECEPTION AND SERVICE: 14

ATMOSPHERE: 15

PRICES: I

Monsieur Vénitien is a painter and teacher, Madame Vénitien is a ceramist, and the two of them are the most unusual
innkeepers in the Paris area.

A few years ago they fell madly in love with a dilapidated
building that was pitifully waiting for the end on a little
square in the village of Chevreuse, away from the state highway and the curiosity of Sunday drivers. This ruin had at least
one claim to fame: its age. The Saint-Saturnin priory had in
fact been built in the tenth century and abandoned at the end
of the sixteenth.

The painter and his wife undertook the restoration of this
admirable building (which was in such bad condition that it
couldn't even be used as a garage), having only fervent love,
very discerning taste and definitely limited funds at their disposal.

When they had at last restored the priory's austere beauty,
they got the idea of actually living there and opening a club.

There was no opening-day cocktail party, there was no publicity, but everything eventually gets around, even in the Chevreuse Valley. Word traveled along the grapevine that there
was a marvelous place only eighteen miles from Paris, where
one could sit beneath Romanesque arches listening to Bach
and eating ribs of beef in front of a huge fireplace.

Today the club has over five hundred members. Joining it is
both simple and very complicated: neither money nor fame
counts. Admission depends on how nice you look and how
well you behave. But this is always very graciously handled,
and besides, some mysterious process sees to it that only those

people who will be welcome at the Prieuré are ever attracted there.

Still, you can't just turn up on the spur of the moment. You have to give them at least half a day's notice that you're coming, since the Vénitiens don't want to be slaves to their club and may be away. Above all, the cloister is very often busy with receptions and dinners given by engineers from Saclay, doctors and manufacturers, who make up the majority of the regular customers.

The staff has been reduced to a minimum; a charming old servant acts as waitress, Monsieur Vénitien takes care of the wine and his wife does the cooking. It's no use asking for the menu; there isn't any. You eat what the lady of the house felt like making. One night this will be quiche lorraine and ribs of beef, another time, chicken roasted on a spit. It's not *grande cuisine,* but good home cooking. The prices, moreover, are exemplary in their reasonableness: a meal costs 20 francs ($4), plus wine and service.

But what can't be calculated—provided of course that you are sensitive to it and don't behave as if this were just another restaurant—is the inimitable atmosphere and discreet friendliness which reign in this resurrected priory.

> Le Prieuré Saint-Saturnin, place de l'église Saint-Martin, Chevreuse. Telephone: 952.17.15. Reservations necessary. (Eighteen miles from Paris, in the Chevreuse Valley.)

Louveciennes

Président Show Boat *

WINE: 11

DÉCOR: 16 ·

RECEPTION AND SERVICE: 14

ATMOSPHERE: 16

PRICES: 1

Let's get out of Paris, drive past the fabulous machine at Marly which pumps water to the Palace of Versailles, and have dinner on the Seine. And, of all things, let's have a good dinner in a place which was designed to be fashionable and might so easily have been nothing else.

It seems it pitches a little when cyclones rage in the Seine Valley. But it also seems that the Président Show Boat (named after those famous Mississippi paddle wheelers which used to be a kind of floating casino) can actually move—with propellers, since the paddle wheels are fake—and that on nice days you can go for a cruise toward Pontoise and Bercy.

But even when firmly moored, it's a wonderful boat, a three-story barge. The hold is completely equipped to give exhausted businessmen the feeling of being on vacation on the Côte d'Azur: salt-water swimming pool, massage tables, a room for sun treatments, a gym, powerful showers, a hairdresser and even a little drugstore (on the main floor).

The long 'tween-decks dining room, done in dark wood pierced with portholes, has its own bar and dance floor and is extremely pleasant. You look out at the Seine as you dine; you dance to Dixieland music and have reasonably priced drinks in glasses that are set in hanging, nonskid trays.

Finally, you can sleep in the sun on the upper deck while your kidneys en brochette are being broiled. This is where the kitchen, or, more exactly, the grill, is located, since the Président Show Boat serves nothing but broiled meat. And also a nice little Landes pâté and a foie gras (the owner comes from the southwest) which would be the envy of many more famous restaurants. The meat is extraordinary. It comes from a strange character, a kind of gentleman-butcher who, when he isn't out riding or playing golf, slaughters the animals (which he raises in Normandy) in his beautiful house in Croissy and then judiciously parcels out the meat.

Thanks to the exceptional quality of the meat, a lamb saddle or rib of beef, followed by flamed crêpes, make for a lovely evening on the river.

Le Président Show Boat, quai Conti, Louveciennes. Telephone: 969.11.29. Open until 2:00 A.M.

Marly-le-Roi

Le Vieux Marly ***

WINE: 14

DÉCOR: 10

RECEPTION AND SERVICE: 12

ATMOSPHERE: 10

PRICES: E

We first became acquainted with Le Vieux Marly three years ago. Since then we have had lunch and dinner there, together, separately and with friends, and each time we have left with joy in our hearts and an unforgettable taste in our months. And each time we wonder whether Monsieur Guillot may not simply be one of the finest chefs in the world. You probably think we're exaggerating, carried away by streams of his marvelous Musigny. Well, stock up on money (sublime food is never cheap, so you should count on paying about 50 francs—$10— without the wine), and go see for yourself. Telephone first for a reservation and let them know what time you'll be there ("Good food doesn't wait," proclaims Monsieur Guillot). And he isn't kidding: he refuses to serve latecomers or people who are in too much of a hurry. Getting there is easy and fast: it takes barely ten minutes to drive to Marly from the Autoroute de l'Ouest tunnel. Now then, if you don't have a meal fit for a king at a roomy table in one of the nondescript but appealing little country rooms, it only means that you have an awfully vulgar palate or that some ghastly catastrophe has prevented Monsieur Guillot from lighting the extraordinary stove in the little kitchen where he cooks his feuilletés and game. And don't be afraid to order dishes which would make you fear for your health in other restaurants. Monsieur Guillot's sauces never contain any flour or cooked fat. They are emulsions, marvelously balanced sauces which this tightrope walker of a cook whips up with a magician's dexterity—and a secret. Sample the terrine of foie gras of duck, amazingly smooth and fragrant, the very surprising feuilleté of asparagus tips (or the many other feuilletés—foie gras, lobster, oysters—all as light as air). Then have one of his sumptuous game dishes: his partridge, three-quarters roasted and then finished in a Dutch oven, with port wine sauce and fresh artichoke bottoms, or his hare, not exactly "à la royale" but no less royal for that. (Telephone ahead to reserve your hare, and hurry up: Monsieur Guillot stops making it after October 15 because he doesn't want to increase the number of items on his menu and he has to make room for pheasant with port and later for his fabulous noisettes de chevreuil with grapes.) Finally there are the desserts: more feuilletés, sherbets, tarts, expert pastry, or simply fresh "butterflies" served with excellent coffee, made as few places know how.

Monsieur Guillot has served as cook for dukes and princes and even for the famous, eccentric writer Raymond Roussel (the author of *Locus Solus*), to whom he used to present several dozen different dishes between noon and five o'clock, which had been prepared exclusively for Roussel (he never had anyone to lunch). You too will be treated like a prince at Le Vieux Marly, if you know how to wait and respectfully eat your food with a sage's humility and dignity. But stay away from this place before you are thrown out (gentle Monsieur Guillot wouldn't be the least embarrassed) if you only like steak-frites or if you are a slave to fashion. Monsieur Guillot will never be "fashionable," thank heaven.

> Le Vieux Marly, place de la Mairie, Marly-le-Roi. Telephone: 969.07.70. Closed on Thursdays and in July and August. Reservations absolutely necessary. (Fifteen minutes from the Pont de St. Cloud, via the Autoroute de l'Ouest.)

Neuilly-sur-Seine

Les Pieds Dans l'Eau

CUISINE: 9

DÉCOR: 11

RECEPTION AND SERVICE: 12

ATMOSPHERE: 16

PRICES: I

Does the idea of trout fishing strike a responsive chord in you? Or bowling a game beneath a fig tree? Or dining at the water's edge? Ten minutes away from the Etoile?

Once you have discovered Les Pieds Dans l'Eau you'll wonder how you ever could have missed this little corner of heaven. But it's true that Parisians have very few reasons to wander around the Ile de la Jatte, all bristling with factory smokestacks.

This is just what happened, though, to two American women one evening, and the encounter made Jean Baron's fortune.

Jean, who used to be a bartender in some of the large hotels, is a black-haired Provençal with a shrewd twinkle in his eye. He wasn't unhappy with the way things were going at his little bistro in Neuilly, but he dreamed of indulging his double passion: angling and tree-shaded siestas. Five years ago, during a stroll on the Ile de la Jatte, his heart skipped a beat. He had caught sight of a fig tree at the water's edge, a real fig tree like the ones in his native Midi, together with four weeping willows and four poplars. There was also a dilapidated little beer joint where local workers used to go for a snack.

He bought the whole thing for a song, set out a row of pans in the dining room for rainy days (the roof was a sieve), and cooked to order for his friends, who include doctors as well as plumbers. It was a sort of casual club where one could bowl or dance to the music of a player piano.

For relaxation Jean would dip his fishing line in the water, which led to the discovery that there are trout in the Seine (he caught seventeen last season, one of which weighed two and a half pounds, and a friend of his even captured a salmon!). One evening two completely lost American women stumbled in when everything was in full swing. One of them was a delightful and very elegant lady. When she saw all those people having fun, she declared: "Come on, let's stay." And, pointing to the other guests, she told Jean: "Everything's on me." The party went full-steam ahead until four in the morning, when Jean, who was already treating the stranger like an old friend, brought her the bill. It amounted to 700 francs ($140). "But that's impossible!" she exclaimed. "You see, honey," said Jean, "you think you're Rockefeller and you end up not being able to pay."

The woman burst out laughing. "But I *am* Mrs. Nelson Rockefeller," she replied, and thanking him warmly, wrote out a check (a photocopy is now enthroned over the bar). If she seemed surprised, it was only because she had spent $700 in a sinister, luxurious *boîte* the night before. She came back a few days later with an American newspaperwoman and soon all the *bon vivants* of Tout-Paris, from Jacques Tati to Francis Blanche, had discovered Les Pieds Dans L'Eau.

Jean and his wife Jeanne have somewhat transformed their bistro, to be sure, but fame has not gone to their heads, even though for some time now you've had to fight to get a table. You don't come here for gourmet thrills. For $5 you get a meal which could easily be better, but mainly you are treating yourself to the most amazing change of scene to be found in Paris.

Les Pieds Dans l'Eau, 39 boulevard du Parc, Ile de la Jatte (Neuilly). Telephone: MAI 19.73. Closed on Sundays and from August 15 to September 15. Open until 10:30 P.M.

Le Tremblay-sur-Mauldre

Auberge de la Dauberie

CUISINE: 9

WINE: 9

DÉCOR: 15

RECEPTION AND SERVICE: 12

ATMOSPHERE: 15

PRICES: E

Hereby hangs a very moral tale: the story of a showgirl who was lucky enough not to marry a millionaire. Every night for years she rhythmically kicked her faultless legs from the Lido to Las Vegas, and flashed that triumphant smile which makes the uninitiated think that showgirls never have any gas bills to pay.

But as her successes piled up, a picture was taking shape in that blond head covered with sequins and plumes—the touching, bucolic picture of a rose-covered cottage and a heart that's true.

Colette Risbourg already had the heart: it belonged to her husband, Dominique the magician. So all she needed was the rose-covered cottage. They found it nestled in a wooded valley at Saint-Rémy-l'Honoré. All that was missing were the roses— plus a roof, walls, doors, windows, running water; in a word, almost everything.

From that day on Dominique and his wife were performing for the local mason, plumber, carpenter and electrician, who had first claim on their salaries as artists.

When the Dauberie (the name of the place) was finally finished, the showgirl and her magician found themselves transformed into hotel owners.

All this happened two years ago. Today La Dauberie is one of the most captivating and exquisite inns in the Ile de France.

Colette might have been an interior decorator. This tall, rather shy young woman applied her excellent taste to unearthing pretty, old romantic furniture and composing an uncloyingly voluptuous décor from fabrics and refined curios, while her husband filled the garden with flowers and fruit trees.

As you might guess, the keys to this little paradise are solid gold; the rooms (of which there are eight) fetch from 85 to 100 francs ($17 to $20), plus breakfast, and you can't hope to have a meal for less than 45 francs ($9).

When the inn first opened, the menu was much too long. Dominique and his wife have very wisely pared it down, and their great specialties remain scrambled eggs with truffles, seafood au gratin, loin of lamb, duckling Montmorency and an acceptable broiled lobster.

So there you have a nice little weekend for 300 to 400 francs ($60 to $80). But when you take a pretty woman to La Dauberie—even if she's your wife—you don't insult her by thinking about the bill.

> Auberge de la Dauberie, Les Mousseaux (Yvelines). Telephone: 57. Closed Tuesdays and in February. (About twenty-five minutes away from Paris, via the Autoroute de l'Ouest.)

Black List

We didn't want to be too nasty in this guidebook and do needless damage to restaurants already doomed by their own mediocrity, with no help from us. But Paris has a certain number of spots whose reputation—sustained by powerful publicity —may attract innocent tourists and give them a terrible let-down.

So we think that the little negative list which follows is just as useful as the list of recommended restaurants. We don't mean that the food you get there is always very bad or that the proprietors of these "meccas" are crooks. But even so, we still don't want you to waste your money or your time.

JOUR ET NUIT: no charm, lots of noise, mediocre.

L'ORÉE DU BOIS: bad food, horrible floor show.

ROTISSERIE PÉRIGOURDINE: overrated for many years now.

DAGORNO, L'HORLOGE, LE BOEUF COURONNÉ: oddly thought to be especially good meat places.

MÈRE CATHERINE: Montmartre tourist trap.

ANNA: fun at times, but the proprietress is insufferable.

MEDITERRANÉE: ex-good restaurant.

JARDINS DE L'ÉTOILE: "top food" in the sense it is served on the top floor.

ROND-POINT DES CHAMPS-ELYSÉES: except for drinks.

NOVY: unauthentic and overpriced Russian.

CAFÉ DE LA PAIX: but the sidewalk café and the décor are fun.

TABLE DU ROY: fine food like you get at the circus.

MOUTON DE PANURGE: tasteless obscenity.

Part II

CAFÉS AND BARS

RIGHT BANK

Champs-Elysées (*8ᵉ*, *16ᵉ*)

American Legion

Antique penny machines are attached to the walls of this venerable and very charming bar, lost at the rear of a graceless court. These little instruments—the only ones like them in Paris—offer Parisians living proof that America wasn't born yesterday, since even its current vending machine kings had their forebears.

Near the bar, old American Legionnaires in mufti sometimes display faded, bicolored glengarries from "the first last war." They drink sadly, waiting for a regeneration of Atlantic relations which they promise to christen joyously. The gravity they try to impose on their rallying center while they wait for that day is very often shattered by the stormy arrival of reporters, photographers and rewrite-men from the area, who have no sense of respect and an amazing capacity for laughter at any price.

> American Legion, 49 rue Pierre Charron (8ᵉ), BAL 41.93. Open until 11:30; Sundays until 9:00 P.M.

George V Bar

Rodolphe Slavik reigns here. Some of the greatest cocktail experts consider this thin, charming and very dignified Czech bartender the best "mixer" in the world.

The George V bar is very vast. It is topped by a cupola, and its beige walls, covered here and there by long ball-fringed drapes, occasionally give way to niches. One of these is the setting for an immense tapestry by Lucien Coutaud, who also composed the strange floral decoration for the seats in a similar flight of fancy.

But the right place to display yourself is near the black-enameled bar, whose entrance is protected by a heavy glass balustrade. Typical California "talent scouts" transparently pretend to be busy businessmen while manufacturers struggle to lead the potential starlets, brought here by the former, away from the proper Hollywood paths.

The real habitués are all blondes. They are pushing forty, smoke, and smile endlessly—at the future, no doubt, or else at the rich Brazilians who eye them while twirling a cocktail glass between their fingers.

This glorious, muted bar is a little sad. It's a haven of sumptuous comfort, but the air seems too rarified for anything of Paris' real life ever to penetrate here. The only thing that disturbs the unhurried passage of time is the waiters' conversation: they are all crazy about cars.

> George V Bar, 31 avenue Georges V (8e), BAL 35.30. Open until midnight.

La Belle Ferronnière

The uninspired luxury of this café was glorified into a temple of whispered information during the fifties by the constant presence of reporters from *Paris-Match* and *Europe 1*.

Models, starlets, hairdressers and young beauties of indeterminate profession take over the terrace around noon and at six o'clock. They have a haughty look, a croissant, a lemonade and patience about making the big time. They are the only ones who remember that Roger Vadim used to officiate here between two appointments at *Paris-Match,* and they make all their entrances and exits in profile (the best side), waiting for a camera flash that never comes or a handsome boy who always does.

Then, toward nine o'clock, the pseudo-photographers come

to pick up these pseudo-starlets. They carry their equipment in aluminum cases which are much too shiny to be real. Their bustling around doesn't fool anyone, though. Cut-rate reporters, stand-ins, colorless new false witnesses to a genuine old Paris whose marvels and mysteries they know nothing about—these "might-have-beens" heedlessly stretch the day's last hazy light, whose fading just adds brilliance to their dreams.

Le Belle Ferronnière, 52 rue Pierre Charron (8e), BAL 03.82. Open daily until 1:30 A.M.

Le Calavados

Two medieval halberds flank the door which leads to this haunt of playboys who come here to invoke the spirit of their patron saint, Rubirosa. Old Saint-Germain-des-Prés aristocrats, multimillionaires from avenue Foch, and all those who are desperately trying to become attached to these two inexpugnable groups, have representatives here every evening. Everything is peaceful and voluptuous in this spot, which is still frequented by pretty—very pretty—women and animated by Joe Turner's very good piano when the South American ensembles have finally done their whiny ethnic "bit."

Le Calavados, 40 avenue Pierre Ier de Serbie (8e), BAL 95.38. Open day and night.

The Sir Winston Churchill Pub

This is Slavik's most straightforward and authentic decorating job. The train "compartments" where one can get a little privacy, the strange decorative pictures (a mixture of Bosch and Leonor Fini), the caressing light, silent carpets, simple woodwork (we're talking now about the basement, which we think is much more successful than the cluttered, glaring ground floor)—all this creates a feeling of genuineness, full of the charm we are always so happy to rediscover in London.

The choice of drinks is intelligent and very varied: some fifty-odd kinds of whiskey, good gin, port and beer, including an excellent dark Watney's ale (Watney's also put up the capital, by the way).

The only thing wrong with the downstairs pub is its prices, which may be the same as other places in Paris but still seem very high to English people in our capital. These customers are indispensable to the Winston Churchill, however, if owner Monsieur Probst wants it to be a real English pub, as he claims, and not merely the caricature of one.

> The Sir Winston Churchill Pub, 5 rue de Presbourg (16ᵉ), KLE 75.35. Open daily until 2:30 A.M.

Chez Tania

Tania is the great heroine of the rue de Ponthieu. Her singing transforms the basement of a delightfully romantic little building into a tiny bit of Russia. The ground-floor discothèque, which is so dark that Afro-American customers lose their brothers in it, finds her welcoming placid papas and businessmen out on the town.

The main attraction at Chez Tania is Tania herself, who queens it over a flock of unretiring damsels who enjoy being treated to splits of champagne by gentlemen who want to show them a little affection—and a few etchings.

> Chez Tania, 43 rue de Ponthieu (8ᵉ), ELY 13.37. Open until 4:00 A.M. Closed Sundays.

Concorde, Vendôme, Opéra, (Iᵉʳ, 2ᵉ, 8ᵉ, 9ᵉ)

Ritz Bar

You can't fly in the face of Ritz customers' habits—not even if your name is Charles Ritz.

Three years ago the great Oscar Ritz's son and successor thought it would be a good idea to completely transform the famous bar on the rue Cambon, so dear to Hemingway. The charming Monsieur Ritz is no longer in knee pants—even though he has the finest electric trains in the world—but he loves life, color, exoticism. The bar, which witnessed the comings and goings of the entire Ritz universe, was sober and subdued.

He turned everything upside down, put in a sky-blue ceiling

bordered with flowers and tropical plants, ordered pink and maroon glass plaques from Murano, installed white leather banquettes and green-enameled tables. It was gay, it was different . . . and it was a flop.

Old customers no longer recognized their bar: even Graham Greene (who lives in London and drinks in Paris) voiced his disapproval by remarking that the new décor was "superficial." Coming from such a solid pillar of the bar, the criticism carried weight.

Charles Ritz's greatest virtue is that he is always ready to correct an error. Were the Ritzians sulking? Well, we can't have that, can we? The painters, carpet layers and electricians (the Ritz has its own complete staff of artisans) would just have to come back. They removed the virgin forest hanging from the ceiling, the green chairs became maroon, and after a few other changes, the Cambon bar recaptured the favor of the Ritzians who, from Monsieur Dubonnet to Michèle Morgan, confide their desire for a Chivas Regal or a pick-me-up to the charming bartender Louis.

Right across from it is the "little bar"—it merits long hours of study if you are sensitive to the atmosphere of a real English bar, which is both prim and fraternal. This is the domain of "old regulars" of a kind they don't make any more. This "year-round parking" consists largely of distinguished members of the Anglo-Saxon colony, elite drinkers who need constant lubrication. They respect one god: Bertin, the bartender, who speaks English with a Midi accent and whips up the most ingenious mixtures like nobody else can.

But don't get the bright idea of asking him for a champagne cocktail. He'll make it for you, but with a look full of silent reproach. For him—and how right he is!—champagne is either good, in which case you drink it as is, or bad, in which case you don't drink it at all.

Ask him instead for the Ritz Special, a marvelous cocktail of his own invention. We managed to pinch the recipe: one-sixth crème de cacao, one-sixth kirsch and, for the other two-thirds, cognac and sweet Italian vermouth in a ratio that will vary according to your taste and how you happen to feel at the time.

Ritz Bar, 38 rue Cambon (Ier), OPE 28.20. Open daily until 10:00 P.M.

Café de la Paix

Ever since the Liberation, Americans have made the Café de la Paix their most solid bridgehead and have transformed the sidewalk terrace into the most amazing, most colorful, most picturesque landing beach.

All the flowered hats, neckties decorated with naked women, intellectuals in berets and pretty, idle, long-legged girls that ever came out of Oklahoma and Michigan find their way, and each other, there. Friends who haven't seen each other in twenty years fall into one another's arms while young Don Juans of the boulevard execute ingenious maneuvers designed to make the beautiful lone strangers fall into theirs.

But Paris, too, contributes something to the show. The Café de la Paix is the last refuge of those old boulevardiers who have managed to survive all disasters. Little shifty-eyed fellows pass by on the sidewalk, going up to solitary gentlemen with a pack of photographs in the palm of their hand. Reproductions from the Louvre . . .

It really takes a lot to startle the waiters at the Café de la Paix, some of whom have been there for thirty or forty years. Harry Truman, Salvador Dali, Maréchal de Lattre, General Leclerc, Maurice Chevalier, Raimu, Jouvet, Josephine Baker, Serge Lifar, Maria Callas, and also Chagall, who had all his meals here while he was painting the famous Opéra ceiling, have all been served here, either out on the terrace or in the amazing gilded, ornate salons.

A regular little army—280 people—sees to it that 250 places are set every day in the main dining room and 500 in the luxurious Pacifique snack bar, not to mention all the breakfasts, teas, and apéritifs produced by this fantastic "factory of *la vie Parisienne.*"

The only famous man who still manages to elude them is General De Gaulle. Not completely, though.

On August 25, 1944, a French officer landed at the Café de la Paix, where the ice cream still bore traces of bullets, and ordered a cold plate to take out—De Gaulle's first cold plate in liberated Paris.

Café de la Paix, 12 boulevard des Capucines (9e), OPE 35.44. Open until 1:30 A.M.; service until 1:00.

La Factorerie

This is a sort of ship reminiscent of Noah's Ark, stranded out near the Madeleine in a forest haunted by every exotic mystery.

You reach the bar by way of pine staircases which wind around boutiques heaped with treasures (on sale during the day) that make you dream of Java, Sumatra, Borneo, Bali . . .

Way upstairs, between purring Tibesti leopards and Malaysian gibbons dancing in their immense glass cave, you drink cocktails with melodious names and dream of South Sea voyages. This is the newest, most unusual and quite possibly the most winning bar in Paris.

> La Factorerie, 5 boulevard Malesherbes (8ᵉ), ANJ 96.86. Bar open until 9:30 P.M. Closed Saturdays and Sundays.

Harry's Bar

There isn't a drinker of any consequence in the entire world who doesn't know, at least by name, this large hallway on the Rue Daunou. The windows are protected by leading, the dark mahogany walls are decorated with antique bank notes, American university pennants and coats of arms with the colors of the great English colleges.

Andy MacElhone is the director of this sacred temple, which was founded by jockey Ted Sloan together with a New York café owner named Clancey.

The latter had the rust-colored façade with its fluted columns shipped over from the United States and got in touch with the man who was to leave his name and fame to the first American bar in Paris. This was Harry, Andy's extraordinary father. But let's let Andy tell it.

"At that time the New York Bar didn't go by my father's name. Racing buffs were about the only people who ever went there before the war made 'Sank Roo Doe Noo' [5 rue Daunou] the daily gathering place for American aviators from the glorious 'La Fayette' squadron. Guynemer and a lot of the heroes from the 'War to End All Wars' got into the habit of coming here. But Harry, who had tended the bar in New York's Plaza Hotel for a while, was serving in the Royal Navy.

"He could briefly be seen mixing very fortifying drinks at Ciro's in London after peace was signed. But the drinkers of Tout-Paris were impatiently awaiting him. So my father came back to his old spot between the Opéra and the rue de la Paix and used all his magic to make the Roaring 'Twenties roar even louder. This is where Scott Fitzgerald mulled over his principal works as, from morning till night, he chewed on olive pits from the very numerous dry martinis that were his main source of nourishment. Gershwin took notes in one corner for his 'American in Paris' while Hemingway talked boxing, the Prince of Wales talked fashion, and the Dolly Sisters talked about themselves.

"A secret society, which today numbers 134 members, was dreamed up here: 'The International Bar Flies.'

"Eisenhower made a second headquarters of the place, which is where the first French 'hot dog' was served in 1925. Suzanne Lenglen, Jack Dempsey, Primo Carnera (whose gloves hang over the bar), and Georges Carpentier were long-time denizens of this lair, while Sinclair Lewis and Ramon Novarro proved competent quaffers whenever they were in town.

"Then came the 'Forties and the war . . ." Andy MacElhone falters. He muses, hunts for a word, finds it and finally decides to say nothing. It was Andy who gradually took charge of the great bar after the war, while his father, by then an old man, devoted more and more time to rest. He died nine years ago.

Andy turned Harry's Bar into a hangout for reporters, intellectuals, rugby players and writers. Jean-Paul Sartre, Marcel Achard, Jacques Prévert and Henri Jeanson used to run into each other there almost every day during the fifties. You can still see them—very late at night—showing the Right Bank's nocturnal splendors to foreign authors or actors. The welcome mat is always out for Jeanne Moreau, Gene Kelly and Thornton Wilder. Even the Beatles thought it worthwhile to send in their names to the long basement room to hear the old Negro piano player, Charlie Lewis, do the same ragtimes which he helped introduce to the French thirty years ago, at the time when Henri, the oldest bartender at Harry's, was on his first maneuvers here.

"Chubby" Bob, Georges the Lyonnais and Marc, known as

"Bordeaux" Marc, circulate between the tables and suggest their panaceas to the new customers who are always very surprised by their friendliness and hospitality.

Nothing ever comes or goes in our thoughtful, thirsty old city that Andy and his sextet of nimble, attentive waiters do not hear about, rejoice or commiserate about, and, in any case, know about.

> Harry's Bar, 5 rue Daunou (2e), OPE 73.00. Open daily from 10:30 A.M. to 5:00 A.M.

New Continental Bar

The New Continental Bar, recently installed in the Hotel Continental which Garnier (the architect of the Opéra) built out of staff, stucco, gold and marble pastries, is one of the capital's secret meeting places. You're just as likely to run into the hotel's regular clients (Prince Victor Emmanuel, Princess d'Arenberg, the Archduke of Hapsburg-Lorraine, the mayor of Baghdad or New York, Orson Welles and Frank Sinatra) as you are Tout-Paris.

The atmosphere is extraordinarily restful and luxurious amid this setting of dark wood, mustard carpet, olive draperies, green plants and quilted velvet sofas and chairs, softly lit by Tiffany lamps. You can have a quick meal (about 20 francs) to the sound of background music or simply drink one of the twenty cocktails that are the bartender's pride.

> Hotel Continental, 3 rue de Castiglione (Ier), OPE 18.00. Open daily until 2:00 A.M.

Les Halles (*Ier*, *4^e*)

Bar des B.O.F.

We thought twice before giving you the address of Jean's picturesque bistro. If we decided to do so it's because we know that no short-lived fad is going to turn his head.

For this white-haired, loud-voiced Swiss peasant from Valais (he'll tell you with a certain pride that his family dates back to

1570) is the high priest in his Bar des B.O.F. (Butter, Eggs, Cheese) where he set himself up nearly ten years ago after serving as *sommelier* in several large hotels.

Jean is no literary stereotype. His real love is wine, his wine. If he followed his own inclinations he wouldn't sell a drop. Sunday, his day off, is spent with his vats, drawing off and caring for his wine. And when he serves, he does it with solicitous, precise, affectionate gestures.

What he has to serve is pure, healthy, proper Beaujolais which he gets right from the estate and bottles himself: Juliénas, Morgon, Chenas, old Saint-Emilion and even a very honorable *vin ordinaire*.

And he is probably the only person in Paris who sells twenty- or thirty-year-old Byrrh, aged in his own cellar. We're not crazy about this apéritif, but his is really amazing, reminiscent of good madeira.

His customers—the cheese and flower vendors from the nearby Halles—are likable and lots of fun. If you coax him, Jean may let you visit his sanctuary, the three-story cellar.

> Bar des B.O.F., 7 rue des Innocents (Ier). Open from 3:00 A.M. to 7:00 P.M.

Café Curieux

Alcide Levert made a museum of bad taste out of this den tucked away among deserted old mansions. For forty years that former barge stevedore hung around auctions in order to stock up on old objects which no antique-hunter would touch. Père Alcide, dressed in striped pants and sheltered by the rolled brim of his derby, kept his quick eye out for the decorated plates, old chandeliers and genre paintings depicting seaports or Napoleon's retreat from Russia; today these adorn all the walls and the ceiling of this café filled with tall bronze statues, neo-Renaissance chairs and sturdy porters from Les Halles.

Alcide Levert is no more. His successors—Annie, the owner, who was born in Innsbruck, and her husband, a not overly gracious Breton—aren't nearly so picturesque, but the Café Curieux is still one of the great curiosities of Paris night life. Artists, socialites, actors and bums stand at the bar drinking the cup that cheers or sit behind the billiards at the large Henri II table which brings together pushcart peddlers, clerks from the Préfecture, truckdrivers and starlets.

Café Curieux, 14 rue Saint-Merri (4ᵉ), ARC 75.97. Open until 1:00 A.M.

Pigalle (9ᵉ)

La Casita

It resembles a lot of the surrounding bars as closely as two drops of water in the Pigalle fountain; in fact, it's exactly like the little Jet d'Eau (fountain) which, come night, also attracts some dreamlike creatures shepherded by a magnificent Eurasian woman. But we won't linger over the latter establishment (which was the first "English bar" in the Paris of the Gay Nineties and a favorite haunt of Toulouse-Lautrec), since a capricious fate insists on closing it every so often for "renovation."

La Casita's sprightly regulars form its permanent nightly welcoming committee. These ladies—all in very good shape—use even more wile than the employees to attract customers, whom they treat with unflagging affection. No one can deny the diligence of these vestals in demonstrating a lively, spontaneous interest in the first comer, whoever he might be.

La Casita is undoubtedly better supplied than any other bar with enchanting members of the fair sex, duly counted by our vigilant Vice Squad.

The resolutely gay, neo-Spanish main room is adorned with painted compositions and picturesque accessories, and furnished with a long, very deep sofa and club chairs arranged in front of the bar, which is administered by a robust barmaid in black. These seats are the scene of outspoken negotiations for the variously priced and varyingly furtive embraces that have given Pigalle its very French reputation. It is a district of gloomy pleasures where everything has its price and nothing is free, so that we can't bring ourselves to praise it.

La Casita, 34 rue Victor Massé (9ᵉ). Open daily until 5:00 A.M.

Clichy (71ᵉ)

Bar Belge

Frenchmen have a superiority complex when it comes to beer. To them it's nothing more than an inexpensive beverage which you drink at the counter or at home without giving it much thought. But who is aware that Belgium alone has more than three thousand different beers, and that they have their good and bad years just like wine? Who has ever heard of Archduke Special, Abbaye de Leffe Triple or Chimay Special Trappist?

Only real beer drinkers, and they're also sure to know the Bar Belge, which you have to go a long way to find on avenue de Saint-Ouen, and especially its amazing owner Julien Forêt.

This wry Belgian with a glint in his eye was a butcher in Les Halles and a lyric singer whenever the occasion presented itself. But he also had another passion: beer. He himself drinks very little of it—so as not to gain weight—but he tends his crûs with touching concern. Aided by his wife (an impressive Bretonne who would have delighted Rubens) and a waiter who used to be maître d' at the Belgian Embassy in Paris, Forêt religiously serves some thirty deluxe beers, each at the proper temperature and in differently shaped glasses. He also has Ardenne *charcuterie,* square Boulogne salami and real Dutch cheese.

The time to go to the Bar Belge is at night, after a show. At times Julien Forêt invites some of his old singer friends for lyrical orgies which leave you (literally) reeling.

> Bar Belge, 75 avenue de Saint-Ouen (17ᵉ), MAR 41.01. Closed Mondays. Open until 1:30 A.M.

LEFT BANK

Ile Saint-Louis (4^e)

Berthillon

The speciality of this old bistro on the Ile Saint-Louis, which you could walk past a dozen times without noticing, isn't wine, but ice cream and sherbet. It was known only to local residents when we first came upon it four years ago. We were stupefied to discover that it had the best ice cream and sherbet in Paris, but were somewhat uneasy about giving this marvelous address to our newspaper and *Guide Julliard* readers. We were even more uneasy when the Berthillons had to call the police to direct the flow of customers struggling to get in on New Year's Eve.

Now we feel better: the place has been snowed under with orders ever since, but nothing else has changed. The bistro is the same as ever. Monsieur Berthillon still makes his ice cream and sherbet single-handedly in a room no bigger than a closet (he doesn't want to hire any help for fear of having his secrets stolen), his wife still does all the selling and packing, and his mother-in-law, an old country woman all dressed in black, still works her fingers to the bone peeling pounds of fresh fruit every day. Their only luxury is that they now are closed two days a week.

Monsieur Berthillon has been approached several times with offers to finance his expansion and each time he refuses, convinced that he would end up sacrificing quality to quantity. He doesn't care about the money; his only pleasure is a job well done. Not an ounce of artificial ingredients ever goes into his sherbets and ice creams. The former contain nothing but individually selected fresh fruits and the latter, equally fresh dairy products.

Berthillon's ice cream is likely to seem a bit "thin" to American palates accustomed to very creamy brands. Actually, it's exceptionally delicate (particularly the rum and marron glacé flavors). But it's better to begin your experiment with the sherbets. Whether you choose black-currant, pear, pineapple, tangerine, wild strawberry, raspberry or melon (according to season), you'll think you're biting into the fruit itself every time. Not even Howard Johnson—and we are very partial to his commercial ice cream—can manage to convince us of the superiority of fruit concentrates, artificial coloring and powdered milk!

You have to telephone Berthillon's in advance if you want ice cream to take home, but you can readily go and enjoy it right there, in maximal discomfort.

> Berthillon, 31 rue Saint-Louis-en-l'Ile (4ᵉ), ODE 31.61. Closed on Mondays and Tuesdays.

Saint-Germain-des-Prés (6ᵉ, 7ᵉ)

Bar du Pont-Royal

Wealthy publishers pursue their after-hours search for new authors at the rear of this oak-paneled basement, done in the "deluxe hostelry" style favored by decorators right after the Libération. Writers from all over give this dark, solemn bar its reputation as a literary haven. You can see authors with frankly opposing views conversing here, when they would feel obliged to forego even a nod of greeting anywhere else.

Novelist-reporters meet here for one final "last drink." But times have certainly changed. Now that there are no longer any serious differences between right and left wings in the world of scribblers, shoptalk has replaced the evenings of virulent discussion very much in vogue during the Algerian war.

Bar du Pont-Royal, 7 rue de Montalembert (7e). Open daily until 12:30 A.M.

Deux Magots

Each of the two mandarins seems to have his own set of customers. The first consists of drinkers who complain loudly that their orders aren't taken or served fast enough. The second includes everyone who tries his utmost not to attract the waiters' attention, knowing how indifferent they are to anything likely to disturb their collective evening reverie. Among the latter is a subgroup of virtuosos who practice the art and technique of making one simple café filtre last from seven o'clock until midnight.

Nobody knows the exact origin of the two heavy Chinese statues which give the Deux Magots its name and which have long been looking down from their column on the comings and goings of the ultrapoliticized clientele who commune in silent, though passionate, perusal of Le Monde.

The mid-1800's witnessed the opening of a notions and baby-clothes shop here under the sign of Les Deux Magots. The proprietor's thankless physique inspired people envious of his prosperity to a series of charming jests. The one which legend has preserved deserves to be passed on: it consisted of asking the shopkeeper where his partner, the second mandarin, was.

Rémy de Gourmont, Léautaud and other editors of the Mercure de France made this café a habit. It was they who saw (or said they saw) Alfred Jarry pull a long pistol out of his pocket one day and fire point blank at a window before saying to the beautiful stranger at the opposite table, "Well, now that the ice is broken, let's have a little chat . . ."

For a long time the Academy of Fine Arts delegated its most conscientious pipe-smokers to the salon, while the French Academy sent its bearded representatives, who were exasperated by the presence of an impish author-diplomat and cocktail drinker, Jean Giraudoux, whom Fargue greeted from the table where Derain and Despiau had just joined him. Alcanter de Brahm, a strange character who called himself a "punctualist," struggled to persuade all the chroniclers present to adopt the creation to which he had devoted his entire life—the "irony mark."

Louis Aragon, who had been banished from the large terrace because the manager was outraged at seeing a man wear an open shirt and no tie, paraded up and down in front of the door to the accompanying drumbeat of Surrealist writer Philippe Soupault.

Sartre and Simone de Beauvoir used to show up on the huge terrace opposite the steeple of Saint-Germain-des-Prés at a time when, it's true, you could run into them almost anywhere. This is where André Breton met them after his return from America. He tried to regroup his old friends here, together with young writers and painters fascinated by his untrammeled spirit and his fame. An old waiter, Paul Raynaud's double, surveyed them from the slits of his suspicious eyes.

The reputation of the Deux Magots owes a lot to these illustrious patrons. From Belleville to Grenelle, everyone knew that a café had just proclaimed itself "the rendezvous of the intellectual elite." After that, ambitious hairdressers sat down to read *Les Temps Modernes* together around the imitation mahogany tables, and mechanics gathered to discuss the future of abstract painting. And tourists from everywhere came to thrill at the sight of pseudo-painters and not-quite poets.

Deux Magots, 170 boulevard Saint-Germain (6e), LIT 55.25. Open daily until 2:00 A.M.

Flore

We might as well come right out with it: the Flore is a great literary café. It is the envy of foreigners who send representatives here by the thousands from the beginning of May to the end of August. During the months without *r* you hardly hear a word of French spoken on the long terrace of this highly esteemed melting pot of French letters.

Emile, the tall, ruddy manager, and a dark, bald little old waiter named Pascal, see that they don't get too dry.

But you can't talk about the Flore without mentioning the owner, Boubal. This fine fellow, who today is assisted by his son-in-law Durand, bravely answers to the nickname "The Little Corporal," bestowed on him for reasons that are now forgotten. For at least a quarter of a century he's been running this café, which was founded at the end of the Second Empire (at that time you entered from the rue Saint-Benoît) and soon became a favorite haunt of Huysmans and Rémy de Gourmont. The staff of *Action Française* had its headquarters here a little later. Young rightists gathered around Maurras and Bainville (who wrote their editorials here) to plan their anti-Dreyfusard moves in the midst of placid domino players and austere *Temps* readers. And every Tuesday from five to eight o'clock Maurice Barrès and Bourget used to meet here with Morréas.

They were followed by Apollinaire, who encouraged the three great founders of Surrealism and on this very spot began the revue *Les Soirées de Paris*. Then came World War I and its aftermath. Léon-Paul Fargue put in a regular appearance until an orchestra was hired to rock the Flore with vibrant melodies and attract new customers. This only lasted a season or two. Fargue returned, followed by all the finest poets then in Paris.

That interesting war broke out. This is when Boubal emerged from an obscure brasserie in Les Halles to take over the management of this café whose name will remain linked to the history of French thought. Sartre, Audiberti, Simone de Beauvoir, Albert Camus, actors, directors and movie makers gathered here every day to work during the darkest days of the Occupation. This whole little world of people driven by the need to express themselves in times hardly favorable to the formulation of subversive—or simply "advanced"—ideas, would some day make this spot famous.

Boubal thought it would be a good idea to convert his old first-floor apartment into a bar-salon. He covered the walls with plaid fabric and light English-style woodwork. The little "queens" from La Reine Blanche (a homosexual café across the street) immediately proved unfaithful. They thronged to give their new allegiance to the Flore, which up until then had had very little to do with them. They eventually established their winter headquarters upstairs and then annexed the side-walk terrace in summer. After that, all the scandal sheets raised the café to the rank of international homosexual center, and the real Flore had to take refuge in its original stronghold: the large ground-floor room where various generations of Parisian men of letters and even more varied ones of eternal, notorious frauds still confront each other beneath the eyes of foreigners guided by their "travel experts."

> Flore, 172 boulevard Saint-Germain (6e), LIT 55.26. Open daily until 2:00 A.M.

Le Nuage

They say that nothing ever happens now in Saint-Germain-des-Prés. It's true that the great postwar tumult calmed down long ago. But some of the most prominent people from that period of existential memory, which was dedicated to every form of liberation, can still be found on rue Bernard Palissy, preserved in alcohol, as it were.

With the coming of night, writers of every race, tongue and school gather between Le Nuage's billiard-green walls. Françoise Sagan meets Edward Albee here, while very young people sit in the carefully gauged shadows and murmur their analysis of the future of French democracy to interested Negroes who have come to see their friend Jojo, the bizarre, bearded and taciturn bartender.

For a long time this bar was run single-handedly by the painter Simone Dat, but it now has two heads. The Puerto Rican poet Juan Romero is determined to make it recapture its momentarily faded glory. He welcomes you beneath a large glass case enclosing the medals won by Laurens cigarettes at international expositions, a case which long adorned the palace of the late King Farouk.

> Le Nuage, 5 rue Bernard Palissy (6e), BAB 56.25. Open every evening from 7:00 P.M. to 4:30 A.M.

Au Sauvignon

This very ordinary bistro has been a meeting place for wine lovers from Saint-German-des-Prés for almost a dozen years.

Henri Vergnes and his wife, Alice, spend the day pouring out the most honest Brouilly, Sancerre, Quincy or Puligny-Montrachet on the market. Brigitte Bardot, Anna Karina (Jean-Luc Godard's ex-wife) and the poet Jacques Prévert sometimes come to stand at Monsieur Vergnes' counter while he lovingly makes them wonderful sandwiches from country bread and Auvergne cold cuts, which outclass many an elegant, pretentious and overpriced lunch.

Au Sauvignon, 80 rue des Saints-Pères (6e), LIT 49.02. Closed Sundays.

Le Village

Le Village was so famous that its name remains associated with Lipp, the Deux Magots and the Flore in the postwar and postmidnight glory of Saint-Germain-des-Prés.

The décor is the same as ever, although it is now yellow with the years that have grayed the hair of the young/old forty-year-olds who come in every night to rekindle their memory of times when everything seemed permissible. The charming Carydes brothers have managed to preserve the atmosphere—suitably stifling—which prevailed in their establishment during those last wild years. And not even the notable decline in their customers' quantity and quality has completely dissipated that atmosphere.

The Carydes' soft Parisian accent disguises the fact that their parents were of Greek origin and that they themselves were born at the foot of the unique steeple at Colombey-les-deux-Eglises (General De Gaulle's village). You can of course order whiskey as you sit on one of the supple, sinuous red banquettes beneath a tole lantern flanked by effigies of cats. However, they also serve an ingenious cocktail maison and some very simple home cooking, consisting mainly of roast beef or veal, antipasto and soups (about 20 francs a meal).

Under no circumstances should you mention life in the *quartier* around the fifties. Tears of nostalgia will only impede the service, which officially ends at two thirty in the morning but usually drags on till dawn.

Le Village, 7 rue Gozlin (6e), DAN 80.19. Open until 2:30 A.M.

Place Saint-Michel (5^e)

Le Petit Bar

Less sordid than Chez Popoff, and also less apt to be closed down, this "Little Bar" welcomes the most neatly combed and less spectacularly sloppy beatniks from the La Huchette neighborhood. Square young chips off the solid bourgeois block sometimes come in from the "nice section" for a look and a little slumming in this den. Their progress with passing foreign damsels is aided by the management's brutal rule denying admission to anyone—boy or girl—with long flowing locks, or to anyone wearing jeans, whose carefully bleached blue sometimes can be glimpsed between the food spots.

> Le Petit Bar, 4 place du Petit Pont (5^e), DAN 16.37. Open daily until 2:00 A.M.

Chez Popoff

You won't find this in any tourist handbook. The façade and walls are flaking off and its low ceiling and rough-hewn tables and benches are straight out of Zola's *Dramshop*. Its one of the most sinister and rundown bistros in Paris. It's also one of the most deservedly famous wine shops.

Popoff's happens to be closed at the time of this writing, for reasons we prefer to skip. But it's sure to reopen some day, and so we think we ought to tell you about it.

Most Parisians have never heard of Chez Popoff. But whenever one of those wild-haired young vagabonds, squeezed into grayish T-shirts and faded jeans, who hitchhike here, there and everywhere with bouncing knapsack and flying beard, runs into a like specimen in San Francisco, Hamburg, Rotterdam or New Delhi and wants to get together in Paris, there's just one place that comes to mind. It's this ancient "Vins et Charbons" on rue de la Huchette, which ranks as the European center for antisocial beatniks.

Tyrolian knapsacks and sailors' duffel bags pile up in the back room while their owners are out looking for a room or lying in the sun on the banks of the Seine.

Even though many of them consider grime the emblem of social protest, a few Vikings, still conditioned by their native Scandinavia, crowd around the washbasin (soap and towels are free).

These glorious youths, most of whom come from Northern Europe or the English-speaking countries, spend hours sprawled on the benches, waiting for heaven only knows what over a cup of coffee that has long been drained. When they're hungry they buy a piece of bread from the baker across the street and salami or olives from the grocer next door, then come back for a picnic under the proprietor's paternal eye.

For Monsieur Popoff is a broad-minded man and prides himself on his understanding and affection for footloose youngsters. "You've got to help the kids out," he says in his gentle voice. And whenever a Finn with thick, curly locks wants to buy a cigarette from him, he takes his pack from his pocket and graciously offers him a Gauloise.

Despite the reassuring presence of this native of Salonika and the no less efficient eye of his wife, who is as Breton as they come, Police Headquarters has made Popoff's off-limits for anyone under eighteen; the vagabonds' International which hangs out here make the mistake of not sufficiently disdaining marijuana and LSD.

> Chez Popoff, 8 rue de la Huchette (5^e), ODE 96.14. Open at the discretion of the police.

Montparnasse (6^e, 14^e)

La Coupole

Everybody who played a major or minor role in making pre-war Montparnasse the electric place it was—all of whom were in some way responsible for the last great period of French art—was sent flying on the winds of terror by the general state of collapse and the German occupation. Many, indeed most, of the painters and sculptors who had made a name for themselves between 1927 (the date La Coupole was founded) and the war were of foreign or Jewish origin. They had to "bow out," as we know. And La Coupole had to wait until the mid-fifties before it began to attract the successors of the people who had made it one of the most exhilarating places in the world. Those successors were the "internationalist" artists, trailed both by bourgeois dying to be shocked and socialites eager to get inside information about the very latest artistic trends.

Today as yesterday, judging by Giraudoux, Hemingway and Miller, La Coupole attracts artists of all backgrounds and tendencies, and writers of widely varying ages and audiences. To the left of the entrance is the brasserie where Soutine used to fortify himself; to the right is the huge restaurant of which Kisling, with his entourage of movie stars, was once the waggish leading light. A sort of fountain, used mostly as a place to put dishes, occupies the center of the room. This is the drinking trough, the focal point for beer drinkers whose favorite activity consists of gravely putting the world to rights from noon until after midnight. The rest of the customers are a motley crowd, composed mainly of voracious, loquacious gallery owners; boys and girls whose world-weary expressions are intended to convince one another that they are creative geniuses driven to despair by the world's stubborn indifference; fashion models of masculine, feminine and indeterminate gender leading their favorite photographers between the square tables; politicians who come to unwind among the "nuts" after a day in Parliament; and finally architects, who can be recognized by the bow tie which sets off the smooth pink of their wealthy speculator's faces, who occasionally manipulate a drawing pen and come here to pay homage to Le Corbusier, who used to dine—often alone—in front of the narrow kitchen doorway.

The second class of habitués at this great artistic pow-wow seems to have nothing in common with the first except the opinion that the food is mediocre, if not downright abominable. One might of course point out to them that nothing is forcing them to eat here every night. But they get such keen enjoyment out of seeing and being seen in this den where everyone puts on a show, that nothing in the world could ever induce them to abandon their role of spectator-actor.

As for the cooking, no matter what they say, it is satisfactory classical, a little uneven, and the service is often very slow.

Occasionally—and the occasions are becoming more and more frequent—you hear that the present La Coupole is going to be remodeled. Rumor has it that a new building will replace the shameless two-story expression of the hopeless taste of some untalented architect in a period that had some fine ones. The future building would link boulevard du Montparnasse with rue Delambre, and roof over La Coupole's abandoned summer garden, now protected by a tall, dreary fence.

The only thing still to be mentioned are the paintings which adorn the tops of the restaurant's twelve square columns. They have been praised so often that we urge you to see them. You will undoubtedly share our feeling that a phenomenal counter-intuition presided over their selection. How else can one explain why the vital center of Montparnasse came to be decorated by nothing but grade-Z daubers, barbarous imitators and prettifiers devoid of even the most elementary talent, when the greatest painters of the period were living in the neighborhood when the café was being built? It's a negative miracle for which there is no justification, not even the presence of a miserable little work slapped together by Othon Friesz who, if not a terribly important painter, was at least at the top of his form at the end of the twenties. His "composition" is sinister indeed. Who was it that said that the painter's hell is paved with grim resentment against blind shopkeepers?

La Coupole, 102 boulevard du Montparnasse (14e), DAN 95.90. Open until 2:30 A.M.

Le Select

This very lively café-bar first opened in 1923 and has preserved intact the beige décor accentuated with graceful floral motifs and the feverish atmosphere of the wild years of which remains old Montparnasse's authentic, living vestige. Right until the beginning of World War II graceful young men leaded by Jean Cocteau would linger here until cockcrow spurred them homeward to an early bedtime with one another. Raymond Coffin took over the destiny of this glorious rallying point for the usually imported but inexportable members of all lost generations. Raymond Coffin comes from Picardy and won't let anyone forget it. The Russian-Jewish colony which sends some of its singular representatives here every night finds him exotic, and the artists and film makers, who sit drinking on the long leatherette banquettes until they're "saturated," dutifully introduce him to Jean-Paul Sartre every time the writer drops in for a drink with his neighbor Simone de Beauvoir.

Le Select, 99 boulevard du Montparnasse (6e), LIT 38.24. Open daily until 2:00 A.M.

Gobelins, Porte d'Italie (5ᵉ, 13ᵉ)

Chaudet (See SHOPPING, *Wine and Spirits,* p. 323.)

Part III

NIGHT LIFE

DANCE HALLS

Not much is left of those little dance halls which flourished at the beginning of the century, survived between the wars, and finally succumbed to the joint attack of discothèques and the jerk. These temples of accordion music and good-natured debauchery are closing down one after another. A few still stubbornly refuse to die, however. Summer tourists are brought around to some of these relics, which then indulge in unbridled fakery. But if you have an opportunity to go back in the off-season, say to rue de Lappe, you'll be amazed to discover a world which is undoubtedly speeding toward extinction but which is genuine nonetheless, and rather surprising. And then there are still others, the refuge of housemaids and clerks, which generally escape notice but which deserve the attention of curious and not overly blasé visitors.

Balajo

Every night is Saturday for the little dancers who haunt Balajo's immense dance hall, created, or rather renovated, by a former plumber named Jo France. The long signs of ornate neon tubing which this highly colorful character installed along the sides of the alley known as "rue" de Lappe have put to flight the old darkness-loving hoods who used their knives to dispute the tired favors of suburban Venuses at the beginning of the century.

Anxious to preserve the picturesque nature of his establishment, Jo France replaced the hoods for a while with a few characters in caps and red neckerchiefs. He could only congratulate himself on his judicious recruitment: the street fights which used to break out every day between the last surviving apaches have now come to an end.

All's well that ends well. The Balajo, the temple of the accordion, attracts its former habitués' children and grandchildren, who have remained faithful to the time-tested, rather undifferentiated, but vertiginous repertory of the *musettes*.

Boys and girls—not all young, but all lonely—try to catch each other's eye. The former go to a lot of trouble to wriggle between the tables during the large orchestra's breaks, stare blatantly at promising partners and finally accomplish their mission by finding someone to dance with.

The walls, overdecorated with harbor scenes reminiscent of some old out-of-the-way district, are pierced with windows where the silhouettes of girls with their own ideas about fashion are outlined against the light.

A uniformly ultramarine sky, punctuated with sparkling constellations, covers the Balajo's entire ceiling, where figures from the Other World reel to the music of *chaloupées* while down below ordinary folk have made this old Balajo their own again—in the winter, that is, for during the summer it is still invaded by groggy herds of tourists from the "Paris by Night" buses.

> Balajo, 9 rue de Lappe (11e), ROQ 07.87. Open every night from 9:00 until 12:30; Saturdays until 5:00 A.M.

Bal Fleuri

The only thing missing in the Bal Fleuri is Fellini's dream camera. You enter through a café; the ballroom is hidden way in the back, behind a partition. Fluttering streamers of faded crepe paper hang from the ceiling, and a reflecting globe keeps revolving. The floor creaks beneath the dancers' feet and semidarkness uniformly reigns.

Tall Martinicans, who dance as nobody else can, grip insatiable fat white mommas of the "retired usher" variety, who seem extremely happy to be swaying to the calypsos and bi guines meted out by three panting West Indians who work as office boys at the social security office during the day.

Bal Fleuri, 6 rue des Patriarches (5ᵉ), POR 31.06. Dancing on Saturdays from 9:00 P.M. to 5:00 A.M. and Sundays from 4:00 P.M. until 11:30 P.M.

Au Petit Balcon

Au Petit Balcon is undoubtedly the only *bal musette* in Paris which has preserved the main elements of the décor which witnessed its finest hours. Unfortunately, very little dancing goes on now. The groups of tourists who arrive in shifts from nine until after midnight are only interested in the spectacle of men and women disguised as apaches and gigolettes, the better to indulge in shameless jigs and abandon themselves unreservedly to the intoxicating "Java Vache."

From his narrow mezzanine just below the high ceiling, which is enlivened by an extraordinarily complicated wooden trellis—a masterpiece of demented craftsmanship—the accordionist on duty sends cascades of enveloping measures spilling over the giddy ranks of strangers squeezed together like peas in a pod.

This old dance hall will celebrate its two-hundredth anniversary in a few years. It resolutely turns its back on nearby rue de Lappe where everything is changing, since the patrons of the old Auvergnat dance halls (Les Barreaux Verts, Le Bal des Familles) now demand a modernistic aura from an overdose of neon. It is true, however, that unhypocritical tradesmen innocently proclaim the prevailing spirit of this little alley. One of them, a carpenter, advertises "Antiques Made to Order" on the large panel supporting his shopwindow.

Au Petit Balcon, 15 passage Thière (11ᵉ), ROQ 04.86. Open nightly from 9:00 to 2:00 A.M.

DISCOTHÈQUES AND NIGHT CLUBS

Saint-Germain-des-Prés

L'Abbaye

The ugly, beigeish façade of this little *boîte* in bar's clothing faces the north side of the church of Saint-Germain-des-Prés. Young Americans form the basis of its constantly changing clientele, whom a young Negro named Gordon Heath tirelessly thrills by distilling a few folk song masterpieces. Initiates commune in silence or cautiously applaud the star of the house by snapping their fingers, so as not to wake the inhabitants of the building that was erected on the site of the famous Chapel of the Virgin in the Abbey of Saint-Germain.

L'Abbaye, 6 *bis* rue de l'Abbaye (6ᵉ), ODE 27.77. Open from 10 P.M. until 1:00 A.M. Closed on Sundays.

Bilboquet

Little rue Saint-Benoît, the throbbing heart of Saint-Germain-des-Prés, is in constant flux, which means you can never be sure whether a club you mention one day will be transformed or closed the next. The Bilboquet, which occupies the site of Club Saint-Germain (at the height of its glory during the existentialist period), has recently undergone a very successful transformation. Yesterday's jazz cellar has taken on an air of science fiction. Steel, copper, clever lighting and odd transparent statues create a strange atmosphere which would be downright disturbing if the presence of lots of pretty girls in very short skirts didn't quickly reassure you.

The entire building is scheduled to become a "complex" devoted to nocturnal pleasures and will include a cafeteria, boutiques, a movie theater, etc.

As a rule, the Bilboquet doesn't make it too hard for tourists to get in. There is a minimum of 17 francs ($3.40).

Le Bilboquet, 13 rue Saint-Benoît (6ᵉ), LIT 81.84. Open from 10:00 P.M. until dawn.

Carnaby

Castel's? Not a chance of getting in. Régine's? No tables available for you. You belong to that class of (temporary) Parisians who would love to spend an evening at one of the fashionable clubs but can't, since you're not an actor, singer, hairdresser or press agent. So every night Paris is full of nice ordinary middle-class people, anonymous, decent folk wandering around in search of a pretty, pleasant spot to have a drink, a bite or a dance without being turned away like some kind of pariah.

That spot exists: Carnaby. The owner—a sturdy fellow with a mustache—couldn't care less about being "with it"; instead, he has applied his discerning taste to evoking the charm and atmosphere of a private home beneath the building's superb beams. At no time do you feel as if you're in a *boîte* full of strangers. It's like being in a warm, friendly living room filled with nooks and crannies, low tables and voluptuous chairs. The daily papers are at arm's reach, just as in a nice old London club, and if you're alone there's even a pile of mystery novels. There is a television in one corner, and good music quietly pervades the room.

There's a discothèque downstairs in the magnificent cellar where the proprietor has installed his amazing collection of antique locks. No one jostles you. For that matter, no one will ever push or shove in this peaceful Carnaby: the owner vigilantly watches over his customers' well-being, and if he doesn't let you in, it isn't because he deems you unworthy but simply because he refuses to have his club transformed into a sardine can.

Carnaby, 10 rue Servandoni (6e), DAN 99.42. Open every day and all night.

Chez Castel-Club Princesse

Chez Castel. Of all the monuments in Paris, this one, where the jerk rubs elbows with politics, and where mini-skirts call the Academy "darling," has the thinnest patina.

Your titles, your bank account or the cut of your clothes have very little to do with whether you'll be made a party to this essential point. They might keep Nelson Rockefeller out and let his butler in. From the back of his dark corridor Castel needs only a glance to weigh aspiring souls, just like Saint Peter at the gates of Paradise. He has refused admission to King Hussein of Jordan . . . ("Those lousy-looking gorillas of his," he says.)

Owner Jean Castel never went to hotel management school. Obviously. He doesn't go in for any of the usual bowing and scraping, flashing smiles, hyperattentiveness or knowing winks. Enthroned in his corner, glass in hand, he surveys his world with a mammoth's weary, indifferent eye. He's watching the show. No customer will ever be "sacred" to this Ph.D.(rink). Only his friends are sacred, and they are infinitely less numerous than all the people who complacently play up to him.

Everything's authentic at Chez Castel—both the décor and the price gouging. The whole thing might have stepped right out of the prop room at the studio where Max Ophuls made *La Ronde*. Ten years ago the red plush, the walls covered with tooled leather and the Art Nouveau lamps looked daring and original. The surprise is rather less overpowering now that every other bistro is rigged out in 1900's fashion. But Castel refuses to change his décor and he may well be right: he'll never go out of fashion.

The room for dancing is frankly ugly. Castel replies that it doesn't matter, since at night people have all they can do just to see the whiskey glass in their hand. The little bar on the ground floor may end up sharing Maxim's immortality. It gives you that rare feeling of being at home, and this in a décor you would never have in your own house.

Except for the famous grandfather of young (twenty-year-old) Charles De Gaulle, who comes here regularly, and Jean-Paul Sartre, there's not a single celebrity in France who hasn't been to Castel's.

But even more important than the dazzling clientele is Castel's Clan. "They" are there almost every night, casting a mocking eye on new arrivals and saying anything that comes into their heads, provided that it is both funny and nasty, from their perch on the red velvet banquette on the ground floor. Accord-

ing to their own definition, they are "clean-cut gentlemen between the ages of thirty-five and forty-five" and consist of reporters, executives and press agents.

If you're interested in the subject of women, it's very instructive to spend an hour on the ground floor observing these gentlemen of Castel's Clan. The most beautiful women in Paris
arrive, stop, bravely put together a retort or two, and immediately dash off to dance in the shadowy basement. This can't be
explained as the men's hatred of women, since Castel's Clan
doesn't have any more homosexuals than IBM. The truth is
that women are a foreign and rather useless element in this
man's world: they float like drops of oil in a glass of water.
They don't stand a chance of mixing in unless they are exceptionally dull-witted or very sharp indeed.

Three kinds of women have a more or less permanent standing at Castel's: First, the mini-skirts: they can do everything
but talk. And it doesn't really bother them. Second, the stars:
all past, present and future stars from Bardot to Jane Fonda
have appeared at Castel's at least once. Some very peculiar phenomenon makes them forget to be horrible. Third, the young
socialites: these are clearly the most wide-awake of the lot and
the only ones whose exploits don't make good copy.

One last word: Don't bother going here if you don't know
the so-called Tout-Paris. Even if by some miracle you manage
to get in, you'll be unbelievably bored. There is an 18-franc
($2.80) minimum for a whiskey.

> Chez Castel-Club Princesse, 18 rue Princesse (6e), DAN 90.22.
> Open every night.

Cherry Lane

The Cherry Lane is three years old. Other dance spots have
sprung up around this one, as like it as two drops of Chivas
glimpsed at nightfall, and jammed with people who drop in
for a look around before winding up the evening at Annik and
Ralph's.

These two night owls continue to preside, in semi-darkness,
over the fun of tired, dancing youngsters who slake their thirst
with Coca-Cola and the other harmless liqueurs dispensed by

Jean, a bartender of Italian origin who made a name for himself at all the local bars when the *quartier* was at its peak.

Groups of steadfast flirts are scattered around the back room, whose walls are covered with beige stamped velvet. Black enamel prevails everywhere else.

The Cherry Lane is still one of the liveliest—and most inaccessible—"private" dance clubs in Saint-Germain-des-Prés. Rows of novitiate drinkers stand waiting every night for Annik to break down and let them into her lair. None of them would ever risk jostling her, though, for her reputation as a *judoka* has made this powerhouse of charm feared in the rue de Rennes neighborhood.

Drinks start at 5 francs ($1).

> Cherry Lane, 8 rue des Ciseaux (6e), DAN 28.28. Open every night from 11:00 P.M.

Djuri

An adroit guitarist and a powerful, polyglot and sensitive singer, Djuri Cortez—whose name is a good indication of his multinationality—interprets all sorts of Russian, South American, Gypsy, Romanian, Spanish, Yiddish, Greek and Israeli songs in his intimate little club.

> Djuri, 6 rue des Canettes (6e), DAN 60.15. Open from 10 P.M. until 2:00 A.M. Closed Mondays.

La Guitare

This isn't Madrid's El Duendo or even La Zambra in Torremolinos, and even less a little *tablão* in Seville; you won't see any superb *cuadro* of overage guitarists, gossipy matrons and tall, willowy Gypsies seated in a semicircle on a large stage.

La Guitare on rue Hautefeuille is only a kind of alley, a *callejon* in an Andalusian village, lined with drowsy spectators who are gradually stirred, then conquered by the little *cuadro's* enthusiasm and talent.

The show at La Guitare doesn't get bogged down by facility or cheap picturesqueness. Conchita Arranda, the tiny dancer who has been seen here for several years, has a grace, skill and fervor which almost raise her to the level of the great Spanish stars, and the other pretty dancer, Carmen, is gifted with a voice that is piercing, true and as loud as one could wish for singing folk (but not flamenco) songs.

Salvador Vargas, the handsome Gypsy who dances the *zapateado,* may be a little too heavy for a clean delineation of the rapid, delicate stamping, but in the second half of the show (around twelve thirty) his feet grow wings.

Finally, the *cuadro*'s two leaders, Bendito and Cascalla, shrewd, pudgy little gentlemen, beat out admirable rhythms with their hands, dance in fun but not inelegantly, and render a generally authentic *cante jondo* with their fine voices, one hushed and the other violent. Drinks are 15 francs ($3).

La Guitare, 14 rue Hautefeuille (6e), DAN 41.11. Performances every night but Sunday, from 10:30 P.M. to 1:30 A.M.

La Rive Gauche

The last holdouts from "old" Saint-Germain-des-Prés took refuge here a little over ten years ago in an attempt to escape the tourists who came to watch them downing their five o'clock (P.M.) breakfast in the sidewalk cafés around that famous intersection. Sartre became a regular customer at Club Rive Gauche, and Françoise Sagan an older one.

The dark décor has vanished, as has the old Saint-Germain spirit, beneath a tangle of enormous vines and small-scale tropical tree trunks. Louis is there to welcome you every night from ten until dawn. Louis is the maître d' and hails from the Midi; Touré, the emcee of this club, where the writers are now outnumbered by little starlets, titled lady socialites and up-and-coming young executives, comes from even farther south. He tells them all about his native Guinea and about the ups and downs of a "soda jerk's" life. An excellent stereo, pleasant air conditioning and faultless service attract a calmer, more subdued crowd than Régine's or Castel's, and the old tradition of flirting still quietly survives.

La Rive Gauche, 11 rue Bernard Palissy (6e), BAB 51.70. Open nightly from 10:00 P.M. until dawn.

Stardust

Don't let appearances fool you. The Stardust is a (private) club which looks like a lot of other (private) clubs. It's open to anyone whose attire is correct enough to pass muster with Marie-Ange, the pretty blond gatekeeper who laughs at everything and knows how to put customers in their proper place. You dance at the Stardust, have a bite to eat (*plat du jour* for 8 francs), a drink and a good time, without so much as a second thought, until three o'clock.

At that exact moment the whole place rocks. The ground-floor restaurant is stormed. The vaulted cellar is filled with a flood of chattering people: the Tout-Paris of clubs and cabarets meets here to pursue their study of the nocturnal economics of cocktails, wine and liqueurs as far as possible into the night. Régine watches Castel, Castel eyes the Blue Bell Girls, the Blue Bell Girls inspect the strip teasers from the Crazy Horse Saloon who, like everyone else, come here after "office hours."

Out on the dance floor people wedged shoulder to shoulder stubbornly mark time, without much hope of achieving anything much in the way of choreography. Giami Talamo, the director of this fabulous establishment, leaves them to their own devices. He's given up taking part in the general "dancerei" when things get "hot," since the congestion prevents him from properly expressing (with flailing arms) his Neapolitan origin and his fondness for the jerk, monkey and other ear-splitting music. This is the music that Patrice (undoubtedly the "swingingest" deejay in Paris) broadcasts in the wildest disorder, with "all systems go." There's one young kid who goes to bed early with his alarm set for four in the morning, in order to be there when everything's "Groovy" at the Stardust, a (private) club which its habitués never leave until it's time for breakfast, just when the rue Guénégaud is waking up to the sound of iron shutters being raised. Drinks cost 12 francs ($2.40).

Stardust, 10 rue Guénégaud (6e), ODE 98.56. Open from 10:00 P.M.

Montparnasse

Régine-New Jimmy's

For a time it seemed that *boîtes* were on the way out, Castel's and New Jimmy's included. But Régine outlasts all fads; besides, she's the one who starts them. Régine rescued New Jimmy's (one of her many enterprises) with a raft of wild parties where guests came dressed as bums, Russians or "professional" women, and her little basement snack bar awash with cheap red wine and sausages. Just like her old friendly enemy Castel, with whom she continues to rule the nights of Paris. Régine, however, is the exact opposite of Castel. She is irrepressible and tireless; he's close-mouthed and nicely indolent. She sends her feet flying to the beat of the latest tunes; he sends toasts flying to the health of his pals. Régine lives in a world of Rolls-Royces, caviar and multimillionaires; his world consists of all-night sessions with pals who may be rich or broke but who are always ready for a good time. Castel's is a men's club; Régine's, a club for pretty women.

The Jet Set made a worldly, sophisticated fief of Régine-New Jimmy's four glistening black walls, but now members of the upper middle class and the business world also have an entrée.

However, you'll still be treated to the fascinating, and disappointing, sight of pretty girls running a blasé eye over this "fun" place, in the pause between dances.

Admission is always reserved for Régine's friends and acquaintances, but the screening process is stiffest on Saturday.

Régine-New Jimmy's, 124 boulevard du Montparnasse (6e), DAN 74.14. Open from 10:30 P.M. Closed Sundays.

Champs-Elysées

L'Etoile de Moscou

You shouldn't be surprised by this new star, rising almost fifty years after the arrival of the last White Russian. The Moscow Star is really just the old Novy in a new setting. Monsieur and Madame Novy (Nadia and Victor Novsky) were hired here, together with their orchestra, Russian chorus, maîtres d' and chef, after being forced to leave rue Faustin-Hélie where they had reigned for years.

So Simon Voltys' tireless violin is still sending chills up and down the ladies' spines, just as it did on those lovely evenings when writer Joseph Kessel used to make a meal of champagne at Novy. All night long the staff of artists—Georges Streha on the balalaika, the singer Tamara (who is more convincing when she keeps her voice low than when she tries to be thrilling), the outstanding basso Boris Nemiroff, and Volodia Poliakov, an extraordinary eighty-year-old Gypsy who could double for Alfred Hitchcock—add flavor and spice to the rather classical food which is honestly prepared and quickly served. (Dinner starts at 60 francs—$12.)

But Franco-Russian society and the Soviet colony who passed through Novy, as did most world celebrities from Lyndon Johnson to Marlene Dietrich, know very well that the high point of the show comes around midnight when the old emigrés, seated around candlelit tables, start to sing their country's old songs together, with the dignity of priests performing a sacred ritual.

> L'Etoile de Moscou, 6 rue Arsène Houssaye (8e), ELY 63.12.
> Open every evening from 8:30 P.M. until dawn.

Gaslight

It may be rather silly for newly arrived American tourists to go to a throughly, typically American night club in the middle of Paris, but you'll certainly give your French friends a treat by bringing them here.

You can't just walk into the Gaslight as if it were a barn. You have to have a key, which will admit you to the five Gaslight clubs—in Paris, New York, Los Angeles, Chicago and Washington.

You show up at the rue du Colisée one night and knock at the door. If you're a good-looking man (women can't become members), a charming miss in a short fringed tutu, fishnet stockings and plunging neckline will flash her ultra-white smile and ask you to come in. A pianist is playing "old favorites" in the bar. You are led to the basement, and all of a sudden you're in New York.

Pretty, attentive girls (they're also skittish and unapproachable) show you to a seat beneath 1925 lamps of colored glass in a room where dreamy skyscrapers rise on all four walls. An orchestra is playing jitterbugs. Pudgy gentlemen from Texas or Marseille chat loudly, play the slot machines, dance off in one corner with their pretty wives and drink lots of bourbon. The atmosphere is unusual, curious, noisy and fraternal.

Gaslight, 41 rue du Colisée (8e), BAL 38.30. Open from 6:00 P.M. until 3:00 A.M.; Saturdays until 4:00 A.M.

JAZZ

Right Bank

Blue Note

The only club in Paris which regularly presents two alternating bands, in a long, narrow room whose walls are covered with velvet and imitation animal skins. Comfort is at a minimum. (Don't sit on the chairs, and watch out for the springs in the banquettes.) The best modern-jazz musicians come to play here whenever they are in Paris. The brilliant, casual Bud Powell is gone, but the club's regulars still include drummer Kenny Clarke, guitarist Jimmy Gourley, Mark Hemmeler at the piano and Pierre Sim on bass, on the one hand, and on the other, the trio led by blind saxophonist Michel Roques. Drinks are 18 francs ($3.60).

Blue Note, 27 rue d'Artois (8ᵉ), BAL 18.92. Open from 10:00 P.M. to 4:00 A.M.

La Cigale

Boisterous Blacks sip nice little "whites" as they skip around near the bar of this old corner café. It's a very odd place, both because of the mixed character of its peppery habitués and the mild—indeed, declining—quality of the jazz bands which take turns performing here, and which range from New Orleans to "Old Beaugency," and even down to the mongrel rock heard at county fairs.

Our solid, solitary compatriots don't make much of an impression beside the graceful movements of African and West Indian couples. They observe the action, refuse to take part in the exotic frenzy and fall asleep, after stoutly voicing their limp disapproval to no one in particular, and concluding, "This isn't for us." Drinks start at 5 francs ($1).

La Cigale, 124 boulevard Rochechouart (18ᵉ), MON 59.29. Open every evening; the band is there from 9:15 P.M. to 2:00 A.M.

Living Room

A blazing fire and swinging sound. It's as snug as the inside of a grand piano, all wood and green carpet, the most intimate jazz den in Paris.

Art Simmons sits on one side of the hearth, like a story teller of old, evoking tender scenes on his piano to a whisper of drums and the approving murmur of the string bass. Glass in hand, you watch the dancing flames. Your nerves give in and relax. From time to time Art Simmons gets up to gulp a Coke at the bar (he hasn't touched liquor for three years now), and the keyboard disappears beneath the gigantic hands of his partner Aaron Bridgers, the man who can capture three whole octaves between his fingers!

The host, Joslin Bingham ("Joss" to his old customers), counts the eighth notes. After so many million, he buys another piano. He's on his fourth—in three and a half years.

The Living Room becomes a musician's hangout after two o'clock in the morning. Kenny Clarke, Chet Baker, Art Taylor and Memphis Slim arrive with their clarinets or saxes under their arms. On some nights the jam session is fabulous, since this is where gentlemen like Miles Davis, Count Basie and Duke Ellington hide out among friends, after a concert at Salle Pleyel. When they're in Paris, they're at the Living Room—you can count on it.

> Living Room, 25 rue du Colisée (8e), ELY 25.29. Open from 10:00 P.M. till 4:00 A.M. Closed Sundays.

Slow Club

This is a haven for old-style and middle-period jazz, with the excellent soprano sax Marc Laferrière and Eddie Bernard, a warm-hearted, eccentric character who is one of today's best pianists in the J.P. Johnson tradition. Tuesdays through Fridays Claude Luter also appears at the Slow Club, where his shrill, shuddering clarinet brings back the dear dead days of the Lorientais, the *boîte* which launched Saint-Germain-des-Prés. You can either dance like you did in the fifties or else just gaze through half-closed eyes at the musicians, who look right through you.

> Slow Club, 130 rue de Rivoli (Ier), GUT 84.30. Open from 9:30 P.M. to 2:00 A.M. Closed Mondays.

Left Bank

Caméléon

Earnest students, modern-jazz fans, artists and lonely souls all come to this vaulted cellar with musical instruments hanging on the walls to listen to the Daniel Humair Trio or other excellent French musicians. It's nice and comfortable every day but Saturday, when it's jammed. Pascal Fang, the owner, sometimes has the musicians stay on after the *cave* is empty, in order to abandon himself in solitude to their beat. Drinks cost 10 francs ($2).

> Caméléon, 57 rue Saint-André-des-Arts (6ᵉ), DAN 64.40. Open from 10:00 P.M. until 2:00 A.M. Closed on Tuesdays.

Caveau de la Huchette

The last French Dixieland and New Orleans groups set penniless kids dancing in this picturesque old cellar. (They dance all the more because the amazing discomfort of the wooden benches makes sitting impossible.) Cover and minimum are 7.50 francs ($1.50).

> Caveau de la Huchette, 5 rue de la Huchette (5ᵉ), DAN 65.05. Open every night from 9:00 P.M. until 1:00 A.M.

Le Chat Qui Pêche

No one—or almost no one—but real fans knows about Le Chat Qui Pêche. And you really have to be a dyed-in-the-wool jazz buff to spend a night perched on half of a wooden stool with your ears ringing, your eyes smarting from the smoke, and your heart bursting with dissonances as you listen religiously to the princes of the contemporary syncopated beat. But this "cat" isn't fishing for teenyboppers who want to dance. Not once in thirteen years during which the greatest names in world jazz have filed through her shadowy cellar, has Mme Ricard relaxed her guard or admitted anyone who wasn't a genuine jazz lover.

Nothing destined Mme Ricard to become a high priestess of Negro music. Until 1954 all she knew about jazz was what any well-born woman from Avignon might know.

Then one fine day she found herself proprietress of Le Chat Qui Pêche. A bar, musicians, customers, scuffles—it all went very well. She started off with a guitarist who was living on a sandwich every other day. She was his first conquest. Today he no longer needs her help: he's the painter Soto. After Eric Dolpy, the holiest of all the sacred cows of "free jazz," she can now hear Dom Cherry, his successor and almost his equal, every night.

The greatest jazz tenors are regulars at Mme Ricard's. They listen to her criticism and advice like schoolboys, kiss her and call her "mama."

She now lives only for jazz and her musicians. But jazz doesn't mean riffraff or beatniks, and she sometimes throws more people out of her cellar than she lets in.

Cover and minimum are 15 francs ($3).

Le Chat Qui Pêche, 4 rue de la Huchette (5ᵉ), DAN 23.06. Open every night from 9:30 P.M. until 2:00 A.M. Closed Wednesdays.

Jazzland

In one of the cellars at the Grande Sévérine, drummer Art Taylor does all he can to keep the audience of young French and American intellectuals from hearing the ultramodern group bawling away behind him. And he succeeds, which is lucky for our ears, much too accustomed to suaver harmonies, but not so good for our nerves. Drinks cost 15 francs ($3).

Jazzland, 7 rue Saint-Séverin (5ᵉ), DAN 15.54. From 10:00 P.M. until 4:00 A.M. Closed on Thursdays.

Pub Chez Félix

This winter, jazz on the Left Bank decided to make its home at Chez Félix. And the later it gets, the better it gets. This is where Maxime Saury and Claude Luter, Jacques Dutronc or José Ferrer come with their musicians after a performance, to eat a grillade and "take off" downstairs with Di Donato's band. The atmosphere is heady and the place really swings. About 30 francs ($6) for a meal.

Pub Chez Félix, 23 rue Mouffetard (5ᵉ), POR 68.78. Open until 6:00 A.M.

For people who speak French

The most entertaining and wittiest cabarets in Paris are the ones which tourists unfortunately don't know about. This is true first because the concierges in the large hotels, the travel agents and all the greedy fauna which gravitate around them neglect to send tourists there. The second reason, and it's a good one, is that unless you understand French perfectly, you're sure to be bored listening to comedians and singers whose talent is most evident in the quality of their material or lyrics.

Le Cheval d'Or

Monsieur Léon—a mustached fifty-year-old—hasn't changed a thing inside his Cheval d'Or. After twelve years of loyal service to young French singers, it's still the only cabaret in Paris where the Left Bank spirit, which prevailed right after World War II, not only endures but keeps on getting better.

Adding the height of his behind-the-counter perch to his own small stature, Monsieur Léon—the discoverer of Raymond Davos, Annie Sylvestre, Petit-Bobo, Ricet-Barrier and the delightful Roger Riffard, surveys the progress of the show to which he has devoted every possible effort, and the silent comings and goings of the audience of regulars whom he cares for like a father.

Monsieur Léon is a lucky man. One might criticize him, of course, for not looking hard enough for new headliners. Everyone who became famous here at the end of the fifties still takes turns appearing on the narrow stage with its yellow backdrop. And it's always just as much fun to hear them. Drinks priced from 10 francs ($2).

> Le Cheval d'Or, 33 rue Descartes (5e), MED 50.11. Show starts around 11:15.

Comptoir des Canettes-Chez Georges

This is a cellar, the latest "reconstructed" bastion of the golden age of Saint-Germain-des-Prés. On the ground floor the

Canettes grocery counter welcomes the neighborhood's flaming youth, here to do a little late shopping.

The show has quality. Chez Georges' ranking members are named Jacques Marchais, Paul Hébert, Anne Vanderlove, Hélène Martin, Malchican and Germano Rochas. Each is remarkable in his own way.

Singer Georges Chelon, who was discovered here by a record company, now and then takes over part of the evening's musical entertainment before returning to Buffalo or Clermont-Ferrand, in that wide, wide world which eagerly looks forward to his appearances.

This cozy club is one of the most active centers in Paris for intelligible, well-written songs.

> Comptoir des Canettes-Chez Georges, 11 rue des Canettes (6e), DAN 79.15. Open daily until 2:00 A.M.

La Contrescarpe

This café-cabaret on pretty little place de la Contrescarpe, where one of the oldest streets in Paris—rue Mouffetard—begins its picturesque descent, attracts a crowd of well-behaved, politely anarchistic young people who earnestly applaud songs about the sufferings of the poor and the oppressed, written by singer-composers who don't lack talent but are none the richer for it.

A fantastic comedian, completely unknown even in Paris, now and then puts on absurd and brilliantly insane little skits. His name is Angelo Gardi—and he also happens to be almost incomprehensible.

Drinks are priced from 5 francs ($1).

> La Contrescarpe, place de la Contrescarpe (5e), MED 44.63. Shows beginning at 10:00 P.M. Closed on Sundays.

René Cousinier

This little known and absolutely extraordinary spot is no hotbed of lubricity or temple given over to black masses. Regular patrons of René Cousinier will even tell you that his show is one of the frankest and healthiest in Paris. And we think so too, being somewhat hip and not terribly prudish.

But watch out! Once seated at a little wooden table in this truly ugly ground-floor room, some of our readers who pride themselves on their liberality will still be dismayed by René's vocabulary and some of his preoccupations, which are as thoroughly obscene as anything you could imagine in a barracks.

Nevertheless, the elegant girls in the audience and the young men with "Government Trainee" written all over them relax and enjoy themselves after the first conscientiously healthy blush and sickly smile.

René Cousinier, who for more than fifteen years has single-handedly kept his audience gasping for three hours every night (what a fantastic performance!), has a wildly diverse background. He is basically a Sephardic *pied noir,* with Italian, Russian, Oxonian and Islamo-Christian taints. This is combined with an amazing knowledge of medicine and theology, a brilliant gift for mimicking accents, terrifying facial mobility, a sharp memory, a bottle imp's ability to land on his feet, skillful piano playing and dazzling intelligence.

Even his crudest phraseology conceals a logic, indeed a cosmogony, which not only make him a sex educator far from Freud's beaten track and a great raconteur of Jewish, North African, Corsican and coarse stories, but also a kind of prophet for whom Mary Magdalen is not the only divinity.

We won't tell you René Cousinier's exact address since the police forbid giving too many details about him, but any café at the foot of Butte Montmartre can fill you in.

Drinks from 8 francs ($1.40).

> René Cousinier, between rue Caulaincourt and rue Constance (18e). Opens at 10 P.M. Closed on Mondays.

Galérie 55

An evening at Galérie 55 is one of the best ways to gauge the exact status of humor in Paris. The most freewheeling comics, like Raymond Devos, Pierre Doris or Jacques Fabri, all made a name for themselves on the narrow platform of this Comédie Française of laughter, at a time when they were just getting started or completely unknown. Now that they're famous they occasionally come back to the Galérie to try out their latest brainstorms—the song or comedy routine they'll later deliver on a larger stage—between the acts of fledgling future stars.

Galérie 55 is a tiny place. It's hot, it's uncomfortable and it's full every evening, so it's a good idea to have a reservation. Drinks from 20 francs ($4).

Galérie 55, 55 rue de Seine (6e), DAN 63.51. Shows beginning at 11:00 P.M. Closed Sundays.

Extravaganzas

Casino de Paris

"Varna: the Watteau, the Gaston Baty, the Diaghilev of the music hall; Varna the magician, Varna the poet, the extraordinary Varna!" The critical blurbs make you itch with impatience as you sit in front of the curtain dripping with gold. If you have a few minutes while the orchestra tunes its violins, take advantage of them to read the editorial: "The Casino de Paris is the loveliest bouquet of stars in the Paris sky." You think they might be exaggerating? Not a bit. Just look at this firmament: Gaby Deslys, Maurice Chevalier, Mistinguett, Josephine Baker, Cécile Sorel, Tino Rossi, Edith Piaf, Lynda Gloria . . . and finally, Line Renaud, since there's no way to avoid mentioning her.

Hurry up! The orchestra is going into the overture, the Wicked Witch is about to raise the curtain, and enchantment will suddenly give way to the most ghastly, most vulgar, most mediocre spectacle one is priviledged to witness in Paris.

Slapdash make-up, miserable choreography, stingy sets, quavering sound effects, elephantine transitions . . . but as soon as Madame Line Renaud makes her appearance, the audience suddenly seems transported to the heights of artistic emotion. And what does Madame Renaud do? She says hello in twelve languages, pats a bald head in the front row, sits in the lap of some poor guy who'd like to . . . but . . . , throws chocolate *louis* to the audience. She also sings (often taped), and last of all, she displays herself, which is the worst of all. Everybody's happy: the Herr Doktor, the English grocer, the Dutch butter-

and-egg man, the Japanese manufacturer. They don't completely fill the hall—far from it, even on Saturday night—but the belly laughs and ecstatic exclamations exploding from every part of the room, in or out of time to the antics on stage, undoubtedly spell success and, for want of anything else, a very dependable gold mine for the show's producers. Poor foreigners, poor Casino de Paris.

(We must point out, however, that Line Renaud has finally left the Casino de Paris . . .)

> Casino de Paris, 16 rue de Clichy (9e), TRI 26.22. Performance every night at 8:30. Tickets start at 10 francs ($2).

Folies Bergère

"Layz Follies Burdjayre, please!" is what the first G.I. to reach Paris in 1944 is supposed to have said.

That fine American soldier could take his children there to-day. After symbolizing naughty Paris in the eyes of the world for almost a century, the venerable hall on the rue Richer now only welcomes families out painting the town red. They're hardly courting apoplexy, whether winter brings them in from Brittany or Périgord, or summer (when it's Standing Room Only) draws them from Berg-op-Zoom or Baton Rouge. It's no longer possible to tell the Folies from a children's matinée, except for a few reassuringly passive chorus girls.

Gone are the days when little ladies from the neighborhood launched fruitful if fleeting romances from the famous runway. Our puritanical era has once and for all cleaned up those few square yards which were the envy of the entire world.

The Folies now belong to history, both world and worldly. The theater first opened in 1869 and soon became the scene of epic electoral and patriotic meetings organized by politicians of the period. With the return of peace it finally resumed its primary function: combining extravaganzas, two-headed women and real Zulu witch doctors, following the example set by the London Alhambra. The Folies remained the brightest jewel in the diadem of Parisian pleasures for four generations. It was here that the first "review"—a series of attractions tied together by the antics of a French Ma and Pa Kettle—was presented in 1886. It was here that the great *monstres* of the music hall (Paulus, Yvette Guilbert, Cléo de Mérode, Mistinguett, Maurice Chevalier, Dranem, Fernandel, Josephine Baker) got their first start or received their ultimate consecration. And it was here that the idea of undressing women and loading them with feathers began in the 1900's, thus launching the spectacular "girlie show" where singers or boxers shared the stage with the most beautiful anatomies of the period. Not even the literary lights disdained these games: Colette herself did not hesitate to display her well-rounded nudity.

Paul Derval was to bring the genre to perfection. The Casino de Paris was the only place in Europe that could rival the lavishness of the Folies between the two World Wars.

Snubbed by our recording stars, who prefer the Olympia's microphones to the stairs of the rue Richer, this Mecca of rhinestones and ostrich plumes has today become an old lady tirelessly repeating the tunes of her youth. But the old lady still can shake a leg. The producer, Michel Gyarmathy, valiantly continues to expend a wealth of ingenuity in reconstructing the courts of Louis XV or Cleopatra, Earthly Paradise or Franz Lehar's Vienna, within the stage's twenty-foot depth. (It's precisely to make up for that narrowness that they use the famous staircases so much.) Wildly extravagant costumes, plumes and paillettes, waterfalls and wooden horses, mannequins lowered from the flies and chorus girls parading around the balcony always guarantee a fine time for big children starved for fairy tales.

Even though it's now nothing more than a wax museum, this vast, obsolete and faded hall will long continue to be taken for the very heart of Gay Paree.

> Folies Bergère, 32 rue Richer (9ᵉ), PRO 98.49. Nightly performance at 8:30. Tickets from 8 francs (on the runway) to 30 francs.

Le Lido

The Lido is almost forty years old. It's hard to remember what this immense cave, which the entire world soon came to think of as the heart of Paris, offered the wild *entre-deux-guerres* public of 1929. There was a swimming pool, a Turkish bath and, last of all, a cabaret which was the only thing left when Joseph and Louis Clérico bought the whole business in 1945.

That date marked the beginning of the reign of Pierre-Louis Guérin, whose first act was to redecorate the huge hall in "Venetian" style.

Why do fifteen hundred or two thousand spectators come here every night? For the naked women? But they're so decorous you can even show them to your children. To admire the Blue Bells? They have ceased to be the program's drawing card. The answer is much simpler: the Lido packs them in every night on the strength of a reputation which is justified by the tiniest details, the thirty-sixth costume off near the wings, and the fastest stopgap routines. Oddly enough, the most famous cabaret in Paris is also the best one.

There is no intermission, not a moment's pause. A cascade of flame succeeds the luminous play of fountains and a skating rink with real ice has been set up in the middle of the hall before you've even managed to pour yourself a goblet of champagne.

Behind the curtain a devilish director keeps the clever transitions and torrents of plumes and lights moving with split-second precision. The "call girl" in the wings has seven seconds to become the "initiate" in the Chinese scene and less than half that time to transform herself into the favorite in the Opium Dream.

But these extravaganzas aren't the best thing on the program. You remember very little of all these music and costume orgies because, whatever the title or style, the show is also—and mainly—a guarantee that you will be witnessing acrobats such as you've never seen before, a fantastic magician, a peerless juggler or contortionist.

In addition, it's one of the rare spots in Paris where tourists, either from the provinces or from abroad, aren't treated like dirt (except by the ladies sipping a drink at the bar, whose main function is to induce innocents to spend more than they have in their wallets).

Le Lido, 78 Champs-Elysées (8e), ELY 11.61. Open every night at 8:30; shows go on at 11:00 and 1:00. Reserve a table near the stage because you can't see very much from the back of the room. The obligatory split of champagne costs $9.70; dinner, $15.

Le Moulin Rouge

At the Lido a very naked woman lolls on the back of a cardboard panther. At the Moulin Rouge her grace is rivaled by a real panther on stage. These two "false" rivals (both the Lido and the Moulin Rouge belong to the same owner) match each other pound for pound of plumes, ton for ton of rhinestones, kilowatt for kilowatt of multicolored lights, and the result is a draw. If the Lido wins for its variety show, jugglers and spectacles, the Moulin Rouge is way ahead in inventive staging, original costumes and sets, and the quality of its ballets, several of which take place in the giant, transparent swimming pool.

For years the Moulin Rouge seemed to have lost its bearings. It staged gloomy spectacles to the rhythm of a half-hearted cancan. The girls at the Moulin Rouge still kick as they used to in Toulouse-Lautrec's day, but the cancan itself has been updated. And even if extravaganzas tend to make you yawn, you'll leave this rejuvenated old shrine of high Parisian folklore feeling quite satisfied. (Dinner here is not a must; it's better to eat next-door at Proust's.)

Le Moulin Rouge, place Blanche (18e), MON 00.19. Dinner at 9:00; shows at 11:00 P.M. and 1:00 A.M.

Striptease

Crazy Horse Saloon

"The temple of the flesh, the Comédie Française of striptease." For fourteen years the Crazy Horse Saloon's naughty reputation has been channeling all the foreigners and provincials whooping it up in Paris into its Western-style setting, with its garnet velvet, oil lamps and "Wanted" posters.

Parisians turn up their noses and pass by. Well, they shouldn't. The show at the Crazy Horse is the most refined, the most explosive, the most unusual one we know. It's a masterpiece of intelligence, humor and sophistication.

There are no plump blonde lovelies here unhooking their bodices with a bawdy leer. Instead, you have supple-bodied girls transformed into mythical, mysterious, distant creatures by the lighting, poses and props. They become symbols of disembodied sensuality, bordering on abstract art.

Producers of such shows hadn't come up with anything new since "The Chinese Screen," "The Japanese Mirror" and "The Bride's First Night" used to send shivers up our grandfathers' spines. But Alain Bernardin is an esthete who loves women as Cézanne loved apples, and he has created a new art form: civilized eroticism.

After a stab at the restaurant and antique business, Alain Bernardin got the idea, in 1951, of opening a *boîte* where he would take his friends who kept asking, "What's on for tonight?"

He named his place the Crazy Horse after the famous Indian chief, and presented an unsuccessful show parodying the Wild West. He only began making news when he put on a benefit for the Abbé Pierre's charities, where Paris saw its first striptease.

Even then the idea didn't go over until Bernardin realized that he should present several girls instead of just one. His girls were the most beautiful in Paris, and still are. The discretion, almost the distinction, the delicate art which he made their hallmark, with the help of bizarre projections, mysterious lighting and sharp advice, saved the Crazy Horse's striptease when everywhere else it floundered and wallowed in the most flagrant vulgarity.

The Crazy Horse Saloon is a training school for stars. From first to last the strippers all have names which are likely to crop up in the movies or Parisian social life: Yoko Tani, Rita Renoir, Rita Cadillac, Dodo de Hambourg, Bertha Von Paraboum, etc.

The show consists of alternating striptease numbers and international cabaret performers who are always funny. There is dancing after the show, but you're squeezed together like sardines.

Drinks are 35 francs ($7) in the main room and 22 francs ($4.40) at the bar.

> Crazy Horse Saloon, 12 avenue George V (8e), BAL 69.69. Shows start at 11:15 and last until about 2:00 A.M.

Crescendo

Solid, well-balanced "shedding" alternates with international variety acts. The girls are absolutely splendid and their numbers "with it" and very erotic, although they lack the Crazy Horse wit. A dense crowd of fairly young and very receptive foreigners throngs to watch the ladies unveil.

Whiskey costs 20 francs ($4) at the bar, 35 francs ($7) in the main room.

> Crescendo, 40 rue du Colisée (8e), BAL 11.68. Shows at 11:00, 12:15 and 1:45.

Kit Kat

At night all cats are orange at the Kit Kat. These felines, who accentuate the animality of their sunset-colored tutus, fishnet stockings and vertiginous necklines with a caudal appendage and little ears, are the main attraction of a new Montparnasse night club, baptized a "saloon" and devoted to striptease.

Nitpickers may find something familiar here and, in particular, may glimpse longer Bunny ears behind those of the cats. Florence, ex-captain of the Blue Bell Girls and granddaughter of the composer Mendelssohn, looks after this litter of kittens. She's beautiful and gracious, but we don't think she's right. Her cats don't have much humor and are pretty ridiculous.

This doesn't prevent solitary gentlemen from lapping it all up in the long, narrow red room flanked by lots of little bars. The cats, who act as waitresses, hat-check girls and cigarette girls, are allowed to exchange confidences with the customers. But we've been assured that any gentleman who tries to paw them will be told to scat.

For consolation, the customers can watch the strippers, who shed every hour on the hour from midnight until four (the last show is on film). The shows, staged by Billy Thomson, who also does the late show at the Lido, are very imaginative, with good color and sound effects. The women are very talented at being naked. We're sorry we're so allergic to cats. When all is said and done, man, and even more his mate, are still very superior mammals, just as the dictionary says.

Kit Kat, 23 rue Bréa (6e), DAN 95.73. Open from 10:00 until dawn.

Lucky Strip

The décor is red, of course, but there's also blue velvet, dark wood and a bar done up like a pub. The little sofas are very comfortable and the row of "dishes" at the bar is tasty, if not overly piquant. The Scottish bagpiper's striptease sends the ladies into giggling fits. The gentlemen find the girl acrobat-contortionist interesting. The pretty blondes are bored. No more than we were. Still, the Lucky Strip is worth a visit between twelve fifteen and twelve thirty, when you can still and as always admire the great Dodo de Hambourg, one of the pioneers at the Crazy Horse.

Drinks start at 12 francs at the bar, 25 francs in the main room.

Lucky Strip, 4 rue Arsène Houssaye (8e), BAL 56.66. Shows from 10:00 until dawn.

For men only

Senator Fulbright did French tourism a great service by warning his compatriots of the mortal danger which *la vie Parisienne* poses to their virtue. Such a warning, added to the solid reputation of Paris abroad as a sinner's paradise, can't help making honest folks' mouths water.

Unfortunately, we have to pour a little water on the fire which is already consuming our bachelor readers. Paris is no longer quite the "hot" town one thinks.

Is this change to be attributed to the virtuous presence of

Madame de Gaulle in the Elysée Palace? Isn't it said that the police energetically cleared the "strollers" off the sidewalk on the famous rue Godot de Mauroy when the General's wife went shopping around the Madeleine? And, furthermore, didn't this street cleaning continue until, about two years ago, almost all the sidewalks in the capital had returned to their "virgin" state, as if touched by a magic wand?

Official statistics nevertheless reveal that the number of ladies who live by their charms hasn't stopped growing since the good old "houses" which our king Saint Louis established in France were shut down after World War II. Well?

Well, it's very simple: the ladies now discreetly suggest what used to be openly advertised. Except for some streets in Les Halles, like rue Quincampoix, you never see women cooling their heels and calling after anything that wanders by in pants. But you needn't worry about the future of the profession: they're not far away. They've taken refuge behind the doors of shady-looking little hotels where they, so to speak, get down to work. And it's a pretty odd sight to see bunches of men glued in front of these sordid hotels, pressing their noses to the window out of sheer curiosity or, on the other hand, with a very firm purpose.

As you might guess, these ladies belong to the lowest rank of the profession. They specialize in mass-produced pleasure and are content to make a modest profit ($4 to $10). Their favorite territory is (and has been since the Middle Ages) the entire old district around Les Halles. The most typical street in this respect is the rue Saint-Denis, where one improbable café or hotel follows another between the alleyways and secret passages, and where you can sometimes spot surprisingly young and beautiful girls among the love-scarred veterans with thirty or forty years' active service on the asphalt front. The "Paris by Night" buses still don't include rue Saint-Denis in their schedule. They might just as well, since there's no risk involved, at least not if you're content merely to walk around.

The little streets bordering place Pigalle and boulevard de Clichy (namely, rues Guelma, Germain-Picon and du Midi, not to mention rue Pigalle) offer a similar spectacle: filthy little hotels with mobs of men in front of them. But the "beauties" here are of an even lower grade, and if you continue your stroll along boulevard de Rochechouart to what is known as the Goutte d'Or district, a real North African slum, you will sink to the lowest depths of something which is hard to associate with love, a demoralizing sight not especially recommended for peaceful tourists.

The *Amazons*

Let's get back up to the surface—and not the sidewalk this time, but the street itself. It happens that a rather unusual phenomenon has occurred within the last few years: love is now being sold from cars. Wheels have replaced legs. This innovation has two principal advantages for the interested parties. First, automobiles make them relatively respectable, and pretty much protect them from the police (although the *gendarmes* are perfectly aware of the drivers' real business). Second, a woman at the wheel of a beautiful car does have a lot more class than a Mrs. Goodbody slogging along a sidewalk. Then, too, cars still enjoy a somewhat magical prestige in France. These *amazons* (that's what they're called) acquired new letters patent of nobility when they moved from the sidewalks into Citroëns. The practical result is that they now charge a little more from their deeply impressed clientele.

The *amazons,* some of whom drive Mercedes or sports cars, have three main territories for their friendly activities. The first is the Champs-Elysées and especially avenue George V, where on some nights you can watch a regular round robin of "well-furnished" cars (the driver usually has a teammate who continues circulating while her comrade fulfills a contract in a nearby hotel room, unless the two of them happen to be engaged by some enlightened connoisseur). Second, boulevard de la Madeleine (and just behind it, on rue Godot de Mauroy) and boulevard des Capucines as far as the Opéra (a point of interest: the *amazons* around the Opéra are tireless workers and are often still there at five in the morning); and finally, the Bois de Boulogne.

Bois de Boulogne

During the period between the two wars lots of strange things went on in the vast Bois de Boulogne, whose principal function is to provide a measure of fresh air for our darling children. The thickets afforded glimpses of instructive bacchanals and group activities which bore only the most tenuous relationship to Boy Scout field trips. But once again the police rushed to the aid of virtue. Today the Bois de Boulogne is a network of police patrols and anyone foolish enough to take a stroll through the underbrush after dark will immediately find himself seized by the collar. On the other hand, it's perfectly legal to go for a drive in the Bois. If you go over by the Porte Maillot, the Allée de Longchamp or the Porte des Sablons road on the first fine days of spring, you'll observe cars constantly going to and fro, moving very slowly, occasionally signaling with their lights, crossing each other's paths and sometimes pulling up next to one another before starting off together in the same direction. There are lots of luxury cars occupied by nice-looking couples whose innocent obsession is to avoid solitude, even in love. They have no trouble finding other couples suffering from an identical phobia, for which they jointly seek a remedy in some hospitable abode. A charming little hotel in the 17th *arrondissement* (often closed by the police) has, moreover, made a specialty of welcoming these dynamic couples. To insure the complete success of the treatment, the proprietress of this establishment has gone so far as to remove the locks from all the doors; a delightful local custom makes "share and share alike" the order of the day.

The above-mentioned couples usually have no financial motives; with them it's art for art's sake. But the Bois de Boulogne has lots of motorized damsels whose intentions aren't the least bit ambiguous: love—in groups of two, three, four or ten— means money. And don't worry: they make sure you know it right away (the Caravelles range in price from 100 to 200 francs —$20 to $40). Only never agree to use the car as the scene of these fleeting pleasures; if the police happen to come by, you risk arrest for outraging public decency.

Saint-Germain-des-Prés

In the end, the only section which has almost escaped the industrialization of love is the one with most libertine reputation: Saint-Germain-des-Prés.

No "professional" woman has yet dared operate from the terrace of the Flore (male prostitution flourishes here, however) or pace the rue Saint-Benoît. Why the devil should people pay for something they can get for free? After all, the bars, restaurants and discothèques are filled with swarms of girls who aren't stand-offish and would like nothing better than to start a conversation with someone who appeals to them. This doesn't guarantee that you'll be eating breakfast together the next day, but if you're not a bad-looking guy and know how to make a girl laugh, your first move should obviously be to try your luck in Saint-Germain-des-Prés.

Watch out, though, for a certain category of girls who hang out in a few cafés like the Pergola. They are very sharp, favor beatnik getup and aren't shy about jumping into bed. Actually they're just little gangsters in petticoats waiting for a chance to get a hold of their naïve swain's wallet—if they don't leave that up to their boy friends, who burst into the room at the right psychological moment to rob the poor guy or sometimes even blackmail him. Luckily, these practices are pretty much the exception and Saint-Germain-des-Prés is full of girls who want nothing more than dinner, a drink and a little companionship.

Since our subject happens to be the ethereal heights of passion, we should say a word or two about the spots where you have the best chance of seeing and possibly meeting pretty girls (who will end up costing you a lot more with their virtue than mercenary women with their immorality).

True Romance

If you stroll down rue du Faubourg Saint-Honoré between noon and five o'clock, you won't know where to look next. There are just too many beautiful, elegant girls window-shopping there in perfect good faith. Unfortunately they're not the type you pick up in the street. Your only chance is to follow them into Hermès or Lanvin and offer them the entire store.

The area around Cook's Travel Agency on place de la Madeleine is a likely spot, provided you forget about trying to seduce French girls and are willing to fraternize with other Americans or else with German, English, Swedish and—why not?—Japanese girls. A little further on, near the Opéra, the American Express and the outdoor terrace of the Café de la Paix are equally good hunting grounds for all but native "birds." Along the same lines, certain connoisseurs deem it very worthwhile to be at the Alliance Française on boulevard Raspail or the Civilisation Française course at the Sorbonne when classes let out.

But what if you won't settle for anything less than a "real French" romance? Before you give up entirely (Parisiennes are much more puritanical than is generally believed), you might take a stroll along boulevard Saint-Michel in the Latin Quarter. The students, real or imitation, won't necessarily refuse your invitation to a drink, if you keep your ulterior motives from showing. The Champs-Elysées area is another good hunting ground. Right on the Champs itself, the terraces of big cafés like the Colisée, the Marignan, etc., have lots of foreigners, but also some French girls who may be alone and looking for a good time. (But be careful of girls who make the first move: they are professionals, little *bourgeoises* out to earn a new dress or handbag before going home to their innocently waiting husband and children. These part-time prostitutes are known as "shooting stars.") At lunchtime the cafés and snack bars on the Champs-Elysées are overrun with salesgirls, hairdressers, etc., who come here for a hard-boiled egg and a ham sandwich. Don't think they have anything against caviar and champagne; just turn on the charm and they'll be delighted to have you take them to a good restaurant that evening.

There is a very high percentage of pretty girls at the Champs-Elysées Drugstore. Most of them are already someone else's property, but give it a whirl anyway. You should also try sitting on the terrace of one of the three cafés which are most popular with models and mini-starlets, if only to feast your eyes. The first is located opposite Dior, at the corner of rue Marignan and avenue Montaigne; the second, on the same avenue, is the Bar des Théâtres, and the third, on rue Pierre-Charron, is La Belle Ferronnière. (See CAFES AND BARS, p. 168.)

All your attempts at seduction have failed. You've given up on free love but are too refined to settle for a B-girl from the Lido, a bar girl from rue de Ponthieu or rue Daunou or one of the Hotel George V's clients who feign idleness by staring into a gin fizz. There's one solution.

Call Girls

No one will be surprised to learn that call girls have quickly made a place for themselves in France's modernization plan. They have even become an essential cog in Parisian life, although one doesn't always realize it.

There are some minor networks, of course, whose phone numbers can be supplied by hotel concierges, bartenders and night club doormen. They are not particularly interesting, since their employees occupy a very middling rank among professional love makers. On the other hand, there are also some deluxe organizations which have beautiful, elegant and not necessarily brainless girls working for them. The most famous of these (we can't give you the address, but inhabitants of the rue Marignan are not unaware of its existence) is run by a very remarkable woman with high-placed friends and more or less exclusive rights to the prettiest girls for sale in Paris. They are more or less "cover girls," more or less actresses, and for an average of 200 to 300 francs ($40 to $60) they will receive any gentleman whom their boss, Mme C., sends over after a simple phone call.

These new-style courtesans are very carefully screened and are supposed to possess all the worldly virtues. They must be tastefully dressed, well bred, speak foreign languages (and anyhow, many of them are foreigners themselves: Germans, Swedes, Italians) and be "presentable" in every way. They make such a good impression in society that important, responsible firms often call them when their executives have to take foreign clients out to restaurants and night clubs. The girls are introduced as personal friends, and the manufacturer from the Ruhr or Milan is so proud of making a conquest that he's completely taken in. The same thing happened to a very famous young American politican whom French journalists took to dinner with an enchanting creature. He had no way of knowing that the lady was only fulfilling one of many contracts when she "succumbed" to his charm that very night.

These girls can be hired by the hour, by the evening or even by the week. They spend their vacations in multimillionaires' villas on the Côte d'Azur and are summoned to London, Dusseldorf and even Moscow for "consultation." One day they disappear, either to get married or because they have caught the eye of some producer who offers them a role. But it doesn't matter: they are immediately replaced by other girls who are just as pretty, just as elegant and just as determined to get all they can out of life.

THE THIRD SEX

Restaurants and bars

Le Coup de Frein

A 1900's "touch" has crept into this black and orange den which has been catering to bachelors of both incompatible sexes for about ten years now. Sleek voyeuristic shopkeepers often come to lose themselves in this hideaway of lost people, doubtless hoping for "something to happen" one day. But the habitués' tastes, aspirations and code of behavior are so clearly and frankly formulated that no ambiguity could ever creep in and so no conflicts are to be expected or feared.

The menu is abundant, the prices reasonable ($4 to $5), and the atmosphere "naughty but nice." All in all, a very odd place.

Le Coup de Frein, 88 rue Lepic (18e), ORN 90.06. Closed Tuesdays. Service until 3:00 A.M.

Le Fiacre

Louis couldn't possibly squeeze any more people into his circle of customer-friends. His Fiacre is bursting at the seams, and the pace hasn't shown any signs of slackening for a good ten years.

The languid striplings who come and go on both floors of this very "special" den, which Louis runs with a maestro's touch, all look like carbon copies of the ones who were here on opening day. There are just more of them—and they're said to be more grasping.

Countesses, artists' wives and a few girls who think that "those fellows" make good friends (because they have no ulterior motives) find people here with whom they can talk clothes without appearing frivolous. "With it" designers really owe it to themselves to bring their associates and suppliers here.

Effusive relationships spring up between tall, long-haired lummoxes on the stairway leading to the restaurant, which goes wild a little after the stroke of midnight.

Anything—well, almost anything—goes then. Decorators, film makers, antique dealers, writers and ladies' hairdressers spontaneously improvise thousands of skits that mercilessly parody the tiniest defects of their outside acquaintances' female companions.

But Louis, a moustached Méridional, knows just how far below the belt they can be allowed to hit, now that fashion decrees low waists for men.

The Fiacre has a new coffered ceiling and a strictly defined ceiling on "proper" impropriety. The waiters, for their part, are very courteous, and their activities are supervised by the boss, known as "Louis-du-Fiacre." He is hospitable, discreet, vigilant and devoid of prejudices: he's been seen to welcome a somewhat voyeuristic but presentable couple, consisting of equal parts men and women.

Le Fiacre, 4 rue du Cherche-Midi (6e), LIT 09.79. Open from 9:00 until 3:00 A.M. Closed on Mondays.

Chez Narcisse

Gleaming copper pots and pans lend a rustic glow to the walls of a village inn reproduced on the ground floor of a building in a sordid little street near the Gare de Lyon, surrounded by the shady looking hotels and secret opium dens of the Chinese population. Gentlemen who are so carefully dressed that it is pointless to speak of them as "elegant" go slumming here under the mocking, sometimes even conniving eyes of the railroad employees who stand at the bar enjoying a glass of red wine and a good long laugh at the "follies" of the owner and his gay clientele. The food is uninteresting, but this very special collusion between capital and labor may be worth a trip over here.

Chez Narcisse, Passage Moulin (12ᵉ), DID 59.21. Closed Wednesdays. Service until midnight.

Pimm's

Undulating blond Fabrice directs this two-story bar while keeping one (languid) eye on the cash register. Fabrice (this is probably a surname; some people prefer to him as "Del Dingo," which is slang for screwball or, in this case, screwbelle) is determined to make a resolutely "in" atmosphere prevail here. This up-and-coming young executive keeps abreast of developments in the habits of which he is both exponent and proponent among his customers, who, it is true, are "converts" of long standing. Their studied casualness impedes the free flow of obscenities which used to constitute the charm of the Fiacre. But ever since "teases" started coming to Louis' place, his old customers (the most hard to please and well to-do) have been forced to seek a peaceful refuge on the other bank, in this duplex which lends itself to the affirmation of their mistaken, and certainly misguided, claim to be "men of the world."

The carpet-covered walls and the male nude which adorns the basement bar provide the setting in which emcee Philippe Petit, who used to be famous—in certain generally rather twisted circles—for his ferocious verve, establishes an atmosphere of good fellowship among a legion of murmuring members of the "intersex," all evidently glad to get off by themselves here. Philippe Petit is a brilliant conversationalist, who uses all his resources to conjure away his customers' blues by vying with them in the arena of the unmentionable. Cultivated, subtle, falsely igenuous, dazzling, chatty, touching, and deliberately grotesque, Petit is undoubtedly the funniest and most cynical of all the "bawds" in Paris.

Drinks start at 10 francs.

> Pimm's, 3 rue Sainte-Anne (Ier), RIC 91.25. Open every night from 10:00 until dawn.

Cabarets

Madame Arthur

At Madame Arthur they knock themselves out trying to be indecent. On stage, mannikins, or rather mannequins in their best bib and tucker, engage in obscenity bouts which would certainly have shocked Granny, and wiggle their busts, newly developed thanks to the ministrations of paraffin artists. Well-informed sources tell us that hormones do the "rest" . . . Despite the show's rather meticulous attention to detail, the ambiguous little divas in this good-natured cabaret still haven't gone "Moroccan," where it appears that extremely zealous pruners keep their lancets busy flattening out superfluous bumps. These cut-rate surgeons have a carefully calculated scale of prices and consider any jewel negotiable.

At Madame Arthur's (who, needless to say, is not a woman) Nature's oversights are corrected by highly qualified native orthopedists. On the rue des Martyrs, the ways of love are all detours, and there are no halfway points. Ear-splitting obscenities abruptly follow murmured confidences. All the names are feminized, but the humor is strictly from the barracks, even though its uniform is an evening gown or mini-skirt. These are worn—and later not worn—while one of the three fat, kilted waiters (the one who promptly answers to the pretty name Violette) unleashes a string of salacious madrigals at some stupefied old man. Everyone laughs. Sylvain, Cynthia, Gipsy and plump Baghera aren't distracted from adjusting their borrowed charms before undressing to the accompaniment of their own vague survey of chansonettes from the thirties and from the toilers of the '33's.

This would all add up to a very mild show if it weren't for Madame Arthur. His name is Maslowa, and everything's grist for his mill. He introduces all the performers, and his own performance flashes with sublime brilliance. Delicacy is not his strong point. His mastery of double entendre and stubborn lack of measure remove any ambiguity from even his briefest comments. This rough, crafty, pathetic old clown can be frightening at times. His audience, who will laugh at anything while digesting their dinner, at first try to fling back some monstrous retorts, but before long they are swamped, silenced, stupefied by the stream of enormities proffered by the vehement Maslowa. Passing drinkers start to feel superfluous. At the end of the evening a squadron of angels—patron saints of hebetude—flit to and fro in this black, sequin-studded Pigallian den where a mad, almost unbearable, and unquestionably very talented ham obligingly debases himself.

Madame Arthur, 75 *bis* rue des Martyrs (18e), ORN 48.27. Open nightly at 11:00.

Brasserie aux Cascades

You have to like this sort of thing. The show, which bald Alsatian Louis Hommel presents as a nocturne for the customers (mostly truckdrivers) at his Brasserie aux Cascades, is certainly a strange one. But some of our most delicate couturiers and pixyish, blonde lady journalists are wild about it.

The regular customers also participate in the show, of course. The curtain-raiser consists of Jo Tchad's nostalgic songs about his native Lake Chad, which he composes himself and plays on the guitar. He is followed by accordionist Mario Robin. This grave musician, a *chaloupée* virtuoso, sometimes plays dance music for the audience, too. But these tried and true numbers are only the preamble. The local star, Armando, is yet to come.

Armando is a swell fellow who had his shining hour right

after the Liberation, in places like Maxim's in Cannes, the Excelsior in Nantes and the old (and now destroyed) Café de la Paix in Toulon.

A former metal fitter, Armando first discovered his gift in Germany, from which he was deported. But it's time we filled you in on the details. Armando appears dressed in a blue satin mini-skirt trimmed with silver braid to emphasize his (borrowed?) curves. With his legs sheathed in dark stockings held up by a pink belt (whose delicate garters can often be appreciated) and black shoes on his feet, Armando makes a sprightly prima donna. A blond wig adds the crowning touch.

This strange creature isn't keen on questions about the morals of female impersonators, and quickly forestalls them. "I'm a father, you know. My daughter, who's eighteen, just got married. It makes home pretty sad for me and my wife. But what can you do, that's life." Armando would undoubtedly have to brush away a tear if the strict rule that "the show must go on" didn't force him to wear a cheerful face in his trying profession, put his best foot forward (and his hand out), and embellish his repertory with the most meticulous simpering.

The congregation of Armando's cap-wearing admirers often joins voices in this repertory, which includes "La Boiteuse" ("The Girl with the Limp"), "Le Dénicheur" ("Robbing the Nest"), and the proud "Marche de la Deuxième Division Blindée" ("March of the Second Tank Division"), along with other off-color melodies. This *chanteuse* with the voice of boulevard Rochechouart knows how to touch a simple heart with a song and strives to breathe new life into our proud Gallic traditions with a few ambiguous but good-natured accents.

Brasserie aux Cascades, 60 boulevard Rochechouart (18e), MON 63.75. Closed Thursdays.

Carrousel

Whether they go by the name of Sophie, Michèle, Florence, Capucine or Fétiche, the numerous, stereotyped creatures who come to display their feminine curves in this unmysterious cavern are all men who strain their wits alternately denying and insisting on that fact. Nevertheless, the Carrousel is not the hotbed of "vice-versa" which all the foreigners who go there seeking some titillation or other expect it to be. The audience as a whole provides a more unusual and varied show than the stage. It consists mostly of "normal" and seemingly decent couples of varying ages, sizes and origins. It's no trick to leave them goggle-eyed.

Every evening you can hear customers oohing and aahing over the fact that a big, lanky fellow, who got his snub nose from a well-known plastic surgeon, also had his chest refashioned with silicone injections. The audience's surprise is very surprising, to say the least. Everything here is contrived to make the gentlemen look like ladies, and to make sure everyone knows who's what. The absence of an emcee of the caliber of the one who makes Madame Arthur's a center of side-splitting enormity weighs very heavily in this room, where simpering masculine-feminines do uninspired imitations of Marilyn Monroe, Régine, Line Renaud, Maria Callas (who are adored by transvestites), and of strip teasers from all over.

Carrousel is destined to provide morose flings for placid papas from every hick town in the world and for their wives, who are stupefied by the frank (and safe) audacity of variety acts which couldn't get a toe in the door anywhere else.

Carrousel, 29 rue Vavin (6e), DAN 66.33. Opens at 10:30 P.M.

Elle et Lui

This club is the exact opposite of the Carrousel next door. In fact, the two share the basement of a single building. "She and He" is "she" promoted to "he" by the dingy miracle of exploited confusion. Humor? Not a trace. For the gentlemanly ladies are indeed the opposite of the ladylike gentlemen in their total lack of that virtue.

At the end of the evening you are treated to a display of emotion by a few execrable singers (Maria Vincent excepted). A delicious whiff of hell emanates from the standard number, which combines a stripper's rather chilly charms with those of two clearly characterized young ladies, one of whom, dressed like a young hood, whips her sprightly, consenting partner with the gestures of a frenzied lumberjack.

Members of the fair sex, dressed in faded blue suits and vests, act as daughters of the house. They wait on tables, promptly distribute drinks and superbly fill the role assigned them by the management, namely, to make a fuss over bejeweled forty-year-olds with affectionate dispositions. The audience is by far the most surprising thing about this spectacle. Besides the heroines already mentioned, who come here to find a lady's home companion, you also see men, old regulars whose nocturnal behavior for the most part seems free both of peculiarities and mystery. They observe, doubtless make comparisons, and sip whiskies until dawn. Now and then they invite one of the club's stars to have a drink. For these many lingering voyeurs turn out not to keep a very close watch on what they spend, to say the least.

> Elle et Lui, 31 rue Vavin (6e), MED 29.52. Opens at 10:30; show starts at midnight.

La Montagne

La Montagne dates back many years as a somewhat sordid temple of the "other" world. But the passing years have blurred all distinctions and have undermined customs one would have thought most solidly entrenched. Modern mores no longer balk at calling an assistant bookkeeper in petticoats "mister" or a crew-cut steno "miss" in this well-behaved *bal musette,* where by force of habit they still half-heartedly distill "wild" obscenities.

Buxom Georgette Anys acts as mistress of ceremonies and exchanges quips with Brandini and Kid Camille, two middle-aged transvestites who blithely open the show in this dark room decorated with old movie posters.

Way up on the loggia, the three instrumentalists assigned to set all the intermissions to music force jigs into a rock beat and the latest pop tunes into jig time. With their help the confusion reaches such a point that men start dancing with women. But everything gets straightened out again when it's time for bed.

> La Montagne, 46 rue de la Montagne Sainte-Geneviève (5e), ODE 15.59. Closed Mondays. Open from 10:00 until dawn. Shows starting at 11:00.

Chez Moune

This is a "feminine" cabaret. Middle-aged ladies contrive nonetheless to invalidate that convenient definition. They dress in strict suits and vests and make and break their little ménages with all the charm of surly stevedores. These women— or, better, men—deliberately encourage confusion. Natural affinities quickly become "unnatural tastes" and Lesbos annexes Cythera as soon as the music stops playing.

But the sight of passion is not itself passionately interesting. These diligent priestesses of a love which, so they say, dares not speak its name anywhere else, speak theirs in terms that are much too clear for any healthy voyeur to want to look any deeper.

Chez Moune, 54 rue Pigalle (9e), PIG 64.64. Open nightly from 10:00 until dawn. Show at 11:30.

Part IV

HOTELS

The French love to tell the whole world how to cook. And the fact is that they haven't yet met their master in that discipline. Given half a chance, however, they'd also take themselves for model hotel keepers. And Parisian hotel owners even manage to find excuses for their decrepit installations, banal décor, negligent service and excessive prices. In particular, they cite the country's fiscal policies and staggering taxes. And they're right. France, which up until World War II had the biggest hotel business in the world, is today trying to make up for tourist losses by a frenzy of taxation. And there's no doubt that the government is much to blame for killing the golden goose.

Still, the hotel owners themselves are far from innocent. A great many of them, influenced at first-hand or second-hand by memories of those great golden days, have refused to comply with the demands of modern living in everything but their joyous pursuit of spiraling prices. When, sometimes with the help of government subsidies, they are finally goaded into modernizing, repainting their leprous walls and replacing plumbing that predates the invention of hot water, they often can't wait to install the ugliest, most depressing modern "improvements." Neon and chrome replace the old broken chandeliers, and the hotel owners think that's that.

The situation in Paris is complicated by the fact that ever since the war the housing problem has caused homeless families to fill countless little hotels. The chain reaction following this phenomenon has had repercussions even in the luxury hotels, flooded in turn by a clientele which wouldn't have dared set foot in them twenty years ago, but now has no other choice. Believe us, if the manager of any large Parisian hotel complains of money problems, he should look to inefficient management rather than insufficient business as the cause.

The real trouble is that Parisian hotels are almost always full, from January 1 through December 31. So why bother restoring and modernizing, why go to any expense when even the dreariest rooms, furnished with a tired mattress and illuminated by a twenty-five-watt bulb, are always desperately in demand?

We have no taste for masochism. But neither are we inclined to act the ostrich or the peacock. It would be pointless to follow the lead of some other countries, whose hotel business is nothing to envy (follow our glance across the Channel . . .), and pretend that everything's fine when everything's in a pretty bad way. We ought rather to assure our readers that, conscious of our sorry state, we have every reason to be enthusiastic if we happen to discover a charming little hotel or come to the defense of a luxury palace which is struggling to survive. You can therefore put complete faith in our absolute impartiality as you read the descriptions of the few hotels we do recommend.

It goes without saying that we haven't visited every single hotel in Paris, and that there are certainly some charming, very comfortable, economical, refined places we haven't mentioned. All the same, if you don't find the name of some very well known hotels here, it's probably because we didn't think they deserved to figure on a list of places where we hope you'll be happy in Paris, according to your preferences and your means.

Besides, some hotels have become well known for very strange reasons. The 9th *arrondissement* near the Folies Bergère (which probably explains it) is swarming with countless extremely modest hotels. A great many tourists make the mistake of thinking that this depressing district represents the norm in French hotels and the heart of Paris as well. This misunderstanding is all the more unfortunate since the population consists almost exclusively of European refugees from North Africa, who certainly have some right to be called French but who nevertheless are not real Parisians.

For that matter, we can't recommend too strongly that sophisticated tourists give up any ideas they might have about venturing outside the well-known tourist districts. Those "unspoiled" areas often have unspoiled records for ruthlessly victimizing tourists. It is sometimes good to get away from the

Champs-Elysées, Saint-Germain-des-Prés and especially Mont-martre. We know, alas, that the most discriminating travelers will still make a beeline for this adulterated honey, which is why we have tried to clear the ground by describing the best hotels in these blessed sections. And anyhow, one must admit that these areas are exactly where good hotels are the thickest.

Last of all, a word about prices. French hotels have a reputation for being expensive. This is true—but what advanced countries have inexpensive ones? New York, in particular, has nothing to brag about, and it's hard to see why our American friends think they deserve to have a room in one of the world's most beautiful cities for less than half of what it would cost them at home. All right, we don't usually have air conditioning, but on the other hand you can ring for room service in France without having the valet take it as a personal affront. This may be because the French don't consider a valet's job ignominious—not that they think it overwhelmingly aristocratic either.

And then, as you'll see, a few of our hotel owners—the ones who are a credit to us—know how to receive a client like a friend, arrange a bouquet of flowers, welcome him with the outstretched arms of an (authentic) Louis XV chair, open a window onto a bird-filled garden and listen to his war memories with a kindly smile. Such things are priceless. And they often happen to be the least expensive.

RIGHT BANK

Champs-Elysées (8ᵉ)
LUXURY HOTELS

- -

Bristol

The Bristol's elegant décor, furnished with antiques or very fine reproductions, comfortable rooms, each endowed with its own magnificent bathroom, luxurious suites (fifty of them), and elegant clientele make it one of the few genuine palaces in Paris. And it is one of only two which are under the personal management of their owner. The agreeable Monsieur Jamet's attentive "master's touch" makes itself felt at every moment in the impeccable condition of the entire place as well as in the faultless service. Renovations are made every year.

Clientele: almost all the foreign politicians and passing diplomats (who are thus only a hundred yards from the Elysée), as well as American high society.

Two hundred rooms, all with bath; some also have air conditioning. Prices: high, but justifiably so. Single rooms, with breakfast included but not counting 25 percent extra for service and taxes, are 120 francs ($24); doubles are 220 francs ($44), and suites run from 395 francs ($79) for bedroom and living room to 1,000 francs ($200). Number 721, for example, is a duplex with private elevator and includes a living room, dining room, office and three bedrooms.

Hotel Bristol, 112 Faubourg Saint-Honoré (8e), ELY 23.15.

George V

From the outside the George V looks like one of those massive "continental" palaces from the period between the wars, the kind that remind you a little of a 1930's New York skyscraper nipped in the bud. The immense, newly redecorated lobby is nothing extraordinary, but at least it has the great merit of understatement, without the all-to-familiar clutter of ticket windows, armchairs, etc. The great gallery leading to the elevators is totally successful in its use of Louis XIV tapestries and Baroque statues, while the elevators themselves attain a peak of refinement with their red leather walls. The drawing rooms and small salons are elegant and quietly comfortable. But your heart sinks the higher you go. The corridors on each floor are painted in the dismal neutral shades which seem to be a secret shared by hotels the world over.

Enormous pipes run the length of the top-floor ceilings. You'd think you were in the hold of an ocean liner. The furniture is contemporary; it has no particular charm or style but is in perfect condition. Most of the rooms are decorated with charming watercolors by Vertès, and the upper floors have a wonderful view of Paris.

The rooms are big, sometimes even immense. The first-floor suites have entrance halls which alone measure a good forty square yards. The problem of furnishing them has been intelligently solved, thanks to very large armoires and especially to extremely clever glass-fronted drawers. The bed linen is absolutely new. There is a little wall safe. On the other hand, there is no radio or television set, although one can be sent up free of charge in a matter of minutes. The bathrooms are in the process of being remodeled. The plumbing is in excellent condition, despite its antediluvian character. And they are not content with giving you a mere bath towel; every guest receives a real bathrobe and four towels. But why is there only one little bar of soap? The heating is excellent. Still, it's a shame that a palace like this is neither air conditioned nor soundproof.

You are given a perfect welcome and seated before a little end table to fill out your registration form. Nothing officious about it. The day is past when some oil baron could demand mauve curtains and pale green chairs. The clientele has sobered down and no longer dares act eccentric. But the minute he steps into his room (which at the very least includes an entrance hall and bath), today's client has almost the entire hotel staff at his disposal. He presses the buzzer and ten minutes later his shoes have been shined, his suit pressed, his bath drawn and the linen put in order. And of all unlikely things, not one of the staff acts as if he's waiting for a tip. Five hundred and fifty employees are at the constant beck and call of the hotel's four-hundred clients (when full). The only slip-up is that the laundry is closed between seven at night and nine in the morning. What's more, a file is kept on the tastes and fancies of regular clients. Does Mr. Smith suffer from asthma? He'll find a horsehair pillow waiting for him. Or flowers. Or a bottle of ice water. Or a detective story. Or a television set.

Among the hotel's faithful clients we should mention Gina Lollobrigida, Vittorio de Sica, Paul Getty, Simenon, and Sam Spiegel. It follows that you are very likely to find people with less firmly established reputations around and even inside the hotel, in the persons of single women with time on their hands but not necessarily with a room at the George V.

Last of all, excellent, very elegant luxury hotel food, prepared under the supervision of Chef Vauthieu, is served in a rather overly majestic setting, except in summer when one can have lunch beneath the parasols in the charming patio. In our opinion, the prices are out of line, even for a very great hotel (the check easily skirts 100 francs—$20!). The hors d'oeuvres, classical dishes like beef heart Prince Albert, and wines are faultless, as is the expert service. (The restaurant is of course open to nonresidents of the hotel.)

Two hundred rooms or suites, all with bath. A single room costs 120 francs ($24) a night and a double, 200 francs ($40). A bedroom and living room suite costs 280 francs ($56); with living room and two bedrooms, it comes to 350 francs ($70). And you have to add another 25 percent for service and taxes. The George V has the same rates winter and summer, but gives a 30 percent reduction if you stay more than a week. In addition to its two hundred rooms, the George V also rents fifty-two residential apartments (one to four rooms, plus kitchenette) which enjoy all the hotel's services and cost 30 percent less than equivalent rooms.

George V, 31 avenue George V (8e), BAL 35.30.

Plaza-Athénée

This ought to be one of the best luxury hotels in Paris. It certainly has a marvelous location; it is patronized by a very select clientele of North and South Americans (Henry Ford, the Rockefellers) and Oriental monarchs (the Shah of Persia, King Hussein of Jordan); the service is excellent (nothing prevents you from ordering a steak at two in the morning, and clients are regularly treated to fresh flowers); the salons and flower-filled courtyards are pleasantly luxurious; finally, the hotel undergoes yearly revisions and is extremely well kept up.

Unfortunately it also has rooms (two hundred and ten, all with bath). These are huge, but cold and unimaginatively decorated. Some of them—done in terribly dated "modern"—are simply ghastly. The others, blessed with neo-Louis XV furniture, are marvelously banal and devoid of any charm or warmth. As for the bathrooms—which are so-so—the newer they are, the narrower they are.

The manager assures us that his clientele appreciates his establishment's "traditional stamp." Does this prove that the customer isn't always right?

Prices: doubles: 150 to 180 francs, plus 25 percent; suites start at 300 francs.

Plaza-Athenée, 25 avenue Montaigne (8e), BAL 43.30.

Raphaël

The Oriental rugs (real or imitation) on the marble floors, the pillars and paneling, the old paintings and reproductions of antique furniture all combine to make this a classical palace whose special virtue is quietness, even though it's just a stone's throw from the Etoile. The rooms are sumptuously decorated and furnished (mostly in Empire style), and always come with twin beds and a (usually modern) bath.

Prices: 124 francs ($24.80) facing the courtyard, 144 francs ($28.80) facing rue Lapérouse. The most sought-after rooms are the ones with a so-called "alcove" (living room and bedroom), which overlook avenue des Portugais. These go for between 196 and 220 francs ($39.20 to $44), to which you have to add another 25 percent for service and taxes. But you're certain to have the entire Italian-American movie world, from Rossellini to Howard Hawks and from La Magnani to Claudia Cardinale, next door or down the hall.

Raphaël, 17 avenue Kléber (16e), KLE 07.70.

San Régis

With its magnificent antiques, its paintings and its curios, this is one of the most luxurious and elegantly decorated hotels in Paris. It is located on a quiet street a stone's throw from the Champs-Elysées, and is patronized by Ursula Andress, Carol Baker and James Mason. American magnates also are regular clients, as is the family of the Grand Duke of Luxemburg. All fifty rooms come with bath, and each is differently furnished with infinitely tasteful antiques. Very friendly welcome and good service.

Prices: singles from 80 to 90 francs ($16 to $18); doubles, 110 to 120 francs ($22 to $24). In season rooms have to be booked a month in advance.

San Régis, 12 rue Jean-Goujon (8e), ELY 41.90.

Champs-Elysées (8e)

VERY COMFORTABLE

Bellman

A pleasant little hotel patronized by members of the international entertainment and fashion worlds. Cheerful rooms, furnished in period style, each with private bath. The bar is an outpost for reporters from *Paris-Match* and the *Europe No. 1* network.

Prices: singles from 70 to 90 francs ($14 to $18), doubles at 110 francs and 120 francs ($$22 and $24), service and taxes included.

Bellman, 37 rue François Ier (8e), ELY 62.51.

Stockholm

This hotel is part of Sweden House and is therefore patronized mainly by Scandinavians. The rooms could stand some renovation and general brightening up, so as not to contradict the cheerful impression created by the pleasant Scandinavian décor in the lobby and lounge.

Prices: single rooms with bath, 65 francs ($13); doubles, 85 francs and 90 francs ($17 and $18), plus 25 percent for service and taxes.

Stockholm, 24 rue Vernet (8é), BAL 04.24.

La Tremoïlle

Big old-fashioned rooms, plumbing which functions well despite its (many) years. English people and provincial adherents of Olde France are very fond of this hotel.

Prices: 100 francs ($20) for a single room with bath, 125 francs ($25) for a double; service and taxes are included.

La Tremoïlle, 14 rue de la Tremoïlle (8ᵉ), ELY 97.21.

Etoile, Passy, Neuilly, (16ᵉ)
LUXURY HOTELS

Majestic

Located in a narrow, almost deserted street, the Majestic is one of the few places in Paris where one completely forgets the noise of the city. Not a sound ever disturbs the cotton-wool atmosphere of the seven floors where Monsieur Varichon has installed twenty-two studios and suites (decorated in Louis XV and Directoire styles), which would be the envy of many star-studded palaces. The prices are obviously out of the average tourist's range: 110 francs ($22)—breakfast, taxes and services included—for a studio with twin beds, bath, kitchenette, entrance hall and lots of closets (130 francs for two people). But these high prices are justified by the comfortable rooms and perfect service.

A suite will cost you either 170 francs or 190 francs ($34 or $38), depending on whether you are alone or with another person. We especially recommend the top-floor suite, which doesn't look anything like a hotel room, not even a very sumptuous one. There is an entry with a little balcony, and a large living room with a sleeping alcove in which a double bed is ensconced. There is gold moiré on the walls, a purple carpet on the floor, period furniture and gilded Louis XV chairs. Large windows open onto a flowered French-style balcony. The suite also includes a small modern kitchen, but customers can have their meals served in their rooms. Since the Majestic has neither bar nor restaurant, the Hotel Raphaël, which is strictly in the same class, takes care of the food and refreshment for the lucky occupants of these dream rooms.

Majestic, 29 rue Dumont-d'Urville (16ᵉ), KLE 34.28.

Etoile, Passy, Neuilly, (*16ᵉ*)
VERY COMFORTABLE

Alexander

A completely new and delightful little hotel, decorated with a great deal of taste. The extremely feminine rooms are papered from floor to ceiling in pretty flowered patterns and the bathrooms are gay and modern. Even the corridors have fabric-covered walls, which not only create a warm, cozy atmosphere but muffle the street noises as well. The reception is friendly, the clientele (out-of-towners and foreigners) elegant. All rooms are with bath.

Prices: 57 francs ($11.40) for a single, 68 francs ($13.60) for a double, with taxes, service and breakfast included.

Alexander, 102 avenue Victor-Hugo (16ᵉ), PAS 19.86.

Jardin de Neuilly

With its garden, trees, old beams, comfortable rooms papered in pink toile de Jouy or paisley patterns, wooden stairways and cheerful service, this is nothing other than a real country inn five minutes away from the Etoile.

Twenty-nine rooms with lavatory, shower or complete bath. Two floors, no elevator. Grill. Most of the rooms have television. A few studios with fully equipped kitchenettes. Prices: rooms with shower but no bath, 60 francs and 75 francs ($12 and $15); single with bath, 85 francs ($17); double with bath, 90 francs ($18); service, taxes and breakfast included.

Making a country excursion less than a mile from home is a crazy idea, so it's probably a good one, too.

Jardin de Neuilly, 5 rue Paul-Déroulède, Neuilly-sur-Seine, MAI 51.62.

Massenet

A very quiet hotel in a bourgeois apartment building in Passy. The décor of the spacious rooms is anodyne but fairly pleasant. Half the rooms overlook the garden.

Rates: singles, 55 francs ($11); doubles, 80.30 francs ($16.60), with service, taxes and breakfast included.

Massenet, 5 *bis* rue Massenet (16e), AUT 53.61.

Résidence du Bois

This is a little private mansion near the Bois where the rooms, furnished in various periods, look out onto a marvelous garden as luxuriant as Eden. The hotel is a private residence whose owners (he's a former manufacturer) have broken with firmly established traditions by making quiet, luxury and beauty available to their guests.

You can choose to live in a Napoleon III room where each piece of furniture, curio or crystal chandelier is the fruit of long searching through antique stores and, above all, of perfect taste. Or, again, in a delightful little garden-level apartment done in Romantic style, with an inner stairway leading to the bedroom.

Remarkably comfortable bathrooms and unobtrusive service go hand-in-hand with this luxury. And there is also the good home cooking to be enjoyed beneath the garden's shady trees.

Seventeen rooms and three apartments. Double rooms: from 90 to 120 francs ($18 to $24), including service, taxes and breakfast. The suites cost from 150 to 180 francs ($30 to $36), taxes and service included. You can park at a garage opposite the hotel (it costs extra, though).

Résidence du Bois, 16 rue Chalgrin (16e), PAS 50.59.

Résidence Foch

In less than two years the Résidence Foch has become one of the best, most elegant little deluxe hotels in Paris, patronized mostly by foreign diplomats and businessmen.

The fifteen suites in this middle-class apartment building, hidden away on a quiet street a few steps from the Bois de Boulogne, are all in perfect taste: pretty reproductions of antique furniture, damask-covered walls, pastel carpets, ultramodern bathrooms. On the top floor there is a marvelous duplex with a little kitchen that enables one to be "at home away from home."

Every detail bespeaks the greatest refinement as, for example, the "jewel box" coat room covered with flowered wallpaper and fitted with completely gilded appointments.

The very well trained staff is worthy of the "great houses" on the avenue Foch. Parking is no problem. Television on request at no extra charge.

The hotel practices the all-inclusive rate system (with breakfast). Singles cost 100 francs ($20), doubles, 140 francs ($28). A duplex rents for 250 francs ($50).

Résidence Foch, 10 rue Marbeau (16e), PAS 92.10.

Madeleine, Concorde, Vendôme, Palais Royal (I*er*, 2*e*, 8*e*)
LUXURY HOTELS
- -

Continental

A mecca for the Wehrmacht high command during the Occupation, the Continental was slumbering beneath the glorious dust of its golden age. It was brought back to life by a Dutch concern and, more recently, by the American Intercontinental, and is at present putting on a bright new face and once again becoming one of the pleasantest luxury hotels in Paris. Big projects are in the works, including the creation of one hundred fifty new rooms and several restaurants. But they very wisely intend to preserve the hotel's own antiquated charm which dates from the *Belle Epoque*. The great Garnier salon, brimming with gold and stuccowork and the twin brother of the one Garnier designed for the Paris Opera, was gone over with a fine-tooth comb but fortunately will escape the wrecker's ball. As for the interior garden, with its fountain and its border of Corinthian columns, it is an oasis of peace and coolness only a few steps away from the noisy rue de Rivoli.

Not all the rooms have been renovated as yet, but they soon will be. Make sure to ask for one of the new rooms when you make your reservation.

Single rooms: 95 to 105 francs. Doubles: 120 to 175 francs

Suites: 250 to 305 francs. Plus 15 percent service charge. All the rooms are with bath.

Continental, 3 rue de Castiglione (Ier), OPE 18.00.

Crillon

A lot of Parisians still think that the Crillon, with its authentic, sumptuous old exterior, is a government building like its neighbor, the Ministry of the Navy. But, honestly, it's a hotel. Since it once was privately owned, however, its interior gardens, delightful balconies overlooking place de la Concorde, high ceilings, well-trained staff and discreet management still preserve an old-fashioned, peaceful dignity which puts it at the opposite end of the scale from a certain unfortunate trend toward futuristic hostelry. And a clientele of refined Americans appreciates this very much.

The Hotel Crillon, like the perfectly symmetrical Ministry of the Navy, was erected in 1758 by Jacques-Ange Gabriel. Beneath this exterior lurk a few ground-floor drawing rooms which could well do with a fresh coat of paint. The furniture and décor are pompous and without any real grace. But everything is gradually being done over. And since the Louis XVI style wasn't as vulnerable as Louis XV to the overzealous chisels and lathes of 1900's cabinetmakers, the rooms have an atmosphere of intimate elegance and good taste. And then there is the view of the most beautiful plaza in the world.

The Crillon has the most modern sanitation of all the luxury hotels in Paris, even if a few little singles do have only a shower. All the bathrooms are recent (five years old at the most), pleasant, well equipped and perfectly comfortable, done in an uninspired but unaggressive pale green. The bed linen, heating and towels are beyond reproach. The racket from place de la Concorde will wake you up early in spite of the enormously thick walls, except in the rooms which open onto the charming inner courts.

With the exception of the annoying proof-of-identity ritual at the front desk, both reception and service are faultless: extremely punctual, affable and intelligent. The staff is not above accepting tips.

The many banquets and receptions make the Crillon somewhat of a circus at times, but the basic clientele has a good deal of class. The immediate proximity of the English and American embassies attracts quantities of Anglo-Saxons who are not necessarily terribly well-to-do but are always well bred. The bewitching Concorde and the hotel's central location in the luxury shopping district do the rest, and foreigners make up the great majority of its clients. They include a lot of diplomats and official guests of the government, as well as Charlie Chaplin, Gloria Swanson, the King of Morocco, etc.

The grill is pleasant and has interesting food, while the bar is a convenient meeting place for Embassy people. The little American bar in the basement, with walls covered in brown imitation leather, is intimate and sometimes affords glimpses of pretty women. The breakfast coffee is somewhat bitter and the butter in rather short supply, but it is served exactly on time.

Two hundred and twenty-eight rooms and suites. A single with shower, bath and toilet is 100 francs ($20); a double (with the same facilities) costs 165 francs ($33) and a one- or two-person suite comes to 180 to 420 francs ($36 to $84). The off-season rates may be 10 to 20 percent lower. There is a 25 percent charge for service and taxes; 6.50 francs for breakfast. Free parking (on place de la Concorde), hairdresser, ticket bureau, currency exchange.

Crillon, 10 place de la Concorde (8e), ANJ 24.10.

Lotti

An elegant, recently modernized palace, much appreciated by the Italian and British aristocracies. The rooms come in a wide variety of styles and dimensions but are all extremely comfortable. The service is courteous and attentive. The Cadran bar is a favorite haunt of international businessmen.

Rates: singles, 70 to 90 francs ($14 to $18); doubles, 100 to 160 francs ($20 to $32), plus 25 percent for service and taxes.

Lotti, 7–9 rue Castiglione (Ier), RIC 93.84.

Ritz

This isn't a hotel, not even a ritzy one. It's a monument.

"One's first impression," wrote Léon-Paul Fargue, "is that the Ritz is a tranquil palace where nothing more serious than an incorrect place setting or dropped fork ever disturbs the ritual. An almost Buddhic no man's land with maître d's gliding about like the perfect priests of an absolutely superior religion."

This is the only hotel fortunate enough to be located, first of all, on one of the most beautiful squares in the world, and second, in a historical residence. For the Ritz happens to occupy the Hotel de Gramont, which was built in 1705 for Anne de Gramont ("an old trollop," according to Saint-Simon; she was a kleptomaniac too). You rather expect to find signed furniture, luxurious tapestries and prize curios inside. But a hotel owner, even if his name is Ritz, is no Maecenas.

The lobby and dining rooms are furnished with reproductions of Louis XV pieces, which are solid enough but nothing special from the point of view of craftsmanship. It would also be nice to see a few attractive paintings and some less insipid carpets (even copies) in the downstairs rooms (the lovely Psyche salon is an exception).

The shopping arcade, where luxury stores display their wares in dismal showcases, cries out for some serious rethinking.

On the other hand, Monsieur Ritz's taste has been used to extraordinary effect in the interior garden, which is just as luxuriant in winter as in summer. The most beautiful suites are on the second floor, on the place Vendôme side. They are listed by the Bureau of Fine Arts and they deserve the honor. One of them, done in First Empire "Egyptian" style (and this time everything is authentic) is worthy of a museum. But we think the most charming is little suite "F" (for one person), which contains marvelous Louis XVI paneling.

As for the rooms, there is nothing sumptuous about the white-painted wooden furniture, copper bedsteads, engraved bronze wall sconces and ruffled lampshades, but they do have a lot of charm. This is largely due to the soft colors (champagne, pink champagne or azure), the quality of the lighting and the perfect condition of the furniture and fabrics (the carpet is a little worn, however).

The beds are luxurious, the linen impeccable. The wardrobe closets are huge, but the hangers are not wide enough. Many of the rooms interconnect and noise sometimes travels from one room to another despite all precautions. One of us was able to catch every word of a stormy telephone conversation conducted one midnight by a Spanish woman next-door. No radio or television. The bathrooms are being done over. As well they might. The rooms are overheated, in our opinion, but it's true that the richer one gets, the chillier one becomes.

This is the "lap of luxury": five hundred employees are on constant call for the two hundred clients. And if that's not enough, the latter can bring along their own help. Sixty servants' rooms are set aside for this purpose, each with a buzzer directly connecting it to the master quarters. And to service the great second-floor suites, the servants' rooms have been installed close by, to reduce the distance separating the domestics from their dear masters.

All the same, we couldn't get a tie pressed at 6:58 P.M. The valet service stops at 6:30.

"This peaceful Ritz," to quote Fargue once more, "so well designed to bring psychological repose to the great of the world, is actually abuzz with novels, adorned with pathetic biographies." Like Maxim's, the Ritz has witnessed a parade of the world's leading lights, from Marcel Proust to Coco Chanel (who has lived there since . . . a very long time ago), from the Begum to Barbara Hutton. Besides, you don't stop at the Ritz; you rise to it.

The oldest client is undoubtedly that lady who moved into a luxury suite before World War I and whom increasing age and declining funds have now brought to a little room under the eaves.

The era of great eccentrics may be past, but all the same an American woman was seen landing at the Ritz a few months ago followed by forty trunks—trunks, that is, not suitcases.

The most surprising thing about these clients, who have the means to indulge their every whim, is their exemplary kindness and discretion, as all the Ritz staff will unanimously agree. But that's also the miracle of the Ritz.

Rates: singles, 110 to 160 francs; doubles, 150 to 200 francs. Suites from 240 francs to 785 francs, plus 15 percent. (Servants' rooms: 16 to 38 francs.) Breakfast: 9.50 francs.

Ritz, 15 place Vendôme (Ier), OPE 28.30.

Meurice

One of the finest palaces in Paris, patronized by the international upper crust. In the last few years this hotel, which used to be the favorite of all the crowned heads, has undertaken extensive renovations. Many of the rooms have been tastefully redecorated and all the bathrooms have been redone. They are in pink marble, ultramodern, ingeniously arranged: in a word, superb. Only the suites have a view of the Tuilerie Gardens.

One of the latter, the immense Number 108 is historic. This is where General von Choltitz, Governor of Paris during the German Occupation, had his office. Before that, King Alphonse XIII of Spain lived out his exile in the same rooms, and today Salvador Dali and Mrs. Florence Gould fight over it whenever they are passing through the capital.

There are two hundred twenty-five rooms. Singles from 80 to 100 francs ($16 to $20) out of season (November to March), 100 to 120 francs ($20 to $24) in season. Doubles: 120 to 140 francs ($24 to $28) out of season, 160 to 200 francs ($32 to $40) in season. Suites: 180 to 340 francs ($36 to $68) in the off-season, 220 to 480 francs ($44 to $96) in season. There is a 15 percent service supplement.

Meurice, 228 rue de Rivoli (Ier), OPE 32.40.

Madeleine, Concorde, Vendôme, Palais Royal (Ier, 2e, 8e)
VERY COMFORTABLE

Castiglione

The Castiglione enjoys a good location in the middle of all the Faubourg Saint-Honoré's great boutiques. It was renovated three years ago and has a rather modern décor. There are one hundred and ten somewhat drab, but well-cared-for rooms.

Rates: single with bath, 85 francs ($17); double, 98 francs ($19.60), all inclusive.

Castiglione, 40 rue du Faubourg Saint-Hororé (8e), ANJ 07.50.

Castille

Well situated between rue du Faubourg Saint-Honoré and the *Grands Boulevards,* it is highly esteemed by foreign tourists. The rooms are quite large, but the décor is uninspired. There is a pretty flowered terrace.

Rates: 34 to 65 francs ($6.80 to $13) for one person and 39 to 90 francs ($7.80 to $18) for two, service and taxes included.

Castille, 37 rue Cambon (Ier), OPE 48.20.

Louvois

An excellent hotel, comfortable and tasteful, situated on a charming square in front of the National Library. The rooms (one hundred and sixty-five) provide an entertaining panorama of styles from Louis XV to 1925. Some twenty-odd rooms have magnificent, ultramodern, ultrarefined bathrooms; the others, vast and well kept up, are older. The service is attentive and friendly. There is a pleasant bar and pretty little drawing rooms adorned with antique furniture and paintings.

Rates: singles, 70 francs ($14); doubles, 102.50 francs ($20.50), including bath, taxes, service and breakfast.

Louvois, I rue Lulli (2e), RIC 64.41.

Regina

An island of peace and calm lies hidden right in the middle of the uproar and traffic jams on the rue de Rivoli, with nothing but a gilded sign to call it to the attention of tourists. The Hotel Regina, located above the arcade just in front of the statue of Jeanne d'Arc, is the ideal refuge for anyone who loves the scenery of Paris.

From the upper floors, and especially from the dormer rooms with their delightful little balconies set into the mansard roof, you survey a wonderful panorama stretching from the Tuilerie Gardens to the Eiffel Tower. Suspended thus in the sky, customers of the Regina can play at the *vie de Bohème* while continuing to enjoy the services of a four-star hotel.

Unfortunately, not all the one hundred and fifty-four rooms or suites face the Tuileries (but at least you're assured of peace and quiet), but they do all share the cushioned comfort of this excellent hotel. The antique furniture, crystal chandeliers, paneling and Louis XV elevator cage combine to create an atmosphere which may seem a little antiquated at times, but the peaceful warmth comes as a pleasant surprise after the hectic rue de Rivoli.

Rates: single room with bath, 90 francs ($18); double, 109 francs ($21.80); suites, 160 to 220 francs ($32 to $44). Prices include breakfast, taxes and service.

Regina, 2 place des Pyramides (Ier), OPE 74.00.

Roblin

This homey, somewhat sad hotel, a few steps away from the Madeleine, has a predominantly English clientele. The rooms are spacious and very well kept up; some are furnished with extremely handsome Empire period pieces. There are a few beautiful modern baths.

Rates: single with bath, 70 francs ($14); double, 85 francs ($17); breakfast, taxes and service included.

Roblin, 6 rue Chauveau-Lagarde (8e), ANJ 57.00.

Vendôme

The Ritz's little neighbor also has a view of the most beautiful square in the world, even if you have to hang out of the window to see it. But you have to pay for it: 86.25 francs ($17.25) for a single with bath and 130 francs ($26) for a double (all inclusive). In addition to the view, this hotel also has a very pleasant old-fashioned charm, huge rooms furnished with reproductions and efficient service. The clientele is quite elegant.

Vendôme, 1 place Vendôme (Ier), OPE 48.24.

Le Marais (3^e)

PLAIN BUT COMFORTABLE

Parc-Royal

Although the Marais may shine for its private mansions and glimpses of Old Paris, its hotel resources certainly don't offer any particular attraction for tourists. Up to the present, the Hotel du Parc-Royal on the rue de Turenne has been the only place where one could spend the night without the risk of being eaten alive. This is why Mme Cortès's venture, which would be banal in almost any other section, is almost an event in this one.

When, some two years ago, this energetic hostess ransomed a *pension* with decay oozing from every crack, she resolved to clean it, repaint it, modernize the plumbing, buy all new bed linens, in short, make it habitable for clients familiar with the uses of soap.

This little hotel—which is also called the Parc-Royal—will not, of course, be much of a thrill for tourists accustomed to the splendors of four-star establishments. On the other hand, people satisfied with very modest but spic-and-span accommodations will find it enchanting to sleep in an outbuilding of a sixteenth-century seignorial mansion, a few steps away from the Musée Carnavalet, National Archives and place des Vosges (16 francs for one person or 22 francs for two—$3.20 or $4.40, breakfast and taxes included). There are seventeen rooms.

Parc-Royal, 17 rue du Parc-Royal (3e), TUR 84.50.

Montmartre (18e)

Terrass-Hotel

A room in the Terrass-Hotel gives you a simultaneous view of the Panthéon, Invalides, Eiffel Tower and Arch of Triumph. Don't go scanning the heavens for a skyscraper which has sprung up overnight. The Terrass-Hotel has been around since 1912, and is located in a rather remote section where the Butte Montmartre first starts upward (which explains its elevation), just behind the immense Montmartre cemetery, which guarantees its inviolable view.

But this extraordinary panorama isn't the only pleasant feature of the Terrass's hundred and eight rooms and thirteen suites, all recently redone with baths, showers and toilets. The owner, Monsieur Hurand, hasn't felt it necessary to give in to the craze for Napoleon III wallpaper, antique furniture, copies of *objets d'art* or ball-fringed curtains. The strictly modern décor is all but invisible, a proof of any hotel owner's respect for his clients' taste.

As for the restaurant and bar, their plaid carpets, paneled walls and large fireplaces are much more reminiscent of a manor house than of the icy opulence of a luxury hotel.

Rates: single, 65 francs ($13); doubles from 80 to 90 francs ($16 to $18); suites, 100 francs ($20); breakfast, taxes and service included.

Terrass-Hotel, 12 rue Joseph-de-Maistre (18e), MON 17.69.

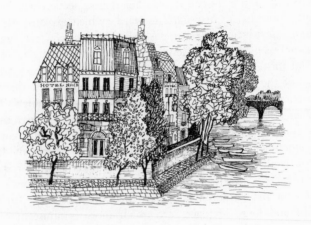

LEFT BANK

Eiffel Tower–Invalides (*15^e*, *7^e*)
LUXURY HOTELS
- -

Paris Hilton

There are two kinds of Americans: the ones who refuse to stay anywhere but the Hilton and the ones who wouldn't touch it with a ten-foot pole. Obviously, our sympathies lie with the second kind. But let's be honest: even if the service is some times surprising, even if the interior decoration by Raymond Loewy is not very exciting and the food at the "Toit de Paris" is elegantly uninteresting, the rooms, on the other hand, are spacious, comfortable, nicely arranged and quiet, and the meet ing rooms and conference halls are certainly the best equipped of any in Paris.

The prices are about the same as at the Ritz, which, per sonally, gives us something to think about.

Paris Hilton, 18 avenue de Suffren (15e), BRE 92.00.

Saint-Germain-des-Prés, Odéon, Saint-Michel (5ᵉ, 6ᵉ, 7ᵉ)

VERY COMFORTABLE

Cayré

Many artists and writers have followed the lead of Bernanos, Nikos Kazantzakis and Pablo Casals by stopping at this excellent, traditional hotel in the heart of the publishing district. Furthermore, most of the clients—both French and foreign—are old regulars (some of thirty years' standing) who appreciate Monsieur and Mme Cayré's warm, friendly welcome, the attentive service, and the rooms, which are a little old-fashioned but endowed with very modern baths.

Rates: singles with bath, 62.50 francs ($12.50); doubles, 80 francs ($16); taxes, service and breakfast included.

Cayré, 4 boulevard Raspail (7ᵉ), BAB 10.82.

Le Colbert

It's not every day that you can contemplate Notre-Dame from bed, but the rooms in the left wing of the Colbert, on rue de l'Hotel-Colbert, have just such a treat in store for clients. The hotel façade was completely restored under the supervision of the Bureau of Fine Arts and fully preserves its period authenticity. The building dates principally from the eighteenth century, but certain parts of it go back as far as 1500. The present garden occupies the site of an animal hospital supported by the Duke of Windsor.

Each of the Colbert's forty-two rooms has double sound-proofing and either a shower or bathtub, with separate lavatory. The rooms are charming and simple, but tastefully arranged: toile de Jouy wallpaper, large, recessed wardrobes and glass wall cabinets with stylized Louis XVI motifs, bathroom tiles which match the color of each room. The sheets are fine and smooth—unfortunately not always the case in many hotels, which still use ordinary stiff, scratchy sheets.

Rates: singles, 60 francs ($12); doubles, 80 francs ($16), including taxes, service and breakfast.

Le Colbert, 7 rue de l'Hotel-Colbert (5ᵉ), ODE 72.58.

Grand Hotel Littré

This hotel was leased to the United States Army up until last year and has just been completely renovated. Its one hundred twenty very quiet rooms are a stone's throw from Montparnasse; each is cheerful, comfortable and comes with bath. The lobby and salons are quite luxurious.

Rates: singles cost 62 francs ($12.40), doubles, 87 francs ($17.40). Service, taxes and breakfast are included.

Grand Hotel Littré, 9 rue Littré (6ᵉ), BAB 71.74.

L'Hôtel

Artists and esthetes, Romeos and Casanovas will erect a statue in their hearts to Guy-Louis Duboucheron.

After sixteen months of work, this former actor has just opened the most delicate, most precious, most discreet haven on either bank for them. It's the old Hôtel d'Alsace, a stone's throw from the Ecole des Beaux Arts.

Professors, writers looking for a publisher, painters somewhat low on funds used to like to stay in this classical country-German hotel where Oscar Wilde died in 1900. The new owner now hopes to attract the same customers (who have, however, "made it," since the price of a room varies between 130 and 250 francs) to his snug, secret and supremely refined oasis.

One has to admit that they didn't pinch any pennies. The old single-story structure, which the great architect Ledoux erected in the garden of the La Rochefoucauld mansion at the end of the eighteenth century, had extra floors added to it in 1835. It was almost entirely rebuilt by an American architect, Robin Westbrook, and totally redecorated by Guy-Louis Duboucheron. The "well," which runs through all five floors and used to remind one of a prison courtyard (it's the old rotunda from Ledoux's pavilion, with the walls built up), was reconstructed in the spirit of triumphant Directoire, complete with stuccowork, pilasters, medallions and rounded vaults.

All of the twenty-five rooms laid out around this rotunda are done in linen velvet in colors ranging from crimson to pine green, from "blush pink" to "leopardskin." And every room has a refrigerator, direct telephone line (there are even extensions in the bathrooms, themselves paneled with colored marble), television set and AM-FM radio. The rooms are small but the sumptuous fabrics and quality of the furniture (everything is an antique) make them jewelboxes of exceptional luxury and charm. And everyone can let his own taste determine the style and color scheme which suit him best, from the most sober to the most lavish.

The cellars have been made into private drawing rooms where one can eat and drink until 2:00 A.M. The garden, equipped with a pool that is illuminated at night, constitutes an unlooked-for island of greenery in the midst of the old houses. And the street side offers passers-by its trophies and garlands, which have been restored according to the canons of the late eighteenth century.

That's still not all. This dream hotel also has two suites available on the fifth floor, overlooking the Church of Saint-Germain-des-Prés and the Ecole des Beaux Arts, where multimillionaires (the suites cost 350 and 400 francs per day) can cultivate the heady sensation of being real "locals." And lovers of the unusual can ask for the room furnished with wild mirrored bed, armchair and secretary that Jean-Gabriel Domergue designed for Mistinguett some forty years ago, or else the room in which Oscar Wilde died and which Guy-Louis Duboucheron has just redecorated with numerous mementos of the author.

L'Hôtel, 13 rue des Beaux-Arts (6e), MED 89.20.

Isly

This will never be a luxury residence, and you won't see any antiques, or even reproductions, but the walls and ceilings of the rooms (of which there are thirty) are entirely covered with delightful flowered wallpaper. Each has its own bathroom or shower, or at the very least, a comfortable lavatory. The furniture is nothing to get excited about; it is sensibly modern and functional. Anyhow, you hardly notice it; the main thing is the very pleasant atmosphere which reigns in these rooms, thanks to the colors used in the fabrics and carpets as well as to the carefully thought out lighting.

It's marvelously located, since it's on Rue Jacob. Reception and service are very friendly, and they spare no effort to make your life easier. Thus, even if the hotel doesn't serve meals, it's always possible to avoid going to bed on an empty stomach. Paris really should have lots of little hotels like this.

Rates: single room with lavatory, 30 francs ($6); double with bath, 50 francs ($10). Tucked under the eaves there is an enchanting little suite consisting of bedroom, living room and bath, for 100 francs ($20). All prices include taxes, breakfast and service.

Isly, 29 rue Jacob (6ᵉ), DAN 64.41.

Lys

A picturesque, inexpensive hotel in tiptop condition, in the heart of the Latin Quarter. When Monsieur Walter Steffen bought this little seventeenth-century house more than fifteen years ago, the roof had caved in, the walls were cracked, the windows falling off their hinges. A real wreck. In a few years the hovel became a very decent hotel: shower or lavatory in all twenty-one rooms, each of which is decorated in a different, but usually rustic style. Students and foreign tourists, fascinated by its nearness to boulevard Saint-Michel, pass the address along in whispers. Naturally, you have to reserve your room several weeks in advance.

Rates: singles from 17 to 30 francs ($3.40 to $6); doubles from 24 to 35 francs ($4.80 to $7); taxes, service and breakfast included.

Lys, 23 rue Serpente (6ᵉ), DAN 97.57.

Nice et des Beaux-Arts

Deep in the heart of Oklahoma or the wilds of Scotland, the native who is setting off for Paris will always find a compatriot to tell him: "I know a terrific little hotel over there. It's the Hotel de Nice on rue des Beaux-Arts. Ask for Mademoiselle Biguet."

Among Anglo-Saxons this hotel is a Parisian institution almost as renowned as the Ritz or the Eiffel Tower. It's one of those famous "little hotels" which often are more instrumental in giving a city a friendly reputation than the luxury palaces.

The Hotel de Nice has belonged to the same owner, Monsieur Oliveaux, for thirty-three years. But the soul of the place is Mademoiselle Biguet. This lady "of a certain age" is all smiles, and is responsible for the simple, unostentatious setting which gives Anglo-Saxon tourists the treasured feeling of being at home.

A big fire blazes away in the lobby. The armchairs are strictly standard, but a few handsome old pieces in a cozy country style plunge the Major or elderly American lady into a homey atmosphere. The rooms are simply but tastefully decorated. The walls are covered with pretty wallpaper and the curtains and bedspreads are made of the same fabric (red, blue or green satin, or brocade). A genuine antique—chiffonier, commode, etc.—lends a discreet nobility to each of the thirty-five rooms. And the welcome and service are nothing less than perfect. Mlle Biguet lavishes stores of kindness and attention on every guest. She'll fix you a hard-boiled egg at midnight, have flowers in your room when you arrive, drive you to the station or airport if necessary.

A feature which is rare in France, and extremely convenient: the Hotel de Nice rents out studios with bath and kitchen in a nearby building. These are independent of the hotel but benefit from all its services (prices start at 1,000 francs—$200—per month).

A single room with bath costs 55 francs ($11); doubles with bath, 65 francs ($13); taxes, service and breakfast are all included.

Nice et des Beaux-Arts, 4 *bis* rue des Beaux-Arts (6e); DAN 54.05.

Saints-Pères

In an old mansion next to Saint-Germain-des-Prés, this hotel has just been entirely renovated. Uninspired modern furniture. Pleasant flowered patio. Forty rooms, all with bath.

Rates: singles, 60 francs ($12); doubles, 65 to 75 francs ($13 to $15); taxes, service and breakfast included.

Saints-Pères, 65 rue des Saints-Pères (6e), LIT 44.45.

Saint-Simon

When, in 1954, Mme Grouillé transformed a gloomy *pension* into an adorable residence filled with flowers and old furniture, she never even thought of advertising. Two or three American couples who happened to stay there did it for her. When they got back to the United States they gave their friends such an enthusiastic description of the Saint-Simon that, the following year, the hotel had to turn people away and soon had made a name for itself in the American press. From then on, all trans-atlantic intellectuals and diplomats—from Edward Albee (*Who's Afraid of Virginia Woolf?*) to Mr. Bruce, the Ambas-sador in London—book rooms here when they are stopping over in Paris.

You don't generally "stop over" at the Hotel Saint-Simon, however. You stay a month, two months, six months, some-times even the entire year, like that seventy-year-old American woman who takes courses at the Alliance Française . . .

Demi-pension is obligatory, but it's a duty which is far from painful: we can testify that the food is excellent. And the guests are delighted at this chance to get to know one another.

The thirty-six rooms are furnished with antiques (Mme Grouillé's husband is in the business) and endowed with every comfort. Some of them cost only 20 francs ($4) but these are almost impossible to get. The others run to around 45 francs ($9), which includes breakfast and lunch (or dinner). And 60 francs ($12) entitles you to one of the charming little suites with windows opening onto a garden.

Saint-Simon, 14 rue Saint-Simon (7ᵉ), LIT 35.66.

Saumur

Even if he's not native to the profession, M. de Kergolay is a native of the *quartier*. He was born and lived for a long time in a little town house which his mother owned on this very rue de Bellechasse, and his desire to acquire a hotel in the vicinity was born one day after some especially bitter appraisals of the impoverished state of the French hotel business in general and Parisian hotels in particular.

His wish was not long in coming true, for he found the

Hôtel de Saumur and immediately bought it. All that he kept of this run-down old rooming house were the walls and the signboard. All the interior walls were knocked down and the room layouts completely redesigned, after which the decorators set to work with instructions not to scrimp on the quality of the fabrics or furniture.

The latter all comes from the London flea markets, and was restored in Paris. At its worst, all of this furniture—roll-top desks, barrel chairs, gueridons and tables—at least has the enormous advantage of going unnoticed.

Thick carpets cover the floors of the rooms, thus furthering the concern for soundproofing which provided for plate-glass windowpanes a quarter-inch thick and particularly effective metal joints until such time as double windows are installed. Curtains in rooms facing the street are lined with separate black veiling which enables one to obtain complete darkness. It is then that the remarkably installed and calculated lighting manages to disorient us enough to make us think that we are no longer in a hotel but almost in our room at home. Nicely framed colored engravings hang from walls covered with painted canvas or handsome wallpaper.

M. de Kergolay has tried to turn his place into a little family-style hotel that matches the luxury and service of the best "palaces." His prices will therefore come as less of a surprise if you keep this ambition in mind: 60 francs for a single with shower, 70 francs for a double, and 75 francs for a double with bath. Suites cost 100 francs (120 francs for three people, with sofa-bed), and all these prices include taxes and breakfast.

Saumur, 22 rue de Bellechasse (7e), INV 43.27.

Scandinavia

Way back in the seventeenth century there was a Scandinavian Inn admirably situated on the broad rue de Tournon between Saint-Germain-des-Prés and the Luxemburg Gardens. It was restored in 1960 and today is a charming residence with a long picture window, broad beams and heavy stones, antique furniture (mostly Louis XIII), thick green carpets and velvet hangings, the product of very studied but sober taste.

There are five floors of rooms (no elevator), all of which are furnished with antiques and beds made either of wrought iron or very beautifully carved wood. Pictures of "ancestors" adorn the walls, and the lighting fixtures are concealed in weapons suspended from the beams. The rich velvet hangings lend warmth to the well-known chilliness of this style and the wooden beams do not in the least detract from the stateliness of the décor.

You reach the top floor by means of a little stairway which leads to two charming rooms, each with a little flowered balcony. All the twenty-two rooms have extremely modern bathrooms with private toilets, so the rates are basically rather reasonable: a double costs 55 francs ($11), including taxes and (very friendly) service. No restaurant or meal service in the rooms.

Scandinavia, 27 rue de Tournon (6e), MED 45.20.

Part V

SHOPPING

We don't claim that this section will give you a detailed analysis of shopping in Paris. We have preferred to limit ourselves to those shops and articles which are most likely to interest American tourists, either because of their prices or their uniqueness. Here as elsewhere we have tried to point out the best places we know of, which doesn't mean that the others are bad.

Miniature cars

Multi-Sports

No garage could ever compete with Monsieur Greilsamer's store. Almost a thousand different automobiles, from the Roaring Twenties Panhard to Jim Clark's Lotus, make up the fabulous stable of small-scale models which he offers his clientele of car buffs. Some of these are real collector's items, like Hitler's armored Mercedes, four inches long, which is well worth a trifling 1,000 francs ($200).

Multi-Sports, 94 boulevard de Sebastopol (3ᵉ), ARC 11.25.

Antique and fancy jewelry

Boutique des Bijoux Anciens

This is a classical jewelry shop with green silk on the walls and Louis XVI armchairs. The only difference is that Monsieur Sartorio sells nothing but antique jewelry.

He'll explain how to recognize the various periods. The inner rims of eighteenth-century rings are overlaid with gold, which prevents the stones from showing through. He'll show you the First Empire's cameos and precious stones. Very light-weight jewelry during the Restoration (silver was scarce); then, the richest period of all, Napoleon III, characterized by its enamelwork and the diamonds and rubies in settings hand-woven from different kinds of gold. Last of all, the little rings, lockets, ropes and "mourning jewelry" of the 1900's.

All of these miniature works of art can be found at Monsieur Sartorio's, at prices ranging from 30 francs ($6) for baby brace-lets (some 1900's rings cost no more than 100 francs—$20) to 1,000 francs ($200) and beyond for exquisite rings set with fine stones.

> Boutique des Bijoux Anciens, 16 boulevard Raspail (7ᵉ), LIT 51.56.

L'Eternel Retour

In her little two-year-old boutique Mme Moalic fans the flames of her customers' desires with antique jewelry (one hundred years old): rococo Napoleon III rings, brooches set with semiprecious stones, coral bracelets, etc., and other, more opulent pieces which estate auctions have placed in her hands: a watch circled with brilliants; a sapphire and diamond brooch.

> L'Eternel Retour, 37 rue de Ponthieu (8ᵉ), ELY 24.47.

Galérie du Siècle

The whole world knows the name Torun. The silver jewelry —rings, pendants, collars—designed by this tall, beautiful Swedish girl has indeed circled the globe.

> Galérie du Siècle, 168 boulevard Saint-Germain (6ᵉ), DAN 98.09.

Huguette Leroy

The sign over this minuscule shop reads "Parfumerie". But even though the owner, Mme Huguette Leroy, continues to sell the great names in perfume, for more than twenty years her real specialty has been fanciful jewelry made from semi-precious stones.

In addition to the famous Chanel-style jewelry, which always creates a sensation, Mme Leroy also has very nice copies of designs by great Parisian jewelers.

Huguette Leroy, 50 rue François Ier (8^e), BAL 12.45.

Jacques Gautier

Jacques Gautier's famous necklaces made of enamel set in old silver, men's jewelry, and the electronic diadems and heart which this explorer of new forms presented at New York's "April in Paris" ball.

Jacques Gautier, 36 rue Jacob (6^e), BAB 36.58.

Les Arcades du Marais

Jacques Lacroix's superb modern silver jewelry. (Also see GIFTS, p. 276.)

Les Arcades du Marais, 13 place des Vosges (3^e), TUR 76.03.

Marc Garland

Are men less romantic than they used to be? In any case, Marc Garland—an antique dealer on the rue du Bac—declares they now show less enthusiasm about buying jewelry for their ladyloves. And he thinks the blame must be laid at the feet of the weaker sex, for whom the merits of a refrigerator outweigh those of a lovely stone. This is doubtless because those practical souls aren't familiar with the antique jewelry sold by Marc Garland.

"Modern jewelry is lifeless," he says, "because it passes through the hands of several specialists. But most antique pieces—up until the Revolution—were 'modeled' by a single craftsman, who stamped them with his own individuality."

He has sumptuous jewels, like that Louis XVI watch in the shape of two enamel cherries (one for the watch, the other for perfume), as well as very simple pieces such as little gold rings set with pearls, opals, diamonds, sapphires or rubies (from 100 to 300 francs—$20 to $60), or a bangle bracelet with a baroque pearl set off by two diamonds (a Russian piece from 1830, priced at 1,500 francs—$300). And he has a lover's fervor whenever he describes any of his jewelry to you.

Marc Garland, 23 rue du Bac (7ᵉ), BAB 50.57.

Michel Périnet

Thirty years ago jewelers used to take them apart and melt them down in order to reuse the stones and precious metals. Fashion had absolutely no use for them, and the children of the great ladies of the early 1900's considered them wildly un-wearable old junk.

The rare 1900's jewelry which is still on the market is com-ing into its own again today. Collectors snatch it up at stagger-ing prices. Last summer's international exhibition at Ostend brought together the most beautiful examples, including those owned by Nubar Gulbenkian, who possesses the world's great-est collection.

"It's easy to explain this new fad," says Michel Périnet, one of the leading specialists in antique jewelry in Paris. "In con-temporary jewelry the only thing that counts is the market value of the stones. Wearing a piece of jewelry today amounts to displaying one's wealth. The value of the materials has re-placed the value of craftsmanship.

"What will be left of most modern jewelry? Gold, platinum, pebbles. But in the old days they made beautiful objects, works of art, whose prices depended much more on the quality of the workmanship, the delicacy of the engraving, the use of imagination, than on the cost of the materials.

"Anyone can buy a diamond from a lapidary and stick a setting around it," he adds, "but who will ever make Sarah Bernhardt's bracelet for us again?"

This bracelet is the star of his collection, as it was of the jewelry section in a recent antiques show. Picture an enameled gold serpent, with little pink brilliants and carved opals, wind-ing around your wrist, its head resting on top of your hand, held in position by delicate chains between the fingers.

This unique piece of jewelry, which no woman would dare to wear today, is the dream of every collector. As is the enormous "breastplate" designed by Mucha, which consists of a woman's face crowned with pearls and opals, dripping with clusters of baroque pearls sheathed in gold, each of them different from the rest, with an ivory miniature as a pendant.

"You see," says Michel Périnet, "unlike their successors, the great jewelers of the early nineteen hundreds made no attempt to seek out expensive stones. They mostly used baroque pearls (which today would seem monstrous), opals, enamelwork, ivory. They created radically new, completely original shapes which had no relation to the past. I mean, of course, the great jewelers of the period: Lalique, Fouquet and Vever."

This great creative period lasted only a few years: from 1897 until 1909. As early as 1904, pure Art Nouveau was already tainted by the influence of the Renaissance. And true collector's items were extremely rare even then.

Besides these unique marvels, you can also find little 1900's rings at Michel Périnet's. The design may be a little "impure," but they are still a good value (around 500 francs—$100).

Going back further into the past, Michel Périnet also has Napoleon III and Charles X jewelry (brooches made of quivering flowers, lockets, cameos, lapis lazuli encrusted with roses, etc.).

"When I think that, for some socialites, nothing counts but the market value of their anonymous precious stones!" he says, as he lovingly contemplates these masterpieces of bygone days. "Those poor creatures, thinking jewelry is just another name for money. As if a rock, no matter how costly, could ever rival the creation of a true artist."

Michel Périnet, 26 rue Danielle-Casanova (2ᵉ), OPE 70.78.

Bathroom accessories

Au Bain de Diane

Michel de Lacour—a former art student—has been revolutionizing the art and comfort of bathrooms for several years now. At Au Bain de Diane you'll find incredible two-person bathtubs and a vast line of bronze fixtures hammered and engraved by craftsmen in conformity with seventeenth-century techniques. These taps, shaped like dolphins, swans or fauns' faces, are plated with chrome, silver or gold, and often set with quartz, agate, onyx or lapis lazuli.

Au Bain de Diane, 2 rue de Miromesnil (8e), ANJ 29.73.

Gift shops—French arts and crafts

Instead of buying horrible souvenirs like the Eiffel Towers and other "art" objects to be had on every street corner, concentrate on real handicrafts from the French provinces. Here are a few excellent addresses.

Jacques Anquetil

This man, who expends untold efforts on behalf of French artisans, has created one of the most alluring boutiques in Paris. Everything he sells—enamels, fabrics, jewelry, dolls, etc. —is the work of real craftsmen.

Jacques Anquetil, 258 boulevard Saint-Germain (7e), INV 54.25.

Boutique d'Arts Populaires

Gabriel Largeteau, a former professor in a technical training school, prospected throughout France to put together this collection of Limousin basketwork, Berry earthenware, homespun from Béarn, larchwood articles whittled by Savoyard herdsmen, and all the products, rough or refined, of a great art which is now coming back to life.

Boutique d'Arts Populaires, 5 rue Bréa (6e), ODE 52.74.

Club des Artisans

A faithful, exciting survey of high-class French craftsmanship.

Club des Artisans, 13 rue des Canettes (6e), MED 44.63.

Geneviève Dupeux

Wonderful handwoven fabrics.

Geneviève Dupeux, 3 rue de Tournon (6e), DAN 25.71.

Boutique Jansen

It's been ten years since Jansen, the great antique dealer and decorator on the rue Royale, first had the idea of opening an antique and gift boutique, which is the most marvelous gift shop in Paris.

Don't be frightened by the name. March right into Jansen's, cross two superbly furnished salons and go up the few steps leading to the large room set aside for this shop. By "shop" Jansen means a collection of small furnishings and curios of all categories and prices, from the simplest (a 10-franc—$2—ashtray, for example), to the most sumptuous.

Princess Caetani, who has managed the shop since it opened, spends a good part of the year traveling here, there and everywhere, as far away as Africa and the Far East. She brings back "finds" from each of the countries she visits. These often represent a combination of her imagination and the skills of local artisans, who then create exclusive models for the Jansen boutique.

The shop can't be put into any definite category. It isn't austere; it isn't kooky. But there is no doubt about its faultless taste.

It has lots of practical things for a man's office, a boat, a country home, a newly decorated room, etc. Little antique furnishings or handsome reproductions. Engravings, old boxes made of horn, wood or silver, decorated papier-mâché trays, andirons, wooden chests, ceramics, mugs, lamps, sconces, crystal, silverware, etc.

In conclusion, we'd say that you're always sure to find the right gift at Jansen's, even if it's an inexpensive one.

Boutique Jansen, 9 rue Royale (8e), ANJ 65.35.

Boutique du Palais-Royal

Beneath the arches on the garden side of the Palais Royal, Mme Anna Joliet, the vibrant, imaginative owner of the Boutique du Palais-Royal, presents all sorts of unusual or zany objects: kaleidoscopes, bottle-imps, etc.

> Boutique du Palais-Royal, 9 rue de Beaujolais (Ier), GUT 28.22. Open every day from 10 A.M. to 7 P.M. (with the exception of Monday mornings).

Deyrolle

Ever since the thirties, when people got the idea of using the beauties of nature to decorate the most sophisticated apartments, it has been impossible to keep track of all the aesthetes with growing piles of rare or unusual minerals in their living rooms.

Thus it was that, in the space of a few decades, Deyrolle's— which for over a century had been exclusively concerned with supplying schools and colleges—became one of the privileged sources for fashionable decorators.

Everyone will find his heart's delight here in the vast rooms chock-full of rough or polished shells, exotic stuffed birds, rare butterflies and, especially, minerals.

The assiduous patronage of Dali (for rhinoceros horns), couturier Yves Saint-Laurent or painter Bernard Buffet hasn't seemed a sufficient reason for the manager, Georges Groult-Deyrolle, to inflate his prices. "We're not antique dealers," he says.

> Deyrolle, 46 rue du Bac (7^e), LIT 81.93. Open every day but Monday, from 9:00 to 12:30 and from 2:00 to 6:30.

Diptyque

Desmond Knox Leet, Christiane Montadre and Yves Cou-slant sell lots of different things—all of which they make themselves—in this quiet, charming little shop. The very pretty hand-painted fabrics decorating the walls, for example. But everything's pretty here, from the kaleidoscopes to the dragon-shaped kites, passing through the engravings, pomanders (oranges stuck with cloves) and rose-petal sachets.

> Diptyque, 34 boulevard Saint-Germain (5e), ODE 88.90.

L'Epi d'Or

This used to be a charming bakery. The décor hasn't changed, but instead of bread they now sell an assortment of cute, old-fashioned little objects (both antiques and reproductions) for decorating a table or bathroom.

L'Epi d'Or, 7 rue Saint-Jacques (5e), MED 08.47.

La Gadgetière; À London

Marianne Frey, the daughter of a Minister and herself the Empress of Gadgets, has thousands of more or less useful, zany "thingamabobs" which, to our great surprise, often turn out to be French. The president of the famous New York store Hammacher-Schlemmer recently admitted that about 70 percent of the gadgets sold in New York come from Europe (France and Germany); all the Americans do is develop and "patent" them.

La Gadgetière, 1 rue Georges-Bizet (corner of avenue Marceau) (16e), POI 61.31. Right next to La Gadgetière is À London— also run by Marianne Frey—where you can find kicky English objects: alarm clocks without hands, dishtowel aprons, etc. À London, 1 rue Goethe (16e), POI 61.31.

Lubin

This great *parfumeur* on the rue Royale has amazing selection of antique bottles and precious old boxes, as well as fantastic scented raw-silk scarves, printed in very soft shades, and flannel cloths, also scented, which, when slipped beneath a pile of linen, will keep it fragrant for an entire year.

Lubin, 11 rue Royale (8e), ANJ 41.72.

Janie Pradier

The great specialist in those "little nothings" which add a touch of unwonted gaiety to everyday life: dolls for grownups, pillows hand-embroidered with irresistible 1900's characters, "touchstones" for nervous businessmen, paper lanterns shaped like animals, etc.

Janie Pradier, 78 rue de Seine (6e), ODE 37.47 and 31 rue des Poissonniers, Neuilly-sur-Seine, MER 39.00.

Pulcinella

Antique objects, jewelry, dresses and handwoven fabrics in a cute little store.

Pulcinella, 10 rue Vignon (9ᵉ), OPE 95.01.

Rigaud

A pretty shop full of useful presents and little antique curios, generally English.

Rigaud, 51 rue François Iᵉʳ (8ᵉ), BAL 20.70.

Saint-Gill

Gérald de Eynde strokes the long-grained Morocco leathers in his little store on avenue Mozart, delightedly opens an enormous stationery chest, manipulates the drawers, reveals its false bottom for secret documents, and, with controlled lyricism, enumerates the thousand visible and invisible beauties of all his leather objects. "When you see such wonders," says he, "what does price matter?"

Of course, his florentined desk appointments (blotters, note pads, stamp pads, cigar boxes, etc.), boxes, travel kits, custom-made suitcases (for around 5,000 francs—$1,000), silver or vermeil articles, are intended only for very wealthy customers. And they, moreover, have to be able to appreciate these luxury gifts, executed by peerless craftsmen.

Saint-Gill, 18 avenue Mozart (16ᵉ), BAG 97.77.

La Shoppinière

The picturesque districts of Belleville and La Maub have a pair of twin shops where one can find funny, useful, typically French little gifts in addition to American gadgets.

La Shoppinière, 138 rue de Belleville (20ᵉ), MEN 42.22, and 7 rue Lanneau (5ᵉ), DAN 81.55.

Vuitton

This famous luggage dealer also sells graceful little people who dance the minuet or gavotte beneath a bell glass. Marquesses, shepherdesses and dandies are all made of painted kidney beans, chenille and period fabrics by two women working in an old mill in the Sarthe.

Vuitton, 7 *bis* avenue Marceau (16ᵉ), ELY 47.00.

Ladies' hats

Jean Barthet

He's a genius at self-promotion, but he also has taste and originality, undimmed by years of success. His customers are famous actresses, but also the Comtesse de Paris.

Jean Barthet, 107 Faubourg Saint-Honoré (8ᵉ), ELY 28.05.

Jean-Claude Brosseau

Hatter to models and stylish young women.

Jean-Claude Brosseau, 64 rue Vaneau (7ᵉ), BAB 42.94.

Paulette

Hats for crowned (or deposed) heads. Well-bred classicism or eccentricity.

Paulette, 53 avenue Franklin-Roosevelt (8ᵉ), ELY 88.79.

Marie Jaleska

Majestic, fanciful, irresistibly funny, Marie Jaleska holds court in the quiet parlor of a charming town house. The princesses, countesses and heiresses of Tout-Paris rummage through her cupboards and try on everything that strikes their fancy: mainly dressy hats made of feathers, tulle, veiling or mink (from 100 francs—$20).

Marie Jaleska, 22 boulevard Flandrin (16ᵉ), TRO 38.77.

Daniel Masson

You never see his name in fashion magazines. He doesn't sell hats to Soraya or the Comtesse de Paris. Instead of being housed in a sumptuous salon, his shop is tucked away in a basement on rue de la Pompe. But Daniel Masson creates the prettiest, most "well-balanced" and most becoming hats, all at eminently feasible prices (about 150 francs—$30).

Daniel Masson, 171 rue de la Pompe (16e), KLE 55.36.

Ladies' shoes

Adige

Chanel-type shoes.

Adige, 26 rue Cambon (8e), OPE 40.60.

Bredin et Mirault

Way off amid the provincial charms of Belleville's little houses and tiny gardens, two young men design complete collections of ladies' shoes. They rarely repeat themselves and have something for everyone in their almost infinite selection. (About 200 francs—$40.)

Bredin et Mirault, 49 rue de Pixèrécourt (20e), MEN 75.00.

Carel

Young, very modish styles.

Carel, 29 boulevard Saint-Michel (5e), ODE 20.46, and 122 Champs-Elysées (8e), BAL 95.70.

Carvil

All their styles have lots of imagination and originality.

Carvil, 22 rue Royale (Ier), RIC 92.57; 87 avenue Paul-Doumer (16e), JAS 86.28; 67 rue Pierre-Charron (8e), ELY 05.30.

Céline

This children's and girls' shoemaker has extremely elegant adult customers. Princess Paola and Grace of Monaco shop here. Sophisticated moccasins.

Céline, 237 Faubourg Saint-Honoré (8e), WAG 15.25; 3 avenue Victor-Hugo (16e), PAS 57.81; 47 avenue Franklin-Roosevelt (8e), BAL 08.27.

Durer

The streets aren't overrun with Durer shoes, because they're all exclusive models. Both classic and fancy-free styles, always in the best of taste.

Durer, 74 Champs-Elysées (8e), ELY 90.41.

Charles Jourdan

You'll think you've walked into a country inn: exposed beams, stone fireplace, copper cauldrons full of flowers. The only unusual feature of this rustic décor are the famous Charles Jourdan shoes, always at the height of fashion.

Charles Jourdan, 12 rue du Faubourg Saint-Honoré (8e), ANJ 35.22.

Au Soulier d'Or

If you don't want to wear the same shoes as everybody else but still can't afford the stiff prices of custom shoemakers, you should do the same as many elegant men and women who aren't rolling in money. That is, entrust your precious little feet to the Soulier d'Or, where you'll find exclusive styles and can order a different size for each foot, if one happens to be larger than the other.

Au Soulier d'Or, 9 boulevard Malesherbes (8e), ANJ 09.92.

Renast

Designs all his own models. A very fine selection of classical and up-to-the-minute styles.

Renast, 22 rue du Vieux-Colombier (6e), LIT 52.12; 33 rue Tronchet (8e), ANJ 03.56.

Roger Vivier

This great shoemaker, the finest in France, possesses footprints of the world's four thousand most elegant women, from Empress Farah Dibah to Sophia Loren, all of whom are his customers. Roger Vivier manages to combine daring with good taste and does not succumb either to extravagance or routine. There is a handsome ready-to-wear department, in addition to the custom-made shoes.

Roger Vivier, 24 rue François Ier (8^e), BAL 81.81.

Men's shoes—the great shoemakers

Hellstern

An ultrachic and ultratraditional establishment. Their most popular style was designed at the end of the last century. Custom shoes only.

Hellstern, 82 place Vendôme (Ier), OPE 60.74.

John Lobb

The House of Lobb was founded in 1850 by John Lobb, an Australian shoemaker who soon emigrated to London. The business of shoeing the world's noblest feet has occupied generations of John Lobbs ever since. They supply the Duke of Edinburgh, President Johnson, the Shah of Iran, the Emperor of Ethiopia, Arabian oil magnates, a good number of French Ministers, and the greatest movie actors, from the late Gary Cooper to Yul Brynner. Lobb is simply the greatest shoemaker in the world.

Bustling little Monsieur Lemare in a navy-blue suit, and the very tall Monsieur Dickinson, wearing a leather apron, rule the store's French branch near the Elysée Palace. Knowing the Almanach de Gotha from heel to toe is the least of their merits. Their real claim to fame is their shoes. It's hardly necessary to say that these are all handmade to order. And this manufacture is quite a work of art, which requires about two months for a new customer.

Monsieur Dickinson first examines the feet to be shod. Their shape not only tells him the nationality of their owner but, more important, the height of the arch, placement of the toes, distribution of weight, etc. He then makes a sketch, and the real work begins. The last-maker makes two wooden lasts (one for each foot). The cutter draws up the pattern and cuts the skins for the stitchers to make uppers, which craftsmen then sew onto the soles. After one or two fittings, the shoes are ready at last.

You don't have to be a fetishist to fall on your knees before the wonderful leathers, superb craftsmanship, colors and styles. The naturally crackled skins are polished to an inimitable patina, which gives them the utter chic of not seeming new, shiny, showy—in a word, "cheap."

Lobb prides itself on "not caring a fig for fashion." But this classicism still doesn't prevent them from giving their shoes a slender line or creating a thousand variations on the oxford and pump.

Up until now we have been talking about ordinary shoes. But Lobb is one of the few places that work with polished calf. This unshiny, matte, absolutely unfragile leather is highly prized for hunt boots. To give it a gloss you take a mutton bone, or better yet, a stag bone, and rub the leather with it for three or four hours. After two years of this you can hope to obtain a real mirror finish. Polished calf, unfortunately, is used less and less frequently.

You are now itching to go into Lobb's, but you don't have the nerve. You're wrong: it will only cost you 6 francs ($1.20) to admire this fabulous footwear, sample a little of that typically British atmosphere, wallow in all that wonderful, anachronistic luxury. Six francs is the price of a jar of Lobb's exclusive shoe polish. As Monsieur Lemare says, it does the same thing for shoes as face cream does for a woman. When you apply it to leather it's actually the leather that shines, not just the polish.

Furthermore, since the days are gone when Russian grand dukes used to buy up twenty-five pairs of shoes in five minutes, Monsieur Lemare will tell you that a great many of his customers are men who have discovered that, even though Lobb's prices are high, in the long run they end up spending no more here than they would for ready-made shoes, since a Lobb shoe lasts ten years.

And anyway, they have another very important advantage: since they already have a fine patina when you buy them, think of the money you'll save on not having to keep a valet to work up this sheen!

John Lobb, 47 rue du Faubourg Saint-Honoré (8e), ANJ 24.45.

Men's shoes—ready-to-wear

Bally

French- and Swiss-made. Very classical, excellent quality.

Bally, 11 boulevard de la Madeleine (8e), OPE 27.79; 3 boulevard Saint-Michel (5e), ODE 19.28; 143 rue de la Pompe (16e), PAS 45.43, and ten other stores in Paris.

Carvil

The great specialist in Italian-style shoes. Very high prices.

Carvil, 67 rue Pierre-Charron (8e), ELY 05.30.

Lanvin

Only one or two Italian styles, but these are incomparably beautiful and supple.

Lanvin, 15 rue du Faubourg Saint-Honoré (8e), ANJ 14.40.

Weston

Faithful to its English traditions, Weston's has victoriously resisted the Italian influence. The selection seems best in the casual styles. There is a shoeblack who displays incomparable talent.

Weston, 114 avenue des Champs-Elysées (8e), BAL 26.47.

Cigars

You would not only be committing a sin by bringing Havanas back to the U.S., but a grave error as well, since the customs inspectors would confiscate them as soon as you set foot on American soil. On the other hand, there's no law (unless it's a moral one) against an American smoking Lonsdales and Monté-Cristos while traveling in France.

Paris, however, is far from tops in Cuban cigars. The selection is infinitely smaller than in Geneva or London, either of which is a cigar smoker's paradise. It's true that you can get some ten different makes, but this is not what really matters. A badly kept cigar dries out and loses all its flavor, which is what happens nine times out of ten when you buy a cigar in the first tobacco shop you come across. Paris has very few specialists and the *tabacs* sell tobacco with the same indifference as postage stamps.

The principal specialists, who store their cigars in specially designed cellars and aren't likely to sell you a dry Havana, are the following:

> La Civette, 157 rue Saint-Honoré (Ier), GUT 79.66 (a charming shop dating back to the eighteenth century), and Le Drugstore, 133 Champs-Elysées (8e), BAL 94.40.

Ladies' hairdressers

Carita

The Carita sisters, Rosy and Maria, just about monopolize the hairdos of feminine Tout-Paris. Every imaginable care is lavished on you with consummate art, and the prices are no higher than anywhere else.

> Carita, 11 rue du Faubourg Saint-Honoré (8e), ANJ 79.00; Hotel Hilton, 18 avenue de Suffren (15e), BRE 00.26.

Katcha

Others may consider his profession frivolous, but André Katcha doesn't take it lightly. This athletic forty-year-old really throws himself into his work. You have to watch him cut hair: it's a ritual with gestures that seem equally inspired by legendary toreros, South African witch doctors and ecstatic mediums. He subjects each customer to intense scrutiny, mentally analyzes the shape of her face and placement of her features and . . . cuts.

All is hushed—even the canaries—while the master operates in the large salon which he has never felt any need to redecorate and which he has occupied ever since he went into business.

Katcha has some peculiar reactions. How else can one explain, for example, that nowadays he only charges 30 francs ($6) for a cut when fifteen years ago it would have cost a fortune (5,000 francs—$1,000)?

Katcha, 9 rue du Cirque (8ᵉ), ELY 37.31.

Other good addresses:

Alexandre, 120 rue du Faubourg Saint-Honoré (8ᵉ), ELY 40.09.

Alexander the Great, who does the hair for all Tout-Paris: the Comtesse de Paris, Farah Dibah, etc.

Arden, 7 place Vendôme (Iᵉʳ), OPE 42.42.

Charles of the Ritz, 51 avenue Montaigne (8ᵉ), ELY 55.39.

Dessange, 37 avenue Franklin-Roosevelt (8ᵉ); ELY 31.31.

Lintermans, 28 rue du Faubourg Saint-Honoré (8ᵉ), ANJ 17.84.

Lorca, 3 avenue Matignon (8ᵉ), BAL 57. 90.

Madeleine Plaz, 1 avenue du Président-Wilson (16ᵉ), KLE 88.00.

Roger Pasquier, 40 avenue Pierre-Iᵉʳ-de-Serbie (8ᵉ), ELY 38.11.

Jean-Louis Saint-Roch, 56 avenue Paul-Doumer (16ᵉ), TRO 47.13.

Helena Rubinstein, 52 rue du Faubourg Saint-Honoré (8ᵉ), ANJ 65.69.

Cutlery

Peter

They come long or short, round or pointed, thick or thin, stiff or as supple as rattan. Their handles are of molded nylon or carved ivory, their shapes copied from the eighteenth century or inspired by contemporary Scandinavian lines. But whatever the style, use or price, the House of Peter still designs, makes and sells its own kitchen and table knives, just as it's been doing since it opened over a hundred years ago.

Every blade is handcrafted in accordance with traditional techniques. "People often accuse stainless-steel knives of cutting poorly," says Monsieur Peter. "Actually, adding chrome to the steel doesn't do anything to the cutting edge. What counts is, first of all, using good steel, and then not burning it, as usually happens with mass-produced knives which are machine-cut from white-hot sheets. The way we do it, however, is to heat and forge the steel in several steps: it is softened over a charcoal fire and its color never gets beyond cherry red." Another advantage of handcraftsmanship, as understood by the Peter family, is that the fang (the part of the blade which is inserted into the handle) is very long, so that there is no play. If you want to take these knives apart you have to boil them to dissolve the cement which unites blade and handle.

These blades, worthy of Toledo, come mounted in all possible handles: black or white nylon, rosewood, imitation ivory, bamboo, black buffalo horn, mottled horn, ebony, Louis XVI style, with metal trim, blond horn, stag horn, silver plate, ebony and silver, ivory and silver, solid silver. This brings us to such collector's items as the copies of the first knob-handled table knives from the Louis XIV period, or an eighteenth-century service in Saint-Cloud porcelain.

Peter has dazzling sets of razor-sharp blades for both kitchen and table use. Young couples who are setting up house will find an indispensable panoply of steak knives (pointed and serrated), fruit and cheese knives, carving sets, cheese knives (one for hard cheese, another for soft), individual butter spreaders and, of course, all the proper utensils for slicing poultry, roast beef, roast lamb (more supple), ham and salmon (long and flexible), not to mention the knife for fileting sole and the grapefruit knife (serrated and curved), nor to forget the whetstone which will ensure their eternal youth.

"We make lots of contemporary patterns for everyday use," says Monsieur Peter, "but the core of our French and foreign clientele asks mainly for period knives. They're the only ones which go with classical silverware."

Nothing which relates to cutting implements is beyond the ken of this firm of cutler-silversmiths. Thus, they also make (by hand) every imaginable kind of scissors, from huge tailor's shears to pocket clippers and tiny nail scissors, as well as a complete line of manicure and pedicure equipment and marvelous travel, garden and other kits.

Sailors will also find some extremely useful accessories here: a sturdy boatknife, unshackling knife, marlinespike, a floating knife whose safety blade is encased in cork, and a knife with a built-in scale for weighing fish. If you can't find your dream-blade amid this stupendous variety of models, you can always have it made. Whether it is an antique or modern design, the little craftsmen who work exclusively for Peter the Magnificent will make it their duty to execute it for you according to your specifications or sketch.

> Peter, 919 rue du Faubourg Saint-Honoré (8ᵉ), CAR 88.00. Closed Monday mornings.

The great couturiers

We won't give you any descriptions of the great designers' styles, for whatever we might say would be far inferior to the descriptions which fashion magazines never tire of repeating to their readers.

Balmain, 44 rue François Iᵉʳ (8ᵉ), BAL 68.04.

Cardin, 118 rue du Faubourg Saint-Honoré (8ᵉ), BAL 06.23.

Chanel, 31 rue Cambon (Iᵉʳ), OPE 60.21.

Courrèges, 40 rue François Iᵉʳ (8ᵉ), ELY 72.17.

Christian Dior, 30 avenue Montaigne (8ᵉ), ELY 93.64.

Givenchy, 3 avenue George V (8ᵉ), BAL 92.60.

Jacques Heim, 15 avenue Matignon (8ᵉ), BAL 29.58.

Lanvin, 22 rue du Faubourg Saint-Honoré (8ᵉ), ANJ 27.21.

Guy Laroche, 29 avenue Montaigne (8ᵉ), BAL 57.66.

Patou, 7 rue Saint-Florentin (Iᵉʳ), OPE 08.71.

Nina Ricci, 20 rue des Capucines (Iᵉʳ), OPE 67.31.

Yves-Mathieu Saint-Laurent, 30 *bis* rue Spontini (16ᵉ), PAS 43.79.

Other great designers:
Louis Féraud, 88 rue du Faubourg Saint-Honoré (8ᵉ), ANJ 27.29.
Hermès, 24 rue du Faubourg Saint-Honoré (8ᵉ), ANJ 22.10.
Jean-Louis Scherrer, 182 rue du Faubourg Saint-Honoré (8ᵉ), ELY 34.83.
Philippe Venet, 62 rue François Iᵉʳ (8ᵉ), BAL 33.64.

High-fashion boutiques

Most of the great couturiers have a boutique where they sell deluxe ready-to-wear along the lines of their main collection.
The shapes are usually simpler, the fabrics less sumptuous, and the prices much more reasonable. But you still have to count on paying an average of at least 600 francs ($120) for a dress, 1,200 francs ($240) for a suit and 1,100 francs ($220) for a coat.
Naturally, each designer maintains his own particular style.
Balmain, 44 rue François Iᵉʳ (8ᵉ), BAL 68.00.
Cardin, 118 rue du Faubourg Saint-Honoré (8ᵉ). Custom-made clothes from his Eve boutique.
Cardin, 185 boulevard Saint-Germain (6ᵉ), LIT 62.46.
Courrèges, 40 rue François Iᵉʳ (8ᵉ), ELY 72.17.
Dior, 30 avenue Montaigne (8ᵉ), ELY 93.64.
Miss Dior, 11 *bis* rue François Iᵉʳ (8ᵉ), ALM 16.94. A brand-new shop in a contemporary setting. Miss Dior fashions for "modern" women, designed by Marc Bohan's assistant. Dresses, suits, coats, knits, hats, stockings, belts, etc. From 300 to 800 francs.
Louis Féraud, 88 rue du Faubourg Saint-Honoré (8ᵉ), ANJ 27.29.
Lanvin, 22 rue du Faubourg Saint-Honoré (8ᵉ), ANJ 27.21.
Guy Laroche, 29 avenue Montaigne (8ᵉ), BAL 57.66.
Patou, 7 rue Saint-Florentin (8ᵉ), OPE 08.71.

Nina Ricci, 20 rue des Capucines (Ier), OPE o8.71.
Saint-Laurent-Rive-Gauche, 21 rue de Tournon (6e), DAN 07.05.

Ready-to-wear boutiques

New boutiques spring up every day, sometimes in the most unlikely places. But you'll get a good idea of Paris fashion by strolling along Rue du Faubourg Saint-Honoré, Boulevard Saint-Germain and around Saint-Germain-des-Prés, and finally along rue de Sèvres, which has been the center of young fashion thinking for some time now.

Not all the good shops are necessarily in one of these three areas, however, as the following list will testify.

Bistrot-Boutique

In the touching, stepchild section of Ménilmontant, two young women sell pretty, frilly evening dresses adorned with beads or ruffles, between a bar and marble-topped tables. They also have beachwear and very sophisticated slacks.

Bistrot-Boutique, 13 rue des Amandiers (20e), MEN 61.78.

Boutique Knize

Knize, the great men's tailor with a century-old reputation in Vienna, Paris, London and New York, has opened its door a crack to "ladies' wear" while maintaining all the virtues which made it famous: very beautiful fabrics, meticulous tailoring.

Boutique Knize, 10 avenue Matignon (8e), ELY 51.44.

Mihri Fenwick

Mihri Fenwick was a fashion writer for fifteen years and Chanel's *directrice* after that. She's now creating her own designs, often made from Indian saris.

Mihri Fenwick, 11 rue La Boétie (8e), ANJ 26.56.

Galérie Orpiment

The window of Véronique André-Siroux's shop, in the old Marais district, looks like an art gallery. Inside, this enchanting, refined girl creates her hand-painted silk dresses and coats.

Galérie Orpiment, 27 rue Saint-Paul (4e), TUR 90.22.

Marie-Martine

All the little Parisian suits. Beautiful fabrics, uncluttered shapes. Wealthy, young clientele. Brigitte Bardot had a lot to do with getting the shop started.

Marie-Martine, 8 rue de Sèvres (6e), BAB 18.44.

La Mercerie

This little "notions shop" on rue des Fossées-Saint-Bernard operates on the principle of hand-knitting or crocheting unbleached wool into dresses, capes, sweaters, bonnets, stockings, etc., using old-fashioned stitches.

La Mercerie, 32 rue des Fossées-Saint-Bernard (5e), DAN 47.84.

Mic-Mac

The famous Bardot-Sachs team has opened a branch of the Saint-Tropez Mic-Mac in little rue de Tournon, which Saint-Laurent had already adopted for his Rive Gauche boutique. The store sells very "in" outfits for summer and winter wear.

Mic-Mac, 13 rue de Tournon (6e), ODE 44.99.

Pline

A pretty atelier-shop at the back of a romantic courtyard, where one can find gloriously colored Italian silk jersey sheaths at extremely reasonable prices.

Pline, 9 rue Bélidor (17e), GAL 64.04.

Emilio Pucci

Marchese Pucci, the famous Florentine designer, has silk jersey dresses in exclusive patterns of rare colors, wonderful scarves, jewelry, etc., for sale in his shops.

Emilio Pucci, 37 rue Jean-Goujon (8e), ELY 07.70; 4 rue de Castiglione (Ier), RIC 46.71.

Réty

Behind the very simple shopwindow you'll find ready-to-wear clothes which can stand up to *haute couture* fashions. A very varied collection, in excellent taste. Air-conditioned dressing rooms.

Réty, 54 rue du Faubourg Saint-Honoré (8e), ANJ 54.53.

Saint-Frusquin

Instead of ready-to-wear, this shop sells already-worn garments. Very stylish, practically new dresses, suits, coats, and hats are bought and sold in a somewhat kooky atmosphere. Extremely attractive prices (whatever you're asking or offering, or almost).

Saint-Frusquin, 1 villa Juge (15e), BRE 13.56. Second floor.

Saint-Laurent-Rive-Gauche

The boutique, where all of society's and fashion's darlings—both budding and full-blown—rush to pick out very sophisticated, elegant, somewhat "babydoll" clothes designed by the very famous Yves Saint-Laurent.

Saint-Laurent-Rive-Gauche, 21 rue de Tournon (6e), DAN 07.05.

Ken Scott

American by birth, French by predilection (he spent ten years painting in Saint-Germain-des-Prés), Italian by duty (he got his first start in Milan), Ken Scott designs his own fabrics and fashions and then has them made up in his own factories. The little shop he recently opened on the first floor off a courtyard looks more like a town house than a dress boutique.

Ken Scott, 4 rue de la Paix (Ier), RIC 88.63.

Ted

Very pretty, witty weekend clothes in lightweight fabrics, designed by Ted Lapidus.

Ted, 6 place Victor-Hugo (16e), POI 40.19.

Torrente

Dressy dresses, suits and coats of perfect taste and workmanship. Not so long ago they opened a new department, Miss Torrente, where prices are more within reach. One of the best boutiques in Paris.

Torrente, 70 rue du Faubourg Saint-Honoré (8e), BAL 81.27.

Victoire

A new, very fashionable boutique in Louise de Lavallière's enchanting town house on the delightful place des Victoires. It has an exclusive selection of featherweight wool challis dresses, magnificent tweeds, handbags and belts.

Victoire, 12 place des Victoires (2e), LOU 53.29.

In all of the following noisy, nutty, gay boutiques, "with it" girls can find slightly offbeat, "fun," usually tasteful (if sometimes giddy) clothes at relatively low prices, but of a quality which often leaves something to be desired. Both exclusive and nonexclusive styles.

Bistrot du Tricot, 15 rue Boissy d'Anglas (8e) OPE 33.09; 57 rue Bonaparte (6e), DAN 59.13.

Bus Stop, 147 boulevard Saint-Germain (6ᵉ), DAN 04.66.
Dorothée-Bis, 37 rue de Sèvres (6ᵉ), LIT 86.11.
Eva, 121 boulevard Saint-Germain (6ᵉ), DAN 35.25.
Gudule, 72 rue Saint-André-des-Arts (6ᵉ), MED 76.41.
Knack, 104 avenue Victor-Hugo (16ᵉ), KLE 13.06; 85 rue de Rennes (6ᵉ).
Laura, 104 avenue du Général-Leclerc (14ᵉ), VAU 04.98.
Madd, 20 rue Tronchet (9ᵉ), OPE 78.35.
Vog, 34 rue Tronchet (9ᵉ), OPE 13.63.

Designer's resale

Mme Martell Benassit

Frenchwomen still have lots of misgivings. They feel there's something suspicious and humiliating about going to an apartment to buy couturier dresses for two-thirds, half or one-fourth the original price. But Americans, Englishwomen and Italians have long been fans of this formula.

Mme Martell Benassit, who worked in the United States for several years, has good reason to be surprised by the Parisiennes' distrust. All her models come from great fashion houses like Dior, Chanel, Saint-Laurent, Balenciaga, Madeleine de Rauch, Givenchy and Cardin. All are new or almost new: they date from the previous season, which means they are at most three or four months old. Some have been worn two or three times by a mannequin; others, which were ordered and then rejected by fickle customers, are absolutely new.

But don't expect to get these high-fashion creations for a song. You won't find any suits under 1,500 francs ($300), for example, but by and large that's no more than what you pay for fine ready-to-wear.

> Mme Martell Benassit, 18 rue de la Tremoïlle (8ᵉ), ELY 95.00.
> First floor. Closed Saturdays.

Discount

Paris has several shops intended especially for tourists—and Americans in particular—where all the "souvenirs" and "gifts from Paris" can be found at exceedingly low prices.

The most important of these discount stores is:

Michel Swiss

Except for a dozen or so perfumes at only 20 percent off, all items sell for 40 percent less than in ordinary shops. A large selection of perfumes, men's and ladies' clothing, handbags (crocodile and beaded), curios and souvenirs.

Here are some sample prices:

Perfumes: Quadrille by Balenciaga, $5.10 the half-ounce; Jolie Madame by Balmain, $4.80 the half-ounce; Millot's Crêpe de Chine, $4.75 the half-ounce; Bandit by Piguet, $5.85 the half-ounce.

Beaded bags: from $45 to $115; crocodile bags from $200 to $230.

Lanvin shirts, $14.70; Dior ties, $7.90 with matching handkerchief.

These prices are made possible because a special excise tax (Supplementary Value Tax) has been abolished; also, the manufacturer allows further reductions, provided you pay for your purchases exclusively with traveler's checks, foreign drafts or foreign credit cards.

Michel Swiss, 16 rue de la Paix (Ier), OPE 60.36.
Also:
Trebel, 62 rue de Miromesnil (8^e), LAB 53.86.
Gray, 5 rue Scribe (9^e), RIC 00.30.

Deluxe groceries

The finest French and foreign delicacies are likely to be found in these deluxe grocery stores. Three of the firms we mention are all located on place de la Madeleine, which has long been the shrine of Parisian gastronomy.

Battendier

This great delicatessen in Les Halles (right next to Dehillerin) is one of the finest caterers in Paris, and numbers General De Gaulle and the Elysée among its clients. Its great specialties are fresh foie gras (in winter), potted game and skillfully prepared homemade conserves (pheasant, hare, wild boar, thrush, woodcock, and foie gras).

Battendier, 8 rue Coquillière (Ier), CEN 95.50.

Fauchon

For some years now this millionaire's supermarket has wrested first place from its neighbor Hédiard. The most elegant housewives in Paris are regular customers. Fauchon is divided into several departments: Delicatessen, where you'll find a good Scottish salmon and the most estimable brands of tinned foie gras; Wines and Spirits, a fairly vast selection of old vintages and giant bottles (magnums and jeroboams) which are hard to find anywhere else, as well as countless whiskies and champagnes; Grocery—canned goods from the world over, English biscuits, jams and honey from every country. It's certainly the best-stocked grocery department in Paris; Fruits and Vegetables—you can find strawberries at Christmas and cherries in March. This abominably expensive produce is pretty to look at but also pretty tasteless; Confectionery—mediocre chocolates, but the candied fruits from the best confectioner in Cannes are magnificent and succulent.

Fauchon charges luxury prices for all products.

Fauchon, 26 place de la Madeleine (8e), OPE 11.90.

Hédiard

A very old shop where Marcel Proust liked to linger but which has since lost some of its former spellbinding atmosphere, reminiscent of a luxurious, baroque suq. You'll find ex-

otic products from farthest Asia and Africa. Its most appreciated specialties are old rums, ready-made punches, fruit syrups,
fruit jellies and wonderful baskets of candied fruit. There is
also an impressive selection of fine wines.

Hédiard, 21 place de la Madeleine (8ᵉ), ANJ 77.36.

La Maison de la Truffe

In addition to excellent wines, fine delicatessen products and
deluxe preserves, this very fine shop specializes in fresh truffles,
from November to the end of February. Thoughout the entire
year, however, Mme Lemattre sells jars of excellent whole preserved truffles which compare favorably with the fresh ones,
and apparently suffer no loss of their aphrodisiac powers.

La Maison de la Truffe, 19 place de la Madeleine (8ᵉ), ANJ
53.22.

Flowers

Once you cross the threshold of these luxury shops you can
be sure the prices will be prickly but also that the flowers and
arrangements will be of exceptional quality.

Arène, 5 rue Mesnil (16ᵉ), PAS 32.19.

Baumann, 98 boulevard du Montparnasse (14ᵉ), MED 30.98.

Elysées-Fleurs, 50 rue François Iᵉʳ (8ᵉ), ELY 90.58.

George V-Fleurs, 49 avenue George V (8ᵉ), ELY 42.87.

Girard, 110 avenue Victor-Hugo (16ᵉ), PAS 88.44.

Harris, 5 rue Cambon (Iᵉʳ), RIC 70.54.

Lachaume, 10 rue Royale (8ᵉ), OPE 66.11.

Lambert, 5 place de l'Alma (8ᵉ), ELY 49.30.

Moreux, 72 avenue Victor-Hugo (16ᵉ), PAS 58.55.

Orève, 25 rue de la Pompe (16ᵉ), TRO 20.13.

Veyrat, 30 rue de Courcelles (17ᵉ), CAR 37.86.

Dried flowers

- -

These can, of course, be found at any florist's, but here is a specialist who we think surpasses many of the better-known establishments: *Original-Flor,* 37 rue Godot-de-Mauroy (9ᵉ), OPE 26.62.

Finally, we advise taking a turn around the front of the Church of Saint Eustache, if only for the walk and the very pretty scene. This is the site of the flower market, where Parisian florists lay in their supplies. After six thirty in the evening (every day but Sunday), however, it's open to the public. The finest selection is usually gone, of course, and wrapping counts for nothing: they tie up the bouquets in old newspapers, and you would be ill-advised to give them to anyone like that. But the prices are worth the trip—20 to 40 percent less than in florists' shops. On Tuesdays and Fridays green plants and potted flowers are sold in the same place from six to eight at night.)

> Halles aux Fleurs, across from the Church of Saint Eustache (Iᵉʳ).

Scarves

- -

Hermès

The whole world knows their silk squares, printed with old motifs. New designs come out several times a year. Hermès also makes very popular matching hats.

> Hermès, 24 rue du Faubourg Saint-Honoré (8ᵉ), ANJ 22.10.

Lubin

Pretty, scented scarves.

> Lubin, 11 rue Royale (8ᵉ), ANJ 41.72.

Pucci

Pucci's famous silks. Colors and geometric patterns of very great beauty.

> Pucci, 37 rue Jean-Goujon (8e), ELY 07.70; 4 rue de Castiglione (Ier), RIC 46.71.

Saint-Laurent-Rive-Gauche

Lovely geometric patterns.

> Saint-Laurent-Rive-Gauche, 21 rue de Tournon (6e), DAN 07.05.

Gloves

Roger Faré

Roger Faré has been making gloves for the Holy Father ever since the pontificate of Pius XI, but his path to the Vatican was strangely roundabout. Summoned to the Elysée when they wanted to present gloves to Pius XI, Faré ended up at Borniol's, the famous funeral parlor. This happens to be the firm assigned to create the Pope's coat of arms after his election to the pontifical throne.

Roger Faré set up shop on the rue d'Aguesseau in an eighteenth-century town house, formerly occupied by Pauline Borghese. And today he is the most famous glovemaker in the world.

The very first celebrity to become a customer was Marlene Dietrich, soon to be followed by Jacqueline Kennedy, Mrs. Johnson, Princess Grace of Monaco, and Queen Fabiola. Twice a year, Princess Sirikit of Siam orders twenty-four pairs of gloves for every hour in the day.

His secret? It's very simple. "We use scissors to cut out the gloves, exactly as they did in the fifteenth century," says Roger Faré. "And the reason that the French glove industry is still the most elegant in the world is that only French kid—especially from animals that live in winegrowing regions like Beaujolais or Saône-et-Loire—makes the most beautiful gloves."

Roger Faré is not satisfied merely to make gloves; he also collects them. If you ask him, he'll show you his treasures, like the velvet falconer's glove trimmed in gold, with the bird's claw marks still showing, or an enchanting pair of printed leather gloves from the Directoire period, or, again, the immense leather-covered zinc signboard from 1820, which Faré discovered in a curiosity shop near Toulouse.

Roger Faré's gloves are washable, of course. And that's not just an advertising slogan. You can really wash them without doing them any harm. All you have to do is squeeze soapy water through them (using nothing but soap flakes, never any detergents) and then rinse them carefully.

> Roger Faré, 22 rue d'Aguesseau (8ᵉ), ANJ 91.63. His gloves, which start at 30 francs ($6), are also sold at Galéries Lafayette and Au Printemps, as well as in many specialty shops such as Denise Francel, 244 rue de Rivoli.

Hermès

"With men's gloves, the important thing is not how well they look but how perfectly they fulfill their function." At least that's the guiding principle at Hermès.

The august firm in the Faubourg Saint-Honoré never puts a new (and, of course, exclusive) style on sale before it has been wear-tested for several weeks and ruthlessly subjected to all the stresses and strains of its intended purpose (golf, riding, hunting, etc.). This scrupulous care is what makes those famous Hermès gloves incomparable.

So before you give a pair to your friends, find out exactly how they are to be used.

For town, select a handsewn pair in warm, supple reindeer hide, in silk-lined Antilda leather (calf tanned in a special way), in doeskin (tanned sheep) lined with chamois. For evening wear, delicately English-stitched doeskin in gabardine shades, with button closing. Pick woven or perforated lambskin for sport.

To wear while hunting: sorak with lambskin palms and asbestos backing in the fingertips; for repeater rifles, each hand has a different backing.

Riding gloves are made of supple kid or crocheted with leather palms; some of the fingers also have a double leather backing.

For golf, supple leather with perforated tops, gathered and sewn onto elastic.

For gardening, extra supple natural chamoisine or else terry-cloth tops with chamois palms, fastened with a button, very practical for wiping the windshield; finally, ostrich or Mexican peccary, which is the rarest and most beautiful because the skin is unmarred.

Don't worry too much about getting spots on these marvel-ous leather gloves. Should this misfortune befall you, instead of using some miracle product or other, turn the other glove in-side out and vigorously rub the two together. This home rem-edy, which was given to us at Hermès, seems to be sovereign.

Hermès, 24 rue du Faubourg Saint-Honoré (8e), ANJ 22.10.

Huc et Ferret

Monsieur and Madame Huc arrived from their native Mil-lau, the heart of the glove country, over forty years ago. They have been making gloves to order ever since. Their styles range from the simplest, machine-stitched gloves to the most luxuri-ous, cut from the rarest leathers—from carpincho, for example, which is an animal related to the peccary. Naturally, all gloves made of noble materials are handsewn. You can also have gloves made in your own fabric to match a dress, or select a leather from which they will make up both gloves and match-ing purse. Prices start at 25 francs—$5.

Huc et Ferret, 42 rue du Cherche-Midi (6e), LIT 03.39.

Patrice

Men's gloves in wolfskin (soft, supple and incomparably sturdy), ostrich (as thin as tissue paper), peccary, sueded lamb (woven, for example), antelope, reindeer, or chamois, starting at 40 francs ($8). You can also buy all kinds of ladies' gloves for sport or dress wear, in peccary, chamois or glacé kid, for 35 francs ($7) and up.

Patrice, 36 rue Washington (8e), ELY 36.60.

Large department stores

It's very instructive, if not always too much fun (they still haven't discovered air conditioning), to make a tour of Parisian department and chain stores. This will enable you to look over the latest Paris novelties and will also give you a fair idea of general prices.

Two *grands magasins* clearly outclass all the rest in their originality and constant innovation, whether in fashions, furniture, china, etc. They are: Les Galeries Lafayette, 30 boulevard Haussmann (9e), OPE 04.50, and Au Printemps, 64 boulevard Haussmann (9e), TRI 03.10.

The two are right next to each other and it's hard to see much difference between them. We'll simply say that Galeries Lafayette tends to be younger and more adventuresome, while Au Printemps appeals to the elegant, classical members of the Parisian middle class. (Printemps has a Pierre Cardin shop.)

You can make some real finds in these stores, and prices are usually most attractive. But remember that our stores don't have sales the way American stores do. Parisian sales are held at the end of every season, and with some exceptions, the quality of the merchandise is far from superior.

We recommend wandering through Monoprix and Prisunic for small articles, "little" dresses and children's clothing. These once-dismal chain stores have now been renovated, and their wares are often full of ideas, tasteful and always very low-priced.

These branches have the best selection:

Monoprix-Opéra, 21 avenue de l'Opéra (Ier), OPE 74.34.

Nouvelles-Galeries-de-Passy, 50 rue de Passy (16e), JAS 54.80.

Prisunic-Caumartin, 56 rue Caumartin (9e), PIG 79.60.

Prisunic-Courcelles, 159 rue de Courcelles (17e), WAG 87.10.

Prisunic-Elysées, 60 Champs-Elysées (8e), BAL 27.46.

Prisunic-Ternes, 25 avenue des Ternes (17e), ETO 43.76.

*Men's clothing: Shirtmakers and
ready-to-wear shops*

Pierre Cardin Boutique

This great couturier has become Public Enemy Number 1 of the great tailors. They complain that he has vulgarized men's fashion and alienated their young customers, who'd rather buy ready-to-wear with the Cardin label (and a pretty high price tag, too). The Cardin Boutique has clothes of a very different cut and style both from what you'll find at the great tailors (more far-out) and at the famous Diffusion Pierre Cardin (less far-out). Pale or violent colors. Lightweight fabrics, new patterns.

Also shoes, shirts (beautiful dress shirts), hats, ties, etc.

> Pierre Cardin Boutique, 118 rue du Faubourg Saint-Honoré (8e), BAL 06.23.

Cerutti

Newly arrived in Paris, this Italian boutique has rapidly gained a reputation by the elegance, refinement and originality of its suits, sweaters, shirts and shoes. Its style really runs to sportscar owners and apprentice playboys.

> Cerutti, 24 rue Royale (8e), ANJ 63.20.

Au Chardon d'Ecosse

Imported ties and sweaters made from the finest Scottish wool.

> Au Chardon d'Ecosse, 8 rue de Marignan (8e), ELY 38.87.

Boutique Dior

Striped ties, infinitely nicer than the ones sold here, there and everywhere under the Dior label.

> Boutique Dior, 30 avenue Montaigne (8e), ELY 93.64.

Dorian Guy

In our opinion, the finest ready-to-wear shop in Paris. Provided you like English styling, which manager Nick Louvier claims is the only way to look truly elegant. Highly successful clientele. Very handsome materials. Refined, rather expensive shirts. (The custom-made suits, cut from superbly light, warm fabrics, cost as much as at the great tailors.)

Dorian Guy, 36 avenue George V (8e), ELY 45.48.

Eddy

There is no busier thoroughfare than the Lido Arcade, yet Eddy does almost all of his business with regular customers. His prices, elegant décor and top-quality merchanidse intimidate most casual strollers. Very nice ready-to-wear suits. All the suits and shirts come in several different sleeve lengths.

Eddy, Arcades du Lido, 78 avenue des Champs-Elysées (8e), BAL 59.19.

Elysées-Soieries

Has many innovations to its credit besides helping to start the fashion for good-quality manufactured shirts. All shirts come with an extra collar. A good selection of fashionable but not extravagant ready-to-wear clothes.

Elysées-Soieries, 65 avenue des Champs-Elysées (8e), ELY 37.64.

Pierre Faivret

The little dictator of Tout-Paris. Extravagant details added onto what is at times a classical cut. Jean-Paul Belmondo and Charles Aznavour follow the firm's decrees. There is also a large selection of various ready-to-wear articles, all very brightly colored.

Pierre Faivret, 165 rue Saint-Honoré (8e), OPE 26.29.

Lanvin

An immense selection of ties and shirts (ready-made or custom-made). Classical and supremely elegant. The finest shirt-maker in Paris.

> Lanvin, 15 rue du Faubourg Saint-Honoré (8e), ANJ 14.40.

Renoma White House

Maurice and Michel Renoma are the mentors for this very elegant section's golden teenyboppers, to whom they sell clothes full of gaiety, humor and even, to a large extent, taste. The styles are unquestionably rather flashy, limitlessly bold, colorful and inventive. They show a strong American, and even Japanese, influence. The shop enjoys considerable success despite its relatively high prices.

> Renoma White House, 129 *bis* rue de La Pompe (16e), KLE 57.04.

Victoire-Hommes

Ever since men got involved in women's fashions it was only a matter of time before a woman got the idea of designing for men.

A few years ago the talented young stylist Catherine Chaillet opened her ladies' boutique, Victoire. Now it's the men's turn to discover place des Victoires. Catherine Chaillet has just opened a second store just for them, opposite her first one on the other side of the statue of Louis XIV. Her styles are intended for working men who want to add an individual note to their wardrobes and whose taste runs to rather witty lines, materials and colors: slubbed India cotton shirts, linen corduroy slacks in twenty-eight colors, Indian print dressing gowns, etc. All of these items are carefully crafted exclusively for Catherine Chaillet.

> Victoire-Hommes, 3 place des Victoires (Ier), CEN 86.72.

Men's clothing: The Best Tailors

Cifonelli

In business since 1930. Tailors for Tino Rossi and movie actors. Delivery in three weeks, with three fittings. Italian and American cuts.

Cifonelli, 31 rue Marbeuf (8e), BAL 38.84.

Creed

Founded in 1854. Regular customers: the Shah of Iran, the Negus of Ethiopia, Monsieur Couve de Murville. Four fittings; allow three weeks for delivery.

Creed, 7 rue Royale (8e), ANJ 25.56.

Louis Edmond

The Don Quixote of tailors. He struggles against all the Sancho Panzas, as colorless as their thoughts and clothing, who people our streets. He will jokingly suggest magnificent fabrics in antique rose or straw yellow. "My own personal classic is Fra Angelico," exclaims this man from another age.

Louis Edmond, 36 rue Quincampoix (4e), TUR 56.72.

Evzeline

Always ahead of fashion, without ever getting so far out as to be ridiculous. One of the inventors of cuffless trousers, which he is now trying to bring back. Tailors Gilbert Bécaud, members of the French Academy.

Evzeline, 103 rue du Faubourg Saint-Honoré (8e), ELY 09.84.

Johnson et Marié

They do the tailoring for General De Gaulle, the Duke of Windsor, Guy de Rothschild, Henry Cabot Lodge.

Johnson et Marié, 11 rue des Pyramides (Ier), OPE 95.20.

Knize

Knize fashions are forever. Their regular customers include all the "really" elegant men. They also have shirts, ties and a complete line of underclothing.

Knize, 10 avenue Matignon (8e), ELY 51.44.

Lanvin

The utmost elegance and refinement. A lanvin suit shows its class by the fact that you never notice it. The cutters are trained in London. They take twenty-five measurements for the jacket and ten for the trousers.

Lanvin, 15 rue du Faubourg Saint-Honoré (8e), ANJ 14.40.

Larsen

Large selection of casual fabrics. Remarkable classic cut. Customers: Charles Munch, Maurice Chevalier.

Larsen, 7 rue La Boétie (8e), ANJ 07.80.

Opelka

Customers: Rainier of Monaco, Jean Gabin.

Opelka, 53 rue La Boétie (8e), ELY 36.92.

Paul Portes

His customers are leading manufacturers and businessmen.

Paul Portes, 194 rue de Rivoli (Ier), RIC 87.07.

Paul Vauclair

Vauclair tailors General De Gaulle's uniforms. Ambassadors and politicians are regular customers.

Paul Vauclair, 23 rue Royale (8e), ANJ 28.08.

Bookstores

Brentano's

An inexhaustible selection of Anglo-Saxon literature.

Brentano's, 37 avenue de l'Opera (2ᵉ), OPE 60.04.

Galignani

Large English-language department, as well as an immense selection of French books.

Galignani, 224 rue de Rivoli (Iᵉʳ), OPE 56.98.

La Hune

This Saint-Germain-des-Prés bookstore-gallery, run by Bernard Gheerbrandt (a former Agrégation candidate), is one of the liveliest in the capital. You will find a complete panorama of French and foreign publications, with special emphasis on the finest art books.

La Hune, 170 boulevard Saint-Germain (6ᵉ), LIT 35.85. Open until midnight on Wednesdays.

Smith and Son

Excellent English bookstore where one can also taste all the products of the ultimate thing—the five o'clock tea: admirable tea, buns, rolls, toast, scones, muffins, and also grilled herring and eggs with bacon.

Smith and Son, 248 rue de Rivoli (Iᵉʳ), RIC 40.73.

Georges Whitman

This isn't exactly a bookstore; it's a charitable organization. Charity is personified by an American with somewhat disturbing eyes and a long mandarin goatee. He's Georges Whitman, a former Harvard student who's been in Paris since 1951. He was raised in China, has wandered over the face of the earth and has devoted his life to hospitality. His dark, rather squalid shop is the Promised Land for young intellectuals from the world over. Whenever Laurence Durrell and Henry Miller come through Paris, their first stop is Whitman's. Professors, reporters, students, penniless vagabonds make themselves at home, read books they don't buy, pour themselves something to drink, and if they don't have a place to sleep, Whitman—who speaks five languages, including Russian—gives them a bed in one of the seven rooms he has fixed up on the second floor, and never asks a penny for anything.

You won't find anything in his shop but rare, quality works. He reads almost everything that comes into his store and ruthlessly rejects anything he considers "too commercial." Needless to say, he's not exactly coining money under these conditions.

Georges Whitman, 37 rue de la Bûcherie (5e), ODE 32.62. Open until midnight.

Household linens

Colin

This is the opposite of a modern store. Imitation Louis XVI panels painted in faded green and cream. It has "provincial" written all over it. But everything at Colin's is of premium quality, from the "blends" to the fine embroidered linens. There is a complete line of household linen: dishcloths with the dimensions of yesteryear instead of those of a handkerchief, sheets which can be ordered in all lengths and widths, valets' and chefs' aprons, cheesecloth, etc. Mme De Gaulle and the Baronne de Rothschild are faithful customers.

Colin, 10 rue de Saussaies (8e), ANJ 45.60.

La Grande Maison de Blanc

This store remains a bastion of high-quality white goods. You can still find linens in the sizes used by our grandparents. Damask tablecloths are of course a specialty of this illustrious, hundred-year-old firm, which supplies ambassadors and kings with table linens for gala occasions. But the Grand Maison de

Blanc's kingdom doesn't end there: there is a vast selection, and the latest novelties lie next to rare articles of great refinement.

La Grande Maison de Blanc, 8 boulevard des Capucines (9e), OPE 08.60.

Jones

Refined examples of all traditional linens. A very well stocked department of kitchen cloths like they used to make, as well as maids' and nannies' aprons, etc.

Jones, 39 avenue Victor-Hugo (16e), PAS 06.30.

Paule Marrot

Her reputation goes back forty years, but she's younger than the youngest of us. Her imagination seems endlessly creative. She floods the world with her tablecloths, wallpapers and printed upholstery fabrics.

A painter, decorator and colorist, Paule Marrot finds her inspiration in nature. If you're ever invited to visit Nikita Khrushchev, the royal family of Belgium, Jacqueline Kennedy or Karim Aga Khan, you'll be delighted to find Paule Marrot's suns and flowers there. But don't think these little masterpieces are reserved for the wealthy of this world. For example, you can get a pretty table set for 20 francs ($4).

Paule Marrot, 16 rue de l'Arcade (8e), ANJ 12.60. Third floor.

Pénélope

This charming store is tucked away in a courtyard in the Etoile section. Society women take turns volunteering to sell household linen, children's dresses, trousseaus and layettes made by dressmakers and seamstresses who, for various reasons, must work at home and cannot go out. They do exemplary work, worthy of the greatest firms, at very "considered" prices.

Pénélope, 19 avenue Victor-Hugo (16e), KLE 07.60.

La Pince à Linge

Everything at "The Clothespin" is dazzlingly white: the walls, the ceiling of embossed paper, the painted floor, and the snowball-shaped light fixtures. Everything, that is, but the linen, which sparkles with a thousand colors. The basic formula here is coordinated colors for all your linens: table linens, towels, sheets, etc. (Moderate prices.)

La Pince à Linge, 10 rue Saint-Simon (7e), BAB 01.60.

Porthault

Crêpe de Chine, fine lawn, needlepoint, Beauvais embroidery, Milan lace. The taste and luxury which remain the glory of the past. The world-famous House of Porthault didn't want these wonders to disappear, and devotes its efforts to making sheets which are straight out of the Arabian Nights and frequently handsewn. Porthault displays infinite refinement, particularly in their great specialty, prints, which come in thirty-six hundred patterns and six different colors. There are complete bed sets, bath linens, lingerie, tea sets, as well as an entire line of bathroom gadgets and beach coordinates.

Porthault, 18 avenue Montaigne (8e), ELY 17.70.

A La Ville du Puy

The Ville du Puy's wonderful linens are handed down from generation to generation. Since it has to satisfy fashion's fancy, the firm provides a selection of solid-color or printed cotton tablecloths in all sizes, shapes and colors, in addition to the damask tablecloths which are coming back into style. A complete line of plain and fancy linen.

A La Ville du Puy, 36 rue Tronchet (Ier), OPE 13.22; 45 avenue Mozart (16e), 525.39.06.

Ladies' lingerie

Cadolle

In 1886 there was a *corsetière* in Paris named Hermine Cadolle, the great-grandmother of the famous firm's present
owner. Three years later she left for Argentina with her
daughter and trunkfuls of rustling petticoats. The two were
extraordinary businesswomen. When they returned to Paris in
1900, not only were they rich but they had a little item in their
luggage which was going to revolutionize women's fashion: it
was a brassiere, the first one ever.

The Cadolle store on the rue Cambon has been in business
since 1913 and is always full of wealthy ladies who go to the
fourth floor for bathing suits, lingerie and deluxe bras. The
ground floor is given over to ready-made articles which put less
of a strain on one's budget.

Cadolle, 14 rue Cambon (Ier), OPE 64.94.

Candide

She finds her inspiration in dreams. This method shouldn't
surprise anyone too much, since Mme Rouge, who runs the
celebrated Candide, conceives, designs and sells the prettiest
nightgowns imaginable, inspired by the Arabian Nights,
Romeo and Juliet, etc. (Prices start at 100 francs—$20.) This
little store is one of the rallying points for the most distinguished Parisiennes.

Candide, 4 rue de Miromesnil (8e), ANJ 80.55.

Frivolités-Au Bon Choix

There's a tiny store between place Blanche and Pigalle which
always has such a mob of people laughing in front of the window that it's hard to tell exactly what it's selling. But we mus
admit it's a real stopper.

Everything a striptease artist or thrill-seeker could dream o
is exposed to the eyes of passers-by. These are nothing bu
transparent nylon panties, frothy lace, bras (in name only)

suggestive negligées in amazing colors baptized "naughty, naughty," "moonlight," "bewitching." For example, picture a little pair of white panties trimmed with black lace, with a "dayglow pink" hand appliquéd to the front, fastened by little buttons for fingernails.

Nevertheless, the inside of this store looks more like a provincial notions shop than a stripper's paradise.

Frivolités-Au Bon Choix, 56 boulevard de Clichy (18ᵉ), MON 71.29.

Gribiche

Near Saint-Germain-des-Prés is a two-story shopwindow sprouting Ionic columns made of wicker, between which are spread gay young nightgowns, the exclusive designs of a talented young stylist.

Gribiche, 49 rue de Rennes (6ᵉ), LIT 08.71.

Marie-Rose Lebigot

Mme Lebigot makes everything that comes under the heading of ladies' foundations with unusual taste, imagination and graciousness. She launched the demi-bra, the waist cincher (in collaboration with Rochas, who has sold more than fifteen thousand of them in his boutique), the "combination" in collaboration with Fath, etc.

Each individual case fascinates her, and she asserts that there isn't a single woman who couldn't be 60 percent improved, the rest being up to God and hormones. Her great idea is the "combination"; everything depends on the cut and the material. Anyone who's anyone—Mrs. Joseph Kennedy, Ludmilla Tcherina, the Duchess of Windsor—"underclothes" herself at Lebigot's.

Marie-Rose Lebigot, 4 rue de l'Arcade (8ᵉ), ANJ 96.26.

Philomène

Lingerie and dresses from the Gay Nineties and Roaring Twenties. The lingerie is absolutely new and comes from trousseaus which were never used.

Philomène, 15 rue Vavin (6ᵉ), MED 62.01.

Jeanne Pradels

A complete line of ladies' lingerie. A few classic designs, but mostly extremely feminine styles.

> Jeanne Pradels, 1 rue de la Pépinière, corner of rue de Rome (9e), EUR 73.86.

Roger et Gallet

Very pretty young nightgowns. Refined bath linens.

> Roger et Gallet, 62 rue du Faubourg Saint-Honoré (8e), ANJ 28.40.

Kitchen utensils

Dehillerin

Every great chef and cordon blue since 1820 has crossed the threshold of Dehillerin's bronze-green hardware store, highly specialized in the sale (and care) of kitchen accessories. The latest Dehillerin, sporting a crew cut and a gray blouse, carries on the family tradition: he is still the Parisian king of tinned copper. Indeed, no one would think of challenging his right to hold such a title in the most distinguished pantries. And since *noblesse oblige,* we'd have you know that this charming, slender man doesn't permit himself to encourage spending by any of his customers, new or old. According to him, a housewife needs only one copper sauté pan and two copper pots to be able to entertain friends like a cordon blue.

But the copper pots and pans, which he sells in all sizes, are never less than an eighth of an inch thick. And his black frying pans (ranging from four and a half to thirteen inches in diameter)—which you should never wash with detergents if you don't want them to stick—are of a quality which all cooks agree can only be termed incomparable. Dehillerin and his quartet of salesmen have more than standard kitchen utensils to offer. Cooking vessels of all shapes and sizes are displayed on shelves, hung on the walls or suspended from the ceiling.

ogether with long oak or boxwood knives and spatulas, molds
or reshaping cut-up poultry, *broodies* (a sort of hemispherical
up of galvanized iron or stainless steel designed to hold egg
vhites), *mandolines* (instruments for making shoestring pota-
oes), and strange, tall white wire skimmers which they call
"spiders" here.

You'll find a complete line of top-quality kitchen equipment
t Dehillerin's, but don't expect him to supply you with all the
gadgets that abound in the "china" departments of every five-
nd-dime. This hardware dealer, who receives orders from all
over the world and from chefs who arrive in France from everywhere (or anywhere else), is the standard-bearer for the
great traditions of French kitchen equipment.

Dehillerin, 18 rue Coquillière (Ier), CEN 53.13.

Perfume

French perfume needs no further praise. In fact, Americans
are so convinced of its superiority that in recent years they have
been buying out the great French brands just as fast as they
can.

A certain number of these perfumes are bottled right in the
United States. This has a good effect on prices but not necessar-
ly on quality. So American tourists who appreciate excellence
n a product have every reason to continue to buy their perfume in Paris.

The "discount houses" (see p. 297) have the best bargains, of
course, but on the other hand they don't carry all brands.

Thus the only places in Paris where you can buy the famous
Guerlain products (perfume, toilet water, marvelous soap, talc,
face cream, and even scented flannels which let you perfume
your car windows as you wipe them off) are their own stores:
58 Champs-Elysées (8e), 2 place Vendôme (Ier), 93 rue de
Passy (16e) and 29 rue de Sèvres (6e).

If you're not really sure what you want, however, you should
enlist the services of real perfume professionals, people who
can intelligently and patiently guide your choice, taking into

account such factors as age, hair color and exactly what you want the perfume for. They also can recognize Jean Desprez Bal à Versailles (this and Joy are the world's most expensive fragrances) or Arpège by Lanvin, with their eyes closed. Here are a few of these fine perfume specialists:

Catherine, 6 rue de Castiglione (1er).

Delphes, 17 rue de la Paix (2e).

For You, 233 and 380 rue Saint-Honoré (1er).

George Baring, 13 rue Royale (8e).

Hélène Dale, 7 rue Scribe (9e).

Gray, 5 rue Scribe (9e).

Lady M, 38 avenue Victor-Hugo (16e).

Raoul et Curly, 47 avenue de l'Opéra (2e).

Parfumerie Française, 31 rue François Ier (8e).

Handbags

La Bagagerie

Large selection of very fashionable handbags. Young styles. Reasonable prices.

La Bagagerie, 13 rue Tronchet (9e), ANJ 47.71.

Chichen-Itza

The world's most expensive handbag—sheer madness! Jacques Pottier designed and made it for Balenciaga, where it is now available for any president and chairman of the board resigned to giving his wife a 10,000-franc ($2,000) present.

This miracle handbag is made of crocodile, of course, with a solid-gold clasp specially created by a master goldsmith. It's a unique piece; better, it is the "masterpiece" of the great leather goods artist.

But don't worry; this Doctor of Leathers, one of the foremost in Paris, also has a whole collection of handbags, brief cases, wallets, even saddles and watches, at perfectly feasible prices, in his little shop at the back of an old courtyard in the

Faubourg Saint-Honoré. Thus, about 500 francs ($100) will buy a little square bag made of calf, where his customers can stash their complete daily arsenal.

But Jacques Pottier's favorite materials (besides capeskin and ostrich, the only leathers which never deteriorate) are crocodile and especially pangolin, which he was the first in France to use. The skin of this anteater, indigenous to Malaysia and Formosa, is very long wearing but also infinitely supple, and is composed of large lozenge-shaped scales. Pangolin is extremely rare (the natives only take in six hundred skins a month), and priced the same as crocodile. His crocodile skins come from Madagascar and Malaysia and are tanned with aniline, which keeps them "natural" and acquires a patina over the years. He only uses pigmentation (a sort of paint) on white crocodile, which has just started coming into fashion. Jacques Pottier handles these skins—the most beautiful on the market —with the care of a true artist. It would be impossible to describe the secrets of great leatherwork in a few lines, for, in the words of that old craftsman at Hermès, "The soul of a handbag is everything you don't see."

But one example will be enough to give you an idea of the class and quality of everything Pottier does. Whereas some "quality houses" usually put a coarse cowhide stiffener (not to mention metal shafts or just plain cardboard) between leather and lining, Pottier utilizes that extraordinary English calf used to line riding boots.

What, then, is a beautiful handbag? There's no such thing in itself, according to Jacques Pottier, for the beauty of a bag depends on how well it harmonizes with a particular silhouette. What looks good in a store window may not be at all right for the person who is going to carry it.

This insistence on profound harmony is really the primary concern of this great leatherwork master who, with his three craftsmen, labors in the obscurity of his little atelier for the most illustrious names on earth.

Chichen-Itza, 231 rue Saint-Honoré, (Ier), ANJ 80.16.

Duc

Mme Duc's store, decorated along eighteenth-century lines displays handbags which she herself designs and has made by the cream of Parisian leatherworkers.

Mme Duc launched the long handle which makes handbags so convenient to carry, and every year she designs eight or ten new models, each adorned with a shield representing a (ducal) crown surmounted by an acanthus leaf. Any of her bags can be made to order within ten days in all sorts of materials (calf, crocodile, antelope, satin, etc.).

Duc, 37 rue du Colisée (8e), ELY 94.07.

Hermès

This is the most famous leathergoods store in the world. It even conceals a little museum which nobody knows about (on the fourth floor; ask permission first before going up). The museum consists of a large room with pale paneling, where you'll find magnificently ornamented saddles, Napoleon's stirrups, and an infinite number of trunks with secret compartments, swiveling boxes and miniature gold or vermeil bottles.

The capacious Hermès bag, made right above the store by wonderful craftsmen, is a national institution, as are the famous scarves of which Hermès sells 450,000 a year to cover charming heads all over the world.

Hermès, 24 rue du Faubourg Saint-Honoré (8e), ANJ 22.10.

Renard

Monsieur Renard, a true craftsman, makes all his handbags himself at the rear of a courtyard in a building on place du Palais-Bourbon. He works mostly with crocodile, to which he brings the utmost taste and a perfect sense of what "finishing" really means.

Renard, 3 place du Palais-Bourbon (7e), INV 77.87.

Tury

At first glance all you see is antique furniture. A few hand-bags, casually arranged, are barely enough to remind you that you haven't walked into an antique store but a leathergoods shop, one of the most precious and elegant in this neighborhood.

Monsieur Tury, a native of Hungary, designs all the bags (an average of four new styles each season) and cuts the skins which he himself selects. Snakeskin, jacaruxy (a cross between a lizard and a crocodile) and, of course, crocodile, with the fine round scales that are his specialty.

As for the clasps, he wouldn't think of using anything but japan work or gold plate.

Monsieur Tury will show you his infinite range of creations, from the traditional crocodile bag to the classic purse in soft leather, passing through such novelties as pleated satin bags in every color of the rainbow, evening bags of tiny metallic beads or other beaded bags with appliqués from antique kimonos. If you like, he can also make the handbag of your dreams to order in about ten days.

Tury, 10 rue Royale (8e), OPE 44.97.

Wines and spirits

Jean-Baptiste Besse

"My mother used to say, 'I don't know how many chickens I've got, but I know when one's missing.'" With a laugh, Jean-Baptiste Besse, his beret stuck onto his large, shrewd peasant's head, points grandly to the most extravagant pile of bottles to be found in any Parisian cellar. Picture a sixteenth-century house with two cellars, one on top of the other. You plunge into the first by means of a steep, narrow staircase. Then, your explorer's instinct aroused, you make your way through a magma of glass, dust and spiderwebs. Bottles are jumbled together in defiance of the law of gravity: champagnes are coupled with Alsatians, Beaujolais smother ports. And the floor is littered with casualties, the victims of these savage struggles.

But you don't linger here. These are just the little ones, the rank and file, the unknowns. You take another plunge into a second cellar, down a vertiginous stairway. The dust is even thicker, the webs even denser, the scene more turbulent. This is the heart of Besse's "treasury," his mad cemetery whose occupants have the sweetest names in the French language: Chamboll-Musigny, Nuits Saint-Georges, Corton-Charlemagne, Château d'Yquem, Château Latour . . .

We can't unequivocally promise that Père Besse will invite you to travel through his "infernal regions." You have to deserve it; you have to win over this amazing fellow, who is a flabbergasting blend of kindness and peasant cunning, theater sense and humility, this Papa Besse who never finished grade school but whose opinions about wine and things in general delight professors from the nearby Sorbonne and Ecole Polytechnique who drop in to celebrate the cult of wine, friendship and wisdom in his tiny grocery store, cluttered with sardine cans and crates of peas. It so happens that Jaguars and Rolls-Royces have been pulling up in front of his store since we discovered it perched on top of the Montagne Sainte-Geneviève. If their owners fit in and show themselves worthy of his friendship, then everything's fine and it's not unusual for Besse to uncork a very old port or marvelous champagne in their honor, which one drinks while sitting balanced on a heap of bottles. But if the newcomers act uppity, show off their (nonexistent) expertise and treat Besse like an ordinary shopkeeper, he'll either fob off a run-of-the-mill bottle on them or push them toward the door.

But just because you've been accepted doesn't mean he'll sell you his Lafite 1928, Chambolle-Musigny 1934 or Château d'Yquem 1937. Those are collector's items which he prefers to drink himself or give to old friends. Then there is that "noble" wine with the famous name, which Besse distrusts for all sorts of reasons: because it's too expensive, because the vinification isn't impeccable, etc. This is the one he saves for snobs and pretentious customers. And last of all there's the wine which he loves and recommends to anyone wise enough to put himself in Besse's hands. It's always a great vintage, not necessarily from a great year, but always a terrific buy.

You might as well know that his personal favorite is a Clos
d'Estournel Bordeaux. Not because it's the best, but because it
was the first good wine he ever drank as a child in his father's
mill in the Lozère. The label looked so pretty and the taste was
so enticing that his vocation was formed that very day.

> Jean-Baptiste Besse, 48 rue de la Montagne Sainte-Geneviève (5e),
> no telephone. Closed Mondays.

J.-B. Chaudet

His first name is Jean-Baptiste, just like Besse. And like
Besse, this tall Savoyard with a merry smile and Herculean
proportions has devoted his whole life to the religion of wine.

For years his shop, hidden away near the Jardin des Plantes,
attracted only local customers and a few connoisseurs who
knew that in this modest shop they would find one of the finest
selections of wine in Paris and the fraternal welcome of a man
in love with his work. Now that Chaudet has been interviewed
on radio and television and is known to every Parisian and all
wine-loving visitors to the city, he has become something of a
star. Not that fame has gone to his head. His gnarled body is
still girded with a long leather apron and he still bustles back
and forth between cellar and store, washing bottles, piling
crates into his tri-car (he makes the deliveries himself when he
has time) and handing out samples of wine at the bar. Chaudet does have one advantage over Besse in that he possesses a
liquor license. As a matter of fact, this has gotten him into
some trouble, since the brimming glasses he insisted on pouring (for the same price) were more generous than the law
allowed. His charming wife, Paulette (who loves her husband
a lot more than wine), officiates behind the bar, which is always
overrun by a very motley clientele of doctors, construction
workers, and painters and sculptors from Montparnasse
(César is a faithful customer). Chaudet's is the only bar in
Paris that serves great wines (Sauternes, Burgundies, etc.)
which elsewhere are sold only by the bottle. He's always ready
to uncork a bottle and give a taste to anyone who shows a
sincere interest in that wine and is thinking of ordering some
from him.

Careful, methodical classification and testing reign here as much as disorder rules at Besse's. Indeed, no wine ever gets into Chaudet's without his first tasting it. He always keeps abreast of the winegrowing industry, and there are few Frenchmen who can tell you, as he can, whether such and such a Burgundy was honestly made or how well an old Bordeaux from ten or fifteen years back has aged. (A "good year" is actually never *definitive:* the 1947 which used to be magnificent now frequently causes unpleasant surprises, and the 1948 which started out very mediocre is often superb at present.) Every year Chaudet travels all around France, which makes it possible for him personally to choose the best wines right at the winegrower's. He is very suspicious of wines sold by wholesalers and does almost all his business with little winegrowers from Burgundy and the Loire, who have proven their honesty and the quality of their products.

One of his greatest merits, in our opinion, is not so much that he can sell you a Chambertin from a good year (which is within the scope of any shopkeeper), but that he has a considerable selection of rather rare and, in any case, unfamiliar wines which he sells at very reasonable prices. Naturally, you'll find real Beaujolais, Muscadets and unadulterated Sancerres at his place, but he also has delicious Savoy wines, very fine ones from Touraine, surprising *passetougrain* Burgundies, and many other supposedly modest vintages which generally escape notice by Parisians whose tastes, in the end, are highly conventional and very much ruled by fashion.

Once you have become a friend of Chaudet's you may be granted the privilege of tasting some of the spirits in his personal cache: plum brandy, Bugey marc, old calvados or pear brandy, made as only a few winegrowers from another age still know how to make them—men who, like Chaudet himself, haven't renounced their love of art.

> J.-B. Chaudet, 20 rue Geoffroy Saint-Hilaire (5e), POR 23.98. Closed on Sundays.

Danflou

An elegant entresol in a beautiful old house in the Concorde district. Monsieur Danflou, a smiling, elegant young gentleman, doesn't remind you in the least of Besse or Chaudet. His sincerity and competence are every bit as profound, however, even if he expresses them in a worldly way. The great specialty of this old firm, unknown to the general public, is not wine but spirits in every form. There is no better guarantee than the name Danflou on a label. All of their products come directly from craftsmen who know nothing of disastrous industrial methods.

Monsieur Danflou will be glad to give you a little course on spirits. You may learn, for instance, that the impressive "V.S.O.P." inscribed on some cognac labels doesn't mean a thing (except, he adds with a smile, "Very Saleable Old Product"), that a "Three Stars" fine has been aged in the wood for three years (which is very little indeed) and that, generally speaking, the year alone won't tell you much unless you know for certain that the brandy has aged in wooden barrels for at least forty years. (Of course, we're not talking about the white brandies—pear, mirabelle, plum—which do not "age" and must be bottled very quickly.) He'll also teach you to beware of certain so-called "very old" calvados, which has been artificially aged by adding caramel. And he will disclose that white brandy should never be chilled in the refrigerator but rather in a glass rotated in crushed ice; on the other hand, any alcohol aged in wood has to be warmed in the hand, never any other way.

One thing you can be sure of, in any case, is that the bottle you buy from Monsieur Danflou will bring back nostalgic memories of this secret little store hidden behind the rue de Rivoli.

> Danflou, 36 rue du Mont-Thabor (Ier), OPE 77.19. Closed on Sundays.

China

The rue de Paradis (in the 10th *arrondissement*) is the realm of porcelain, faience and glassware. One shop stops where another begins. The choice is immense but the "taste" extremely varied: Limoges, porcelaine de Paris, Baccarat, Saint-Louis, Daum crystal, etc.

Madronet-Contemporain

Contemporary table services from the famous German firm of Rosenthal.

Madronet-Contemporain, 26 rue de Paradis (10e), PRO 34.59.

Clara Fandor

Plain white and decorated (Limoges) china. Exclusive patterns. They will make up sets to order with your initials or any pattern in black or in color.

Clara Fandor, 18 rue Mazarine (6e), MED 05.38.

L'Echoppe

The best selection of contemporary china, in one of the prettiest modern stores in Paris.

L'Echoppe, 51 rue de Seine (6e), ODE 57.65.

Claude Perras

Lovely china by Scandinavian and German designers.

Claude Perras, 34 rue Saint-Louis-en-l'Ile (4e), DAN 78.88.

Lalique

Widely renowned crystal. Exclusive patterns.

Lalique, 11 rue Royale (8e), ANJ 33.70.

Rosenthal-Studio Haus-Delvaux

China, tableware and glasses in shapes that are both sensible and sensitive, designed by the great European "plasticians": Tapio Wirkhala, Bjorn Wimmblad, Hans Theo Baumann, etc.

Rosenthal-Studio Haus-Delvaux, 18 rue Royale (8e), OPE 85.95.

Part VI

ANTIQUES

For some time now Parisian antique dealers have been complaining that they no longer can find anything good. The problem is very relative. An American visiting France for the first time is, on the contrary, pleasantly surprised by the abundant selection he sees in the shops of these whimpering dealers.

It does so happen that very valuable objects rarely stay in France, but head rapidly for New York or Chicago. There's still a lot left, though, and it's more than enough to gladden the hearts of lesser collectors or people who simply enjoy beautiful things. A serious problem has nonetheless arisen in France as elsewhere, namely, the proliferation of forgeries, whether of paintings, antique bronzes, furniture or curios. Knowledge and flair are becoming more and more essential to obtain a work of exemplary quality, and, alas, not even the greatest experts are proof against unfortunate errors from time to time. You simply have to be prudent when the price of your prospective purchase goes over a certain figure. How? There's no choice: either you're a real connoisseur and can risk buying anywhere at all, or you can't trust blindly in your own judgment. In that case there is a golden rule which you absolutely have to follow: Buy only from a real specialist. You may end up paying a little more than if you went into the first second-hand store you laid eyes on (and besides, that's not always true), but you'll have the double guarantee that (1) ninety-nine times out of a hundred the object will be genuine, and (2) if it turns out to be false in spite of everything, the dealer will respect the certificate of authenticity he gave you and won't make any fuss about taking it back.

This is why we prefer to give you only a few good addresses instead of drawing up endless lists of antique dealers. We repeat: these people sometimes make mistakes, but we can guarantee that they practice their profession with a maximum of honesty and scruples. If any of them ever takes it into his head to disobey the laws of business ethics, just let us know. You can be sure he'll be chewing his nails after the "publicity" we'll give him.

Our list is not definitive, of course. Paris has thousands of antique and second-hand stores, and we don't pretend to know them all. There are undoubtedly some excellent stores which we may have missed but, incomplete or not, we'd rather stick with the ones we know.

You can find antique stores almost anywhere in Paris. But there is one privileged section where you can take a most agreeable stroll into the past, even if you don't feel like buying anything. This section is on the Left Bank, between boulevard Saint-Germain and the Seine.

Stroll along boulevard Saint-Germain. Turn left onto rue Bonaparte, then right onto rue Jacob. A little further down this street, to your right, you'll find rue Furstenberg and the enchanting little square of the same name where Delacroix had his studio (open to the public). Walk around the square. The shopwindows are full of cute, funny, unusual objects. But watch out: the prices are often steep, since this is a very fashionable spot. It's best to compare and decide later.

Back on rue Jacob, go down it again to your left until you intersect rue Bonaparte, on which you turn right, walk past the Ecole des Beaux Arts and come out onto Quai Malaquais and, further to the left, Quai Voltaire, which has some highly renowned antique shops. Now go up rue de Beaune, which is lined with several excellent stores. By taking either rue de Verneuil or rue de l'Université, both to your right, you'll emerge onto rue du Bac, which in turn leads back to boulevard Saint-Germain. If you're not ruined or crawling on your hands and knees by this time, cross boulevard Saint-Germain. On the other side is boulevard Raspail, then rue de Grenelle or rue de la Chaise to your immediate left, where you'll discover some good shops. Finally, when you come to the end of rue de Grenelle, take a left onto rue des Saints-Pères, which you will leave either at boulevard Saint-Germain or in front of the Seine on

Quai Malaquais, where other quality antique shops await you.

Some other day you can walk along Faubourg Saint-Honoré and rue Saint-Honoré from rue La Boétie to place Vendôme. You'll see some very handsome stores which are likely to intimidate you by their rather solemn appearance. But don't let that fool you. On several different occasions we've noticed that prices here are sometimes lower than in the flea market, and the quality usually much higher.

But we wouldn't want to claim this is a fixed rule.

Just as we will classify antique dealers by specialties, we thought it might prove helpful to tell you which museums (outside of the Louvre, which has just about everything), can satisfy the tourist's curiosity with collections from that same period.

Antiquities (Egypt, Greece, Rome, Mesopotamia)

The French have relatively little interest in archaeological objects, although the market has expanded within recent years. In any case, if the selection is less vast and less extraordinary than in Switzerland, London or even New York, prices are generally lower. And when you compare the price of a beautiful Roman statue or Egyptian stele with what is being asked for second-rate Impressionists, you're likely to conclude that fashion's fancies are fanciful indeed.

But you still have to be careful: forgeries sprout like weeds in the field of antiquities, and you should only place your confidence in dealers with a profound scientific knowledge of this terribly complex art.

Galérie Archéologie

Elie Borowski, who studied at the Ecole du Louvre and was assistant curator at the Toronto Museum, is the world's greatest dealer in Greek and Near Eastern antiquities. His town house in Basel has three floors crammed with the rarest works of art, from which he supplies the greatest museums of Europe and America. He recently opened a little store in Paris that is much less of a treasure house than the one in Basel but in which you can have just as much confidence.

Galérie Archéologie, 40 rue du Bac (7e), LIT 61.60.

Gérard Lévy

This young antique dealer, a graduate of the Ecole du Louvre, isn't exclusively interested in antiquities (see *Art Nouveau,* p. 364), but it's a field he knows well and never stops studying. You'll find a little bit of everything here (Egypt, Greece, Rome, Sumer, Louristan, etc.), at all prices. He is scrupulosity itself, and will guide your choice both intelligently and honestly.

Gérard Lévy, 17 rue de Beaune (7e), BAB 80.19.

Marianne Maspéro

This young woman is related to the great archaeologist Maspéro, loaded with diplomas and passionately interested in her profession. She has an irreproachable stock of Greek and Egyptian articles, an appreciable number of which end up in museums.

Marianne Maspéro, 48 boulevard Malesherbes (8e), LAB 08.59.

Orient-Occident

Jean-Loup Despras is a true scholar: he can read Egyptian hieroglyphs fluently and is always being consulted about the authenticity or meaning of Egyptian art objects that turn up on the Paris market. A young man but not a very talkative one, he's not much interested in the commercial aspect of his profession and hardly bothers to have his gallery repainted. He lives in another world, which is where you have to join him if you want to see the most beautiful Egyptian art available in Paris.

Orient-Occident, 5 rue des Saints-Pères (6e), LIT 66.48.

Gold and silver plate

A certain number of dealers specialize in antique silver, but the majority also handle second-hand silver, i.e., from the late nineteenth and early twentieth centuries. Flatware in these shops often costs half of what you'd pay for new table silver.

English silverware is certainly more plentiful, since it was never melted down in quantity, as French silver was in the eighteenth century, to bolster government finances. Nevertheless, you can often get better bargains in Paris than in England.

Baur

Old pieces, beautiful, high-class silverware.
> Baur, 32 rue La Boétie (8ᵉ), ELY 19.16.

Christofle

The great silver-plate specialist for over a hundred years. They also have a department devoted to fine antique gold.
> Christofle, 12 rue Royale (8ᵉ), OPE 70.43.

Helft

An old firm, much esteemed by good middle-class Parisians. Nice antique silver, brooches, jewelry, candle holders, tea services, etc.
> Helft, 366 rue Saint-Honoré (Iᵉʳ), OPE 88.01.

Joséphine

A great specialist in antique gold and silver, especially from the eighteenth century.
> Joséphine, 1 rue Bonaparte (6ᵉ), DAN 49.73.

Kugel

One of the greatest antique dealers of our time. His taste, refinement, stock and prices attract great French and foreign

collectors to his town house (20 rue Amélie, 7ᵉ) or his store on
the rue de la Paix. At Kugel's you'll see a remarkable assortment of gold plate, miniatures, gold boxes and collector's items.

Kugel, 7 rue de la Paix (2ᵉ), OPE 61.04.

Musée de l'Argenterie (Museum of Silver), Christofle Factory,
112 rue Ambroise-Croizat, Saint-Denis, PLA 15.30.

A complete panorama of French silver up to the present day.
All the pieces are very faithful copies.

Musée des Arts Décoratifs (Museum of Decorative Art), 107
rue de Rivoli (Iᵉʳ), OPE 49.68. Closed Tuesdays.

Arms

The antique-weapons market has experienced an impressive
development over the past ten years. Prices haven't stopped
climbing, but in spite of everything there is still a rather vast
selection.

Au Bon Vieux Chic

Monsieur Johnson (his father was American) is the foremost weapons specialist in France and perhaps in Europe. Ever
since he was a child he has been shut up in this dilapidated
store, shrine for weapon collectors since the eighteenth century. His oldest pieces go back to the twelfth century, but
they are not necessarily the most expensive: some Colts easily
bring 20,000 to 30,000 francs ($4,000 to $6,000). It would take
weeks to see all of Monsieur Johnson's treasures, not to mention the ones hidden away in his cellar, which he only shows to
rare initiates. Do you know who are the most enthusiastic fans
of these antique instruments of death? Not soldiers, not hunters, but doctors and surgeons. Freud is definitely still with us.

Au Bon Vieux Chic, 16 quai du Louvre (Iᵉʳ), CEN 56.61.

Musée de l'Armée (Army Museum), Hôtel des Invalides, Esplanade des Invalides (7ᵉ), INV 27.81. Closed on Tuesdays.

This museum, the only one of its kind in the world, houses a fantastic collection of weapons from the Middle Ages to the present. The section devoted to the armor of the kings of France, especially from the Renaissance, is particularly impressive.

Primitive art (Africa, Oceania, America)

Galérie Arts des Amériques

With his chiseled features, shrewd eyes, thick peasant hands and self-proclaimed thirst for gold, adventure and freedom, Robert Vergnes bursts with life, like everyone who lives by risking it. He has lived in the depths of the virgin forests of Central America, digging like mad, turning over ton after ton of earth. His profession was that of *huaquero*. This is a Spanish-American word meaning tomb, and a *huaquero* is someone who looks for tombs. For several months now he has been transformed into a respectable antique dealer, who displays and sells his best finds in a little shop all done in blue.

Archaeologists aren't too fond of this adventurer who goes off to dig holes in the depths of the virgin forest and makes his own rules. He couldn't care less, and goes right on replenishing his little store with the pre-Columbian objects that have cost him many a blister.

> Galérie Arts des Amériques, 9 rue de l'Echaudé (6e), MED 18.31.

Kamer

Whenever Nelson Rockefeller or Paul Tishman wants a piece of African, pre-Columbian or Oceanic art, he picks up the phone and calls Henri Kamer. In fifteen years this Parisian, a graduate of the Ecole du Louvre, has become one of the foremost dealers in the world. He left France because the market didn't offer any openings worthy of his ambition, and settled in the United States, for, as he says, "Americans are the only real collectors. What counts most over there isn't an object's price,

decorative value or emotional impact, but its uniqueness."
Nevertheless, Henri and Hélène Kamer's two galleries (New
York and Palm Beach) and five-story Manhattan town house
stuffed with rare objects have just produced a new offshoot: a
luxurious gallery on the banks of the Seine. Does this mean
that the French have become the collectors which, in Kamer's
opinion, they are not? No; it's simply that Hélène Kamer can't
do without Paris, so her husband gave her this lovely "play-
thing," doubtless in the secret hope that the French are some
day bound to remember that they were the ones who first discovered and launched Negro art some fifty years ago.

Kamer, 9 quai Malaquais (6ᵉ), LIT 54.60.

Le Corneur et Roudillon

With consummate art, these two partners have assembled
more than a thousand pieces of Negro and pre-Columbian art,
many of them noteworthy, in their attractive gallery.

Le Corneur et Roudillon, 206 boulevard Saint-Germain (6ᵉ), LIT
55.54.

Charles Ratton

With Kamer, Ratton is the world's leading specialist in
Negro art, which he was the first to launch in France. He
amasses his treasures in a huge apartment where you go by
appointment. His passion for Africa does not exclude others,
however; you'll also find very beautiful archaeological objects
as well as some luxury curios.

Charles Ratton, 14 rue de Marignan (8ᵉ), ELY 58.21.

Jacques Kerchache

Jacques Kerchache learned his trade from the late, celebrated
Pierre Loeb, who revealed Oceanic art to the French. At
twenty-five, Kerchache is already a great collector and highly
esteemed dealer. His expertise covers a wide range, since he is
equally interested in Mexico and British Columbia as in the
Marquesas Islands and Dahomey. When the Musée de
l'Homme (Museum of Anthropology) held an exhibit called

"One Hundred Masterpieces," there was only one name in the catalog: Jacques Kerchache.

Jacques Kerchache, 53 rue de Seine (6ᵉ), ODE 87.79.

Musée de l'Homme, Palais de Chaillot, place du Trocadéro (16ᵉ), PAS 74.46. Closed Tuesdays.

A remarkable museum, both scientific and educational. The exhibits, which include very rich collections of African, American and Oceanic art, are arranged with the utmost clarity.

Asia (China, Japan, India, Cambodia, Siam)

Michel Beurdeley

Whenever Michel Beurdeley takes part in an antique show—whether in Paris, Florence, Brussels or London—you can be sure that he will have one of the two or three handsomest and most admired booths. This distinguished, refined gentleman is one of the world's leading authorities on Chinese art, particularly porcelain. His customers include the cream of international society, whom he receives by appointment in his sumptuous apartment near the Elysée Palace.

Michel Beurdeley, 4 rue de l'Elysée (8ᵉ), ANJ 97.49.

Jean-Michel Beurdeley

He's his father's son, but no "Daddy's boy." At twenty-four, this antique dealer with the playboy physique has unusually fine taste and judgment. His gallery is one of the most alluring in all Paris. He frequently changes the interior layout by means of a system of movable panels and display units, and concentrates each time on presenting different objects centered around specific themes. All civilizations (Greek, Roman, Egyptian, etc.) are represented in his gallery, but his heart belongs to Asia, particularly ancient China and Japan. However, everything from the fine collector's items to objects priced at 200 to 300 francs ($40 to $60) have both quality and individuality.

Jean-Michel Beurdeley, 200 boulevard Saint-Germain (6ᵉ), LIT 97.86.

C. T. Loo

This extravagant Chinese palace, stuck smack in the middle of bourgeois Paris, was converted in 1928 from a Louis XV town house where Charles Dickens lived after the Franco-Prussian War. Ching Tsai Loo, who ruled this Pekingese palace until his death in 1957, was undoubtedly the greatest Chinese art dealer of the century. It's true that there was no problem then about bringing fifteen-foot-high sculptures or priceless Chang bronzes back from China. Miss Loo is now in charge of this vast establishment which some hard-to-please enthusiasts claim is only the shadow of its former self, but which is still rich enough to make you wonder whether you're not in a museum.

It would be far from true to say that your presence is ardently desired here. In this silent, ghost-haunted palace they prefer great collectors and museum curators to simple tourists out to buy a teapot.

C. T. Loo, 48 rue de Courcelles (8ᵉ), CAR 53.15.

Moreau-Gobard

If all antique dealers were in the same class as Jean-Claude Moreau-Gobard, no one would have to worry about the future of the profession. Not a single criticism can be leveled at him. He is an expert whom it is impossible to stump, no matter whether the subject is ancient Chinese bronzes, Khmer sculpture or Hindu art; a dealer whose prices couldn't be fairer (to compare them with those of any New York dealer will set you dreaming); a collector who never allows himself to show a customer any object whose authenticity is not absolutely certain; and finally, an esthete who much prefers to describe the background of his pieces for your admiration than to sell them.

His store is rather antiquated, but it's hard to tear oneself away, especially when he has just received a shipment from India, Siam or Indonesia.

His cupboards conceal jades and bronzes worth hundreds of thousands, but you certainly don't have to be a millionaire to become a customer. You will even be surprised at the (relatively) low cost of some beautiful antiques compared with mediocre "modern" souvenirs which became worthless the minute you buy them.

Moreau-Gobard, 16 avenue George V (8ᵉ), ELY 44.86.

Janette Ostier

This gallery, situated under the arcades of the magnificent place des Vosges and run by a charming and very erudite woman, is devoted to Japanese art. Janette Ostier was one of the very first in France to awaken interest in Japanese curios, painting and drawing, some ten years ago. Masks, lacquer boxes, screens: everything here is refined, and displayed with exemplary taste.

Janette Ostier, 26 place des Vosges (2ᵉ), TUR 28.57.

Josette Schulmann

While her husband makes and sells ultramodern furniture, this smiling young woman spends her days in the company of Hindu gods and Chinese bronzes. Her objects are of good quality and sell for reasonable prices.

Josette, 17 rue de Grenelle (6ᵉ), LIT 09.42.

Musée Cernuschi, 7 avenue Vélasquez (8ᵉ), LAB 23.31. Closed Tuesdays.

This quiet little museum, located at the entrance to the Parc Monceau, contains magnificent collections of ancient Chinese art (bronzes, pottery, funerary statuettes, etc.) as well as paintings and drawings. They put on very interesting exhibits.

Musée Guimet, 6 place d'Iéna (16ᵉ), KLE 75.96. Closed Tuesdays.

This is the Oriental Art section of the Louvre. You'll find a library, classrooms, record library, etc. And magnificent collections of Chinese, Khmer, Greco-Buddhist, Louristan and Japanese art, unfortunately displayed in a rather shabby setting. But it's still a must for anyone interested in Asia.

Dolls and automatons

Jacques Damiot

This decorator has been very much "it" for twenty years, and is responsible for the success of the 1880's style. He has a sumptuous collection of automatons and will recount their backgrounds to you with tremendous humor.

> Jacques Damiot, 57 rue Jacques Dulud, Neuilly-sur-Seine, MAI 96.16.

Curiosités, 36 rue de l'Université (7e).
Jeanne d'Arc, 9 rue Geoffrey Saint-Hilaire (5e), GOB 75.72. Nineteenth-century dolls.

Musée du Conservatoire des Arts et Métiers (Arts and Crafts Museum), 292 rue Saint-Martin (3e), TUR 37.38. Closed Mondays.

The ruins of the beautiful medieval priory of Saint-Martin-des-Champs house a very rich collection of antique automatons, including the famous "dulcimer player" which once belonged to Marie Antoinette. They "perform" once every three months.

Gilded wood

Marguerite Fondeur

You won't find any newly minted gilded wood from Spain or Italy in the shop of this voluble lady. There cannot be the slightest doubt about the quality or authenticity of her eighteenth- and nineteenth-century objects, but don't expect her to give them away.

> Marguerite Fondeur, 24 rue de Beaune (7e), LIT 84.47.

Music boxes

La Boîte à Musique, 9 rue du Bac (7ᵉ), BAB 01.30.
Closed Monday mornings.

Second-hand stores

There used to be a great distinction between antique dealers,
who sold precious objects to great art patrons, and junk dealers, who sold . . . everything else. Today everybody calls himself an antique dealer, except for a few modest tradesmen who
have the decency not to give the name "antiques" to their odds
and ends, which for that matter are often lots of fun and may
sometimes conceal a little "buried treasure." (See *Flea Markets,*
p. 354.)

Au Beau Marché d'Occasions

Marcel Tardieu, the picturesque king of junk, has amassed a
collection of improbable and often zany furniture and knick-
knacks in the house which the magician Cagliostro made his
home at the end of the eighteenth century.

Au Beau Marché d'Occasions, 99 boulevard Beaumarchais (3ᵉ),
TUR 89.35.

Sénac

Anything and everything, from stuffed Siberian elk heads to
1900's canopy beds, passing through velocipedes and hurdy-
gurdies.

Sénac, 36 *bis* rue Ballu (9ᵉ), PIG 35.82.

Buttons

Boutons Anciens

Thousands of old buttons, including some precious ones from the seventeenth and eighteenth centuries. They are made of embroidered fabric or gilded copper mounted on bone or wood, and used to be sewn with catgut onto men's costumes for decoration. It was not until the Revolution in 1789 that tailors—especially military tailors—started using them to fasten men's clothing. At the beginning of the nineteenth century someone got the idea of giving them a little neck to make it easier to attach and remove them, this time using thread.

These pretty buttons add elegance to a blazer or can even be made into cuff links.

Boutons Anciens, 18 rue d'Anjou (8e), ANJ 11.56.

Bronzes

We're not going to talk about precious, very costly Renaissance bronzes—which can be seen at great dealers like Alavoine, 42 avenue Kléber (16e), or Nicolas Landau, 8 rue du Cirque (8e), by appointment only at ELY 52.01. These are destined for great collections and cannot be of any practical interest to the average art lover. On the other hand, here's an address which will be more fun and less intimidating than the former:

Alain Lesieutre

This young dealer is the only one who specializes in bronze statuettes from the second half of the nineteenth century in France, a period long neglected by art lovers. You'll find bronzes by the great *animalier* Barye, by Carpeaux (who did the "La Danse" group at the Opéra), and even some pieces by Rodin in this charming, minuscule boutique, at prices ranging from 100 francs to 10,000 francs ($20 to $2,000).

Alain Lesieutre, 10 rue Saint-Sulpice (6e), MED 41.03.

Musée Rodin, 77 rue de Varenne (7é), INV 01.34. Closed Tuesdays.

The major part of Rodin's work is very successfully displayed in the setting of a sumptuous Regency mansion surrounded by delightful gardens. The museum has its "hell": the great sculptor's erotic works which, as one might well imagine, are kept out of sight of the general public.

Hunting

Air de Chasse

This very pretty shop specializes in all antiques related to hunting: work by English goldsmiths, silver trophies, bronze animals, engravings, plates with hunting scenes, knives, but also little everyday articles patterned with hunting motifs (paper-knives, ashtrays, knife-rests, napkin rings, etc.) which all make wonderful, original gifts.

The proprietress of this shop is an entrancing young woman, Mme Mondovi, who, oddly enough, doesn't care one bit for hunting.

Air de Chasse, 8 rue des Saints-Pères (7e), LIT 65.68.

Musée de la Chasse (Museum of Hunting), 60 rue des Archives (3e), LOU 90.66.

The beautiful Guénégaud mansion (seventeenth century) has recently been renovated at great expense by a couple of hunters, the Sommers, to accommodate a hunting museum of incomparable luxury and refinement. In addition to paintings, photographs and trophies from the world over, you can admire a collection of antique hunting weapons which is the only one of its kind in the world.

Keys, doorhandles and locks

Aubier et Cuny

This tiny shop in the heart of the artisans' district has more than three thousand kinds of door and drawer handles, key tops and finger-plates, from the time of Louis XIV to the present. They will quickly make a perfect copy of anything you select.

> Aubier et Cuny, 74 rue du Faubourg Saint-Antoine (12ᵉ), DID 36.36.

Bricard

The largest imaginable choice of antique locks and keys from France and abroad. Bricard's collection is so rich that he's soon going to start a museum in the Marais.

You can get copies made of most of these models.

> Bricard, 39 rue de Richelieu (Iᵉʳ), RIC 99.39.

Furniture reproductions

The flea market and many "antique" dealers have lots of imitation Louis XV chairs and Louis XIV commodes. Unfortunately, they're not all honest enough to admit it, and you may end up paying stiff prices for partially or even completely faked merchandise. If you don't know enough about the different styles and don't have the means to treat yourself to duly signed furniture, why not go straight to the source? We're going to give you two addresses of absolutely exceptional craftsmen, who make copies of antique furniture and don't claim to do anything else. It's not their fault if some antique dealers pass their work off as genuine. By dealing with them directly, you'll avoid being swindled in any case, and you'll save money besides.

Luis Ansa

This Argentinian painter, who came to France in 1948, is a great lacquer craftsman whose specialty is French eighteenth-century furniture in the Chinese manner. He sells his low tables for about 600 francs ($120) and his splendid Louis XV "Chinese" commodes for 2,000 francs ($400), which is the same price he charges dealers.

> Luis Ansa, 37 *bis* rue de Montreuil (11e), 344.06.50. Second court, stairway C, third floor.

Mocqué et Fils

This diploma-laden cabinetmaker makes copies of armchairs for museums, palaces and top decorators. His workshop, which has knee-deep shavings, a wonderful smell of wood and not a single piece of machinery, occupies three floors off a courtyard in the old Faubourg Saint-Antoine, the cabinetmakers' district. What they do here is nothing short of marvelous, copying the work of great eighteenth-century artists under the same conditions, by the same methods and in the same spirit. Jean Mocqué is not content simply to use the same stains, execute veneers and marquetry in the same manner, carve every line, molding and ornament by hand, apply a French polish finish and use mortise and tenon joints. He also possesses the most complete documentation in France: the designs for more than ten thousand signed pieces of furniture, all of which are in museums or private collections.

A Directoire chair, the exact replica of the ones in Malmaison, sells for less than 700 francs ($140); a reproduction of a Louis XVI chair by the great Jacob is 650 francs ($130); a Louis XV or XVI commode costs from 3,000 francs to 15,000 francs ($600 to $3,000).

> Mocqué et Fils, 95 rue du Faubourg Saint-Antoine (11e), DID 12.13. By appointment only.

Curiosities

We use this word as a blanket term for all antique dealers specializing in the sale of strange, unusual, bizarre objects, which sometimes are also real works of art. (See *Luxury Curios,* p. 351.)

Le Cabinet de Curiosité

Enchanting panels from a late-eighteenth-century pharmacy run the length of the walls. The shelves display precious, exquisite, amusing objects: toys, tools, pipes, ladies' shoes from the Louis XVI period, scientific instruments, etc. You should also ask Monsieur Hébert to show you his file of business cards (German, nineteenth century) which were the forerunners—and so much more attractive!—of today's loathsome handbills. These pretty, illustrated, very decorative documents cost no more than a few francs.

Le Cabinet de Curiosité, 23 rue de Beaune (7e), BAB 59.65.

Comoglio

The zaniest and probably the most poetic shop in Paris. Comoglio supplied Jean Cocteau with the bizarre props he used in his plays and movies. You could spend hours on end in this enchanted kingdom of wrought iron and papier-mâché.

Comoglio, 22 rue Jacob (6e), ODE 65.86.

La Lanterne Magique

Monsieur Chérel, a bald and often scowling little fellow, doesn't cultivate the bizarre out of faddishness. He genuinely loves all the "horrors"—usually from the nineteenth century—with which his fantastic collection is filled: gory posters, miniature factories, naughty photographs, statues made of shells, magic lanterns, etc. The troubling guardian of this troubling world, Monsieur Chérel, doesn't like to sell anything. If he doesn't happen to cotton to you, you won't get anywhere at all.

La Lanterne Magique, 11 rue Coëtlogon (6e), LIT 05.61.

Suzanne Neton

This little white-haired lady hasn't anything of tremendous value, but she does have some endlessly entertaining knick-knacks: a tobacco jar shaped like a face, trompe l'oeil, snuff-boxes, etc. In short, a pretty exciting jumble if you have been bitten by the curio bug.

Suzanne Neton, 8 place Adolphe-Max (9e), PIG 60.63.

Wreckers

Very few tourists think of it, but there are a few wrecking companies right in the middle of Paris where it's fun to rummage around. The remains of houses, villas, sometimes even of dilapidated châteaux which had to be destroyed, are stored in sheds or out in the open, over hundreds and hundreds of yards. Among the mantelpieces, balconies and staircases you also find more portable objects such as candelabra, doors, wrought-iron ornaments, etc. And usually at very low prices.

Fauvet et Bernard, 1 boulevard de la Chapelle (10e), NOR 23.04.

Saussier, 154 rue H.-Barbusse, Argenteuil, 961.10.73.

Pewter and copper

The abundance of imitation pewter should put you on your guard against trading with anyone but a specialist:

Philippe Boucaud

His father was the leading specialist in antique pewter in France. The son carries on the old tradition and will show you his collection of pitchers, mugs and tankards, all of the utmost quality.

Philippe Boucaud, 42 rue du Cherche-Midi (6e), LIT 33.63.

Jacqueline Debay

Antique French and English copper, from jardinières to andirons, passing through bathroom accessories.

Jacqueline Debay, 145 rue de la Pompe (16e), PAS 42.33.

Lematte

An improbable, dusty shop full of pitchers, ladles, candlesticks and oil lamps which Monsieur Lematte grumblingly sells, when he doesn't simply throw his customers out.

Lematte, 14 rue Saint-Sulpice (6e).

Clarck-de Castro

At the rear of a courtyard in a narrow passageway wedged in between Quai de la Rapée and the Gare de Lyon, Jean-Pierre de Castro and Edgar Clarck sell all sorts of rustic antique objects: copper utensils in every size and shape, wrought iron, carriage lamps, scales from the thirteenth and fourteenth centuries, apothecary jars, copper or porcelain oil lamps, etc.

Clarck-de Castro, 2 passage Gentry (12^e), DID 30.93.

Engravings, lithographs, drawings, posters

For a long time French interest in drawings and engravings was limited to a small circle of enthusiastic fans. The market today has considerably expanded; nevertheless, prices are still generally lower than in London, and if you have a good eye you can still unearth some very interesting finds, especially among nineteenth-century French drawings.

A l'Art Ancien

Mme Woog-Meyer specializes in engravings and drawings. If you're curious enough to go rummaging in the back room, you'll find them there by the boxful.

A l'Art Ancien, 344 rue Saint-Honoré (8e), OPE 36.97.

Aymonier

Mme Aymonier is one of the foremost specialists in master drawings from the fifteenth through the eighteenth centuries.

Aymonier, 13 rue des Saints-Pères (6e), BAB 26.61.

Bihn

Large selection of English engravings.

Bihn, 15 quai Voltaire (7e), LIT 91.32.

Breheret

Original lithographs and etchings by contemporary artists (Picasso, Braque, Dufy, Buffet, etc.).

Breheret, 9 quai Malaquais (6e), LIT 47.89.

Cailac

Mademoiselle Cailac is a highly esteemed expert on modern prints and drawings.

Cailac, 13 rue de Seine (6e), DAN 98.88.

Cailleux

A very great specialist in eighteenth-century drawings. Clientele of collectors.

Cailleux, 136 rue du Faubourg Saint-Honoré (8e), ELY 25.24.

Deux Iles

Charming little nineteenth-century drawings at very feasible prices.

Deux Iles, 1 quai aux Fleurs (4e), ODE 67.76.

Documents

Wide choice of posters and lithographs from the *Belle Epoque* (Toulouse-Lautrec, Cappiello, Cheret, etc.).

Documents, 53 rue de Seine (6e), ODE 50.68.

Aux Goûts Réunis

The portfolios of François Fourcade and his associate Madame Cheval contain an impressive selection of drawings from all periods, among which something really marvelous turns up every now and then. Everything is sold at extremely reasonable prices by charming people who adore their work.

Aux Goûts Réunis, 16 rue d'Assas (6e), BAB 70.16.

La Hune

This bookseller (Bernard Gheerbrandt, whom we spoke of earlier) publishes engravings and lithographs by modern masters such as Dubuffet, Hartung, Poliakoff, etc., which are displayed on the second floor of his store. The original is destroyed after a limited number of proofs (between thirty and seventy-five) have been pulled; the prints fetch from 100 to 500 francs ($20 to $100).

La Hune, 170 boulevard Saint-Germain (6^e), LIT 35.85.

Loeb-Larocque

Specializes in engravings depicting landscapes from everywhere.

Loeb-Larocque, 36 rue Le Peletier (9e), TRU 11.18.

La Pochade

On the second floor of this paperback bookstore are lithographs and engravings by modern artists.

La Pochade, 157 boulevard Saint-Germain (6e), LIT 00.14.

Paul Prouté

A million engravings from the fifteenth century to the present, classified by subjects, periods and styles. The atmosphere is impersonal but the selection is large.

Paul Prouté, 74 rue de Seine (6e), DAN 89.90.

Rousseau

A vast selection of old engravings, both in black and white and in color.

Rousseau, 42 rue Lafayette (9e), PRO 84.50.

Even though we promised not to talk about the Louvre, we want to point out that the Drawing and Print Room (*Cabinet des Dessins et des Estampes*) has an extraordinary collection and arranges exhibits which are models of their kind.

Luxury curios

The term covers museum-worthy showpieces and collector's items, well beyond the price range of the average buyer.

Kugel, 20 rue Amélie (7e), INV 15.57. (See *Gold and Silver Plate,* p. 333.)

Nicolas Landau

Even his colleagues agree: Nicolas Landau is a genius. This fantastic antique dealer is of Polish origin and lived for some time in New York. He is endowed with a flair, taste and wit that elevate him far above the ordinary. There are "Landau

things" just as there used to be "Rothschild things." Nicolas
Landau is the source of all intelligent fads (notably the one for
scientific instruments) and exhibits in shows all over the
world. He is now retired from business, but will make an appointment to show you the wonders he has amassed in his
personal apartment: archaeological treasures, Renaissance
bronzes and gold, pottery, sculpture—superb, unique pieces
which you must prove yourself worthy to own.

Nicolas Landau, 8 rue du Cirque (8e), ELY 52.01.

Auctions

Hotel Drouot

The Auctioneers' Association owns this jerry-building,
which dates back to the nineteenth century and has the Paris
monopoly on auctions. The Hotel Drouot is pretty seedy compared to the Parke-Bernet or Sotheby's, but it is still a fascinating place where anyone who loves art, or simply loves to look,
can spend a very exciting afternoon. There are sales every afternoon but Sunday, starting at two o'clock. Auctions of
household articles are held on the ground floor; they are very
picturesque but of no interest to art lovers. Regular auctions—
which cover what is known as "good" furniture—take place
partly on the ground floor and partly on the floor above. The
great auctions, the ones that get written up in the newspapers,
are all supervised by experts (in France, your money is always
refunded if your purchase was falsely or mistakenly labeled).
These sales, which are usually catalogued, take place on the
second floor or at the Palais Galliéra, 10 avenue Pierre-Ier-de-
Serbie (16e). Merchandise is on view in the ground-floor
rooms from ten to eleven o'clock on the morning of the sale
day. Exhibits for the first-floor and Galliéra auctions are held
on the afternoon of the previous day. The auctioneer or one of
his assistants is on hand in the exhibit room and will indicate
the price which the object of your interest ought, in principle,
to bring. You can name your highest bid and instruct him to
buy the article for you.

You make bids by raising your hand or nodding your head. The bidding goes rather quickly and demands strict attention. When the auction is over, you pay for your purchase in cash or by check, and can either take it with you or pick it up in the courtyard of the Hotel Drouot off rue Rossini before eleven o'clock on the following morning. After that it is put away and you will have to pay a storage charge. A forwarding company with an office in the courtyard will deliver your acquisitions to your Paris address. If you want to send them directly to the United States, see a mover approved by the customs office, such as Wingate et Johnston, 8 rue d'Enghien, or Pitt et Scott, 24 rue du Mont-Thabor, for example.

Hotel Drouot, 9 rue Drouot (9e), PRO 18.23.

Musical instruments

Alain Vian

An incredible hodgepodge in the heart of Saint-Germain-des-Prés, sparked by an amazing character named Alain Vian. He is a dead-pan comedian, a former jazz drummer and the brother of Boris Vian, who was one of the leading lights of the *quartier* and was posthumously discovered to be a great novelist as well. The store has an extraordinary collection of antique instruments, from Renaissance viola d'amores to Gay Nineties accordions and dance hall player pianos.

Alain Vian, 8 rue Grégoire-de-Tours (6e), ODE 02.69.

Musée Instrumental, Conservatoire de Musique et Déclamation, 14 rue de Madrid (8e), LAB 29.30.

A very extensive collection of European instruments. Beethoven's clavichord, Lulli's violin, the harp which belonged to Marie Antoinette, numerous harpsichords and five Stradivarius.

Toys

Claude Labarre

This rotund little man with the smooth pate and mischievous expression satisfies his craving for magic by amassing the toys enjoyed by our grandparents. This isn't a store; it's a fairyland where even the most blasé will recapture the sweet savor of childhood amid the old cars, puzzles, magic lanterns, colored pictures and kaleidoscopes.

Claude Labarre, 22 rue Dauphine (6e), ODE 72.62.

Flea markets

Paris has several flea markets, and quite a few of them—such as the ones on place d'Aligre, place de Bicêtre, Porte de Montreuil or Porte Didot—are completely foreign to foreigners. You're not missing much. These markets are picturesque but very poor, and only a few antique dealers and old regulars (who get up early) now and then come across a worthwhile object.

What else is there? The Village Suisse, 52 avenue de la Motte-Piquet (15e), open every day but Monday. It is being totally reorganized and is much too clean for a real flea market.

You see pretty things sold by socialites, at prices which are strictly rue Jacob or Faubourg Saint-Honoré. But it is still a pleasant way to while away the time.

The Marché aux Puces at Porte de Saint-Ouen (Porte de Clignancourt subway line) is much more picturesque, even though it is overrun with tourists. Open Saturday through Monday.

Some three thousand second-hand dealers display every imaginable object. Of course, it's all a matter of having good luck and a good eye, but don't believe the people who peremptorily state: "You never find anything at Les Puces now." This is utterly false: you have only to ask the antique dealers who go rummaging around there at dawn on Saturdays to be convinced that one can still get some very good buys!

Nevertheless, some booths really are more interesting than others. We have tried to situate them according to the five different markets which make up Les Puces.

Marché Vernaison (entrance at 99 rue des Rosiers)

A labyrinth where you meet lots of tourists but also some genuine second-hand dealers.

Booth 16: fairly inexpensive weapons and nice icons; Booth 30: copper utensils; Booth 88: glassware from every period and at every price; Booth 127: Robert, the great specialist in antique toys, telephones and automobile accessories; Booth 139: old dresses and suits; Booth 155: pretty Chinese articles; Booth 173: François Lepage's coins, antiquities and nice eighteenth-century engravings; Booth 175: old clothes; Booth 191: beautiful fans; Booth 257: antique jewelry; Booth 250: precious curios.

At 3 rue Voltaire, between the Vernaison and Biron markets, you'll find the best collection of old paintings in the flea market.

Marché Biron (entrance on rue des Rosiers)

It's known as the Faubourg Saint-Honoré of the flea market. Bargains are rare but you'll see lots of quality merchandise.

Booth 3: cut- or etched-crystal glasses; Booth 11: antique fabrics; Booth 14: carved and gilded wood; Booth 20: Charles Marchal is a good specialist in weapons and military souvenirs; Booth 41: Horace Chambon is another well-known specialist in military curios; Booth 81: locks, doorknobs; Booth 101: watches and funny knickknacks; Booth 111: some good paintings are often hidden among the hackwork; Booth 157: a paradise of frills and furbelows from 1900 and 1925; Booth 166: attractive Russian objects; Booth 181: optical equipment; Booth 183 *bis:* antique glass, pretty little oddities; Booth 199: a real junk store full of clocks, coffeepots, etc.; Booth 200: 1900's *découpages* and funny labels.

Marché Malik (take rue Paul-Bert and turn left)

Booth 32: antique braid and lace; Booth 104: *Hélène Leiba* sells blue jeans and pea jackets to Tout-Paris; Booth 105: the finest Oriental rugs in the flea market. Last of all, there is a wonderful booth selling rare and used books at Number 20 on the outer belt boulevard.

Marché Paul-Bert (entrance at 8 rue Paul-Bert, to your left off rue des Rosiers)

Booths 15, 17 and 19: hodgepodge of odd and funny objects; Booth 38: plates, pitchers and lovely wooden statues; Booth 79: a mountain of knickknacks; Booth 95: occasionally interesting paintings; Booth 145: a little museum of Chinese art patronized by real collectors; Booth 146: chromos and cut-paper pictures; Booth 177: pretty nineteenth-century pictures (horses and ships); Booth 211: a good selection of African art.

Marché Jules-Vallès (entrance at 7 rue Jules-Vallès)

At the corner of rue Paul-Bert, three young men stand out because of their rather questionable taste in selling daggers, armbands and souvenirs from Nazi Germany; Booth 10: all sorts of glasses, mostly antiques; Booth 18: six thousand 78-rpm records in perfect condition, and gramophones besides.

Rocks and minerals

Michel Cachoux

Petrified fireworks. Iridescent or marbled blocks in colors deep as night, risen from the depths of earth and time. Fossilized tree trunks where the wood has disappeared, giving place to silica which reproduces its every lineament. Quartz studded with tourmalines and mica, stibiconite corroded by antimony oxide, amethysts, agates, calcites shaped like stars, organ pipes, and statuettes carved by some mad artist.

Michel Cachoux spends four months of the year hunting for these mineral treasures in Brazil, Ceylon, the United States, Madagascar, the Congo or right in the Alps. He removes them from their matrix, polishes, cuts and displays them in his little store on rue Guénégaud. Sometimes he even entrusts his stones to young artists who set them into structures or incorporate them into mobiles, thus creating a new art form. With the exception of the agate ashtrays, these objects are of course perfectly useless and fall outside any known category. But they should be viewed as a testimony to the prodigious fantasy and incredible richness of the mineral world. Or even as the beginning of an art which unites the slow subterranean work of the ages with the quest for a new aesthetics.

Michel Cachoux, 29 rue Guénégaud (6e), ODE 52.15.

Musée d'Histoire Naturelle (Museum of Natural History), Jardin des Plantes, 57 rue Cuvier (5e), GOB 21.51. Closed on Tuesdays.

A superb mineral collection, one of the richest in the world.

Coins and medals

Until only recently, numismatics was a very exclusive and extremely intimidating religion which, from the outside, gave every appearance of a maniacal passion. Today it has a very vast public, including many young people and enthusiasts with limited incomes. It's possible to build up a very valuable collection without spending too much money, but all the specialists agree on this point: Never buy coins of inferior quality, such as are sold in bulk by some dealers and at the flea market. It's better to buy a single piece of the highest quality. Which is why it's desirable to deal with real numismatists who not only impose strict standards on what they sell but also delight in giving intelligent advice to beginners. Here are two masters of this profession, who serve as experts at all important auctions and are known to collectors throughout the world.

Bourgey, 7 rue Drouot (9ᵉ), PRO 88.67.

Vinchon, 77 rue de Richelieu (2ᵉ), RIC 16.11.

Bibliothèque Nationale (Département des Monnaies et Médailles), 58 rue de Richelieu (2ᵉ), RIC 00.06.

Watches

Au Vieux Cadran

Monsieur Laforet, whose courtesy is of another age, is more of a collector than a businessman. He has to force himself to part with the objects of his passion, a passion which begins with the first watch ever made (about 1510) and ends in 1925. Whether it's a Louis XV watch in gold repoussé which strikes every quarter-hour, a Louis XVI or Directoire watch shaped like a mandolin, butterfly, lyre or scarab, or a 1900's waterlily, it would be impossible not to find the precious object of your dreams at the Vieux Cadran.

Au Vieux Cadran, 59 *ter,* rue Bonaparte (6ᵉ), DAN 01.07.

Jean-Baptiste Diette

Internationally known expert; here you'll find standing and hanging clocks of every period and style.

Jean-Baptiste Diette, 4 avenue Matignon (8ᵉ), ELY 98.90.

Musée du Conservatoire des Arts et Métiers, 292 rue Saint-Martin (3ᵉ), TUR 37.38. Closed Mondays.
Superb collection of antique clocks.
Muséee Cognacq-Jay, 25 boulevard des Capucines (2ᵉ), OPE 55.66. Closed Tuesdays.
The finest collection of watches in Paris.

Opalines

At the end of the eighteenth century Louis XIV ordered silverware to be melted down in order to replenish the state treasury at the end of his reign. For this reason porcelain and faience underwent a remarkable development, and so there is a very vast choice of all styles at all prices.

Art d'Autrefois, 90 rue du Bac (7ᵉ).
Chinese and Delft porcelain.

Aux Vieilles Epoques, 64 rue du Cherche-Midi (6ᵉ).
Compagnie des Indes plates, services in Chantilly, Vieux Rouen, and Limoges porcelain or yellow Marseille faience.

Bernard, 86 rue du Cherche-Midi (6ᵉ), BAB 43.94.
Plates from the French Revolution.

Lecomte-Ullman, 75 rue du Faubourg Saint-Honoré (8ᵉ), ELY 52.23.
A very great specialist in beautiful French porcelain and Dresden china. They give very friendly—and precious—advice to beginning collectors.

Lefebvre, 24 rue du Bac (7ᵉ), BAB 35.01.
Ceramics for great collectors.

Nicolier, 7 quai Voltaire (7ᵉ), LIT 91.02.
This esteemed expert has an enormous stock of porcelain and faience, all of premium quality.

Pierre de Regaini, 6 rue de Beaune (7ᵉ), LIT 42.67.

The greatest collectors recognize their master in this very polite little man who possesses an infinite number of quality pieces: Sèvres, Compagnie des Indes, Moustiers, Marseille, Vieux Paris, etc. He will give you a very detailed explanation of the complex world of porcelain.

Finally, we'd like to call your attention to a firm which, instead of antique porcelain, sells Sèvres or German faïence which can even be hand-decorated with your initials:

Clara Fandor, 18 rue Mazarine (6ᵉ), MED 05.38.

Besides the Musée des Arts Décoratifs, there is the Musée de la Manufacture de Sèvres (Sèvres Factory Museum), 4 Grande Rue, Sèvres. OBS 00.23.

Ceramics from every time and place, but in particular an extremely rare collection of Nevers and Rouen faïence and eighteenth-century fast and slow-fired faïence.

Musée de l'Assistance Publique (Museum of Public Welfare), 47 quai de la Tournelle (5ᵉ), DAN 60.91. Closed on Tuesdays.

A superb collection of ceramic apothecary jars, housed in the enchanting Miramion mansion (seventeenth century), which almost no Parisians know about.

Russia

A la Vieille Cité, 350 rue Saint-Honoré (Iᵉʳ), OPE 38.30.

A delightful old Russian couple sells admirable gold plate, Fabergé jewels, icons and an exceptional collection of delicately crafted eggs from the eighteenth and nineteenth centuries.

Popoff, 86 rue du Faubourg Saint-Honoré (8ᵉ), ANJ 38.44.

Monsieur Popoff began his career at the Russian court and sells ceramics, paintings and icons of fine quality.

Haute Epoque (*Middle Ages, Renaissance, Louis XIII*)

Bresset et Fils, 197 boulevard Saint-Germain (6ᵉ), LIT 18.24; 5 quai Voltaire (7ᵉ), LIT 89.35.

This charming old gentleman, now assisted by his son, is the leading French specialist in *Haute Epoque.* Wood carvings, furniture, sculpture and paintings, all of the finest quality, at prices which often come as a pleasant surprise.

Brimo de Laroussilhe, 58 rue Jouffroy (17ᵉ).

Coquenpot, 25 rue de Bourgogne (7ᵉ), INV 47.16.

Perpitch, 240 boulevard Saint-Germain (7ᵉ), LIT 37.67.

Musée des Arts Décoratifs, 107 rue de Rivoli (Iᵉʳ), OPE 49.68. Closed on Tuesdays.

A very successful new arrangement of the *Haute Epoque* rooms. A model of its kind.

Musée de Cluny, 6 rue Paul-Painlevé (5ᵉ), ODE 24.21.

The most popular museum after the Louvre and the Jeu de Paume (impressionists). It is located in the magnificent old mansion of the abbots of Cluny and extends into the Cluny Roman baths, where the famous Unicorn tapestry ("La Dame à la Licorne") is on display. The twenty-seven rooms devoted to the arts and crafts of the Middle Ages (statues, stained glass, etc.) constitute a most beautiful survey of medieval France.

An incomparable collection of Renaissance pieces has been lying around in storerooms for a century, inaccessible to the general public.

Louis XIV, XV and XVI

The seventeenth and particularly the eighteenth century, the golden age of French furniture, are represented in some fashion at almost all the large antique dealers' and decorators'. To keep you from wasting time, we have only selected first-rate dealers whose furniture is decidedly above average.

The most prestigious is undoubtedly *Samy Chalom,* 38 rue de Faubourg Saint-Honoré (8ᵉ), ELY 17.80, whose basement houses a collection of furniture which attracts multimillion-aires (and simple browsers) from all over the world. We should also mention *Alavoine,* 42 avenue Kléber (16ᵉ), PAS 07.67, the most sumptuous, refined decorator in Paris; Fabre, 19 rue Balzac (8ᵉ), CAR 17.52, whose storerooms are breath-takingly rich; *Kraemer,* 43 rue de Monceau (8ᵉ), LAB 24.46, by appointment only; *Carmontel,* 5 quai Malaquais (6ᵉ), ODE 51.16; *Thenadey,* 1 quai Voltaire (7ᵉ), LIT 62.98; *Buve-lot-Camoin,* 9 quai Voltaire (7ᵉ), LIT 53.40; and *Touzain,* 27 quai Voltaire (7ᵉ), LIT 54.57. That ought to be enough infor-mation to ruin you.

Musée Nissim de Camondo, 63 rue de Monceau (8ᵉ), LAB 12.32. Closed on Tuesdays.

A lovely town house completely decorated and furnished in Louis XVI style. Some of the most beautiful pieces by great eighteenth-century cabinetmakers. Unfortunately, very few people go there to admire them.

Musée Cognacq-Jay, 25 boulevard des Capucines (2ᵉ), OPE 55.56. Closed Tuesdays.

Just as deserted as the preceding one, yet this museum, de-voted to the seventeenth and eighteenth centuries, is a treasure house: paintings, drawings, watch and snuffbox collections.

And, of course, you should also visit the Musée des Arts Décoratifs.

Empire

Here are a few fine specialists in the Napoleon I style which is coming back into favor (furniture, lamps, curios, bronzes):

Au Directoire, 47 rue du Bac (7ᵉ), LIT 00.76.

Mancel, 2 rue du Bac (6ᵉ), LIT 04.34.

À Napoléon, 33 boulevard Raspail (7ᵉ), LIT 20.92.

Musée Marmottan, 2 rue Louis-Boilly (16ᵉ). Open Saturdays and Sundays from 2:00 to 5:00 P.M. Closed from July 15 through September 15.

This museum is almost always closed and practically deserted. It belongs to the French Institute and contains, among other things, Napoleon's bed and a very complete collection of Empire furniture, bronzes and sculpture.

Also go to the Musée des Arts Décoratifs at 107 rue de Rivoli.

Restoration and Charles X

Nicole Gérard, 28 rue Jacob (6ᵉ), DAN 26.43.
Blond wooden furniture and curios.
Imbert, 157 rue du Faubourg Saint-Honoré (8ᵉ), ELY 54.89.
Opalines, nineteenth-century ceramics and very beautiful blond furniture from the 1830's.
Mancel, 2 rue du Bac (7ᵉ), LIT 04.34.
Furniture, porcelain table services, curios. Very high quality.

Napoleon III and Third Republic

Alexandre, 50 rue Saint-Georges (9ᵉ), TRU 35.56.
Amusing papier-mâché objects.
Madeleine Castaing, 21 rue Bonaparte (6ᵉ), ODE 91.71.
Madeleine Castaing has been in fashion for twenty years. She specializes in English and Napoleon III furniture and also carries pretty curios. Her prices, too, are "fashionable."
Jacques Damiot, 57 rue Jacques-Dulud, Neuilly-sur-Seine, MAI 96.16.
Furniture and curios which are often funny, always elegant and never cheap.
Gabrielle Lorie, 21 quai Voltaire (7ᵉ), LIT 27.97.
Black-painted furniture, but mostly curios, opalines and flower paintings with a very romantic grace.

Yveline, 4 rue Furstenberg (6ᵉ), DAN 56.91.

A charming jumble of curios, armchairs, sculpture, screens, lamps, etc., at prices which are unfortunately somewhat less than romantic.

Art Nouveau (1900)

Also known as Modern Style, Style Métro, etc., the art of the 1900's is enjoying a vogue which was carefully nurtured by the great auctioneer Maurice Rheims and a few specialized dealers. After a period of frequently unfair prices, the market has settled down, in the sense that only objects of genuine quality maintain their value, which, however, increases with every year. More than the furniture, which isn't always easy to sell, it's the glassware (vases by Gallé, Daim, etc.), bronzes and jewelry (see above) that find favor with enthusiasts. Painting of the 1900's, in the other hand, seems somewhat underappreciated.

The three top specialists are:

Yvette Barran, 11 rue Bonaparte (6ᵉ), DAN 90.28.

Jacques Denoël, 21 rue Guénégaud (6ᵉ), ODE 65.09.

Gérard Lévy, 17 rue de Beaune (7ᵉ), BAB 80.19.

Musée des Arts Décoratifs, 107 rue de Rivoli (Iᵉʳ), OPE 49.68. Closed Tuesdays.

This superb and too little known museum offers a complete panorama of French furniture from the Middle Ages to the present. The 1900's period has been very successfully recreated.

Musée National d'Art Moderne (National Museum of Modern Art), 11 avenue du Président-Wilson (16ᵉ). Closed Tuesdays.

An entertaining survey of Modern Style decoration and painting. The only trouble is that this "modern" museum is miserably run-down.

OLD PAINTINGS

Large dealers

Several of these specialists enjoy an international reputation. Don't expect to unearth any inexpensive treasures here: they usually sell recognized, catalogued works and they're not in business for their health.

We only make token mention of Wildenstein since this great dealer—or at least his son and heir—has practically ceased all activity in France in order to devote himself to his New York and London galleries.

Cailleux, 136 rue du Faubourg Saint-Honoré (8ᵉ), ELY 25.24.
Paul Cailleux's son and daughter carry on the family tradition, which consists of selling works (chiefly from the eighteenth century) whose high quality is perfectly matched by their prices.

François Heim, 109 rue du Faubourg Saint-Honoré (8ᵉ), BAL 22.38.
He runs the gamut from primitives to the eighteenth century. You often see first-rate works here, which are fought over by museums and great collectors.

Robert Lebel, 14 avenue du Président-Wilson (16ᵉ), PAS 96.71.
An art critic and expert, considered one of the best in his profession, Lebel sees art lovers by appointment only.

Mestrallet, 22 avenue Matignon (8ᵉ), ELY 25.63.
Mestrallet and his father before him have supplied quality paintings (from the fifteenth through the eighteenth centuries) to the most well-to-do Parisians, who never stray from the path of "serious" painting.

Pardo, 160 boulevard Haussmann (8ᵉ), CAR 66.51.
In the course of a few years, this dynamic, enterprising dealer

has carved himself the "lion's share" of the French and Venetian eighteenth-century market. He has an immense stock (over fifteen hundred pictures in his storeroom) of work ranging in quality from average to very good.

Reliable dealers

We obviously don't mean to imply that large dealers aren't also reliable. Rather, this heading covers specialists in old paintings whose reputation hasn't attained the international proportions of those mentioned above.

Aubry, 2 rue des Beaux-Arts (6e), DAN 27.27.
A fine specialist in French nineteenth-century painting (Delacroix, Géricault, Corot, Barbizon School).

Brame, 68 boulevard Malesherbes (8e), LAB 16.89.
Late-nineteenth-century paintings (Degas, Fantin-Latour, Delacroix, Boudin, etc.).

Daber, 103 boulevard Haussmann (8e), ANJ 91.83.
Another expert on the nineteenth century (Courbet, Boudin, Jongkind, etc.).

Fleurville, 62 rue Bonaparte (6^e), DAN 53.32.
Paintings from the sixteenth, seventeenth and eighteenth centuries.

Gairac, 13 rue de Seine (6^e), DAN 53.32.
François Heim's father. Serves as expert at auctions and possesses an interesting stock of old paintings from every school.

Nikolenko, 220 boulevard Saint-Germain (6^e), LIT 20.62.
Even more than his richly framed, ingeniously lighted primitives and Flemish paintings, it's the ancient icons which hold one's attention.

Small galleries

These dealers aren't very well known, either because they are just starting out or because they've never been able to invest important sums, but they have both a good eye and good taste, and people have been known to find some nice "bargains" here. The prices they charge are much less stiff than those of their more famous colleagues; on the other hand, they give no guarantees.

Galérie Bernard-Palissy, 11 rue Bernard-Palissy (6ᵉ), BAB 51.38.
Charming Princess Eristoff sells naïve paintings from the nineteenth century and pretty, decorative still lifes in her picturesque little shop.

Aux Goûts Réunis, 16 rue d'Assas (6ᵉ), BAB 70.16.
We hope that when this book comes out Monsieur Fourcade and Madame Cheval will not yet have carried out their plan, which has one of them going off to write a book on India and the other retiring to the Midi. You immediately become friends of these charming people who are not interested in getting rich at their customers' expense. They have been known to make some rather sensational finds, in which case they like nothing better than to pass these discoveries on to their clients, making a minimal profit in the process. It's the truth, believe it or not.

Gosselin, 25 quai des Grands-Augustins (6ᵉ), DAN 76.19.
You sometimes find nice little nineteenth-century paintings amid the fourth-rate canvases.

Galérie des Deux Iles, 1 quai aux Fleurs (4ᵉ), ODE 67.76.
In addition to inexpensive nineteenth-century drawings, the proprietor—who is himself a painter and an authority on the paintings of neuropaths—has an interesting stock of paintings and pastels by the remarkable, little-known Post-Impressionist Schuffenecker. We don't claim to be prophets, but his work can't help increasing in value.

Marcus, 20 rue Chauchat (9ᵉ), PRO 91.23.

Dealers are the only people who know about this dark little gallery tucked away at the back of a courtyard near the Hotel Drouot. You find anything and everything, including some good canvases now and then.

Musée Cognacq-Jay, 25 boulevard des Capucines (2ᵉ), OPE 55.66. Closed on Tuesdays.

Paintings and drawings from the seventeenth and eighteenth centuries (Rembrandt, Tiepolo, Watteau).

Musée Jacquemart-André, 178 boulevard Haussmann (8ᵉ), CAR 39.64. Closed on Tuesdays.

Treasures of Italian art (frescos by Tiepolo, paintings by Carpaccio and Paolo Uccello), Flemish art (three masterpieces by Rembrandt: "The Disciples at Emmaeus," portraits of Saskia and Doctor Tholinx) and French art (Philippe de Champagne, Fragonard). Long ignored by Parisians, this lovely if somewhat austere museum is now coming back to life.

MODERN PAINTINGS

We won't insult our distinguished readers by sending them off to Montmartre where galleries and genre painters grow like weeds. Since these people have to earn a living too, we won't dwell on the ghastly quality of their productions or the deplorable effect they have had on the appearance of this old artists' village. And anyhow, can one really apply the term "modern painting" to these pitiful works which can only inspire a shrug, but which many tourists make a great fuss over nonetheless?

"Modern" painting is a rather confusing term, since, in Paris, it refers to Impressionism as much as to Pop Art. But we'll do

in Belgium and in Switzerland, displayed in the apartment where he once lived.

Rugs and tapestries

Strange as it seems, the French—the creators of Savonnerie and Aubusson—shy away from rugs. They think it frivolous to spend a lot of money for something you walk on and which they're afraid will wear out. Which is probably why prices are higher in Teheran than in Paris.

Here are a few good specialists:

Roger Bechirian, 47 bis rue du Bois de Boulogne, Neuilly-sur-Seine, MAI 53.18.

This recognized expert sees people only by appointment.

Benadava, 6 rue Royale (8ᵉ), OPE 73.63.
Few rugs, but these are of the finest quality.

Boccara, 184 rue du Faubourg Saint-Honoré (8ᵉ), ELY 84.63.

One of the finest assortments of rugs and tapestries to be found in Paris. You have to see his fabulous collection of Turkish and Persian rugs from the seventeenth century. He refuses to show any Aubussons which, he says, "were merely pale copies of Savonnerie carpets, which at that time were too expensive for the bourgeoisie." And besides, when the Savonnerie started out (under Henri IV) it was nothing but a vulgar business of copying Oriental rugs. Dario Boccara also has a remarkable collection of Flemish Gothic tapestries.

Berthéol, 150 rue de la Pompe (16ᵉ), PAS 51.36.
President of the Oriental Rug Importers Syndicate, Monsieur Berthéol is determined to show nothing but original, quality goods.

Calatchi, 135 boulevard Haussmann (8ᵉ), ELY 80.58.
Deals exclusively in Oriental rugs, of which he possesses some superb examples. His rugs are often displayed in muse-

ums throughout the world, and contemplation of them inspires him to lyrical, ardent comments. Robert de Calatchi isn't shy about telling you that he is the *only* real expert in Paris and perhaps in the world. You may end up believing him when you look at his rugs.

Catan, 129 avenue des Champs-Elysées (8ᵉ), BAL 41.71.
A limited choice of fine Oriental and Savonnerie carpets.

Lefortier, 54 rue du Faubourg Saint-Honoré (8ᵉ), ANJ 43.74.
An old firm specializing in beautiful old tapestries.

Meunier-Batifaud, 38 boulevard Raspail (7ᵉ), LIT 05.78.
A very extensive choice of superb tapestries from the sixteenth through the eighteenth centuries.

Monseigneur l'Ancien, 24 rue de Beaune (7ᵉ), LIT 67.87.
Jacques Behar, an excellent carpet repairer, charges less than many of his colleagues, who are obliged to have repairs done on the outside. He restores the rugs, mends them with old wool and sets the price according to what they cost him. He doesn't sell any "antiques" (rugs made before 1800; they are extremely rare and cost a fortune), but rather "old" (1800 to 1865) and especially "semi-old" (1865 to 1936) carpets. These are not collector's items; instead, they are pretty pieces which no one need be afraid to walk on.

Place Clichy, 93 rue d'Amsterdam (8ᵉ), EUR 54.20.
This large store sells carpeting and rugs by the yard. One tends to forget that it also has an excellent Oriental rug department, including some which really deserve to be in a collection.

Musée des Arts Décoratifs, 107 rue de Rivoli (Iᵉʳ), OPE 49.68. Closed Tuesdays.
Superb collection of French and foreign rugs and tapestries.

Musée de Cluny, 6 rue Paul-Painlevé (5ᵉ), ODE 24.21. Closed Tuesdays.

The masterpieces of medieval French tapestry-making: "La Vie Seigneuriale" and "La Dame à la Licorne." According to the present curator, these tapestries came from Northern France and maybe even Flanders, not, as is commonly believed, from workshops on the banks of the Loire, whose existence is highly problematic.

Musée des Gobelins, 42 avenue des Gobelins (13ᵉ). Open Wednesday, Thursday and Friday afternoons.

You visit rug collections from the seventeenth and eighteenth centuries, as well as the Savonnerie workshops, which are still functioning and where rugs are woven according to age-old techniques.

Textiles, fabrics, laces, old clothes

Brocard, 1 rue Jacques-Coeur (4ᵉ), ARC 16.38.

This workshop looks as if it belongs in another century. And it does: the work is done exactly as it was under the First Empire, when this admirable firm was founded. This is where Napoleon's coronation robes were embroidered (they may show you the original "pattern"). Brocard's main business is repairs, but they also sell precious, costly antique laces.

Fulgence, 74 rue La Boétie (8ᵉ), ELY 05.12.

Since 1890 the Fulgence family has been piling their shelves high with textiles, dresses, church ornaments, hangings, and laces from the sixteenth, seventeenth and eighteenth centuries, some of which are worth a small fortune. Monsieur Fulgence, an "old-clothes dealer" of the highest order, will also show you marvelous men's costumes dating back to the eighteenth century.

Flea Market

The Marché Biron has an immense selection of textiles, trimmings and curtains (Booth 11) and dresses and nightgowns from the *Belle Epoque* (Booth 157). Booths 139 and 178 at the Marché Vernaison sell textiles, dresses, shirts and jumpers, and Hélène Leiba's Booth 104 at the Marché Malik is a very fascinating hodgepodge.

Au Point de Venise, 44 rue du Bac (7e).
Two old spinsters all dressed in lace, who sell nothing but that: handkerchiefs, tablecloths and lace by the yard.

Glassware

Of all collectors, lovers of antique glass are the most unobtrusive and modest. Its very nature—fragile and worrisome—makes glass hardly tempting to fat fortunes looking for an "investment." By a curious paradox, a lot more glass has come down to us from ancient times than from the Middle Ages (the Greeks, Romans and Egyptians all buried their dead with household articles). So for all practical purposes antique glass doesn't go back any further than the sixteenth century, with the exception of ancient pieces. Crystal appeared toward the end of the eighteenth century (Baccarat being the finest in the world), and the nineteenth century witnessed the birth of the great era of cut glass.

Altero, 21 quai Voltaire (7e), LIT 02.71.
A great address for seventeenth- and eighteenth-century glassware.

Max L. Baudot, 5 rue Bourbon-le-Château (6e), ODE 06.78.
A charming antique dealer and remarkable specialist, where you'll find reliable, elegant glass at all prices.

Flea Market
Booth 6 at the Marché Biron: glasses and carafes by the piece or by the dozen.

Part VII

SIGHTSEEING
IN PARIS

EXCURSION BOATS
(BATEAUX-MOUCHES)

A ride down the Seine in a *bateau-mouche* is a classical experience. You'd be wrong to count yourself out on the pretext that you're not an "ordinary tourist."

Of course we miss the excursion boats of yesteryear, which descended the Seine as far as Rouen and were infinitely more picturesque than these big sharks with their pointed plexiglass snouts, looking for all the world like huge plexiglass toys. Of course we miss the soirées of old where everyone on deck whole-heartedly sang along to the sound of an accordion. But the *bateaux-mouches* have the quais along the Seine, Notre-Dame, the Louvre and the Institute for a setting—and that's really not so bad.

A few years ago the food on these boats was so bad that we would have advised you not to have dinner aboard. Fortunately, the cooking has made progress, and even though the bill is rougher than the water you're riding on (50 francs— $10, all inclusive), we heartily urge you to spend an evening on one of the *bateaux-mouches,* of which we must now give you a brief history.

The boats made their appearance on the Seine around 1860, during the reign of Napoleon III. Their creator, Jean-Sébastien Mouche, was honored by generations of dignitaries, and until recently everybody believed in the existence of the excellent Monsieur Mouche. As a matter of fact, there was no such person: he was the product of a monumental hoax. The joke was taken up in all seriousness by Jean Bruel when, in 1950, he launched his fleet on the Seine, which hadn't seen the boats since 1936. In view of the venture's success, the first boats, shabby and charming, were replaced by the five launches we know today, each of which can hold six hundred passengers.

They leave by turns every hour on the half hour from six in the morning to ten at night, or even midnight if the weather is nice, on excursions which vary with the captain's mood, the weather and the time of day. We recommend either the luncheon trip (30 francs—$6—complete) or the two-hour dinner excursion (50 francs) which goes from Pont de Grenelle to Pont Sully. Allow us to describe the itinerary.

Departure from Port de la Conférence (Right Bank, entrance off place de l'Alma to the left of the bridge).

Pont de l'Alma with its Zouave, who has nothing to complain about during the summer since his feet are nice and dry. One wonders why his companion in arms on the other side of the bridge doesn't enjoy the same renown: he certainly looks like a decent enough chap. We then come upon the Museum of Modern Art behind the plane trees on Quai de Tokio (which has changed its name since 1945 when, as everyone knows, France crushed Japan . . .), and its big brother, the Palais de Chaillot, erected after the Trocadéro on the site of the dream castle (it never got beyond the planning stage), the "vastest and most extraordinary in the world" which Napoleon wanted to build for his little boy.

You soon reach the island called Allée des Cygnes. You make a half-turn in front of the little Statue of Liberty, a copy of the one that Bartholdi made for New York. When the boat stops turning you can see Liberty lighting the world, superimposed on the round Radio House building. This is pretty funny, when you know that liberty isn't exactly a characteristic of our official radio network.

If you're having dinner on board, now's the time to place your order, which means you risk missing an immense, odd metal edifice erected in 1889, for no apparent reason, by the engineer Gustave Eiffel. It is known that the ingenious graduate of the Ecole Centrale not only built this tower (on the pretext of giving a high-altitude treatment to his children who were down with whooping cough), but also constructed a sort of studio on the fifth and last floor. Rumor has it that he granted access to young ladies, even if they weren't suffering from children's diseases. A friend reports that, for professional reasons, his cousin had the key to this lofty *pied-à-terre* and used to take innocent damsels up for a look at the view. He always made sure to use the last elevator of the day for the trip up . . .

After the Port du Gros Caillou, which used to be Ile Maquerelle, you soon arrive in front of the Invalides esplanade and soldiers' home. Under Louis XIV the Hotel des Invalides had over seven thousand pensioners; it now houses no more than one hundred-fifty, because of the great decline in casualties during recent wars.

You then discern two sumptuous town houses belonging to the Minister of Foreign Affairs and the President of the National Assembly, followed by the Palais Bourbon, which is known for its Deputies, its Delacroix paintings and the remark made by an eighteenth-century architect: "An example of the art of comfortable private living." You pass beneath the Pont de la Concorde and have the nasty satisfaction of hearing the racket of maddened cars creeping forward while you glide along over the gentle waters.

The management of the *bateaux-mouches* line hasn't arranged for any stop at the floating Deligny pool in order to permit one to take a dip and cheer on the bathing beauties. It's a shame, but you quickly forget your disappointment when confronted by the sumptuous spectacle of the subsequent palace. This charming semicircular pavilion is the Hotel de Salm (seat of the Légion d'Honneur). After that, there is the zany Gare d'Orsay, the Caisse des Dépôts et Consignations (Deposit and Consignment Office) and, after the Pont Royal—the most beautiful bridge in Paris—the eighteenth-century town houses where Madame d'Agout, Condorcet, Musset, Wagner, Baudelaire, Corot, Delacroix, Ingres and Voltaire once lived. Then comes the Hotel de Chimay (by Mansart), which has become part of the Ecole des Beaux-Arts, and a few lovely Louis XIII houses. This is the moment when the cruise presents its crowning jewel: Le Vau's superb Palais Mazarin (the French Institute) which served as a prison for (among others) Dr.

Guillotin, inventor of the guillotine, who was helpless before the Immortals. Seen from the river, this exquisite palace with its famous cupola is indeed a moving sight.

But the boat moves forward in the night. After the little Guénégaud mansion where Bonaparte concealed his fleeting love affairs, there is the wonderful, noble Hotel de la Monnaie. Further on, after the Pont Neuf, the oldest bridge in Paris, you see the low windows of the Lapérouse restaurant, the old houses along Quai des Grands-Augustins and, on the banks, the beginning of the slow parade of lovers and bums, one of whom—who gives his bottle a particularly thorough workout —knows the *bateau-mouche* schedule by heart. After Saint-Michel you come upon beatniks picnicking (in very civil fashion) near the Petit Pont and the real *clochards* from rue de l'Hotel Colbert. For some moments now, the Ile de la Cité, Palais de Justice, Quai des Orfèvres (home of our gracious police force) and the friendly old Préfecture de Police have been passing by on the left. But even if you prefer to look at the charming old houses along the Left Bank quais, you will be abruptly yanked from your reverie by a stampede on deck. "They" have caught sight of Notre-Dame and are devouring it with their zoom lenses. Then the miracle happens. You look at the fine gray stones and say, stupidly and sincerely, "You know, it really *is* beautiful." Sometimes you even shed a tear.

We continue flying along between the blazing, bacchic Tour d'Argent and the wonderful town houses on the Ile Saint-Louis, asleep in the shadows of its old memories. You go around the front of the Hotel Lambert and while other houses, haughty or cheerful, file past in the night, a second stampede tells us that a tightrope walker, a juggler and some musketeers, who put on a nightly show for the *bateaux-mouches,* are performing off the starboard bow, along the Quai des Celestins on the Right Bank. We prefer the Ile's old houses, authentic and perpetually still.

Returning toward Notre-Dame, which the boat lights up with a blazing beacon as a treat for diners at the Tour d'Argent, we come upon the Louvre at the bend near the Vert Galant—the Louvre, which goes on and on, without ever managing to bore us.

The riverside promenade. A few pairs of lovers and a horde of spectators to watch them have fun.

After the Orangerie and the radiant Concorde, which you are at last able to see without having to contemplate your neighbor's bumper, and where crazy-looking cranes outdo the Luxor Obelisk, the boat smells home. It makes short work of the Petit Palais and even the Grand Palais. We come to a stop at last in front of Cours Albert-Ier, but forget to get off the boat. Instead, we remain gazing dreamily into the watery mirror where the moon and the lights of Paris lie trembling. We'd say you'd be very silly to scorn the *bateaux-mouches*.

If you still want to continue your excursion on solid ground, Jean Bruel has cute little cars available, *mini-mokes* equipped with multilingual sound to guide tourists (15 francs—$3—an hour, plus 1 franc—20 cents—per kilometer, but the gas is free).

Bateaux-Mouches, Pont de l'Alma, Right Bank, BAL 96.10.

CITYRAMA

It's ten o'clock in the morning; you're at the corner of the rue de Rivoli and rue du 29 Juillet; things are buzzing. The terrace of the Welcome Café doesn't have a single empty table. A mighty detachment of foreign tourists, mostly Americans, sit silently over sodas, anxiously scanning the horizon or making final adjustments on their cameras. One of them suddenly jumps up, knocking over some chairs in the process, and points to the big bus, emblazoned with the arms of the House of Cityrama, which is slowly pulling into its parking place in the shadow of the arcade. The rush is on. The gaudy crowd hurls itself in a body at the glazed door of the bus like moths around a light bulb; inside, the reviled hostess shields the tape-recorders with her body, and with her finger on the release button, prepares to open the floodgates to the mob.

Such is the first scene in the permanent script. Hour after hour, eleven times a day, the bus stops in front of the Welcome Café's terrace to receive another load of fifty Paris-starved tourists. The 20 francs they have paid entitles them to spend three hours "getting at the meat" of the capital, with the help of commentaries. But why such a mad dash? It didn't take us long to find out. It would seem that the Cityrama bus, that magnificent, self-powered, multilingual jewel-case, has fifty seats, of which only three are really good. We know from experience.

We were the only French people aboard and had managed to reserve seats ahead of time, either by good luck or the most flagrant good management. With no harm intended, we selected two of the three best seats; these are located in the front row of the upper deck, which affords them a panoramic view of 180 degrees. To tell the truth, it didn't take us long to judge them rather low on comfort and short on padding. Be that as it may, once our earphones were adjusted, we put on our dark glasses and lit strong cigars so as not to seem out of place. Then, more or less content, we waited for the bus to start. That's when the hostess pushed the button, the downstairs door swung open and we listened anxiously as the little stairway behind us trembled at every hotly disputed step.

An old lady, doubtless carried forward like spume before the invading wave, immediately snatched the third and last "good" seat. A dozen extremely athletic males close on her heels unequivocally invited us to move back a few seats, which we willingly did under the concerted pressure of their feet on ours and the weight of our nation's solid reputation, which still insists that the French are the politest people on earth. When we questioned the hostess a little later, she stated that it wasn't unusual to witness an exchange of blows for the three seats at the prow of the upper deck.

We'd like to think they are worth the struggle, for the ones we took in the rear were to prove singularly unfit and uncomfortable throughout the entire three-hour tour. While waiting for the bus to fill, the hostess made an inspection tour of the upper deck and asked us to put out our cigars since only cigarettes are allowed. It started to rain and we took advantage of this to remove our sunglasses, so as not to cause the slightest breach in Cityrama's regularity or regulations.

A few phrases continued to crackle beneath us:

"Are you Mr. Briggs?"

"Who are those guys, anyway, Françoise?"

"Guests of the Governor."

"So you're going to take good care of them, huh?"

"Now what's that one over there up to? Is he nuts or is he trying to catch a train?"

"Count them, Jean-Jacques. I'm missing one . . ."

"No more, no more; next time, madame . . ."

The doors close at last, silence reigns, the bus starts moving while martial revolutionary music hails our first stop at the foot of the Obelisk. We press one of the eight levers on the back of the seat, thereby unleashing a flood of theatrical commentary by Monsieur Dubreuil, the director of Cityrama: " 'I die innocent.' . . . The bloody head of Louis XVI . . ."

We're off again, our ears glued to our headset. The earphones are as big as saucers, and since the armature is both too long and too stiff, you have to keep your head constantly bent forward to catch bits and pieces of the nasal text amid the general racket. We are now driving along the quais.

". . . wonderfully peaceful quais shaded by tall trees . . ." At our feet a regiment of power hammers plays a welcoming tattoo. The pavement, broken up by tractors and bristling with fences, presents a scene of merciless trench warfare.

"To your left, the Louvre, a grandiose work . . ." All heads try jointly to execute the "Left, left," but to do this you have to take off the earphones, which grip your head like a helmet. The resulting chaos sends the greasy saucer into your eye or under your nose. At last you see the Louvre, completely covered with green canvas behind which Monsieur Malraux's little launderers are busily at work. The Institute . . . the Pont Neuf, and the place Dauphine, which isn't on our route, but where Monsieur Dubreuil assures us can be found "the sweet melancholy of the provinces . . ."

The Palais de Justice, Notre-Dame, Hotel de Ville, Saint-Gervais and the Marais, where:

"Despite the wrecking ball of progress, there are more than

one hundred private mansions here which can give us a lesson in architecture and good taste."

"Sure, they are very expensive," someone in a loud shirt explains to his wife.

But he'll probably inquire about the price of rooms here and there.

The Bastille! A brief halt. Unfortunately we are right in front of boulevard Henri IV and it's impossible to catch a glimpse of the column which rises behind us. Well, who cares, we'll look at the paving studs instead.

The Tour d'Argent. Every head is raised to look at this summit of world gastronomy. Nowhere else have the faces expressed such respect or admiration. Two hundred snapshots are quickly taken of the glassed-in pergola behind which that fabulous food is prepared, while behind us a concert of honking demands the right of way. Then we're rolling again, this time toward the riverside bookstalls, as the tape-recorder imperturbably sings a hymn to their picturesque, poetic nature. They're mostly all closed.

Saint-Julien-le-Pauvre, Saint-Séverin and rue Saint-Jacques . . . the Sorbonne, the Boul' Mich' (*sic*) and the Panthéon. Stop.

"The admirable pediment, the work of David d'Angers . . ." Too bad. The admirable pediment is likewise veiled. The Luxembourg, Saint-Sulpice. Stop in front of the police station, that is, behind the square's curtain of trees which hide everything but the top of Sevandoni's steeple. Another stop at Saint-Germain-des-Prés where, after a dazzling summary of existentialism, the orator concludes:

"The youth of Saint-Germain-des-Prés has style; this is what youth is all about!"

And for once you really can judge by the evidence.

We move on toward the Beaux-Arts, toward the Palais Bourbon, where more than five hundred Deputies, side by side . . . We're getting a little dry. Luckily there is a stop. Right in the middle of the Champ de Mars, between the Eiffel Tower and the Ecole Militaire, the hostess offers us all sodas with a straw, averaging a mere 1.50 francs (30 cents). Soon we're off again, after learning that the pressure which the Eiffel Tower exerts on its supports is no more than the weight of an average man distributed over the four legs of a chair.

From the Palais de Chaillot, whose architecture, we learn, is not without analogies to Romanesque art, we make for the Etoile, the Champs-Elysées (Tchampss-Eeleezees), Grand and Petit Palais, Faubourg Saint-Honoré, Madeleine . . .

"Ladies and gentlemen, since the route which takes us to Montmartre has no history or monuments of any particular interest . . . we will use the time to listen to a little of that music so dear to the hearts of all Parisians . . ." "A la Bastille" . . . "Viens, Poupole" . . . "Sous les Ponts de Paris" . . .

At last we arrive in front of the basilica. Two dozen other buses have beaten us to it. A fifteen-minute stop; everybody gets out. An army of strolling photographers falls upon them, seizing their prey by the sleeve and dragging them to the steps at the base of the Sacré-Coeur, to immortalize the unique moment which will continue to bloom on night tables in Winnipeg, Dallas or Magdeburg. Unsavory-looking characters advertise mouth-watering folders of "feelthy peectures," pinned to their jacket linings. We head for the nearby shops to stock up on little terra-cotta gamins, gilded Eiffel Towers, copies of Old Masters, postcards. The occupants of the three front seats have left a sentinel. They take turns standing guard. Finally everyone boards the bus once more and we return like a shot to the Welcome terrace, the only interruption being a fleeting, commented vision of the Opéra. It's after one o'clock. Everyone is pleased with our little outing; they slip the hostess a coin and immediately dash off to inquire about fares for the "By Night" and "Cabaret" tours.

Cityrama, 2 rue du 29 Juillet (Ier), RIC 25.09. Buses leave every hour on the hour from 9:00 to 12:00 and from 3:00 to 6:00. The trip costs 20 francs ($4).

GUIDES

Meet the French

What memories will you take away with you from Paris? Of course you will have seen Notre-Dame, the Eiffel Tower, the Sacré-Coeur and Napoleon's tomb, just like everyone else. But what about a stroll through the Marais? What about a chat with a real Parisian, who has something else on his mind than raking in your dollars? What will you really have learned about France?

Guy Barbey and J. A. Prévost, who understand the importance of this problem, launched a very appealing venture, namely, an organization whose aim is to give foreign tourists an "inside look" at Paris and France. Some hundred students, both girls and boys, with a good grasp of English and a broad general background, help tourists who are not satisfied with organized tours to discover old corners of Paris. Each has his own car and never takes more than three or four people at a time. What makes them unique is that they're not simply guides: experience has shown that foreign tourists are much more interested in chatting with French people, asking them about their life, tastes, aspirations, than in learning about the sights they are seeing. In short, they want to establish a real human rapport. And this is exactly what these young people try to do.

The fee for their services obviously depends on the number of hours they devote to you. Count on about $33 a day for a car for three people.

Meet the French, 8 rue Vignon (9ᵉ), 073.30.74.

"Paris by Night"

Several dozen organizations share the thankless task of rescuing the masses of people eager for a taste of our capital's famous night life from the boredom of dismal hotel evenings. We didn't choose Rapid-Pullman. The tour run by this company was thrust upon us with steel-plated courtesy by an

agency obviously interested in doing well. All in all, we had
nothing to complain about. Rapid-Pullman (those two words
fairly well fill the requirements of an age ruled by the signs of
speed and comfort) was as good as its word. In a few hours a
bus blessed with a remarkable suspension carried us into the
thick of Paris night life. We saw bandits perspiring away in
time to the java at the back of a sordid alley; superb, beplumed
nudes dancing in an old mill at the foot of the basilica; and,
last of all, ripe Parisiennes undressing with perverse, incandes-
cent skill at the very bottom of a deep cellar.

This "Enchantment" tour starts with an unusual assigna-
tion: Please meet at nine thirty sharp, ticket in hand, beneath
the fleur-de-lis banner which Joan of Arc flourishes in the
middle of place des Pyramides. Every night the Saint, riveted
to her pedestal, contemplates more than forty buses taking off
for the "hot" streets. For our part, we chose the tour which
offered to regale us consecutively with the Petit Balcon, Moulin
Rouge and Crescendo. Two Mexican ladies, five Englishwomen, four German women, two indefinable couples and a
lone gentleman, sitting somewhat sheepishly in the back, had
already gotten into the bus.

Everybody babbles on merrily. It's impossible not to notice
that the Germans have just come from an orgy of sauerkraut-
eating at Jenny's, that the Englishwomen are denouncing the
flagrantly barbarous way a famous hotel like the "X" makes its
tea, that the Mexicans have had a little something to drink. . . .
We note that this community, reduced to jibbering by the
prospect of the forthcoming pleasures, has donned its most
gorgeous finery. The gentlemen sport fancy handkerchiefs or
carnations while the ladies are inaugurating all their loveliest
jewelry, souvenirs of the rue de Rivoli. One Englishwoman,
topped with a bird's nest and completely inured to the vicissi-
tudes of bargain tours, now and then pulls a bottle of mineral
water out of her newspaper and takes a swig with the best of
grace.

Our guide in turn enters the bus. He's a prepossessing fellow, hardly at all embarrassed by the language barrier. He
comes up to fire a cordial polyglot greeting at each of us and to
check our tickets. Then, mike in hand, he makes more or less
the following speech, as the joyous convoy starts rolling.

"Good evening, ladies and gentlemen. Allow me to introduce us: our driver, Jacques A., and myself, Jacques B. I wish you an excellent evening. We're going to start off with a cabaret that is very typical of an old section of Paris, the Bastille. It's the Petit Balcon, where you'll see the famous apaches, gigolos and gigolettes dancing the java to the sound of an accordion. You'll be able to sample a glass of sparkling wine: the champagne is reserved for our other two stops . . ."

The Petit Balcon's sparkling wine is a rare blend. It leaves deep streaks on the jelly glasses, which barely manage to contain its sulphurous effervescence, and our stomachs remembered it long after the evening was over. Now then, however, that's not the real spectacle. This is to be seen, first of all, in that famous passageway where every bus in the world seems to be keeping an appointment. Lined up one after another on the sidewalk, every half-hour they discharge a flood of candidates for the wine, the white wooden tables, sticky benches and the exhibition put on by half a dozen seedy-looking hoods in the pay of the folklore syndicate. The show doesn't last long. A few coarse javas, a lady bonecrusher leading a fat, dumb-founded Helvetian onto the dance floor and inviting him to undo her blouse. A pretense at a skit is made amid the general hilarity and it's over, finished; you dodge the apache, and make a dash for the bus where the Englishwoman in the bird's nest claims someone has stolen her bottle . . .

"Le gusta los apaches senorita? . . . ah! ah! ah!

"Did you like apaches, ladies? . . . ah! ah! And now . . .

"Vous avez aimé les apaches?" etc. . . .

At the Moulin Rouge it's another story. What a setting! This is the real Paris! You are squeezed in at a table for eight next to the dance floor, completely off to one side. You can see next to nothing, but the ruffles fan your cheeks pleasantly each time they go by and you barely avoid being knocked over by all those lovely girls, driven by the lascivious music to shake their generous bosoms beneath our noses, as they head back on stage from the wings.

The champagne is on the table: two bottles for the eight of us. Which is correct, as far as quantity goes. Three thousand pairs of eyes from the capacity audience converge on the hat of a magician who is conjuring baby chicks out of a spectator's trousers. Which is correct, as far as quality goes. Unfortunately, we must be the only French people astray at the Moulin Rouge, and we miss the better part of the remarks uttered in American from the stage in front of the musicians. Something tells us we didn't miss much. The sparkling wine from the Petit Balcon is furiously upsetting our usual serene objectivity, and we strongly suspect one of our fellow prisoners, an especially hilarious Belgian from Ostend, of stealing that bottle of mineral water. Be that as it may, the Moulin Rouge really puts on one swell show and at the sumptuous finale, where a swarm of chorus girls descend from the ceiling in a balloon, releasing big red balloons upon bald heads and white shoulders, our enthusiasm knows no bounds.

We move on to other pleasures.

"You like Moulin Rouge, ladies? . . . ah! ah!"

The bus rolls silently down toward the Seine. Our next and last stop is the Crescendo.

"You've seen the apaches, you've seen the Moulin Rouge and its splendors, but you can't end this Parisian night without sampling the troubling, vicious (*sic*) atmosphere of a striptease . . ."

A few couples are dancing between the tables in the half-light of this cellar filled with blaring music. A velvety American voice calls for silence and whispers magic words into a mike: "And now, the artless, the troubling, the daring, the perverse . . . Nadia Nora! The little bride of your dreams."

The curtain does indeed open on an enchanting young bride in her white gown and train, who immediately sets to work raising our temperatures and throwing her veils one by one onto a fourposter, instantly put to the test with a few solitary, innocent revels. Two other numbers of the same ilk bring our visit to a close, and we regain the bus with a ration of thrills and a store of images for cold winter nights.

"Le gusta striptease, señor? Eh! eh! . . ."

Yessir, you can really have a ball in Paris.

Rapid-Pullman, 3 place des Pyramides, OPE 81.60. "Paris By Night": 85 francs ($17). (Two options: Moulin Rouge or Lido.)

Part VIII

SOME IMPORTANT
ADDRESSES

United States Embassy
Chancellery: 2 avenue Gabriel (8ᵉ), ANJ 74.60.
Cultural Services: 41 rue du Faubourg Saint-Honoré (8ᵉ), ANJ 74.00.
American Church of Paris, 65 quai d'Orsay (7ᵉ).
American Hospital, 63 boulevard Victor-Hugo, Neuilly-sur-Seine, MAI 68.00.

Airlines

Air France, 119 Champs-Elysées (8ᵉ), BAL 70.50; 2 rue Scribe (2ᵉ), OPE 41.00. For information and reservations, telephone KEL 66.00.

We are not afraid of being a little chauvinistic. Isn't traveling on board a French airplane the best way to beat everyone to France? You'll enjoy French cooking as you fly over the Atlantic (excellent in first class, more ordinary in tourist); you'll drink French wine and champagne; you'll watch a masterpiece (at least we hope so) of French movie-making, and you'll try out your French on the pretty stewardesses. All this, and in good old American planes besides . . .

Offices in the United States: *Boston,* 20 Providence Street (Room 520), 482-4890; *Chicago,* 22 South Michigan Avenue, ST 2-6181; *Los Angeles,* 518 West 6th Street, MA 5-7171; *New York,* 683 Fifth Avenue, 656-6000; 2 Broadway, 765-3000; *San Francisco,* 260 Stockton Street, YU 2-1750; *Washington,* 1120 Connecticut Avenue, FE 7-8374.

Pan-American Airways, 138 Champs-Elysées (8ᵉ), BAL 92.00.

TWA, 101 Champs-Elysées (8ᵉ), BAL 10.83.

Ocean liners

French Line (Compagnie Générale Transatlantique), 6 rue
Auber (9ᵉ), RIC 97.59.
Cunard Line, 6 rue Scribe (9ᵉ), RIC 41.12.
United States Line, 10 rue Auber (9ᵉ), OPE 89.80.

INDEX

ABOUT THE AUTHORS

HENRI GAULT and CHRISTIAN MILLAU direct their own press agency and write for numerous magazines and newspapers here as well as in France and Britain, including *Holiday* *Realités, Paris-Presse,* and *Marie-Claire.* As well, they appear regularly on French radio and television.

MM. Gault and Millau have published eight guides in France, and their *Juilliard Guide de Paris* was a runaway best seller. This present book, *A Parisian's Guide to Paris,* was written especially for an American audience, but the authors have also done a guide to New York, written for French tourists which was featured in both *Newsweek* and *Life.*

Henri Gault, born in 1929, the son of a doctor, abandoned his medical studies for journalism. From 1954 to 1958 he reported on legal matters, entertainment, politics, and music. Since 1958 when he began to write about how to spend one's leisure time his life has become more hectic as he travels widely and works hard writing about the pleasures of eating, drinking, and traveling. He is married and has three children.

Christian Millau, who was born in Paris thirty-nine years ago, is married and the father of three children. His father was a Parisian banker, his mother Russian. M. Millau was graduated from the *Institut d'Etudes Politiques.* He started writing on politics for the prestigious newspaper *Le Monde* when he was eighteen, and has since contributed articles to many literary and artistic journals. The author traveled around the world on a yacht, and during this trip, made a documentary film with Orson Welles for French television. On his return to Paris, he became features editor of the evening *Paris-Presse* and eventually joined forces with Henri Gault, who had started a daily column "Paris Guide" for *Paris-Presse* which was devoted to life's pleasures—gastronomy, night life, and travel.

Next year Random House will publish a new guide to New York which Gault and Millau are currently researching.